THE POLITICAL ECONOMY OF AFRICAN FOREIGN POLICY

THE POLITICAL ECONOMY OF AFRICAN FOREIGN POLICY

COMPARATIVE ANALYSIS

Edited by
TIMOTHY M. SHAW
Director, Centre for African Studies and
Professor of Political Science,
Dalhousie University, Canada

OLAJIDE ALUKO
Dean, Faculty of Administration and
Professor of International Relations,
University of Ife, Nigeria

St. Martin's Press New York

ISBN 0-312-62253-8

Library of Congress Cataloging in Publication Data

Main entry under title:

The Political economy of African foreign policy.

    1. Africa—Foreign relations—1960— .
    2. Africa—Foreign economic relations.
    3. Africa—Economic conditions—1960— .
    4. Africa—Dependency on foreign countries.
I. Shaw, Timothy M.   II. Aluko, Olajide.
DT30.5.P66 1984   327.6   83—13966

ISBN 0-312-62253-8

Contents

Notes on contributors

Olajide Aluko is a Professor of International Relations and Dean of the Faculty of Administration at the University of Ife in Nigeria. With a Ph.D. from the London School of Economics, Dr Aluko is one of Africa's leading students of international affairs. Apart from books on *Ghana and Nigeria, 1957–1970, The Foreign Policies of African States, Essays in Nigerian Foreign Policy,* and *Nigeria and Southern Africa*, his many articles have appeared in *African Affairs, Issue, Millennium, Quarterly Journal of Administration* and *Nigerian Journal of International Studies.*

Marcia M. Burdette is Assistant Professor of Political Science at Fordham University in New York and Visiting Lecturer in African Development Studies at the University of Zambia. With a Ph.D. from Columbia University, Dr Burdette has written for the *Canadian Journal of African Studies*. At Fordham she contributes to both the undergraduate and graduate programmes in political economy.

Naomi Chazan is Senior Lecturer in Political Science at the Hebrew University in Jerusalem and Coordinator of the African Studies Unit at the Truman Research Institute. The author of *An Anatomy of Ghanaian Politics: managing political recession, 1969–1982* (1983), Dr Chazan was recently a Fellow in Radcliffe College at Harvard University. Her work on African, especially West African, politics has appeared in *African Affairs, African Studies Review, Comparative*

Politics, International Journal, Journal of Commonwealth and Comparative Politics and *Political Science Quarterly*.

Christopher Clapham is Senior Lecturer and Head of the Department of Politics at the University of Lancaster, England. He is the author of *Haile-Selassie's Government* (1969), and *Liberia and Sierra Leone: an essay in comparative politics* (1976), and editor of *Foreign Policy Making in Developing States* (1977) and *Private Patronage and Public Power* (1982), as well as writing numerous articles and papers on Ethiopia and the Horn of Africa.

Cyril Kofie Daddieh is a Killam scholar in the doctoral programme at Dalhousie University, Nova Scotia, preparing a thesis on the political economy of agriculture in Ghana. He holds a B.A. from Ripon College and a master's degree in international affairs from Carleton University. His reviews have appeared in *International Journal* and *International Journal of African Historical Studies* and an essay on the future of food in Shaw and Aluko (eds) *Africa Projected* (1984).

Ken Good is presently Senior Lecturer in Political and Administrative Studies at the University of Zambia, having taught previously at the Universities of Papua New Guinea, Port Harcourt and Rhodesia (being expelled from the latter by the Smith regime). Dr Good is the author of several articles on Southern Africa in *African Affairs, Australian and New Zealand Journal of Sociology* and *Journal of Modern African Studies* and co-author of *Development and Dependency: the political economy of Papua New Guinea* (1979).

Richard A. Higgott is now Senior Lecturer in Social and Political Theory at Murdoch University in Western Australia. He holds a Ph.D. from the University of Birmingham, England, has held teaching posts at the Universities of Western Australia and Tasmania and was recently a Fulbright Fellow at Harvard University. Dr Higgott is the author of *Political Development Theory: the contemporary debate* (1983), contributor to *Africa Contemporary Record* (1982), *Australia in World Affairs* (1982) and articles in the *Journal of Modern African Studies, Journal of Commonwealth and Comparative Politics, Review of African Political Economy, Studies in Comparative International Development, Politics, Social Analysis*. He is currently editor of *Australian Outlook* and joint editor of a forthcoming collection of essays entitled *Southeast Asia: the political economy of structural change*.

David H. Johns is Professor of Political Science at San Diego State University in California. His work on African, especially East African, international affairs has appeared in *Journal of Modern African Studies, Sage International Yearbook of Foreign Policy Studies*, Aluko (ed.) *Foreign Policies of African States* and Shaw and Heard (eds) *Politics of Africa*. Following a year's sabbatical in China Dr Johns is currently completing a book on the distinctive international relations of the Third World.

Vincent B. Khapoya is Associate Professor of Political Science at Oakland University in Michigan having been a Lecturer on government at the University of Nairobi. Dr Khapoya's work on African, especially Eastern and Southern African, international affairs has appeared in *Africa Today, Ufahamu, Journal of Modern African Studies* and the *University of Denver Monograph Series in World Affairs*. He holds degrees from the Universities of Oregon and Denver and was born in Kenya.

Nadia Kostiuk is a consultant at the North–South Institute and IDRC in Ottawa, having served recently as a CUSO volunteer in Francistown, Botswana, where she was a district development planner. Ms Kostiuk holds an honours degree in political science and a master's degree in international affairs, both from Carleton University in Ottawa, and has been associated with Crossroads Canadian International.

Olatunde J. B. Ojo holds a Ph.D. from the Graduate School of International Studies at the University of Denver and is Senior Lecturer and Head of Political Science at the University of Port Harcourt in Nigeria. Dr Ojo's work on Nigeria and West Africa has appeared in *Africa Today, African Studies Review, International Organization* and *Orbis*.

Michael G. Schatzberg is now Associate Professor of Comparative Politics and African Studies at the Johns Hopkins University School of Advanced International Studies (SAIS) in Washington, D.C. He is the author of *Politics and Class in Zaire: bureaucracy, business, and beer in Lisala* (1980), and articles in *African Affairs, Journal of Modern African Studies, Comparative Politics, Urban Anthropology, Canadian Journal of African Studies, Comparative Education Review*, and *Cultures et développement*. Dr Schatzberg has taught previously at Virginia Polytechnic Institute and State University and at Dalhousie University, where he was also an associate of the Centre for Foreign Policy Studies.

Timothy M. Shaw is Professor of Political Science and Director of the Centre for African Studies at Dalhousie University in Nova Scotia; he has taught at the universities of Ife, Zambia and Makerere in Africa, and

Carleton and British Columbia in Canada. Dr Shaw holds a Ph.D. from Princeton University and has published on African political economy in a variety of journals, most recently in *Alternatives, International Journal, Journal of Modern African Studies* and *Third World Quarterly*.

Fola Soremekun is Senior Lecturer in History at the University of Ife where he specialises in Southern African, especially Angolan, affairs. Dr Soremekun holds a Ph.D. from Northwestern University, taught previously at the University of Zambia and has essays in *Genève-Afrique*. He is president of the Lusaphone Area Studies Association (LUASA) at Ife and editor of *LUASA Journal*.

Roger J. Southall is a Visiting Professor at the Institute for International Development at the University of Ottawa, having taught previously at the National University in Lesotho. With a doctorate from the University of Birmingham, Dr Southall is the author of *Parties and Politics in Bunyoro, Federalism and Higher Education in East Africa*, and *South Africa's Transkei: the political economy of an 'independent' Bantustan*, along with essays in *African Development, African Affairs, Africa Contemporary Record, Canadian Journal of African Studies, Journal of Modern African Studies, Journal of Southern African Studies, Labour, Capital and Society* and *Race Relations News*.

Preface

This collection has taken considerable time and tolerance to prepare; we hope that, like vintage wine, it's worth the wait. The initial seed for the idea was sown while we were colleagues together for one year in the Department of International Relations at the University of Ife; and that arrangement was itself the result of collaboration in the production of *Foreign Policies of African States*.[1] The present volume is in some senses a 'second generation' or second edition of that text. It results from our respective research in and dissatisfaction with the field of African foreign policy studies;[2] and general developments in that field pointing in the direction of a concern for structure rather than ideology, exchange rather than diplomacy and class rather than personality. In short, this enterprise represents an attempt to go beyond superficial and orthodox investigation towards more fundamental and radical explanation. It will have served its purpose if it advances critical comparative analysis.

The preparation of this collection over four years has put us into debt with many people: colleagues and graduates at Ife and Dalhousie, John Irwin at Gower, secretaries in the Centres for Foreign Policy Studies and African Studies at Dalhousie, and both original and eventual contributors of chapters both included and excluded. To you all — our appreciation for your support and patience. Let us hope that we can all get a little intoxicated on what we trust will be considered to be vintage results: 1984, a good year.

Timothy M. Shaw and Olajide Aluko
Halifax and Ile-Ife
October 1983

Notes

1 Edited by Olajide Aluko with a chapter on Zambia by Timothy M. Shaw (London: Hodder and Stoughton, 1977).
2 See, in particular, Olajide Aluko, 'Necessity and Freedom in Nigerian foreign policy', *Nigerian Journal of International Studies,* vol. 4, nos 1 and 2, January and June 1980, pp. 1–15 and Timothy M. Shaw, 'The political economy of African international relations', *Issue*, vol. 5, no 4, Winter 1975, pp. 29–38, 'Review article. Foreign policy, political economy and the future: reflections on Africa in the world system', *African Affairs* vol. 79, no. 315, April 1980, pp. 260–268, and 'Class, country and corporation: Africa in the capitalist world system' in Donald I. Ray et al. (eds) *Into the 80s: proceedings of the 11th annual conference of the Canadian Association of African Studies, Volume 2* (Vancouver: Tantalus, 1981) pp. 19–37.

Abbreviations

ANC	African National Congress
BDP	Botswana Democratic Party
BLS (also HCT)	Botswana, Lesotho and Swaziland
CFA	African Financial Community (franc zone)
CONCP	Conference of Nationalist Organisations of Portuguese Colonies
CPP	Convention People's Party (Ghana)
ECA	(UN) Economic Commission for Africa
ECOWAS	Economic Community of West African States
EDF	European Development Fund (EEC)
EEC	European Economic Community
FLS	Front Line States
FNLA	National Front for the Liberation of Angola
FRELIMO	Front for the Liberation of Mozambique
IBRD	International Bank for Reconstruction and Development (World Bank)
IMF	International Monetary Fund
MPLA	People's Movement for the Liberation of Angola
NICs	Newly Industrialising Countries
NLC	National Liberation Council (Ghana)
OAU	Organisation of African Unity
OCAM	Communal Organisation for Africa and Mauritius
OECD	Organisation for Economic Cooperation and Development
PDCI	Parti Democratique de la Côte d'Ivoire

PPN	Progressive Party of Niger
PRA	People's Republic of Angola
RSA	Republic of South Africa
SADCC	Southern African Development Coordination Conference
SMC	Supreme Military Council
SWAPO	South West African People's Organisation
TANU	Tanganyika African National Union
UDI	Unilateral Declaration of Independence (Rhodesia)
UMOA	West African Monetary Union
UNIP	United National Independence Party (Zambia)
UNITA	National Union for the Total Independence of Angola
ZANU	Zimbabwe African National Union
ZAPU	Zimbabwe African People's Union

Introduction: towards a political economy of African foreign policy

Timothy M. Shaw and Olajide Aluko

> . . . most international relations work on African can be safely neglected. . . there are also very few studies of African foreign policy that are not both theoretically crude and largely descriptive.[1]

> . . . the primacy of Africa's own history blends and interweaves with exterior histories.[2]

> The historical interest (in the period after independence) lies. . . in the working out of confrontation between the colonial heritage and the pre-colonial heritage, now that the second is free to challenge the first; and, along with that, the resultant development of ideas concerned with searching for a different model. These are the fields of theory and practice within which this history plays out its ongoing and decisive themes into the 1980s and beyond.[3]

Africa stands poised half-way between the achievement of formal independence in the early 1960s and the end of the current century. The last 20 years on the continent have been characterised by disillusionment with the 'imported model' and an intensifying re-evaluation

1

of both development and foreign policies. According to Basil Davidson, 'Broadly, the 1960s were a time of reaction, the 1970s one of new experiment'.[4] The 1980s are likely to constitute, then, a period of experimentation, not least amongst various forms of political economy as national policy goals. But, given the multiplication of studies of African foreign policy, the new decade is also likely to be a period of renewed experimentation amongst various forms of explanation as well as prescription.

Both development and foreign policies themselves and ways of approaching them are in a state of flux. Shifts in the mode of production and shifts in the mode of analysis are clearly interrelated; social science can never escape from the mood of the day. And, given the contemporary intellectual as well as political reconsideration, there is the potential for fruitful interaction between these two modes. As Davidson notes, during the 1970s,

> New departures, new experiments, new achievements combined to induce a sturdy scepticism about any kind of foreign model that might be recommended. There came the development of programmes for constructive change aimed at building indigenous models.[5]

This collection represents an attempt to describe and dissect these changes in Africa as they relate to policy, practice and analysis. Students as well as participants have begun to question established modes of enquiry in addition to orthodox modes of diplomacy. And the contemporary period, half-way between 'independence' and the year 2000, presents a timely occasion at which to pause, reflect, revise and progress: foreign policy analysis as well as foreign policy direction is in need of reconsideration.[6]

The present volume is intended, then, as a contribution to the 'second wave'[7] in Africa at the levels of both scholarship and strategy, a wave that, according to Davidson, was spreading as the 1970s drew to a close: 'the evidence further suggested that this trend towards renewal, towards revolutionary ideas and structures, was now in course of enlargement'.[8] The set of contributors included here consider in part how far the second wave has proceeded in terms of both policy and inquiry; they attempt to reflect the mood — both intellectual and existential — of an Africa half-way between 1960 and the year 2000.[9]

This introductory chapter is intended to situate this ambivalent mood of both disillusion over past results and researches and anticipation over future achievements and analyses. A preliminary section introducing the purposes of the collection is followed by a review of the literature to date and by an overview of the framework for analysis adopted throughout the case studies in this volume.

Purpose

This set of comparative studies has been prepared, then, to review both the state of the nations and the state of the field. It has also been conceived as a teaching device and as an analytical tool. If the approach and analysis adopted here are appropriate and valid, implications and indications for the future will be apparent. These projections should be relevant for discerning the next few years' empirical trends as well as for diagnosing possible policy responses and revisions. So contributions were invited for reasons of intellectual review, instructional utility, policy analysis, conceptual development and predictive potential. They are intended to be a positive response to the recent lament of Mark DeLancey on the deficiencies of the field so far; these include, according to him:

> . . . the high proportion of case studies and single-country studies and the rather small number of really comparative undertakings among researchers. Related to this is a lack of up-to-date, general studies covering the entire scope of African international politics. There is a lack of comparison and a lack of generalisation.[10]

In an attempt to advance comparative analysis and to improve general theory, a political economy approach has been adopted here. Its adoption not only reflects a growing trend in the sub-field but also serves to enhance the utility of these cases because long-term characteristics are examined rather than shorter-term crises. The emphasis here is on what Davidson characterises as 'structure' rather than 'contingence'. For although these are interrelated the 'decisive and structural' are given more prominence than the 'ephemeral and contingent'.[11] Such an approach is adopted not only because it improves the longevity of this book but also because it increases the forcefulness of analysis. Given a concern for comparison, concept and theory, the cases and contributors to be included were selected with special care. Essentially, the criteria for inclusion were two: the character of the state and the character of the scholar.

Countries were selected, then, both to provide comprehensive spread and to reflect intrinsic interest. The claims of balance and curiosity were well satisfied in several instances by incorporating a set of central sub-Saharan states; Angola, Ivory Coast and Tanzania, for example, had to be included because of their size, status and/or salience. Comprehensiveness is taken here to mean variety of political economy rather than size (although Niger and Nigeria are included from opposite ends of this spectrum) or region (although cases are taken from all the major parts of the sub-continent.[12] Given this concern for structural and continuing characteristics, the crucial criterion is clearly variety of

3

political economy. As indicated in the final section of this chapter, Africa's political economies can be divided into two or three types; two or three examples have been included from each of these here. The usefulness of this typology as a basis for comparative analysis should become apparent when cases are contrasted from either within or between these sets of states.

The other important criterion, related to the first, is the intrinsic interest of particular countries, the quality of the foreign policy literature on them and the availability of appropriately critical and informed scholars. In general, the more interesting states have attracted the attention of several capable analysts amongst whom a series of debates has arisen over how to describe and explain 'their' country's respective development and foreign policies. So several states have been included because of their intrinsic interest, foreign policy literature and quality of analysis; Kenya, Nigeria, Tanzania and Zambia[13] meet this set of criteria. Not only are these countries of considerable interest in themselves, but no continental comparative analysis would be complete without mention of them. Moreover, the debates over their own development and foreign policies and problems can usefully inform broader discussion about mode of analysis and response throughout Africa.

To put this selection of cases and concepts into perspective we turn next to a review of the literature before concluding with an overview of the collection's conceptual framework. The approach adopted there is something of a response to the limitations displayed by the literature to date.

Review of salient literature

If the comparative study of foreign policy is underdeveloped in general, it is particularly so in the case of Africa. For despite the multiplicity of states on the continent, few rigorous comparative analyses have been attempted. Moreover, those that have been undertaken have tended to focus on super- rather than substructural features. I. William Zartman, for instance, in his initial, innovative investigation of the 'development' of foreign policies in West Africa in the mid-1960s identified the following set of characteristics: level of nation-building and political development; power capability; primacy of ideology; searching nature; *ad hoc* content; and instability. By contrast, a political economy perspective on foreign policy examines more lasting, structural characteristics such as domestic social system, relationship to external interests and type of development strategy.

4

Meanwhile, the orthodox, realist approach is not totally dormant and may be able to adapt itself to some of the concerns of more critical scholars. Okwudiba Nnoli, for instance, in his creative analysis of *Self Reliance and Foreign Policy in Tanzania* has related Tanzania's loss of innocence to frustration over the lack of power to affect important international issues.[15] So the Arusha Declaration constituted an historic conjuncture at which Tanzania sought to augment its national power by turning inwards and enhancing its own capabilities.[16] *Kujitegemea* (self-reliance) and *ujamaa* (socialism) are taken to be mutually reinforcing and together to improve Tanzania's capacity for external influence over change in either Southern Africa or Amin's Uganda. They are intended 'to maximise independence, promote economic development, and insure socio-political stability in a way that enhances national power'.[17]

Nevertheless, while one or two scholars have attempted to rehabilitate the orthodox approach in general its deficiencies are more apparent than its strengths. DeLancey captures a sense of the inadequacies of the traditional perspective – the 'dominant paradigm' – by noting that in general 'the literature is descriptive and prescriptive. . .very few publications are analytical'.[18] One recent attempt to overcome this unpromising intellectual inheritance is the study of Senegal's foreign policy by W. A. E. Skurnik in which he adapts James Rosenau's pre-theory to an African case.[19] While he finds the general notion of adaptation to be a helpful one, Skurnik argues for a revision to Rosenau's ranking of variables, especially when different issue area distinctions are introduced:

> Systemic variables are found to be most potent in three of the five examples, and domestic variables are most potent in the other two. Contrary to the expectations of the Rosenau model, idiosyncratic variables rank least in importance in each case. The potency of a given variable appears to vary in direct relation to the degree of actual or potential, direct or indirect control over a given issue area by Senegal's foreign policy decision-makers.[20]

Skurnik tends to play down the idiosyncratic variable by contrast to Rosenau or Zartman and instead comes to emphasise the systemic or external: 'both adaptation and change, then, appear largely as responses to threats emanating from, and as a search for opportunities inherent in, the international environment'.[21] This approach leads him to predict a continuity or consistency in Senegal's foreign policy:

> It does not seem that the objectives and general orientation of Senegal's foreign relations will undergo any drastic change. The country's enormous dependence on the outside world, her attach-

ments to those nations most able and willing to help, her emphasis on regional rather than continental cooperation within Africa, her opposition to minority rule in Africa, her insistence that political borders and sovereignty be respected, and her efforts to seek structural changes in the international economy will probably remain the most important concerns of her foreign policy.[22]

But Skurnik's emphasis on 'systemic forces'[23] has a somewhat static and deterministic quality to it. A sensitive political economy approach could help to transcend this limitation by emphasising varieties and degrees of incorporation within a general and common situation of external dominance and subordination.

An awareness of dependence is a prerequisite for such analysis but it is not sufficient by itself because transnational relations take myriad (and often mystifying!) forms. Moreover, we need to relate domestic class formation (itself based on the coexistence of particular modes of production) to such external associations, adopting a more critical perspective towards some of the lacunae identified in the orthodox literature by DeLancey in his review of

> topics upon which little or no study has been done: the South African policies of those governments, the foreign policy formulation process, the attitudes of African elites (and the masses) toward foreign policy objectives and actions, and study of the linkages between domestic and international politics in Africa. . .[25]

The present collection is an attempt to fill these and other gaps apparent in the dominant paradigm; not by extending the range of orthodox cases and concerns, but rather by switching to an alternative mode of analysis. This mode might facilitate exploration and explanation of, for instance, foreign policy making and transnational linkages by situating them in the context of the national component of a world system. By itself, Africa provides a rich range of cases of such national units within global structures. And given the continent's common inheritance and articulation, differences in strategy could be identified and explained.[26]

Africa has the potential, then, to become a popular field of comparative analysis — at sub-national, national, regional and continental levels — in part because of the multiplicity of countries on the continent and in part because of certain common features present amongst these countries. The majority of African states were incorporated into the world system in response to external rather than internal changes. And this vulnerability to pressures and demands from the relatively advanced industrialised states has continued to the present day through the pre-colonial, colonial and post-colonial periods.[27] As Christopher Clapham notes in his own review of African foreign policy studies:

> The states of sub-Saharan Africa have enough in common to make comparative treatment of their foreign policy making process a matter of more than simple geographical convenience. Though their place in the international stratification system and particularly their economic underdevelopment make them very much part of the third world, with the general foreign policy consequences which that implies, they possess in addition features which are distinctly African.[28]

Olajide Aluko has included some elements of this distinctiveness in his framework for the comparative study of African foreign policy, identifying colonial heritage, geographical location and the continued existence of colonialism and white supremacist regimes as factors. He also included the cold war environment as part of the 'external environment' and in the 'domestic setting' incorporated internal political pressures and the nature and ideology of governing elites as well as the national economy.[29] In the present volume, however, the emphasis — that which distinguishes this from other orthodox or revisionist works — is on those continuing elements of substructure that affect policy, that is on political economy, including the impact of colonial and post-colonial incorporation in the world system, the coexistence of modes of production and different class relationships associated with them, and the transnational linkages amongst external and internal social formations.[30]

The essential commonality of these factors in Africa has not led, however, to homogeneous responses. Rather, there are enough differences in social relations, political institutions and ideological formulations for clear distinctions to be made amongst foreign and development policies. At the level of superstructure these may be characterised as more or less radical, more or less pragmatic; while at the level of substructure they may be conceived as more or less socialist, more or less dependent. The former type of distinction is described by Clapham:

> ... for the most part, the similarities between their predicaments on the one hand, and their interests and goals on the other, place before African states a very similar set of choices. These choices, which essentially are set by the tension between the societies and state structures which governing groups control, and the cross-national economic and other linkages on which they necessarily depend, range over many issues between extremes of heroism and pragmatism.[31]

Most studies of foreign policy in Africa to date have concentrated on the idiosyncratic rather than on the institutional and have emphasised contrast rather than commonality. Differences rather than similarities have been identified and superficial actions rather than substructural characteristics examined. In part such emphasis may reflect the utility of foreign policy for the ruling class as a deflection from the pathos and problems of underdevelopment. For it does direct attention away from these features of continuity and constraint that limit both the longer-term orientation of and the shorter-term pay-offs from foreign policy. As Clapham himself notes, foreign affairs for African leaders constitute a form of escape from the claims of patronage and, paradoxically, from the omnipresence of dependence. External relations afford a welcome form of glamour, even if, given the leaderships' inability to treat the dependence that ensnares them, it is a mirage:

> The immediate decision making setting of foreign policy is. . . highly personalised. To African leaders, as to Renaissance monarchs, foreign policy is an attribute of sovereignty which remains in their hands even when important tasks in the domestic political system are delegated. . . International relations offer the chance of an escape into the big time world of global politics, which must be justified rhetorically in terms of world peace or third world development, but in which the activity itself is to a large extent its own reward.[32]

Whilst almost all African states share, as both Aluko and Clapham note, a common inheritance of colonialism, dependence and under-development, there are significant and increasing differences amongst them as well. As Clapham remarks, 'there are, however, important differences in the constraints on African states and the capabilities which they can employ, which in turn affect the degree of independent action open to them'.[33] Variation in constraints and capabilities may best be explained through an examination of political economy, rather than by looking at, say, leadership or ideology in isolation. For constraints and capabilities are really the two sides of a single coin, namely that of the degree of national autonomy and development. But autonomy and development are rare currency in Africa precisely because of its history of incorporation and exploitation. So any abstraction of foreign policy 'choices' on the continent has to take into account salient aspects of the national political economy, which is itself a function or fragment of the world system. Hence the elusiveness or ambiguity of African foreign policy.

Ironically, then, 'foreign policy' is a form of escape from (as well as sometimes a response to) the very dependence that unequal external exchange produces. African leaders seek to transcend the constraints of underdevelopment by participating in a world system that is, in fact, the primary conditioner of their own political economies. Hence the dilemmas of demanding a new international economic order while already being firmly integrated into global transnational networks.[34] However, such contradictions are most apparent and intense at the global level; they are less visible or worrisome at other levels where international institutions and interests can still be 'blamed' for the elusiveness of development and change.

African foreign policy can be categorised, then, according to level of interaction as well as according to type of political economy. The regional and continental, in particular, tend to be rather different from the collective (Third World) and global levels. For notions of 'good neighbourliness' and 'pan-Africanism' operate at the former levels whereas at the latter, ideas of Third World solidarity and North–South cleavage prevail. As Ali Mazrui has noted, two distinctive forms of supranationalism tend to be applied at these two apparently separate levels:

> African diplomatic thought tends to distinguish between two basic forms of supra-national arrangements. These are, firstly, continental supra-nationality in politics and, secondly global supra-nationality in economics.[35]

And, as Clapham points out, the degrees of equality and unity may also vary between these rather different levels:

> The external setting of African foreign policy making falls into two fairly distinct spheres. On the one hand, there is the sphere of equals, comprising other African states and on some occasions states elsewhere in the underdeveloped world. On the other hand, there is the sphere of outsiders, comprising especially the world super-powers and the former colonial powers, with their associates in Eastern and Western Europe and elsewhere. The relations between African states and each of these two categories and the influence which these have on the foreign policy of the state concerned, are different enough to make them worth considering separately.[36]

This discontinuity between intra- and extra-African policy is one which Zartman develops in his classical study within the orthodox tradition: *International Relations in the New Africa*. But regional politics are no longer confined just to political intervention, boundary disputes or the quest for integration along the lines identified by Zartman.[37] Rather, the emergence (or rather the reappearance after a period of quiescence during the immediate pre- and post-colonial periods) of inequalities at this level has led to the growing recognition

9

of structural differentiation.[38] Such contemporary 'sub-imperialist' tendencies, unlike earlier quests for visibility, are likely to be more permanent features of the regional scene, underlying different sets of regional contradictions, coalitions and constitutions.[39] And Zartman, in a substantial, albeit speculative, revision of his earlier view of regional politics in Africa, now recognises the prospects for increased inequality and dominance rather than for integration and interdependence at this level:[40]

> By the 1980s, the spread in the level of power sources is certain to increase, even dramatically. . .several effects are likely to ensue. First, the more developed members may become more attractive to outside influences, even if greater amounts of influence will now be required in order to have an effect. Second, at this stage of development, internal gaps between socio-economic levels are likely to be magnified, as are also gaps between the states which have surged forward and those many others which have been unable to do so. . . the chances for regional leadership are increased.[41]

In other words, regionally dominant states may also be the most vulnerable to internal and international inequalities. Such tendencies of sub-imperial and semi-peripheral actors, as well as their causation, can probably best be understood by situating national, regional and continental institutions in the context of an unequal and ubiquitous global system.[42] A political economy approach offers the possibility of such a holistic, historical and heuristic form of analysis. The concluding section of this initial chapter introduces the basic outlines of such an approach, which is the type of analysis adopted throughout the collection to advance comparative as well as critical study.

Framework of analysis

A political economy approach differs from an orthodox analysis of foreign policy in at least four crucial regards; this is so whether it is applied to African or other cases. First, its *level of analysis* is sub-structural rather than superstructural. Second, its *mode of analysis* is critical and analytic rather than just descriptive. Third, its *method of analysis* is materialist rather than behavioural, concerned with modes and relations of production, with internal and international divisions of labour, and with the identification of inequalities, contradictions and prospects of any new synthesis. And fourth, the *implications* of such analysis are basic: radical change rather than reformism is considered to be essential if a history of dependence, underdevelopment and vulnerability is to be transcended.

In short, with its emphasis on 'structure' rather than 'contingence',[43] a political economy perspective — whether it is 'bourgeois' or 'marxist' — entails a rather fundamental reassessment of Africa's place and potential in the world at the levels of both analysis and *praxis*. As such it is reflective of a growing trend, apparent on the continent itself, of reconsidering established assumptions, relations and projections. A substructural approach draws attention to the core problems of dependence and development which are themselves a preoccupation in an Africa characterised increasingly by social inequalities, political *putschs*, disparate directions and divergent predictions.[44] As Dr Abebayo Adedeji, Executive Secretary of the Economic Commission for Africa (ECA) has warned:

> There is no gainsaying the fact that Africa cannot afford to continue to perform in the field of development during the next decade or two at the same rate as in the last 15 years or so. If it does, the Africa region will be a much poorer relation of the rest of the world than it is now; the gap between it and the rest of the world will be wider, and its economic and technological backwardness will be more pronounced. It is therefore imperative that African states should reformulate their policies and economic strategies and instruments with a view to promoting national and collective self-reliance.[45]

The problematic future of the continent has itself served, then, as an incentive to evaluate critically modes of production and projection.[46] But the form of analysis advocated here has historical in addition to heuristic features.

A political economy perspective on African foreign policy involves an historical as well as a critical and structural component. Such an approach enables contemporary relationships and responses to be put into an appropriate and extended time-frame. The emphasis is on institutional evolution rather than on more ephemeral crises; on economic rather than diplomatic history. Davidson provides such a sense of history and destiny; not one of predestination but rather of time and place:

> Africa today is the product not only of its pre-colonial history, or more recently of the history of the colonial period, but also of a direct trading relationship with the mercantile and early capitalist systems of Europe which began before 1500. . . On this view of historical processes, beginning to be quite widely held by the 1970s, the twentieth century acquires a still more dramatic and

decisive interest. For this emerges as the century in which the Africans not only come out of their isolation and begin to measure where they stand, but learn to analyse their limits and capacities within the wider scene of the world itself, and embark on new destinations.[47]

A political economy approach to foreign (and development) policy conceives of Africa's responses within the context of dependence and underdevelopment. Not that the world system is omnipresent; but its history and evolution have been the primary determinants of African social structures. The articulation of different modes and relations of production between periods, regions and nations has had a varying impact, but Africa's place in the world system should be taken as the starting, and not the concluding, point for any reliable explanation of present policies and strategies.[48] The continent's present history is not predetermined; but its inheritance of dependence cannot be ignored.

Local responses and capabilities vary between decades, classes and countries, but the general inheritance of external, structural dominance cannot be disregarded. Moreover, changes in the world system as well as in particular situations may provide opportunities in addition to obstacles. Steven Langdon and Lynn Mytelka, in their work for the Council on Foreign Relations' 1980s Project, explain the continent's contemporary choices and constraints in the context of its past position, emphasising

> first, how precolonial and colonial economic penetration shaped underdevelopment in Africa and, second, how the industrialisation and regional integration efforts of the postcolonial period have reinforced such patterns. Increasingly in the seventies, though, new strategic options have been emerging for African countries. In particular, changes in the international economy appear to be opening up a new form of economic relationship between African countries and Western Europe, especially around the terms of the Lomé Convention.[49]

But several studies of the 'new' Eurafricanism of Lomé I and II have pointed out the growth of uneven benefits, both between the EEC and ACP and amongst the ACP countries themselves. In general, the richer, bigger and more industrialised states of Africa — the sub-imperial actors of the semi-periphery — have enjoyed access to unequal gains.[50] And it is this type of divergence — at the levels of incorporation, production and distribution — that has come to reflect and reinforce alternative policies and prescriptions on the continent. As the inequalities of external articulation have increased with shifts in the global system itself, so tendencies towards divergent strategies have multiplied. A

12

political economy perspective helps to identify and analyse these various directions.

Africa's responses to an inheritance of dependence and under-development can now be divided essentially into two contemporary types, reflective of the traditional choice between collaboration and confrontation: those countries and classes in favour of further incor-poration into the Western system and those in favour of disengagement from it. The former, incorporationist variety of state and strategy may be called 'state capitalism' whereas the latter, disengagement variety, can be subdivided into two further variations: 'state socialism', involving some change in the balance of relations between external and internal interests and institutions, and 'socialism', involving a more fundamental restructuring at both levels.[51]

These divergences have both increased and intensified from the mid-1970s onwards as the process of liberation has occurred in lusophone Africa; the process of re-evaluating development strategies elsewhere in Africa has spread; and the post-Bretton Woods and post-OPEC era has generated new instabilities, shortages and uncertainties. The latter are revealed in the emergence of, on the one hand, 'inter-imperial rivalries' and, on the other hand, a new set of intermediate states, the 'Newly Influential/Industrialising Countries' (NICs).[52] Taken together, then, the latter phenomena have exacerbated inequalities amongst both strategies and systems in Africa, with new hierarchies arising both within and between states.

Only a few countries and classes on the continent have enjoyed adequate and sustained rates of growth since independence. Africa as a whole has performed less well than the rest of the Third World and several countries have suffered negative rates of growth since the mid-1970s.[53] A few states at the semi-periphery — a particularly privileged type of incorporation — have benefited from the process of semi-industrialisation and have been prepared to play sub-imperial roles to perpetuate their advantages. In general such states espouse a form of capitalism and are permissive towards the national and corporate interests of countries in the capitalist centre;[54] they include Ivory Coast, Kenya, Nigeria and South Africa (see Chapters 5, 6, 8 and 9).

However, the majority of countries in Africa have little or no choice — because of lack of interest externally or the absence of attractive resources or the inadequacies of infrastructure internally — but to become more self-reliant either through negotiation and partnership (state capitalism) or through disengagement and protectionism (state socialism).[55] The former grouping includes Botswana, Ghana, Zaire and Zambia (see Chapters 2, 4, 11 and 12) whereas the latter includes Angola, post-revolutionary Ethiopia, Somalia, Mozambique, Tanzania, and Zimbabwe (see Chapters 1, 3, 10 and 13). Reflecting on these two

13

sub-groupings, Colin Legum has calculated that 'there are now ten African countries which formally adhere to the Marxist system. . . However, there are considerable differences in the systems established in these ten countries, with only the first three (Mozambique, Angola, Guinea-Bissau) adhering to the classical Marxist pattern.'[56]

The divergent developmental and ideological paths already apparent are likely to exacerbate inequalities and tensions on the continent by the year 2000 because of change both inside and outside the continent. For, as Philippe Lemaitre predicts:

> the next 15 to 25 years present relatively positive opportunities for Africa's semi-industrialising countries but a bleak picture for the largely agricultural ones. The minority able to exploit such an opportunity include Algeria, Nigeria, Zaire, the politically special case of South Africa, possibly Egypt, perhaps Zambia and Morocco, one day (but only later in time?) Angola.[57]

As this 'Third' world becomes distinguished from the 'Fourth' and enters into some sort of 'special' relationship with the OECD countries so African unity may be further retarded and the continent's voice rendered discordant.[58] Taking such changes into account, Zartman has predicted, in a considerable revision of this earlier comments on continental homogeneity in Africa (see quotation at note 41 *supra*)[59] that inequalities in Africa will increase during the next decade. So, too, may the prospect of regional dominance and associated forms of authoritarian behaviour. For, as Claude Ake suggests, the choice now facing Africa may not be so much the old one between capitalism and socialism as that between socialism and fascism; the latter tendency being exacerbated by growing internal contradictions in particular state capitalism countries generated by uneven growth through semi-industrialisation and sometimes still expressed in *coups* or *putschs*.[60]

Nevertheless, despite this possibility, the primary choice for Africa at present remains that between more or less autonomy, involving associated socio-economic implications and relations. As Lemaitre identifies it,

> . . . the essential option of African states seems to be between governments controlled by internal middle class groups openly allied to governments and corporations in the industrialised world, and the more 'socialist', more autonomous, and more self-consciously indigenous regimes.[61]

Clearly the foreign, as well as development, policies of such different regimes would themselves be quite distinctive. The former, state capitalist type would tend to be less radical, less non-aligned and more open to transnational associations whereas the latter, state socialist or

14

socialist type would tend to be more radical, more non-aligned and less open to transnationalism.[62]

Basil Davidson, putting such alternative orientations into historical perspective, also proposed a rather similar typology of reactions to the 'imported model' in the 1970s, comparable to that adopted in this collection:

> A first category now consisted of a few regimes with relatively strong economies. Their ruling groups could still add wealth and status to themselves, and, by continuing to grow, hope to become a middle class capable of building an indigenous capitalism. . .
>
> A second category was numerous. These were regimes with relatively weak economies in most or all of which the parliamentary model had decayed into an autocracy, but where, because of economic weakness, ruling groups had no thought of being able to grow into dominant middle classes. Often relying on foreign partners for their survival, these were bureaucratic dictatorships of a peculiarly crude type. . . A third category, few in number, was also composed of regimes with weak economies. . . These were the regimes that had turned away from the given model and its decadent derivatives, and were ready to experiment with democratic politics. . . Within this third category a further division needs to be made. Some among them were independent regimes within the 'neo-colonial' situation. Others were regimes-information within territories which otherwise were still colonies.[63]

And Davidson sees a trend emerging in the 1980s away from the first two types and towards the third: 'the development of programmes for constructive change aimed at building indigenous models; and some of these, in the perspective of the 1980s, were manifestly within an entirely new field of independent thought, having discarded the various simulacra of other people's systems along with the rest of the decorative verbiage of the 1960s.'[64]

This projection has rather profound implications for analysis and for unity in Africa. At the analytic level, it reinforces the movement towards a more critical and sensitive political economy approach which might serve to explain such rejection of the 'imported model' and dependent situation. And at the continental level it points to exponential divergence (probably leading to conflict both within and between states) and related disagreements amongst actors. On the other hand, the increasing adoption of some form of socialism and non-capitalist path of development can be seen as a belated, but nonetheless positive and promising, response to a history of dependence and underdevelopment.[65] Moreover, this response may be rather timely given the tendency towards isolationism in the North, particularly in the United

States. Self-reliance in the 1980s may be an inevitable rather than a preferred or rational choice.[66]

The choice between more and less self-reliance in Africa is related, then, to an ongoing debate, concentrated this time in the advanced industrialised states, between more liberal and more parochial responses to changes in the international division of labour. The former, dominant, internationalist tradition is under attack from the latter, neo-mercantilist perspective. And whereas the establishment liberals still have faith in an 'open' world economy of multinational corporations and external exchange the new protectionists favour isolation and regulation to overcome the threat of deindustrialisation and the fear of impoverishment in the North.[67]

The outcome of this debate about 'inter-imperial rivalries' (essentially Japan and the EEC versus the United States) and the rise of NICs have profound implications for all African states, whether they be middling rich or very poor. This is because, on the one hand, the NICs in Africa — the sub-imperial powers of the semi-periphery — may identify with the OECD and the EEC rather than with the OAU or regional institutions (except to the extent that the latter reinforce rather than challenge dependent social formations[68]); this is the 'internationalists'' dream. However, on the other hand, the NICs in Africa and elsewhere may yet be abandoned by their would-be mentors if parochial and protectionist pressures in the latter become dominant; this is the 'neo-mercantilists'' vision.[69] In the latter instance, self-reliance would become more widespread on the continent as adoption of the imported model and an outward-looking approach were fore-closed. In this case, state socialism would come to replace state capitalism as the dominant characteristic of Africa's political economy in the 1980s.[70]

In any event, no matter what the outcomes of the internationalist versus protectionist debates in both the OAU and OECD, the adoption of a political economy mode of analysis has advantages, relevance and nuance compared with either the traditional approach or its revisionist variant. It is employed in this collection to enhance understanding of African foreign policy, to reflect current realities and trends, and to assist in intra- and extra-African comparisons. It may also, by focusing on substructure rather than superstructure, have a greater longevity than orthodox descriptions. 'Contingence' is by nature transitional and ephemeral; 'structure' is more continuous, providing the conditions and constraints within which particular relationships take place. The concern here is to investigate the *underlying* features of African states' foreign policy by looking at their place in the world system and their responses to this inheritance of dependence and underdevelopment. The emphasis is on currents rather than changes, on constraints rather than choices and on continua rather than crises. Instead of looking at diplomatic incidents and rhetorical flourishes, this analysis examines more continuous transnational linkages and development strategies. This does not mean that particular events or distinctive features are ignored altogether; merely that they are seen in the context of the national component's articulation within the global political economy.

To aid comparative analysis, as well as to advance consistency and continuity, each chapter will cover a common set of features, although treating each of these in a distinctive manner as dictated by national character and data. So each case study will deal with: historical incorporation and inheritance; contemporary dependence and underdevelopment; national political economy in the world system; nature of response through development strategy; relationship between political economy and foreign policy; overview of regional, continental, global and transnational interactions; and future of foreign policy.

This framework constitutes quite a demanding agenda for each author, transcending the limitations and frustrations of the dominant orthodox approach while raising novel and challenging difficulties. However, it is hoped that the adoption of a political economy perspective will advance both the comparative analysis of African foreign (and development) policy and the reconsideration of appropriate policy responses throughout the continent. The intent here is to go beyond the sub-field's somewhat unsatisfactory analytic inheritance as defined by the dominant realist paradigm and identified by Chris Allen's opening citation and thereby to contribute somewhat to a radical redefinition or reinterpretation of African foreign policy; i.e. one that is 'primary, fundamental, of the roots'. This volume is intended, then, to be an addition to the emerging 'radical' alternative in studies of both foreign policy and Africa, according to Peter Waterman's conception of the term:

> ... a major characteristic of conservative African studies is that despite their frequent sophistication and elegance, their findings are banal and trivial. In this sense, any work which ignores the superficial and epiphenomenal, which uncovers basic structures and root problems can and should be considered radical.[71]

Notes

1   Chris Allen, 'A bibliographical guide to the study of the political economy of Africa' in Peter C. W. Gutkind and Immanuel Wallerstein (eds), *Political Economy of Contemporary Africa* (Beverly Hills: Sage, 1976), pp. 298 and 301.

2 Basil Davidson, *Africa in Modern History: the search for a new society* (Harmondsworth: Pelican, 1978), p. 21.

3 *Ibid.*, p. 295.

4 *Ibid.*, p. 300. For more on the need for experimentation to achieve development see Basil Davidson, *Can Africa Survive? Arguments against growth without development* (Boston: Atlantic-Little, Brown, 1974).

5 Davidson, *Africa in Modern History* (note 2), p. 376.

6 See Timothy M. Shaw, 'Review Article. Foreign Policy, Political Economy and the Future: reflections on Africa in the world system', *African Affairs* vol. 79, no. 315, April 1980, pp. 260–268.

7 Contrast the second and third parts of and ideologies discussed in Carl G. Rosberg and Thomas M. Callaghy (eds), *Socialism in Sub-Saharan Africa: a new assessment* (Berkeley: University of California Institute of International Studies, 1979).

8 Davidson, *Africa in Modern History* (note 2), p. 376.

9 On various projections and predictions for this mid-term period see Timothy M. Shaw (ed.), *Alternative Futures for Africa* (Boulder: Westview, 1982).

10 Mark W. DeLancey, 'Current studies in African international relations', *Africana Journal*, vol. 7, no. 3, 1976, p. 220.

11 Davidson, *Africa in Modern History* (note 2), p. 25.

12 The selection also includes, incidentally, Arab and Black African states; Moslem and Christian societies; single- and multi-party regimes; civilian and military governments; countries ruled by original nationalist leaders and others that have experienced a variety of *coups*; societies that are anglophone, francophone or lusophone; countries where Arabic or Swahili are spoken; systems with one or many racial or ethnic groups; and countries in a variety of ecological zones.

13 For debates over the foreign and development policies of Tanzania, Nigeria, and Zambia, for example, see John Saul, 'Tanzania's transition to socialism?' *Canadian Journal of African Studies,* vol. 11, no. 2, 1977, pp. 313–339 and Cranford Pratt, 'Democracy and Socialism in Tanzania: a reply to John Saul', *Canadian Journal of African Studies*, vol. 12, no. 3, 1978, pp. 407–428; Timothy M. Shaw and Orobola Fasehun, 'Nigeria in the world system: alternative approaches, explanations and projections', *Journal of Modern African Studies*, vol. 18, no. 4, December 1980, pp. 551–573; and Douglas G. Anglin and Timothy M. Shaw, *Zambia's Foreign Policy: studies in diplomacy and dependence* (Boulder: Westview, 1979) pp. 409–429 and Timothy M. Shaw, 'Dilemmas of dependence and (under) develop-

ment: conflicts and choices in Zambia's present and prospective foreign policy' *Africa Today*, vol. 26, no. 4, Fourth Quarter 1979, pp. 43–65.

14 See I. William Zartman, *International Relations in the New Africa* (Englewood Cliffs: Prentice-Hall, 1966), pp. 143–149.

15 See Okwudiba Nnoli, *Self Reliance and Foreign Policy in Tanzania: the dynamics of the diplomacy of a new state, 1961 to 1971* (New York: NOK, 1978), especially pp. 1–18.

16 On Tanzania's reorientation and rearticulation see Timothy M. Shaw and Ibrahim S. R. Msabaha, 'From dependency to diversification: Tanzania 1967–1977' in K. Holsti (ed.), *Why Nations Realign: foreign policy restructuring in the post-war world* (London: George Allen & Unwin, 1982), pp. 47–72.

17 Nnoli, *Self Reliance and Foreign Policy in Tanzania* (note 15), p. 14. For more on Tanzania's foreign relations see K. Mathews and S. S. Mushi (eds), *Foreign Policy of Tanzania, 1961–1981: a reader* (Dar es Salaam: Tanzania Publishing House, 1981).

18 Mark W. DeLancey, 'The study of African international relations' in his collection on *Aspects of International Relations in Africa* (Bloomington: Indiana University African Studies Programme, 1979), p. 22.

19 See W.A.E. Skurnik, *The Foreign Policy of Senegal* (Evanston: Northwestern University Press, 1972), pp. 256–275.

20 *Ibid.*, p. 260.

21 *Ibid.*, p. 275. For another attempt to apply Rosenau's approach to an African case see Timothy M. Shaw, 'African states and international stratification: the adaptive foreign policy of Tanzania' in K. Ingham (ed.), *The Foreign Relations of African States* (London: Butterworth, 1974), pp. 213–236.

22 Skurnik, *The Foreign Policy of Senegal* (note 19), p. 293.

23 See *ibid.*, p. 295.

24 For an early attempt to do this see Timothy M. Shaw, 'The political economy of African international relations' *Issue*, vol. 5, no. 4, Winter 1975, pp. 29–38. See also Richard Harris, 'The political economy of Africa – underdevelopment or revolution' in his collection on *The Political Economy of Africa* (Cambridge: Schenkman, 1975), pp. 1–47.

25 DeLancey, 'Current studies in African international relations' (note 10), p. 220. See also his *Annotated Bibliography of African International Relations* (Boulder: Westview, 1980).

26 For attempts to do this see Timothy M. Shaw and Malcolm J. Grieve, 'Dependence or development: a review article on international and internal inequalities in Africa, *Development and Change*, vol. 8, no. 3, July 1977, pp. 377–408, 'Dependence as an

explanation of inequalities in Africa' in Larry Gould and Harry Targ (eds), *Global Dominance and Dependence: readings in theory and research* (Brunswick, Ohio: King's Court, 1980) and 'Dependence as an approach to understanding continuing inequalities in Africa', *Journal of Developing Areas*, vol. 13, no. 3, April 1979, pp. 229–246.

27 For an introduction to these continuities in external or transnational articulations see Timothy M. Shaw, 'The actors in African international politics' in Timothy M. Shaw and Kenneth A. Heard (eds), *The Politics of Africa: dependence and development* (London: Longman, 1979), pp. 357–396.

28 Christopher Clapham, 'Sub-Saharan Africa' in his collection on *Foreign policy making in developing states: a comparative approach* (Farnborough: Saxon House, 1977) p. 98.

29 See Olajide Aluko, 'The determinants of the foreign policies of African states', in his collection on *The Foreign Policies of African States* (London: Hodder & Stoughton, 1977), pp. 1–23.

30 For an overview of such modes of production and analysis see Timothy M. Shaw and M. Catharine Newbury, 'Dependence or interdependence? Africa in the global political economy' in DeLancey (ed.), *Aspects of International Relations in Africa*, pp. 39–89.

31 Clapham, 'Sub-Saharan Africa' (note 28), p. 99.

32 *Ibid.*, p. 87.

33 *Ibid.*, p. 100.

34 On these see Timothy M. Shaw, 'Dependence to (inter) dependence: review of debate on the (New) International Economic Order', *Alternatives*, vol. 4, no. 4, March 1979, pp. 557–578.

35 Ali A. Mazrui, 'African diplomatic thought and supranationality', in Ali A. Mazrui and Hasu H. Patel (eds), *Africa in World Affairs: the next thirty years* (New York: Third Press, 1973), p. 121.

36 Clapham, 'Sub-Saharan Africa' (note 28), p. 90.

37 See Zartman, *International Relations in the New Africa* (note 14), pp. 87–142.

38 See Timothy M. Shaw, 'Discontinuities and inequalities in African international politics', *International Journal*, vol. 30, no. 3, Summer 1975, pp. 369–390.

39 For overviews of these conditions see Timothy M. Shaw, 'Kenya and South Africa: 'sub-imperialist' states' *Orbis*, vol. 21, no. 2, Summer 1977, pp. 375–394 and 'International Stratification in Africa: sub-imperialism in eastern and southern Africa', *Journal of Southern African Affairs*, vol. 2, no. 2, April 1977, pp. 145–165.

40. For a review of these two approaches — the orthodox and the radical — to regionalism in Africa see Timothy M. Shaw, 'Africa' in

Werner J. Feld and Gavin Boyd (eds), *Comparative Regional Systems* (Elmsford, New York: Pergamon, 1980), pp. 355–397.

41   I. William Zartman, 'Africa' in James N. Rosenau, Kenneth W. Thompson and Gavin Boyd (eds), *World Politics: an introduction* (New York: Free Press, 1976), p. 593.

42   For attempts to do this see, for example, Kenneth W. Grundy, 'Regional relations in Southern Africa and the global political economy', in DeLancey (ed.), *Aspects of International Relations in Africa*, pp. 90–125 and Timothy M. Shaw, 'Regional co-operation and conflict in Africa', *International Journal*, vol. 30, no. 4, Autumn 1975, pp. 671–688.

43   See Davidson, *Africa in Modern History* (note 2), pp. 23–27.

44   For an overview of these see Timothy M. Shaw and Don Munton 'Africa's futures: a comparison of forecasts' and Paul Golding and Timothy M. Shaw, 'Alternative scenarios for Africa' in Shaw (ed.), *Alternative Futures for Africa* (note 9), pp. 37–130.

45   Adebayo Adedeji, 'Africa: the crisis of development and the challenge of a new economic order. Address to the fourth meeting of the Conference of Ministers and thirteenth session of the ECA, Kinshasa, February-March 1977' (Addis Ababa, July 1977), pp. 3–4 and 8.

46   For more on this see Timothy M. Shaw, 'On projections, prescriptions and plans: a review of the literature on Africa's future', *Quarterly Journal of Administration*, vol. 14, no. 4, July 1980, pp. 463–483 and 'Introduction: the political economy of Africa's futures' in Shaw (ed.), *Alternative Futures for Africa* (note 9), pp. 1–16.

47   Davidson, *Africa in Modern History* (note 2), pp. 18 and 21.

48   See, for instance, Samir Amin, 'Underdevelopment and dependence in Black Africa: origins and contemporary forms', *Journal of Modern African Studies*, vol. 10, no. 4, December 1972, pp. 503–524, and Immanuel Wallerstein, 'The three stages of African involvement in the world economy' in Peter C.W. Gutkind and Immanuel Wallerstein (eds), *The Political Economy of Contemporary Africa* (Beverly Hills: Sage, 1976), pp. 30–57 and 'Theoretical reprise' in his *The Modern World System* (New York: Academic, 1974), pp. 346–357. See also Immanuel Wallerstein, *The Capitalist World Economy* (Cambridge: University Press, 1979).

49   Steven Langdon and Lynn K. Mytelka, 'Africa in the changing world economy' in Colin Legum et al., *Africa in the 1980s: a continent in crisis* (New York: McGraw-Hill, 1979 for Council on Foreign Relations 1980s Project), p. 193.

50   See, *inter alia*, Michael B. Dolan, 'The Lomé Convention and

Europe's Relationship with the Third World: a critical analysis', *Journal of European Integration*, vol. 1, no. 3, 1978, pp. 369–394, Lynn K. Mytelka, 'The Lomé Convention and the new international division of labour', *Journal of European Integration*, vol. 1, no. 1, September, 1977, pp. 63–76 and Timothy M. Shaw 'EEC–ACP interactions and images as redefinitions of EurAfrica: exemplary, exclusive and/or exploitative?', *Journal of Common Market Studies*, vol. 18, no. 2, December 1979, pp. 135–158.

51 This typology is a refinement of that proposed in Shaw, 'The political economy of African international relations' (note 24).

52 For an overview of post-Bretton Woods difficulties and distinctions see Timothy M. Saw, 'Dependence to (inter) dependence' and 'Towards an international political economy for the 1980s: from dependence to (inter) dependence' (Halifax: Centre for Foreign Policy Studies, 1980).

53 See Adebayo Adedeji, 'Development and economic growth in Africa to the year 2000: alternative projections and policies' in Shaw (ed.), *Alternative Futures for Africa* (note 9), pp. 279–304 and Timothy M. Shaw, 'From dependence to self-reliance: Africa's prospects for the next twenty years', *International Journal,* vol. 35, no. 4, Autumn 1980, pp. 821–844.

54 See Timothy M. Shaw, 'Inequalities and interdependence in Africa and Latin America: sub-imperialism and semi-industrialisation in the semi-periphery', *Cultures et Développement*, vol. 10, no. 2, 1978, pp. 231–263.

55 For definitions and descriptions of these ideal types of political economy see Shaw, 'The political economy of African international relations' (note 24).

56 Colin Legum, 'The year in perspective' in his *Africa Contemporary Record: annual survey and documents, Volume 10, 1977–78* (New York: Africana, 1979), p. xxiii.

57 Philippe Lemaitre, 'Who will rule Africa by the year 2000?' in Helen Kitchen (ed.), *Africa: from mystery to maze* (Lexington: Lexington, 1976. Critical Choices for Americans Volume 11), p. 266.

58 See Timothy M. Shaw, 'The elusiveness of development and welfare: inequalities in the Third World' in Ronald St. John Macdonald, Douglas M. Johnston and Gerald L. Morris (eds), *The International Law and Policy of Human Welfare* (The Netherlands: Sijthoff & Noordhoff, 1978), pp. 81–109.

59 For a review of alternative approaches to regionalism see Timothy M. Shaw, 'Towards a political economy of regional integration and inequality in Africa', *Nigerian Journal of International Studies*, vol. 2, no. 2, October 1978, pp. 1–28.

60 See Claude Ake, *Revolutionary Pressures in Africa* (London: Zed, 1978), p. 107.
61 Lemaitre, 'Who will rule Africa by the year 2000?' (note 51), p. 275.
62 See comparative studies in Aluko (ed.), *The Foreign Policies of African States,* Rosberg and Callaghy (eds), *Socialism in Sub-Saharan Africa,* Lionel Cliffe, 'Underdevelopment or Socialism? A comparative analysis of Kenya and Tanzania' in Harris (ed.), *The Political Economy of Africa* (note 24), pp. 137–185 and Susan A. Gitelson 'Policy options for small states: Kenya and Tanzania reconsidered', *Studies in Comparative International Development,* vol. 12, no. 2, Summer 1977, pp. 29–57.
63 Davidson, *Africa in Modern History* (note 2), p. 329.
64 *Ibid.,* p. 376. See also Goulding and Shaw, 'Alternative scenarios for Africa' and Adedeji, 'Development and economic growth in Africa to the year 2000', in Shaw (ed.), *Alternative Futures for Africa,* and Timothy M. Shaw and Malcolm J. Grieve, 'The political economy of resources: Africa's future in the global environment', *Journal of Modern African Studies,* vol. 16, no. 1, March 1978, pp. 1–32.
65 On such a non-capitalist path see Mai Palmberg (ed.), *Problems of Socialist Orientation in Africa* (Stockholm: Almqvist & Wiksell, 1978).
66 See Julius K. Nyerere, 'The rational choice', in his *Freedom and Development: uhuru na maendeleo* (Dar es Salaam: OUP, 1973), pp. 379–390 and Davidson, *Can Africa Survive?*
67 For a useful typology of state–corporate relations, one that relates to this classical versus conservative debate, see Robert Gilpin, 'The political economy of the multinational corporation: three contrasting perspectives', *American Political Science Review,* vol. 70, no. 1, March 1976, pp. 184–191. He identifies three major perspectives: liberalism, marxism and mercantilism. For a development of this typology see C. Fred Bergsten, Thomas Horst, Theodore H. Moran, *American Multinationals and American Interests* (Washington: Brookings, 1978), pp. 309–353. They identify four types of home country–corporate links – neo-imperialist, neomercantilists, sovereignty-at-bay, and global-reach:

> The first two postulate that the growth of multinationals represents an extension of the power of the home country at the expense (where there is a trade-off) of the host countries. They differ over how much narrow class interest predominates over the public interest in the formation of foreign policy in the home state. The sovereignty-at-bay and global-

reach schools of thought postulate that the growth of multinationals represents an extension of their own power at the expense of the power of home and host countries. They differ over whether multinationals transform the international system for good or for ill (p. 314).

68 For a review of the compatibility or incompatibility of various forms of regionalism at the levels of both analysis and interaction see Shaw, 'Towards a political economy of regional integration and inequality in Africa' and 'EEC–ACP interactions and images as redefinitions of EurAfrica'.

69 See Shaw, 'Towards an international political economy for the 1980s', and Malcolm J. Grieve et al., 'Global problems for Canadians: forecasts and speculations', *Behind the Headlines*, vol. 37, no. 6.

70 On this prospect see Timothy M. Shaw and Malcolm J. Grieve, 'Inequalities and the state in Africa', *Review of Black Political Economy*, vol. 8, no. 1, Fall 1977, pp. 27–42; 'Chronique Bibliographique – The political economy of Africa: internal and international inequalities', *Cultures et Développement,* vol. 10, no. 4, 1978, pp. 609–648, and 'Dependence or development: internal and international inequalities in Africa' in Palmberg (ed.), *Problems of Socialist Orientation in Africa* (note 65), pp. 54–82.

71 Peter Waterman, 'On radicalism in African Studies' in Peter C. W. Gutkind and Peter Waterman (eds), *African Social Studies: a radical reader* (London: Heinemann, 1977), p. 14.

1 Angola*

Fola Soremekun

The People's Republic of Angola (PRA) came into existence on 11 November 1975. This marked the culmination of 13 years of nationalist armed struggle against the Portuguese government and a turbulent year of quick decolonisation,[1] one that had wide external dimensions. Born in international controversy, the People's Republic is yet to have peace and security to pursue properly the normal goals of political, social and economic development. Why? The answer is complex and multifaceted.

The ruling political party in Angola, the MPLA–PT,[2] declared itself to be Marxist–Leninist-oriented shortly after independence and began to embark on instant socialism swinging away from the capitalist mode in the Southern Africa milieu of Western capitalism.[3] By this clear move it appeared to have guaranteed itself perpetual hostility and armed attacks from the minority white regimes of Namibia and South Africa. In Angola itself 90 per cent illiteracy abounded, symbolic of colonial neglect; members of the ruling party were far from being united once independence had been achieved; and party cadres were for the most part still guerillas with little or no experience of running a complex modern government. MPLA–PT had not been put into power

* An earlier version of this chapter was presented at a seminar in the Department of History at the University of Ife in February 1982.

by any electoral process and it still faced opposition by southerners led by Jonas Savimbi's UNITA movement. In the midst of all this, MPLA–PT was trying to intensify its own political following while embarking upon national reconstruction. If foreign policy is but an extension of internal policy, the interplay of these factors in the Angolan case was going to put the declared foreign policy objectives of the ruling party to a severe test.

This chapter has four themes. First, the origins and early ideological tendencies of MPLA–PT as a background to understanding its enunciation of a socialist ideology in 1976. Second, the challenges of the evolution in the party's foreign policy. Third, its Marxist socialist option and the search for national security. And fourth, a brief look at foreign policy after the death of Dr Agostinho Neto.

It is necessary to point out at the outset that research and writing about Angola have remained a perpetual problem. In colonial days scholars faced the constraints imposed by Portuguese fascists. Today we face another set of difficulties similar, ironically, to those of colonial days. Angola's borders had been virtually sealed off from the world except for very few favoured folks, no doubt partly because of the security problem the country faces. When entry is gained one's movements are somewhat restricted. Researchers have found that they can no longer rely on old friendships even though these might have been formed in pre-independence days at a time when the new rulers were exiles. This is partly because under the monolithic party structure now being operated only one source of information is permissible; officials do not like to be interviewed. And it is partly because of the security situation in the country, whereby almost every subject of enquiry is looked upon as a 'state secret': statistics are virtually impossible to cross-check.

Therefore it is incumbent on one to be able to read between the lines, to pick up cues and scrutinise them. It is hope that the material presented here — which cannot be called definitive — will at least give a fair representation of Angola's foreign policy at the time of writing.

Origins and early tendencies

In October 1976 the third plenary meeting of MPLA–PT Central Committee took place to deliberate on matters of importance for the new Angolan nation. The time was particularly auspicious. Seven months previously the second war of national liberation had ended. It had resulted in the expulsion of FNLA and UNITA from the country. So it was necessary for the ruling party to define clearly the path the

26

nation must follow. Angola's foreign policy objectives were defined as follows at the meeting:[4]

1   The establishment and maintenance of diplomatic relations with all countries of the world, on the basis of mutual respect for national sovereignty and territorial integrity, non-aggression and non-interference in internal affairs, equal and reciprocal advantage and peaceful coexistence between states with different social systems;

2   Respect for the principles of the UN and OAU Charters;

3   The safeguarding of political independence and our socialist option.

4   The policy of non-alignment in respect of military blocs set up in the world, basing our action within the Movement of Non-Aligned Countries on strengthening the anti-colonialist and anti-imperialist orientation, for peace, freedom and the independence of peoples and for social progress.

5   The rejection of all international commitments entered into in the name of the Angolan people by the Portuguese colonial government on their annulment in the light of the legislation in force in the PRA.

6   The forbidding of foreign military bases on the national soil.

7   The protection of Angolans abroad and their interests.

8   The strengthening of bonds of friendship and cooperation with the socialist community and with anti-imperialist communities on every continent.

9   The diversification of economic and technico-scientific cooperation.

10   Support for the creation of a New International Economic Order which eliminates the dependence of underdeveloped countries on the developed capitalist countries.

11   Maintaining the traditional spirit of unity and struggle against imperialism and neocolonialism among the former Portuguese colonies and strengthening the bonds of friendship, militant solidarity and multiform cooperation between these states.

12   Militant solidarity with the oppressed peoples and with the national liberation movements, and support for the armed struggle waged by these peoples to win their rights.

13   Solidarity with the struggle of the workers of the whole world on the basis of proletarian internationalism.

14   Support for the actions conducted by the socialist countries and the democratic and progressive forces internationally, to achieve detente and world disarmament and the elimination of sources of tension that imperialism has created or wishes to create

in order to prevent the progress and liberation struggle of the peoples. And

15 Good neighbourly relations with countries adjacent to Angola.

From these objectives we can see that MPLA—PT is 'Marxist—Leninist socialist' and is determined to follow a foreign policy in line with such socialist countries. But it should be noted that some of these objectives are not necessarily distinctive or ideological. They would seem to be fairly normal objectives of most independent African countries. When the 'socialist' veneer has been stripped off them, close to half of the objectives would appear to be almost pedestrian. Yet these represent in essence a final distillation and the history of early foreign policy tendencies of the MPLA—PT. For 20 years, from 1956 when the party was founded, to 1976 when it was in control of Angola as the ruling party, the MPLA—PT had seen itself first as a government in exile and later as the true government which should have power above all other parties like FNLA and UNITA which had also been governments in exile.

The party's belief in itself was and is real. The exigences of the war for national independence and the vicissitudes of winning as wide a sympathy as possible among Angolans and people from all over the world appeared to have led the party into being content with being labelled 'left-leaning'. Much of the struggle against it by hostile forces stemmed from this. Yet this 'left-leaning' tendency is not a pretence; it was genuinely felt from the very beginning. Lucio Lara, the present secretary of the party, has made this clear:

> From the on-set the MPLA's policies were closely related to a scientific socialist orientation, . . . although attempts were made, the formation of a Party was never achieved during the national liberation process. At the height of our national liberation struggle, when the greatest successes were achieved and the prestige of MPLA finally compelled recognition both nationally and internationally, that is in the late 60s and early 70s, the idea of forming a Party arose. But after in-depth analysis. . . it was felt to be premature and perhaps a little unrealistic. It was when we arrived at the legal establishment of the MPLA in Angola and therefore had much more direct contact with the working class which still had little class consciousness, in the course of the Second Liberation War in 1975—76 that what we regard as the minimum conditions for making the MPLA into the MPLA—Workers' Party were created. . . The Second National Liberation War (1975—1976) was a very great lesson for our people. The invasions we suffered raised the class consciousness of the working

28

people and the idea of exploitation and imperialist oppression became very much more clearly understood. Up to then the essential target of our struggle had been colonialist, and imperialism had been something that the Movement and its leaders spoke about but which our people were not very aware of.[5]

A look into the party's constitution and programme reveals the following, symbolic of its eventual socialist orientation and rhetoric. The MPLA–PT pledged itself 'To ally itself with all the progressive forces of the world. . .'; 'To defend. . .the interests of. . . peasants and workers. . . the two most important groups in the country.' It was also determined to 'liquidate private monopoly of production of consumer products' and to 'define the limits of extension of private rural property.'[6] When compared to points 5, 12 and 13 of the above foreign policy objectives, it can be seen that a clear linkage exists between internal and foreign policy.

Between 1960 and 1961 the MPLA–PT government in exile was headquartered in Conakry where it joined CONCP (*Conferencia das Organizacoes Nacionalistas das Colonias Portuguesas*), an association with 'left-wing' links. It was however the association of the Angolan Communist Party with the formation of MPLA that early 'painted' the party as being perhaps pro-communist. It should be noted further that CONCP, which established itself in Casablanca in 1961, led to the associating of MPLA with the 'Casablanca' bloc in Africa, generally regarded at that time to be 'left-wing'.[7] Throughout the period of the struggle for independence in all of the Portuguese-speaking countries of Africa, CONCP members met periodically. Indeed a few days after Angola's independence that body gave support to Neto's international moves to involve Cuba and the Soviet Union in his country's struggle against South Africa, FNLA and UNITA. The significance of point 11 of the foreign policy objectives could then be seen. CONCP still continues to meet: in 1980 it met in Luanda to resolve the problem of a military coup in Guinea-Bissau.

Although, in theory, the Central Committee made national and foreign policy for MPLA–PT, the real driving force within this Committee was Neto and the other members of the Political Bureau. Before Neto's death in September 1979, as throughout most of the history of the MPLA–PT even before independence, the three most poweful men were the president himself, Lucio Lara, and Lopo do Nascimento, although it was from Neto that most policies flowed. Although they had other motives of their own, the leaders of the *Revolta Active* (a dissent group in the party) shortly before independence had bitterly criticised Neto's style of leadership which they said was 'dictatorial'. But his method of operation was seen by many of his followers as the result of his having innovative ideas. As the leader of MPLA—PT, Neto's words were listened to eagerly. As a poet, he towered above most of his contemporaries in the use of the Portuguese language, depicting the lives and vicissitudes of the oppressed peoples of Angola, a stand which made many see him as 'left-wing'.

In his speeches before independence — for example, 'Who is the enemy?' given at Dar es Salaam in February 1974 — Neto identified the enemy of Angola as 'Imperialism which is more than a localised phenomenon in Angola, but at present a universal phenomenon'.[8] Imperialism, he said, was skilful in using various devices to perpetuate itself; it used racism and created privileged classes opposed to the peasants. Angola was not only dominated by Portugal; it was dominated also by the political and economic interests of several world powers including Britain and the United States which were competing to dominate the country's strategic position and its wealth. In a free Angola 'power must be exercised in such a way so that the most exploited masses. . .have control'. . . MPLA's struggle was one against 'imperialist forces'. Reflecting on the world's power blocs he noted that 'it is the socialists who hold high the banner of internationalism and. . . give the most support to the liberation movement. Nonetheless the liberation movements ought to be careful in their dealings with their main helpers, the socialists, so that they could preserve their personalities and reflect the social image of their own individual countries.'

These statements should be seen as the precursors of the sort of foreign policy Angola might have and the direction the MPLA—PT leader might take his party into after independence. Many of Neto's anti-imperialist statements were to be repeated again and again from the OAU-arranged and abortive MPLA—PT Congress of August 1974 in Lusaka to the special congress of Neto's main-line supporters held in Moxico, Angola in late September 1974. There he reminded his audience that 'the solidarity of socialist countries was and is fundamental, it is the principal material base for our combat.'[9] Reflecting on the Lusaka Congress he labelled it a cross-roads in Angolan history 'where the progressive forces sought to overcome the epoch of colonial slavery to enter into a life of liberty and of dignity. . . (whereas). . . the reactionaries wanted to dominate through neo-colonialist formulas'.[10] The party's manifesto, released when it entered Angola in November 1974, did not flag in its condemnation of the evils of imperialism and the efforts of 'reactionary forces' to subvert Angola.[11]

From that point on, and with increasing political rivalry with FNLA and UNITA, the party became more radicalised. The turning point came in March 1975 when FNLA unleashed a particularly stiff offensive against Neto's party. This led to a frantic search for more support by MPLA–PT. The Soviet Union, which had been temporarily cold towards the party because of OAU politics, was then ready to reactivate its support for a party it had been helping for so long. And the intensified efforts of both FNLA and UNITA with South African help and United States acquiescence seemed to have put MPLA–PT into a position that for survival it had to rely on Cuba, the Soviet Union and other socialist countries; but not exclusively so, for Congo (Brazzaville), Guinea, and Nigeria also give substantial help.

Neto was to reminisce on these matters in a major speech in 1978 in Cabinda and to the OAU Conference in Khartoum.[12] In Cabinda, he acknowledged an indebtedness to the Soviet Union and Cuba: 'You comrades know about the enormous volume of the quantity of arms which we received from Soviet Russia. You know that with these arms we are today guaranteeing our independence and our territorial integrity. . . And you know comrades that during that period, during the second war of National Liberation, there was an extraordinarily important element. . .the comrades from Cuba. They were the comrades who came and who helped us make military struggle and who did not hesitate later in increasing their help into other areas. . . of reconstruction'.[13]

Indebtedness to Cuba and to the Soviet Union raised the question of whether or not it might become either necessary or desirable for the President and Angola's foreign policy makers to reciprocate as is normal in international affairs. What effect would this have on the direction and practice of Angola's foreign policy when, on the day of independence, Neto had intoned: 'The foreign policy of the People's Republic of Angola, based on the principles of total independence always followed by the MPLA, will be a policy of non-alignment'.[14] We shall see later how and to what extent this pledge was kept. Would it not be in conflict with points 4 and 14 of MPLA–PT foreign policy objectives? Did Neto and his men in their bid for power tell the Cubans and the Russians to help them when they intended to establish a Marxist–Leninist socialist state in Angola? Every effort made by this researcher to find out has been met by prevarication on the part of MPLA cadres. And the official Cuban version of involvement does not help either.[15]

Perhaps the Angolans did not have to give any assurances to the Russians and the Cubans. The 'left-wing' tendencies of the MPLA–PT, the history of obtaining most help from the socialist states even before independence, plus the prevailing circumstances of the party's struggle for power inside Angola would appear to have been sufficient to reinforce the party's inclinations towards Marxist–Leninism. Neto's declaration to this effect was to come about six months after the end of the second war of national liberation, in October 1976. But a hint to this effect was already given on independence day: 'Putting a final end to colonialism and decisively barring the way to neo-colonialism, the MPLA, at this solemn moment, affirms its firm intention radically to change the present structures. . .'[16]

Colonial legacy and the challenge of evolving a foreign policy

At independence the People's Republic of Angola had no internal political structure based upon a consensus established through the polls. Also the young state inherited a chaotic economy, the remnant of a capitalist system which MPLA—PT had vowed to change. The banks had been looted almost to emptiness, white skilled workers had fled, large amounts of capital had disappeared, diamond mines had been robbed, industrial machinery had been sabotaged, transportation had been crippled, and most of the bridges had been wrecked. Social unrest was noticeable everywhere. The workers were enraged and embittered by the history of past oppression. There was virtually no food. The political, social and economic conditions of Angola at that time were better described than actually experienced.[17] These internal conditions of Angola further fuelled the left-leaning tendencies of MPLA—PT leaders giving them and their supporters visions of a new society and the new people to live in it.

In August 1975 Neto and his cadre launched a generalised resistance — *Resistencia Popular Generalizada*. The *Resistencia* was more than a means of fighting war against invaders; it was also a way of trying to teach socialism to the people. The preface to a popular book then in circulation said:

> If colonialism emerged and if it developed in our country as a violation of the existing structure, it provoked. . . a collection of various forms of reaction. . . The dialectic product of the conflict of interests is the history. . .of people's resistance, it is the formation in the struggle of national consciousness and of the structural and organisational forms which that. . .consciousness implicates.[18]

The role of MPLA—PT in this resistance programme was to use Marxist socialist organisational techniques in trying to create an alternative to the colonial political structure through *Poder Popular* (people's power) to be buttressed by *Poder Economico* (economic power). These went together with a centralised government organisation called CADCO (*Comissao de Apoio e Dinamizacao de Cooperativas*). The link-up between economic and political activities was symbolised in the slogan *Produzir e Resistir*: to produce is to resist. Sub-groups of MPLA—PT were made more dynamic: JMPLA (Youth Wing of the MPLA), OMA

(Women's Organisation), ODP (People's Defence Organisation – People's Militia) and so on.

In the wake of the military and other aid being given by Cuba, the Soviet Union and other socialist countries MPLA came to the point of victory in Angola. Many Angolans were impressed, believing that the socialist system might well be a suitable alternative to the capitalist one they wanted to discard. With a fantastic amount of propaganda through the newspapers, pamphlets and other media, the Angolan public came to accept tight international relations with the socialist countries. Thus Angolan MPLA–PT leaders helped to stimulate and were in turn reinforced by public opinion to reorient their foreign policy toward socialist countries in general and toward Cuba and the Soviet Union in particular.

On independence day Neto had the opportunity to make a formal invitation in a blanket fashion for aid from friendly countries, a move made not without regard to creating a good image for the PRA in the international arena. Before then no Angolan leader even admitted the presence of Cuban or Soviet advisers. In his independence day speech Neto spoke in a manner calculated to please audiences both at home and abroad. At the same time it was a fairly consistent speech, given the political tendencies of his party. It took into account the inter-relatedness of internal and foreign policy. Among other things, Neto pledged to put an end to the legacy of distortions between the sectors of Angolan economy. The economy, he said, would be planned to serve its people, 'never voracious imperialism'. It would also be geared towards becoming 'an inwardly oriented economy'. Both private and foreign economic activities which were useful to the economy and the people would be protected. The rub here was, of course, who but the party could decide the criteria for 'usefulness' of any enterprise. Neto went on, 'The People's Republic of Angola will be open to the whole world as regards its economic relations'. It would accept international cooperation on the unquestioned premise that 'external aid' should not be conditional.

In its domestic reorganisation, the land problem would be tackled and cooperatives and state enterprises would be set up. Externally, the PRA was in the anti-imperialist struggle and would have as its natural allies African countries, socialist countries and all progressive forces in the world. All other generalised principles of international relations were acceptable to the new state. When compared to foreign policy objectives unveiled in 1976 the tone of the independence day speech was very mild indeed.

On the day of independence Angola was in one of the darkest days in its history. There were two governments, one in Luanda, the other in Huambo. As Neto was making his speech, FNLA guns could be heard.

The enemy of the party was less than 12 kilometres away from the north of Luanda; and to the south, the South Africans were less than 60 kilometres away. Neto could not afford to antagonise any nation on earth at that time; he was looking for friends anywhere, even in the United States.

A measure of PRA uncertainty was that the first diplomatic recognition came from an unexpected source: Brazil, not the Soviet Union or even Cuba. And Brazil had hardly supported the nationalist struggle for independence, at least not after 1964. Brazil was believed by many high-ranking Angolans to be nothing but a medium through which the United States act. More diplomatic recognition followed soon afterwards, mainly by members of CONCP and the socialist commonwealth. As the country's security situation improved, so did recognition and aid. Diplomatic recognition by Nigeria in mid-December plus a promise of aid in excess of $100 million was a major boost to the government. The extraordinary OAU summit of January 1976 made certain that Neto and his men were virtually secure, giving an added incentive to FAPLA and the Cubans to get rid of South African, UNITA and FNLA forces throughout the land by March. The first challenge to the MPLA—PT government had been met by skilful international diplomacy and war. It was, however, an unfinished business. Nevertheless, the objective of the MPLA—PT in getting independence seemed to be realisable.

After the achievement of diplomatic recognition the attention of party leaders was turned to restructuring the national economy along Marxist—Leninist lines. Since Angola's economy had been part of the Western system and since the MPLA—PT's tendency was toward Marxist—Leninism it was clear that the leaders would need all their diplomatic skills to try to wrest the economy from 'voracious imperialism'. This called for a delicate internal manoeuvre to win the support of the people to be able to deal with Western multinationals and other businesses in the country.

In February 1976 a Law of State Intervention was passed which identified three sectors for future planning of the economy: state economic units, cooperatives and private enterprise. This set the stage for state control of strategic sectors of the economy, especially those involving multinational companies.[19] When the second war of national liberation was over, the government ordered a survey of leading industrial enterprises. Intensified propaganda against 'imperialists and exploiters' was the order of the day. International enterprises in Angola included the following: Gulf Oil (American), after which one of the worst *muceques* was named, Leyland Motors (British), and Tanganyika Concessions (the British controllers of the Benguela Railroads) etc. Associated with particular enterprises were the following Portuguese individuals:

Manuel Vinhas: Cuca, banks, *Noticia Magazine*, security companies, French capital, animal and poultry feeds.
Engineer Cardoso e Cuuha: Fishing, cattle, beer, flour mills.
Sousa Lara: Sugar, sisal, cotton.
Engineer Fernando Falcao: Building construction.
Fernandes Vieira: Chairman of Association of Commerce and Industry.
Mota Veiga: Import and export, cars, sisal.
Mario Cunha: Coffee, palm oil.
Mauricio Vieirade Brito: Portuguese banking and financial groups.
Sousa Machado: Steel, mines.

The MPLA call was that the exploiters should have their enterprises expropriated and confiscated without compensation. A government survey showed that out of 692 enterprises investigated only 294 were in operation with their former management; the remaining 408, were either abandoned or had to be reorganised by the state. A Nationalisation Act was also passed the same month 'to enable the state to take action with regard to industrial plants which had been abandoned or sabotaged and which were considered important for the economic development of the country'.[20]

The stage was set for a spate of nationalisations, mainly from May to June 1976, just as in early May a significant move was made between PRA and the Soviet Union. The two countries signed a declaration on the basic principles of friendly relations and cooperation, a consular convention, an agreement on cultural and scientific cooperation, a trade agreement, an agreement on economic and technical cooperation, an agreement on cooperation in the fishing industry and an agreement on merchant shipping. This dizzying array of treaties was seen by Angolans as necessary to help give the country some measure of stability in view of its shaky foundation in virtually all fields. This was yet another show of solidarity by a socialist state in the face of adversity; perhaps also it was a wooing gesture and a prelude to a bilateral Treaty of Friendship and Cooperation which was signed in October and cemented with the award of a Lenin Prize to Neto.

On May Day 1976, Angolan workers could begin to see the significance of independence as Angolan leaders were showing their citizens that a people's government could punish exploiters. These moves were popular. But when the air was cleared it revealed that government had been cautious not to violate its own pledge about foreign enterprises which were not Portuguese-owned. Shares owned by non-Portuguese foreign private investors were exempted.[21] Angola's new rulers seemed to believe that rage against Portugal at that point was permissible in international relations, Article 10 of the PRA constitution notwithstanding. According to that the PRA undertook to recognise, protect and guarantee private activities and property, 'even those of foreigners' so long as they were useful to the economy and people. This was probably what Neto felt he had promised on independence day in bilateral Angolan—Portuguese relations:

> The People's Republic of Angola will give special attention to relations with Portugal, and because it wants this to be lasting it is establishing them on a new basis devoid of any colonial vestige. The present dispute with Portugal will be dealt with calmly, so as not to envenom our future relations.[22]

Other anti-Portugal fiscal measures were to follow, further straining relations.

But no such sweeping nationalisation or expropriation moves affected a company such as Gulf Oil, which had been operating in Cabinda before independence. During the second war, in December 1975, the United States government had put pressure on Gulf not to pay profits or taxes due to PRA. Due to Gulf's lobby in Washington — and, in any case since the war was soon over and the United States faced an energy shortage — it was in the United States interest that Gulf operations be reopened. The company was also afraid that should it not move quickly enough its equipment would rot and it might lose its area of operation to the Italians or the French. So in March 1976 Angolan funds were unfrozen and negotiations with the new government were started. These resulted in Gulf reopening its field about May. However, a new company was formed called Cabinda Gulf Oil Company in which 51 per cent of the shares were held by Angola. Gulf Oil International was to handle the marketing.

This agreement was essentially a triumph for common sense on both sides. On the part of Angola there was nothing particularly Marxist-socialist about the move. On the part of the United States, which up to now has refused to recognise the PRA, President Reagan's rhetoric would not make him stop a United States Export—Import Bank loan of about $100 million to Angola to increase oil production in Cabinda from 100,000 barrels a day to 200,000; this deal was signed on 13 July 1981.

For Neto and his cadre the fact of the situation was that good international oil diplomacy demanded that they remember that even before independence oil brought in about 40 per cent of Angola's revenue! Indeed from the end of 1976 up to 1981, in spite of government efforts to ensure that all economic activities be made to reach 1973 levels, the result was that of all the sectors in the confused Angolan economic situation, oil consistently brought in more than 70 per cent of the country's export earnings; yet production by Gulf did not restart until May 1976. Between 1976 and 1980, despite mass harvesting, coffee brought in only $33\frac{1}{3}$ per cent of prewar level income; Angola lost its fourth place as coffee producer to become the eighth.[23] And iron ore appeared permanently out of function: in 1973 it yielded 5.6 million tonnes of ore and in September 1981 when 140,000 tonnes of ore left Angola it came from pre-independence stock. Production has not yet been restarted.[24] Mining was not to resume at the main Kassinga mine until 1983 when it was to be operated by an Austrian concern — Austro-Mineral — which had been examining the mines and carrying out a feasibility study on a new deposit in Central Angola east of Luanda.[25]

Ironically enough the deal with Gulf, which gave Angola a good image abroad as a respecter of international treaties, did not go without considerable criticism in Angola itself, particularly within UNTA (Angolan Union of Workers), the increasingly radicalised shock troops of MPLA—PT. This body and many other Angolans were demanding total takeovers of all capitalist enterprises without compensation. In October 1976 at the closing session of a UNTA conference Neto had to resolve the dilemma of the necessity of a 'left-leaning' government having to deal with a capitalist company like Gulf and others like it: Total, Texaco, Elf and Petrobras. The President claimed that the Angolan people alone could not defeat colonialism and imperialism. Although they had their natural allies — the socialists, the anti-imperialist countries in Africa, and the working class and peasants throughout the world — realism was needed at that point in managing the economy:

> The national economy needs devices to buy medicines, raw materials, tools, food, industrial equipment, means of transport. . . These devices are obtained through sales on the international market, of our mineral products...through the sale of petroleum, iron, diamonds, cement, dried fish. . .coffee, cotton, sisal, etc. Decrees, inflammatory editorials could not resolve the situation in favour of Angola. . . The petroleum of Cabinda is extracted by means of advanced technology. Do we have this technology? No![26]

What needed to be done, therefore, was to renegotiate the contract with Gulf. According to this, the company was obliged to produce as much oil as before: 'It is clear that Gulf will make profit; can we reject that situation? No. . .but we could not avoid that situation without causing new difficulties for Angolan workers and the Angolan people in general. To paralyse now the production of petroleum will be to bring us against the people of Angola, unnecessary hardship. . . This is an example which is valid for the various enterprises which are working here in Angola.' Then in one of the clearest and most forthright declarations, Neto put forth his party's ideology:

> We do not wish to deceive anyone. We do not wish to deceive the foreign monopolists, capitalists, hiding that we are going to follow the road of socialisation of our means of production, of finance, of trade, of services and all that we can socialise as rapidly as possible. When we speak of socialism we are speaking seriously. We are not dealing with the so called 'African Socialism' or 'Bantu Socialism' but of scientific socialism. . .

Neto's attitude towards companies like Gulf was shaped essentially by the belief that industry was the decisive factor in economic and social development because of its high rate of growth and its involvement of other sectors, particularly agriculture, enhancing the value of its products and supplying it with tools and machinery, fertilisers, pesticides and irrigation systems. So far as extractive industries were concerned, priority was to be given to producing essential goods for satisfying the requirements of the people. And in all sectors effort was to be directed towards bringing in maximum foreign currency.[27]

When the Central Committee met as has been previously mentioned in October 1976 and set down PRA foreign policy objectives it was its belief, among other things, that imperialism wanted to maintain the *status quo* in Southern Africa. This would necessitate keeping the Angolan economy under dependent capitalist monopoly by promoting a diplomatic campaign and economic blockade against MPLA—PT to damage its image in international circles. Imperialism was blamed for, among other things, seeking to re-arm 'puppet' groups to make life difficult for the MPLA—PT government. The Central Committee clearly linked the Angolan political and economic situation with foreign affairs, both regional and global:

> Political struggle in the international field cannot be dissociated from action conducted in the interior of the country for the realisation of great objectives fixed in the phase of National Reconstruction: the planting of People's Power, the techno-material bases for the construction of socialism and of economic independence. Diplomatic struggles in the phase of transition toward socialism will have as fundamental objectives to create in the exterior of the country conditions indispensable for the consolidation of national independence and safeguarding the revolutionary gains of Angolan people, without losing the view that external policy constitutes an important front of struggle between bourgeois interests and those of the international proletariat.

Conscious of these bases, national objectives were drawn up, with their tilt toward Marxist-socialist states and policies which such states tended to adopt in their foreign affairs. It was declared firmly that 'The friends of the Angolan people are the socialist states and countries and progressive forces from all continents. Our allies are countries and organisations which helped us or which cooperated with us for reasons of common interest and reciprocity'.[28]

Angola's Marxist-socialist option and the search for national security and unity

The people who ratified the basic policy objectives of Angola's foreign policy were filled with fear; they shared with their country the widespread feeling of insecurity. Having been schooled by long years of clandestine activities, having actually experienced fascism at work and having come close to being annihilated by South African forces they had come to perceive the world as a perpetual conspiracy at work — against them. In the light of the myriad problems Angola was facing, the members of the Central Committee felt they had to define their friends, enemies and allies carefully. Socialist victories won by progressive and democratic forces (among which no doubt was the expulsion of South Africa from Angola) and by the liberation movements had to be consolidated. Meanwhile, imperialism, in desperation, was becoming more aggressive. Aspects of this were the United States' veto preventing PRA from being admitted to the UN, the Western powers trying to set up a South Atlantic Pact, and so forth. Points 3, 8, 12, 13 and particularly 14 — noting 'the tension that imperialism has created or wishes to create to prevent the progress of liberation struggle of the peoples' — clearly reflected the leaders' fears. From independence to the time of writing, Angola has been in a state of perpetual insecurity within and without. It has been compelled by these circumstances to search for security while it tries to unite the country.

Neto's first ever visit as a Head of State outside Angola was in March 1976 to socialist Guinea (Conakry) to attend a summit meeting for the purpose of creating a 'Front for the Consolidation of Anti-Imperialist Forces'. Also present were Luis Cabral of Guinea-Bissau and Fidel Castro of Cuba. Their major concern was the question of Southern Africa and the military situation in Angola. A joint communiqué stated that all the leaders decided to support MPLA: 'Cuba, Guinea and Guinea-Bissau assured President Neto of their decision to furnish the Angolan government with all the help which would be necessary until it reached and maintained complete independence'.[29]

But despite the snowball recognition, diplomatic acknowledgement represented an incomplete success for PRA, for four reasons. First, voting at the crucial OAU summit revealed that African states were split evenly. Half were for MPLA and the other half were against her in a back-handed way: they appeared to be against 'Soviet intervention in Africa' rather than for FNLA and UNITA. This result was due in part to active lobbying by the Soviet Union and the United States; most West European countries remained sceptical about recognition. The British and Americans were particularly sceptical mainly because some of their countrymen had been captured as mercenaries and were slated for trial. PRA's effort in convening an international jury to deal with them together with the issue of mercenarism was an attempt essentially to win a good international image. Nonetheless, in the Western media the international commission was seen as a 'kangaroo court' or as a 'show trial'.

Second, the United States, still dazed in the wake of its debacle in Vietnam, had been unable to respond meaningfully to the Angola crisis except to call for a government of national unity among the three contending parties and for the withdrawal of the Cubans. Up to this moment it continues to stick to these two points as preconditions for a recognition of Angola. The significance of this for internal stability in Angola has been that it encouraged UNITA to continue to have hope of eventually settling with MPLA–PT on its own terms, otherwise there would continue to be perpetual instability. In Southern and Central Africa Zaire was hostile, still licking its wounds, Zambia was lukewarm, still harbouring UNITA people, and South Africa was antagonistic. So as of early 1976 PRA was essentially in a state of local isolation; splendid isolation it was not. It was a situation pregnant with unease.

Third, then, it was not surprising therefore that in May Angola had a very warm bear hug from the Russians in the dizzying array of treaties already alluded to. A Russian writer saw the issue as follows: 'The Soviet people regard Angola as an example of staunchness and courage, and as a symbol of internationalism and the international solidarity of all progressive forces inspiring the peoples of Africa that are still under colonial oppression to intensify the struggle for their national liberation, against the intrigues of imperialism.'[30] The treaty of co-operation was very comprehensive indeed. Both countries agreed to give each other Most Favoured Nation treatment. The treaty was to last for 20 years, unless either party wanted it terminated on one year's notice, in which case it would remain in force for five more years. To date this remains the most far-reaching treaty into which Angola has entered; Angola's insecurity was driving it into the Soviet Union's orbit.

Fourth, finally, failure to enter the UN in mid-1976 was a great blow to the young republic. At the same time the country's membership in several socialist organisations was growing steadily. She joined the Afro-Asian Peoples' Solidarity Organisation, the Afro-Arab Solidarities Conference, the Afro-Asian Writers' Conference and many others. Through these PRA started playing a part in anti-imperialist campaigns and learning to apply socialism. However, the leadership wanted to enjoy the benefits of UN recognition. They wanted the psychological protection as well as real benefits to be gained from the world body. From it they could get expert advice in many areas to help their national reconstruction effort. From it also they could appeal to the world if any nation practised aggression against them. Efforts made by Nigeria on PRA's behalf, which was given the facilities of Nigeria's office in the UN, were thwarted by the United States. The anger of Neto knew no bounds. Lopo do Nascimento was dispatched to the 17th OAU summit of Heads of State in Mauritius in early July to seek OAU solidarity over the issue. He was also to look for any type of help a member state like Angola could get in the light of its location *vis-à-vis* South Africa. Promises of diplomatic support were obtained, but it was not clear what concretely Nascimento got. He nonetheless reminded the OAU of Angola's pledge to help secure the rearguard for the liberation groups in Southern Africa.

The degree of Neto's concern over the issue mirrored the emotionalism of his complaint about it. Speaking at a police passing-out parade in July, Neto revealed feelings of insecurity about the state wondering aloud (against his better judgement) as to why Angolans did not yet understand the politics and the ideology of MPLA—PT. He said that it was the revolutionary duty of organs of defence like the police to defend the people 'through preventing violence or through repression so that the tranquillity of the country may be preserved wherever it is needed.' They needed, however, to be different from the colonial police for then 'when people heard the word police or security it was normal that they unleash in some people a reflex of repulsion.' Then Neto launched into an attack on the United States calling her a 'reactionary, imperialist, international gangster — the United States — vetoed with the complicity of another country — China — the entry of Angola into the UN'. Yet the PRA was an independent and sovereign state:

> The pretext is the presence of comrades from socialist republic of Cuba. Ridiculous argument because the US itself maintains military bases in various countries. . . Where does the problem lie? The problem is that the United States was defeated in Cuba. The problem is that the agents of U.S.A. such as South Africa and all their lackeys. . .installed in the interior of our country were defeated. They were defeated by the Angolan people and thanks to close cooperation and solidarity with the republic of Cuba, the

41

USSR and the People's Republic of Angola. Various defeats disturb the imperialists, various defeats make them lose prestige as international policemen, recruiters of mercenaries and of agents of subversion.[31]

The PRA was indeed admitted to the UN in December 1976 as the passing Ford Administration saw no further point in delaying admission, particularly since virtually all specialised UN bodies had voted to admit the young Angolan state as a member.

Three weeks later, in late July, Neto went on a state visit to Cuba to thank Fidel Castro and to ask for further help to make Angola more secure. Neto emphasised that Cuba and Angola were fighting a common enemy not having to do with race, nationality of location. . . ' the enemy imperialism never disarms.' 'With this imperialist activity the People's Republic of China was logically associated, whose officials and soldiers were in Zaire and accompanied the puppet troops of FNLA in Angola and fought against Angolan people. If China practises socialism as it says we must agree that it has a very strange socialism. . .' (Here indeed Neto was taking part in the Sino-Soviet dispute. It is a matter of record that the Chinese left Zaire before Angola's independence. Till today, however, China, like the United States, has not recognised the PRA.)[32]

Neto appealed for further Cuban aid for the task of national reconstruction, noting that it would lead 'toward consolidation of the Revolution in both countries and toward the triumph of socialism'. The role of Angola in the vanguard of the fight against apartheid was emphasised, noting that socialism must succeed in Angola, which was in the middle of African states supposedly independent 'but still being manipulated by neo-colonialism'. Many of them could not combat apartheid; neither did they understand their position of dependency. 'Political and social progress was only possible in any state when it cuts its ties with imperialism. . .if we are in tune with the dynamics of present events we can arrive at the conclusion that the geographical factor is not the determinant of unity between sovereign states. . .the determinant is political orientation and ideology.'[33]

It was agreed that Cuba would help Angola in a variety of fields: political, military, manpower training, and the development of the sugar and coffee industries. I do not know the number of Cubans in Angola involved in these various fields; neither do I know the number of Angolans who have been and are still being trained in Cuba. The West has emphasised the presence of Cuban troops rather than the presence of other Cubans engaged in the task of national reconstruction. These are there like helpers from other socialist countries such as East Germany, about which little is said in the Western press. The significance of the Cubans to Angola is that their Spanish is intelligible to the Portuguese-speaking Angolans and vice versa. Furthermore the Cubans were able initially to handle the sophisticated weaponry supplied by the Soviet Union; otherwise, this could not have been put into effective use.[34] It is not clear to what extent the Cubans have been engaged in actual combat particularly since 1976. To the Angolan government Cuba's presence continues to be a source of insurance against its overthrow, although this presence has neither prevented nor contained the constant harassment of South African troops who always mask their attacks as if mainly against SWAPO. The South Africans hate communism and want to destroy Angola. It has been a measure of Angola's caution that despite provocations it would not allow its territory to be a cockpit for a hot war between the big powers, a situation which South Africa has wanted to bring about if only to attract more overt United States' help.

Nigeria and Brazil

Angola's predisposition towards the socialist states, her disdain of imperialism and its 'lackeys', and her preoccupation with security led to disdain and indifference towards non-socialist systems. A case in point was the behaviour of Angolan leaders toward Nigeria. Nigeria was an enigma to them; its involvement in the cause of Angolan liberation was not understood although they welcomed the fruits of it. In August 1976 a trade agreement was signed by Nigeria with PRA but nothing came of it. The Angolans allowed the agreement for only two years, to which Nigeria raised no objection, making allowance for the fact that Angola was young and needed time to gather itself together. The Nigerian government did not want to appear to be forcing anything on the Angolans; it even told Nigerian businessmen to stay away from Angola until the country had settled down. Nevertheless, despite such sensitivity, Angola manifested rudeness toward Nigeria: messages from Nigeria's head of state went unanswered; experts were often not allowed to fulfil their duties, some leaving after staying for days without anyone caring for them; it was difficult for Nigerians to get visas to enter Angola whereas visas for Angolans to visit Nigeria were easily obtained; and although the Nigerian government gave scholarships Angolan authorities preferred students to go to socialist countries. It appeared that much of this behaviour reflected efforts by some top Angolans to drive a wedge between the two countries. Although the trade agreement was renewed in 1978 it has so far only been honoured with 9,000 tons of cement exported to Nigeria in late July 1979.

Nigeria's attitude towards Angola remains essentially proper but no more. In the Ministry of External Affairs in Lagos people used to say that Neto had disappointed them. Nigerian leaders appreciated and sympathised with the enormous problems which Angola faced. In the execution of Angola's diplomacy these problems included lack of trained people to man new embassies; indeed, this lack of manpower pervaded every sector of Angolan life. Another problem was inadequate funding for embassies of which there are less than ten in Africa and even fewer outside it. Nigeria is still uncertain as to what its proper role should be towards Angola even in the wake of South Africa's most devastating invasion in August and November 1981. When this happened, a summit of Front Line States was held in Lagos in which much noise was made, and much sympathy expressed, yet from which nothing concrete emerged. The matter was meanwhile in the UN for debate, in which Nigeria's attitude was well described:

> Nigeria's lame and timorous stance was contained in a statement by the country's Foreign Minister Dr. Ishaya Audu. He diffidently said in a feet-dragging manner that Nigeria is undertaking a careful study of the situation in Southern Africa, particularly the invasion of Angola by racist South Africa with a view to taking an official position. He said that Nigeria's position would be made known after the exercise and pledged that his country would always do its best within its resources to assist the liberation movements in Southern Africa; but added that Nigeria could not be expected to carry the burden alone. 'We should be careful not to think of Nigeria as the policeman of Africa. We are not' Dr Audu said.[35]

Brazil's attitude is essentially similar to that of Nigeria, basically because of Angola's attitude. About the only bilateral ties are a petroleum agreement with Petrobras and a Volkswagen factory. Angolan delegations have toured Brazil to ask for help because of language ties, but few Brazilians are willing to go to Angola because of its economic conditions. Besides, the presence of Cubans in the country runs counter to Brazilian interests. Relations with the two countries, like Angolan–Nigerian links, remain proper and strict.

Zaire and Zambia

Let me now turn to Angola's relations with neighbouring states. Angola's search for security with Zaire to the north and Zambia to the east were necessary if she was to break her isolation, and if established economic ties among the three were to continue. The main economic link was the 1,250 mile-long Benguela Railway owned and built by the British company Tanganyika Concessions. Zaire and Zambia need this railway to get their main money-earning export — copper — to the outside world and to get in capital and consumer products. Mobuto had staked much on FNLA in the hope that he might be compensated by some oil deal in Cabinda. When FNLA lost the war Mobuto was in an embarrassing and exposed position. Angola was then behaving as if it did not need the railway as much as her neighbours. What she needed was to be able to earn revenue from Zambian and Zaireian freight charges so that she could improve her foreign exchange position. But she was really worried since the railway was strategic and passed through the most central portion of her territory, one in rebellion as Savimbi of UNITA was intensifying dissident activities and finding favours in Zambia. UNITA was constantly making the railway unoperational by blowing up track or by removing rails.

The tension between Angola and Zaire has a long and chequered history, going back to the early days of the Angola liberation movements. Holden Roberto of FNLA had lived in Zaire for a long time and grown up knowing most of its ruling elite. When his movement was formed it was headquartered in Kinshasa and from there made sorties into Angola starting on 15 March 1961. The United States backed efforts of FNLA were to make sure that 'communist-controlled' MPLA was not allowed to function from Zaire. This tradition was cemented by ties of kinship through marriage between Roberto and the Zaireian ruler. Added to this was the determination of the United States that no rival state to Zaire should be allowed to succeed, not to talk about a 'communist' one in neighbouring Angola.[36] In the last stages of Portuguese rule in Angola thousands of Zaireian troops were infiltrated into Angola in the guise of FNLA troops, from Kinkuzu base in Zaire; mercenaries also entered Angola through Zaire.

Through OAU efforts it was Mobuto who first initiated a move to mend fences after the second war. His emissaries came to Luanda in April 1976 and in June Neto paid a visit to Kinshasa. There was much fanfare, but mutual distrust remained. A communiqué was issued from which we know that the presidents discussed the question of security along their common border; agreed to open liaison offices in each other's country; and talked about the question of communications and reopening the Benguela railway.[37] But nothing has come out of this; nothing, because the Angola side had gone to Kinshasa merely so that it might not appear unreasonable in the eyes of the OAU. Although Neto went to Kinshasa and was received as Head of State Zaire did not formally recognise the PRA until afterwards — in February 1977. This scenario seems to indicate that while Angola was eager to mend fences, Zaire was still playing a diplomatic game. Angola continued to suspect Zaire of, among other things, plotting to overthrow it through 'Operation Cobra' due to take place in September 1977. Besides, Angola charged that Zaire was holding seven of its planes from pre-independence days, had repainted them in Zaireian colours and was using them as its own.[38] (Let us recall here point 14 of Angola's foreign policy objectives.)

And when in March 1977 the Shaba I rebellion broke out Mobuto blamed Angola and Cuba for having trained and dispatched the Katangese gendarmes (former supporters of Tshombe).[39] There was a repeat incident in June 1978 when Castro and Neto again denied Angolan involvement. A significant aspect of this denial was the vehemence with which Castro voiced his non-involvement in the wake of President Carter's seeming determination to confront Cuba: 'We are not a military power. . . We have no nuclear weapons, no navy, no strategic forces. We are just a small country whose most important raw material is its spirit, the willingness of our people to sacrifice and demonstrate solidarity with other peoples. . .'[40] Could Castro and Neto have been involved in a situation which would have made Angola fight a three-sided war: against Zaire, South Africa and UNITA?

The aftermath of the second Shaba invasion was that Mobutu's Zaire was completely broke financially with his army shored up by the Western powers. Zaire's defeat was, to Neto, a triumph of his anti-imperialist foreign policy. Mobutu's Western backers insisted that he seek accommodation with Neto. The go-between for bringing about *rapprochement* was President Yhombi-Opango of Congo (Brazzaville). In August 1978 secret talks were opened and agreement was reached on a wide range of issues concerning commercial, cultural, and economic relations: Zaire was to close FNLA offices and a joint OAU Committee was to help both sides iron out their difficulties.[41]

Angola's attempt to mend fences with Zambia was going on simultaneously with that towards Zaire. In June 1976 an agreement was worked out for the exchange of ambassadors with Zambia and a joint commission was also set up as with Zaire to work out bilateral problems. One of these was Ovimbundu refugees who had fled to Zambia; these were now to be allowed to return. There was also talk about a direct bilateral road link through Zambia's North-Western province. And in November 1976 UNITA offices were closed down in Zambia.

The outstanding problem among the three countries — Angola, Zambia and Zaire — remained the intractable issue of the Benguela Railway. It had to be reopened if only because the shattered Zaireian and Zambian Copperbelts would bring further instability to the region. In 1978 an international loan from the EEC and the Arab Bank for Economic Development was accepted by the three countries for $35.2 million to repair the railway. But it did not start operating again until 1980, and then only intermittently. In that year it carried only 48,000 tons per month, compared to 100,000 tons per month in 1973; it was hoped that it would reach a carriage capacity of 96,000 tons by 1983.

46

UNITA's sabotage still made its impact felt, forcing Zaire and Zambia to rely on the route through South Africa.

European Economic Community

Also of significance in Angola's move to mend fences with her neighbours, particularly with Zaire, was that it brought in its train the beginning of *rapprochement* with European countries which had hitherto been lukewarm or hostile. Of special interest were moves towards reconciliation between Angola and Portugal: the former colonial master recognised its erstwhile colony. In August Presidents Eames and Neto met in Bissau under an arrangement made by Luis Cabral of Guinea-Bissau. Wide-ranging bilateral agreements were reached in the fields of economic development, bilateral trade, culture and technology. Discussions were commenced about nationalised Portuguese assets said to be worth over £2 billion. And Eames agreed not to allow Portugal to be used as a forum for propaganda by Angolan dissidents. Thus Neto's pledge at independence that Angola would draw close to Portugal was redeemed.

Another related foreign policy move soon took place: in September 1978 Henri Simonet, Belgian Foreign Minister, visited Angola. This was significant because before leaving Europe he had consulted with West German Foreign Minister Hans Dietrich Genscher who through him advocated the normalisation of Angolan–West German relations. The sticking point had been a feeling of hostility which had been generated when Zaire allowed the German company OTRAC to have a missile testing range in Shaba. During the visit of the Belgian Minister, Simonet declared he was impressed by the sense of responsibility shown by the Angolan authorities. He declared that Europe and the EEC were desirous of improving economic cooperation with Angola. As a consequence of the Simonet visit Angola requested and received observer status in the renegotiation of the Lomé Convention. And in mid-October 1978 a team from the EEC came to Luanda for talks.

Economic crisis, conjuncture and reorientation

The year 1978 could be seen to be very significant in Angola's external relations. It was the year when she mended fences with her neighbour Zaire, was recognised by Portugal, and opened economic relations with the EEC: the year she began opening herself to the West. The desire to achieve security had been an important catalyst; but it would be totally inadequate as a means to explain the series of moves in light of the preponderant predisposition of PRA towards socialist states.

Another reason was that all had not been going well at home: national reconstruction was flagging, productivity was low, and Angola's socialist friends were giving cause for concern. The country's southern flank was witnessing a resurgence of attacks from early 1978. And there was political wrangling and sabotage at home within MPLA—PT itself. Foreign policy cannot be divorced from political, economic and social activities at home. For the average Angolan the sudden shift in economic fortune was quite incomprehensible. Suddenly people could not buy and sell the way they used to. Party activists raided small shops and forced them to close down; the alternative 'people's shops' were failures. The new shopkeepers would alert their friends who would come early to buy up all the goods; in turn they would have clandestine outlets where they would sell at exorbitant prices. A more common variety of this has been 'auto-consumption'. Workers in a factory have the right to buy so much of the products at reduced rate. Since they could not possibly consume everything purchased they would sell to others. Inflation became rampant; shortages became the vogue.

On the other hand, political leaders did not have to stand in queues as they had their own special shops. In any case when shortages became worse they could shop in foreign countries even though according to Angolan law no one could go out more than once every three years. Farmers refused to produce enough food because they were only being paid ridiculously low prices. Bribery and official corruption became common, particularly in the distribution of goods and of jobs. The distribution network collapsed due to no fault of the government: transportation was in a chaotic condition because of colonial sabotage. And Luanda port had never been efficient.

Productivity was low for many reasons. There were not enough trained people to handle the variety of jobs. The average Angolan worker was supposed to do so many things: work, go to school (there were always campaigns against illiteracy), raise his children, and attend party meetings, all against the backdrop of a vastly diminished infrastructure. The ruling party's own political organisation and orientation were also faulty. They certainly did not orient the people toward working. For instance there were always festivals, which called for rallies, and when any Head of State visited day-to-day activities stopped as everybody sought to entertain him. There were interminable meetings in work places, all of which consumed time and impeded productivity. No wonder 1973's level of economic production has yet to be repeated.

Angola's socialist friends were also giving Angola cause for concern. Neto discovered that Soviet arms were not going to be free gifts. The Russians took Angola's coffee at cheap prices and re-exported it at considerable profit. They would overfish in Angolan waters, so much so that fish became too expensive for Angolans to buy; not until late November 1981 were the Soviets ready to renegotiate the fishing treaty. The East Germans came to Angola to help reconstruct; but of more than 140 road bridges blown up by 1978 only 45 had been rebuilt.[42] It also became clear that retooling many of the country's machines was difficult. The East Germans did not have the actual specification of the machine parts, most of which were under international (i.e. Western) patents.

It then dawned on Angola's leaders that it was necessary to have broad economic relations with the West not just in petroleum. From 1978 on the government started having technical and supply arrangements in the transport field with, for example, Volvo and Scania from Sweden, Land-Rover of Britain, Renault from France, Volkswagen from Brazil, Toyota and Datsun from Japan and Fiat from Italy. Most of Angola's planes had always been from the West.[43] The fleet, which was made up of two Fokker 27s at time of independence in 1975, had increased to 23 by 1979, including 5 Boeing 707, 3 Boeing 737, 4 Antonov 26, 3 Yak 40, and 2 Hercules C-130 planes. Economic relations with the West came to be seen also as one aspect of general foreign policy objectives as Angolans had always wanted to trade with all parts of the world. There was no question of them eating their own rhetoric.

The most disturbing aspect of all Angola's internal problems however was the abortive coup attempt by Nito Alves and Ze Van Dunem on 27 May 1977. The coup attempt was a shock to MPLA leaders because it came less than three weeks after a serious South African raid and bombardment in Southern Angola. Alves' and Van Dunem's dissatisfaction with the way the government was running dated back almost to independence. At the Central Committee Meeting of October 1976 already alluded to, it was resolved that they should be punished for their 'factionalist' activities. Yet on their own they went out to mobilise the people, infiltrating every nook and cranny of the party and government. A report after the coup had been smashed said that the conspirators had done 'mind-poisoning work. . .accompanied by criminal acts of sabotage. . .in all bodies. . .to convince the people that the government was inoperative.'[44] They considered themselves 'leftists' yet they were also accused of racism and regionalism. Alves had been the Minister of Interior, well placed to carry out many of his designs. He had in fact worked out how *Poder Popular* should actually function and had installed many of his own people to operate it.[45] If the revolt had succeeded Neto would have been neutralised and many of his immediate supporters would have been eliminated. In the event, when the revolt was over, the task of building socialism in Angola had to start all over again. *Poder Popular* had suffered a set-back; the party

49

had to start screening all cadres again, in a so-called programme of *rectification*. This onerous task has so far not revived the party as Lucio Lara, party secretary, was to admit even in 1980: 'As regards party organisation, there is not yet a profound awareness of the role of the base cell in controlling the economy of an enterprise, in controlling the life of the state... We came to somewhat pessimistic conclusions.'[46] Aprt from this problem ethnic differences between *mulattos* and blacks exist and are real; MPLA—PT is not a monlithic party.

Another major repercussion of the attempted coup was that thousands were rounded up and killed without trial; thousands disappeared and thousands were jailed. All that was needed to get rid of one's enemy or rival was to call him a 'fraction'. The vehemence of protests about the violence disturbed the President when he discovered that many ugly things which he did not order had been done in his name. Furthermore, while attending the OAU conference in Khartoum in July, he was taken to task by some Heads of State who wondered why he had to kill so many people in his already depopulated country. These incidents and protests had their effect on the President. The Angolan situation seemed to need a reappraisal and only Neto could give the necessary leadership and direction. The need was for peace and harmony at home as well as peace with the state's neighbours. This point was made by the President in September 1978 when addressing the ODP's (People's Militia) 3rd anniversary.

The President began by reminding them of how Angola had defeated colonialism. Angola was now in a new phase trying to make social revolution but was encountering a lot of difficulties. It was necessary to defend ideas from penetration by reactionary agents trying to divert the people; the President was obviously still reacting against the 'fractionists'. Angolans must learn also to defend the revolution 'in relations with other countries'. Furthermore, he went on, 'It is necessary to have relations with all the countries which do not attack us directly'. Obviously this could not be Zaire or South Africa, so the reference must have been to EEC countries with which Angola had just started to reopen economic links. Then he went on to point out the need to develop the regional economy, in spite of differences over political ideology:

> I believe that following our opening to the world in the desire to see our people live in peace, in tranquility so that each day they may not only be thinking of the number of soldiers which we lose but in the number of hectares which we can clear for agriculture — if we could, instead of thinking of buying arms, to buy ploughs, to buy tractors and tools to help the reconstruction — we would have reached the essential objective.[48]

50

Neto went on to list the economic woes of the country. Economic production has generally failed to reach the level of 1973 which the Central Committee wanted. In resolving these problems '. . .we are not going to be leftists, not going to be. . .radical. . . We are not going to attempt as some comrades think to finish completely and at once. . . with private business. . .by individuals.' (Here again the reference to the leftists leaves no doubt that the President was still fighting the 'fractionists' and persuading his followers to abandon them.) He went on to insist that although the party had a preference for collective property, no one should destroy the little farmer who wished to make his farm or the little merchant who wished to own his shop:

> We cannot, we ought not to develop forms of repression to kill initiatives by which small artisans, carpenters or masons who, not understanding yet the benefits of collectivisation, might wish to continue working in an individual manner. That would be only to destroy an important part of production which we desire in the country.

Until all the people understood the benefits of collectivisation and until the country had sufficient equipment to collectivise, the little artisans should be left alone.

Two days later, Neto went to Cabinda on a working visit to meet Yhombi-Opango of Congo (Brazzaville) for talks. There he called for Angola to make a new revolution.[49] If there had been any doubt about what he earlier siad to the ODP this was laid aside in a very candid speech about the need for internal harmony and peace. He offered an olive branch to all Angolans to return home. Those who collaborated with the 'fractionists' were to be freed. This was being done so that every Angolan could contribute to the task of economic development. Neto reminded his cadres that the party functioned to serve the people and not to serve party members alone.

In September a further step was taken in the country's foreign policy of support for SWAPO and other liberation movements: the opening of the regional headquarters of the OAU Liberation Committee in Luanda. This opening marked the beginning of a new era of travail for PRA in which South Africa had a real excuse to intensify raids and to destabilise it by bombing economic targets. The opening marked the second day of another set of raids in which Angolan airspace was violated in the provinces of Kunene and Huila. It was more intense than the May 4 raid in which even the United States administration joined in condemning the South Africans.[50] Angola's new position made her one of the Front Line States with which the Western contact group started to negotiate for the independence of Namibia and through whose efforts UN resolution 435 was obtained. Angola's ability to join in regional cooperation was made possible because of her outward-looking policy and because it suited her self-interest.

This outward policy suggests to me that Neto was already changing some of the ideological stands he used to take. Above all he had a broader perspective, reflective of the needs and interests of his country. During the rest of his administration the major issues which pre-occupied him in foreign affairs were the question of Namibia, national unity and security, the condition of the party and the intense suffering of Angolans during the constant South African raids. And although there was a United States administration which appeared well disposed towards Africa the demands which the Americans were making as preconditions for recognition remained essentially the same. They still wanted the Cubans to be removed and Neto to make a pact with UNITA. Another overture of this nature came in mid-February 1979 and was again rejected. Neto then conducted an initiative of his own towards Savimbi but he was unable to complete it before his death. It would have been foolish for Neto to throw away his trump card — the Cubans — without getting anything in return and run the risk of destabilising his country further. Diplomatic relations with the United States were not worthwhile if he had to do that.

During the last few weeks of his life Neto managed to host Dr Kurt Waldheim, Secretary-General of the United Nations, and to attend the Monrovia OAU summit. He then embarked on a tour of several of Angola's provinces. His speeches during this period mirrored even more vividly the country's perennial problems. Soon after this his health deteriorated rapidly; he died on 19 September 1979 in Moscow.

After Neto

The exit of Neto from the Angolan scene has left a void which is difficult to fill. No one else in Angola had either his personality or his stature to initiate ideas and carry them through. Upon his death Neto has been made the 'Immortal Guide' of the Angolan Revolution, which meant that all other successors must always look back to him. The present incumbent — José Eduardo dos Santos — is rather young and inexperienced; he is more of a manager than an initiator. It has been his lot to try to pull all of the various shades of opinion in the party together.

As far as the conduct of Angolan foreign affairs is concerned, matters have remained the same in Southern Africa. The outward-looking policy, however, continues to attract Western investment. This was the theme which Pedro Pacavira, Minister of Agriculture, emphasised in his press conference in London in October 1980. There has been one seemingly major embarrassment to the government: the support given to Soviet involvement in Afghanistan. However, even this event could be understood in terms of Cuban and Soviet pressure given their position in Angola; and, indeed, it coincided with the 14th point of Angola's foreign policy objectives and as a gesture towards the United States.

Looking into the internal political and economic background to sustain foreign policy, we notice still the same hardships and the same marginal rise in productivity. Angola is still dependent on oil as a revenue earner which in turn depends much on the expertise of the West through the multinationals. More than 70 per cent of national income derives from this single product. And yet the necessity of fighting a war against internal dissent in the form of UNITA (supported by South Africa) costs the country more than 50 per cent of these foreign earnings.[51] The nefarious efforts of UNITA need to be appreciated in that it was able to carry on nationwide infiltration and sabotage in 1979–1980. To resist UNITA, MPLA needed armaments which had to be paid for in hard currency. Angola's potential wealth allows her to continue to pay large amounts for war material but this is conditional upon continued high prices for exports in the international market. Recently, however, with falls in the price of Angolan oil by $6.00 per barrel (June 1980–1981), and in the price of coffee by more than 50 per cent the country will be facing even tougher times ahead.[52]

The election of Reagan with his anti-communist stance meant that 'cold war' tension between the superpowers would increase the United States' tilt towards South Africa. This has already resulted in making the United States feel it could do whatever it liked in Southern Africa and sent shivers down the spines of Angola's leaders. The uncertainty which Angola faced was underlined by Paulo Jorge, Minister of External Affairs, who called on the United States government to declare its intentions. Angola, for herself, only wanted peace and tranquillity in which to develop. However, Angola, he said, would be forced to fight back and to ask for outside help in doing so if attacked.[53] But as already noted on 23 August 1981 South Africa occupied a large portion of Southern Angola, devastating it in the process. In the United Nations the United States cast a veto against a vote censuring South Africa.

Increased pressure is also being put on Angola by some American legislators who now want the Clark Amendment repealed. This amendment was tagged on to a foreign aid appropriation bill in 1975 to prevent the United States President from sending arms to UNITA. In December 1981 Jonas Savimbi was allowed to enter the United States having made sure beforehand that he had sabotaged Angola's only refinery in Luanda. After an audience with United States Under-

Secretary of State for African Affairs, Chester Crocker, the latter was quoted as saying that the new administration considered UNITA 'a legitimate political factor in Angolan affairs'. For his part, Savimbi was arguing that he had a role to play in the Namibia settlement since he had military forces in Southern Angola, where 'neutral' forces were to be deployed before any Namibia election.

The Savimbi visit raised a great deal of controversy both inside and outside the United States. Reagan wanted to help Savimbi by trying to get the Clark Amendment revoked, offering the excuse that it limited presidential powers in the conduct of foreign affairs. But the House of Representatives has so far refused to follow the example of the Senate. The Savimbi visit was to drum up support for revocation in the House. But United States black groups like the Congressional Black Caucus and Transaction were lobbying to retain the Amendment.[54]

About the same time Alexander Haig was putting pressure on Cuba in Latin America. Yet amidst all this, the United States and other Western states in the contact group said they were still trying to solve the Namibian question so crucial for Angola's future. Yet in the wake of the late November 1981 mercenary attempt to topple the Seychelles government in which South African acquiesced, it seemed difficult to predict what would eventually happen in Namibia and what role the Angolans and Cubans — with Soviet help — might be forced to play. One thing is certain: Neto's successor is facing one of his toughest times in trying to resolve this complex international issue to Angola's advantage.

Conclusion

Although Angola's general foreign policy orientation can be traced to the 'left-wing' tendencies of the MPLA—PT, her actual policy objectives have been motivated more by the search for national security, unity, and development than by any other factor. In terms of political and social mobilisation the preference of Angolan leaders is still for Marxist-socialist methods. This preference is based on their own long experience of Angola under colonial political domination. If they had had their way they would have opted for those developmental methods emanating from their socialist friends. But Neto discovered that it was impossible for Angola to do away with the Western economic presence, especially its much desired technology, given some of the realities of his country's post-independence situation. In choosing to deal with the West, he was merely being pragmatic.

To search for ideological consistency in every move any government makes is to demand the impossible. In today's world few nations' foreign policy actions are completely in agreement with their avowed principles or objectives. Angola's foreign policy goals have been defined as they should be: from the angle of national self-interest. The result, as is now apparent, is that the country's economic development cannot ignore or exclude the West as more than 70 per cent of its trade and economic projects are with it, while just 20 per cent depends on the East. On the other hand, the country's tilt towards the latter block is quite clear in political and social matters. Whether these two sets of factors balance out and what they would eventually mean in Angola's overall scheme of things, remains to be seen.

This chapter also shows that internal politics affect external policy and vice versa. Much of the suffering in Angola today, whether internally or externally located, has been due as much to unavoidable circumstances as to precipitous action born of inexperienced leadership. For example, if Marxist–Leninist socialism is the goal for the people of Angola can it be imposed immediately? Could Angolans cope with such revolutionary change? If imperialism must be fought as a foreign policy objective is it wise always to make so much noise about it? And should Angola really jeopardise its sovereignty to get freedom for Namibia?

The weakness of Angola's foreign policy stems essentially from the problem of internal disunity. A major example of this was Neto's and his cadres' initial assumption that they could bring UNITA to heel through military means alone. For six years this policy has not worked due as much to their miscalculation of the sinister forces at work within Southern Africa as to their misunderstanding of the limits to which their socialist friends would go in trying to effect changes in the region. If Angolans themselves to not want their country to be a cockpit for an East–West hot war, then the Soviet Union and the United States do not want their allies to push them into such a conflict either. In this case, then, how do we reconcile MPLA–PT's rhetoric of 'militant solidarity' with this reality? A free Namibia would hold at least a partial key to the problem of internal disunity in Angola, which cannot be resolved without the UNITA factor. Although a Namibia settlement might help free Angola from obnoxious raids from South Africa it is not certain, given the perfidy of some African states, that others might indeed not become substitute channels of arms for UNITA. This is why it may now be necessary for the Angolan government to review its cold attitude towards African states which do not necessarily share its political ideology.

Notes

1   *Angola: O Governo De Transicao* (Luanda: Ministerio de Infor-macao de Angola n.d.) A very useful book of documents.

2   People's Movement for the Liberation of Angola-Partido Travalho (Worker's Party); hereafter to be refered to as MPLA—PT. The party amended its name during the first post-independence con-gress, December 1977.

3   *Angola: Socialism at birth* (London: Magic, 1980) *passim.*

4   *Documentos: Terceira Reuniao Plenario do Comite Central do MPLA. Luanda 23-29 Octobro 1976* (Luanda: Edicao do Secre-tariado do Bureau Politico do MPLA, n.d.) See *Discurso do Camarada Presidente*, pp. 3—6 and *Resolucao sobre os principios directores das relacoes exteriores*, pp. 51—55.

5   'Strengthening The Party in Angola' Lucio Lara interviewed by Mozambican newspaper *Noticias*, 11 November 1980. This inter-view is reprinted in *People's Power*, vol. 17, Spring 1981, pp. 23—35; quote is from pp. 23—24.

6   *MPLA: Programa Estatutos* etc. (Luanda: Edicao do D.O,R., n.d.), pp. 3 and 7.

7   See John A. Marcum, *The Angolan Revolution, Volume II: exile politics and guerrilla warfare, 1962—1976* (Cambridge, Mass: M.I.T. Press, 1978), pp. 14—15 and George M. Houser, 'Nationalist Organisations in Angola: Status of a Revolt' in John A. Davis and James K. Baker (eds), *Southern Africa in Transition* (New York: Praeger, 1966), p. 166.

8   'Quem e o lnimigo. . .qual e o nosso objectivo' Discurso, Agostinho Neto. Conferencia feita na Universidade de Dar es Salaam, 7 February 1974. The language and rhetoric of this speech can be compared favourably with those of party's statutes, constitution, programme of action and preamble to the Central Committee's Resolution concerning Angola's foreign policy objectives.

9   *MPLA: Programa Estatutos* etc. (note 6), p. 47.

10   'Alocucao do Camarada Presidente Agosthino Neto', Conferencia Inter-regional de Militante do MPLA, 7 October 1974.

11   Comicio do MPLA 'Declaracao Politica', *O Angolense* (Luanda), 15 November 1974.

12   Discurso do Camarada Presidente, Agostinho Neto No Plenario da Cimeira da OUA Khartoum, 18—21 July 1978.

13   Agostinho Neto, 'Precisamos de fazer uma nova revolucao' Discurso Proferido no Cambinda 15/9/78 *Jornal de Angola* (Luanda), 16 September 1978.

14   Agostinho Neto, 'The Proclamation of Independence: Zero Hours 11 November 1975', in Minfa, *Angola 11 de Novembro de 1975,*

(Documents of Independence), pp. 119–125 *passim*.

15 Gabriel Garcia Marquez 'Cuba in Angola: Operation Carlotta', *Prensa Latina*, vol. 166, 1 April 1977, typescript, and Robin Halett, 'The South African Intervention in Angola, 1975–76', *African Affairs*, vol. 77, no. 308, July 1978, pp. 347–356.

16 Neto, 'The Proclamation of Independence' (note 14), p. 122.

17 Even from the time of the Government of Transition parlous economic conditions had given Neto a lot of concern. The Minister of the Economy made his complaint known: Vasco Viera de Almeida, 'Eu ACUSO', *O Angolense* (Luanda), 11 July 1975.

18 'Prefacio' *Resistencia Popular Generalizada* (Luanda: Ministerio da Informacao, 1975). In his independence day speech Neto's statement on this issue is almost identical with the passage just cited: 'Our anti-imperialist struggle, in the form of resistance, is the expression of an irremediable class contradiction pitting the Angolan people's interests against those of international imperialism' *Angola*, p. 123.

19 *Angola: Reconstrucao Nacional* n.p. chapter on Industry and Energy.

20 *Ibid.*

21 Here is a list showing the extent of Angolan state participation in foreign-owned enterprises in May 1976:

Petroleum	51%	Soap	55%
Diamonds	61%	Building	100%
Sugar	100%	Paper and pulp	100%
Cement	5%	Metal containers	98%
Margarine	76%	Matches	67%
Beer	85%	Plywood	100%
Shipbuilding and repair	100%	Bicycles and mopeds	100%

Source: *Angola: Reconstrucao Nacional* n.p.

22. Neto, 'The Proclamation of Independence' *Angola* (note 14), p. 122.

23 *Angola: Socialism at Birth* (note 3), p. 21.

24 *Africa*, no. 122, October 1981, p. 144.

25 *Jornal de Angola*, 16 August 1981.

26 'Pela Independencia Economica, Discurso do Cda Presidente A. Neto na Sessao do Encerramento da Segunda Conferencia Nacional dos Trabalhadores Angolanos, 18 de Outubro de 1976', *Coleccao Resistencia Texto*, 9.

27 *Angola: Reconstrucao Nacional*.

28 'Preamble to Foreign Policy Objectives'. For citation see note 4 above.

29 *O Angolense*, 20 March 1976.

30. K. Uralov, *Angola's Just Cause*, p. 25.
31   *O Angolense*, 3 July 1976.
32   For aspects of Sino—Soviet rivalry over Angola see Colin Legum and Tony Hodges, *After Angola* (London: Rex Collings, 1976), pp. 22—25.
33   *O Angolense*, 31 July 1976.
34   For an interesting discussion of this issue of foreign troops see President Julius Nyerere, 'Foreign Troops in Africa' *Africa Report*, vol. 23, no. 4, July—August 1978, pp. 10—13. See also Neiva Moreira and Beatriz Bissio, *Os Cubanos Na Africa* (Sao Paulo: Flobal Editora, 1979), *passim*.
35   *Times International* (Lagos), 14 September 1981, p. 6.
36   Senate Hearings 'Subcommittee on African Affairs on U.S. Involvement in Civil War in Angola,' *Angola: Hearings* (Washington: US Government Printing Office, 1976), p.109.
37   'Documento: Communicado Conjunto das Delegacoes da Republica Popular de Angola e da Republica do Zaire, que reuniram em Kinshasa de 28 a 30 de Junho de 1976' *O Angolense*, 10 July 1976.
38   Agostinho Neto, 'Discurso, 24/2/77', *Coleccao Resistencia*, Texto 16, and Lucio Lara, 'Discurso No Comicio de Repudio a Operacao Cobra. . .5/3/77' *Coleccao Resistencia*, Texto 14.
39   *Time*, 4 April 1977, p. 23. See also 'Address by Comrade Paulo Jorge at the O.A.U. Summit. Libreville, 24/6/77,' *MPLA Information Bulletin*, vol. 4, July 1977 and Nyerere, 'Foreign troops in Africa'.
40   *Time*, 26 June 1978.
41   *Jornal de Angola*, 22 August 1978.
42   *Africa*, December 1980, p. 93.
43   *Ibid*., p. 91.
44   'Report of the Political Bureau. . .on the attempted *coup d'etat* of 27 May 1977', *MPLA Information Bulletin*, vol. 4, July 1977.
45   *Lei Do Poder Popular* (Luanda: Ministerio da Informacao, February 1976). Of importance is the preface, which was the speech of Nito Alves on introducing this law.
46   'Strengthening the Party in Angola. Interview with Lucio Lara Beira' *Noticias*, vol. 1, November 11 1980. Translated and reprinted in *People's Power*, vol. 17, pp. 23—35; quote is from p. 27.
47   Agostinho Neto, 'O que e O Fraccionismo', *Coleccao Resistencia*, Texto 19, 12 June 1977.
48   *Jornal de Angola*, 14 September 1978.
49   Agostinho Neto, Discurso: Precisamos de fazer uma nova revolucao', *Jornal de Angola*, 16 September 1978.
50   *Africa Report*, July—August 1978, p. 39.

51 Lucio Lara's *Noticeas* interview, *ibid.*, p. 31. See also José Eduardo Dos Santos in a speech on 15 July 1981 to the People's Assembly.

52 *People's Power*, vol. 18, Summer 1981, p. 25.

53 *Jornal de Angola*, 2 April 1981.

54 V.O.A. 10 December 1981, 6 hours GMT. This programme quoted from *Washington Post*, 'Editorial: The Savimbi factor' and *New York Times* 'Editorial: Keep the Amendment'. See also Caryle Murphy 'U.S. edges closer to alignment with white South Africa', *Washington Post*, 15 September 1981; Sammy O. Otuonye, 'The Aid of Subversive Adventures', *Daily Times* (Lagos), 6 November 1981; and 'Editorial: America and Puppet Savimbi', *New Nigerian* (Kaduna), 10 December 1981.

2 Botswana

Nadia Kostiuk

Introduction: the inheritance of colonialism

As the years since independence celebrations in underdeveloped African countries begin to number in the twenties and even thirties, it becomes increasingly difficult for many observers to identify the colonial inheritance as the primary source of the numerous problems faced by these states. The problems tend to be attributed instead to idiosyncratic variables within the individual countries, or within the Third World as a whole. Without denying that such variables do contribute to under-development, the root of the problem is attributed to another cause by this writer. The underdeveloped economy is all too often haunted by a colonial inheritance which has seriously restricted its ability to develop other than as a primary producer, subject to the whims of the inter-national market, and unable (or unwilling) to improve the lives of the majority of its citizens.

This chapter focuses on the foreign policy of the Republic of Botswana, a sparsely populated, land-locked country in Southern Africa. Multi-party state, staunch member of the Organisation of African Unity, Front Line State in the Zimbabwean liberation struggle, key actor in the budding Southern African Development Coordination

Conference (SADCC), a country with bounteous natural resources, yet Botswana has been thrust by history into a dependent peripheral relationship within both the Southern African region and the international economic system as a whole.

Botswana's unenviable geopolitical and economic position and her response to such constraints have been the subject of numerous studies, although a political economy critique still forms only a small part of the literature. It is inevitable that most works have focused on Botswana's complex relationship with the South African system, as that system has a very real stranglehold upon her fragile economy, and it is also the medium through which Botswana interacts with much of the rest of the global economy.

Early observers marvelled at Botswana's very existence as a national entity, and presented a highly orthodox view of her foreign policy. For Richard Dale two very important features of Botswana's foreign policy were the presentation of the image of a tranquil, non-violent, non-racial alternative to her racialist neighbours, and the refusal to behave as a client state of a larger power.[1] Such an approach neglected both the complexities of Botswana's domestic situation and the harsh reality that although she does not wish to behave as a client state, her choices in this matter are rather limited.

Christopher Colclough and Stephen McCarthy present the most comprehensive study to date of Botswana's political economy.[2] Their presentation, though descriptive rather than analytical in nature, documents the degree to which Botswana is incorporated into the South African economy, and shows the growing domestic gap between social classes. Such a gap, which neglects the deterioration of the condition of the poor in absolute terms, grew over the period of time when Botswana's mineral-based economy was one of the healthiest in Africa.[3]

The need for internally integrated, balanced economies capable of providing productive employment for nations' populations has been presented forcefully by numerous authors. Ann and Neva Seidman argue such a stance in their look at multinationals in Southern Africa.[4] Percy Selwyn has written about the enormous constraints faced by dependent states in attempting to diversify their economies.[5] Jack Parson looks at Botswana specifically as a capitalist 'labour reserve', and provides a concise history of incorporation into the international capitalist economy.[6] He presents some planning and policy options for a reorientation toward rural-based small-scale development, but he concedes the great difficulty of achieving much given the very serious problems presented by the existing distribution of class power, and the overwhelming impact of South Africa upon developments in Botswana.[7]

It is clear that Botswana's dependency is such that no simple short-term solutions can possibly apply. Only a larger global and regional transformation can bring about fundamental changes within Botswana, but Botswana must have a role in bringing about that change. Therefore, it is necessary to study the important internal and external dynamics which make her response to her dependent situation such as it is.

Historical incorporation

The formal independence of the British Bechuanaland Protectorate from Great Britain was proclaimed on 30 September 1966. The new Republic of Botswana, with approximately six hundred thousand people, was created. That such an event came to pass was in itself a feat, as the protectorate's viability as a state had been long questioned internationally, although the Tswana nation has occupied the territory of the present state of Botswana since it migrated there from the Transvaal, South Africa, in the eighteenth and nineteenth centuries.[8] It had been hoped, particularly by the Republic of South Africa, that Bechuanaland would be incorporated into that Republic, thereby greatly augmenting the proportion of land allocated to blacks.[9]

The *de jure* political incorporation of Bechuanaland did not occur, nor was it necessary, as a cautious, traditionalist, conciliatory government was duly elected by the people of Botswana. The economic dominance of South Africa, forged since the advent of colonialism, ensured compliance from the little state, which was completely surrounded by racialist minority regimes at that time.[10]

Bechuanaland had been made a Protectorate in 1885, after several decades of conflict over its status between the British and the Boers of the Transvaal State. Bechuanaland was coveted for its mineral wealth — gold and diamonds had already been discovered there — as a 'Road to the North' for missionaries and traders, and as an extra territory for superfluous blacks. Only when the British became concerned about being pushed out of South Africa by the Boers and the Germans in Namibia did they act to keep most of Bechuanaland in their own hands.

'Protectorate' was too glorious and generous a term for the 80 years which followed. At first much of the governing power was given *de facto* to Cecil Rhodes and his British South Africa Company — an early start to a dependence upon multinational enterprises. This allowed the British to protect their colonial interests without expending any funds.[11] There was little infrastructure provided, nor were there any developments of any other type. However, the Tswana were expected to pay the costs of being 'protected' from the outset.[12] For a 10 per cent commission, traditional chiefs were in charge of collecting a hut tax from their people.[13] Although the amounts collected never managed to pay fully for the costs involved, for the Batswana the consequences of such regressive taxation have lasted to this day. So have the fortunes started by the chiefs' commissions.

Those people with no source of cash had to seek wage employment. Job opportunities were not being created within the Protectorate as the colonial administration, composed primarily of South Africans, believed that the territory existed in order to supply South Africa with labour power.[14] At the same time as the Batswana struggled to earn their hut taxes, they were incorporated further into a cash economy by the lure of imported consumer goods from South Africa. The easy availability of these products lessened the people's self-sufficiency and discouraged local initiatives in the manufacturing sector. In such a way were the strong regional links formed for this open and vulnerable dependent economy.

Throughout the first half of this century South Africa harboured hopes that Bechuanaland and the other High Commission Territories — Lesotho and Swaziland — would join the ranks of the 'bantustans'. The election of the racialist Nationalist Party of South Africa in 1948 acted as a strong deterrent for the Territories. By 1959 the appointment of a High Commissioner who strongly supported self-government seemed to ensure a politically independent future for Bechuanaland.[15]

In the first national elections held in March 1965 the conservative Botswana Democratic Party, led by Seretse Khama, the hereditary leader of Botswana's largest tribe, won 28 of 31 seats:

> The new Prime Minister reaffirmed his intention to welcome investment from all countries, including South Africa and Rhodesia, and emphasized his belief that economics and politics remained distinct. He indicated that under his government, Bechuanaland would seek membership in the United Nations, the Organisation of African Unity, and the Commonwealth, and would also be favourably disposed toward an economic grouping of Southern African states.[16]

However, Khama immediately sought to forge alternative economic links with Zambia, thereby giving 'substance to his pre-election promise that South Africa and other nations would be used so long as necessary', in keeping with his declared policy of 'putting Bechuanaland's survival above all else'.[17]

Southern Rhodesia's Unilateral Declaration of Independence (UDI) in 1965 (see Chapter 13) illustrated quickly to the new government the constraints under which Botswana had to live: worried that a military struggle would spill over; with no significant military power of its own;

and concerned about endangering its political and economic relations both with white South Africa and its own white settlers. Eighteen years later, the same concerns loom on an even larger scale as the battle for the last bastion slowly heats up. An additional factor this time around is the internal dynamics of Botswana.

The political economy of Botswana

In just 17 years Botswana has changed from being perceived as a marginally viable state to becoming an 'African growth economy.'[18] While external perceptions may have changed, the reality of a highly dualistic economy has not. Botswana may be experiencing one of the fastest growth rates in Africa because of the recent exploitation of its vast mineral deposits, but such growth is heavily dependent on the whims of the international market.[19] It also has an internal social and political structure which is broadening the gap between the wealthy few and the poor majority.

Botswana's prospects for development are curtailed by a number of major factors: first, its subordinate status with regard to South Africa has far-reaching implications for virtually every aspect of Botswana's political economy. The response by the government to both external constraints and domestic problems is another factor, as its basic orientation is traditional and conservative. The ruling Botswana Democratic Party (BDP) which has been in power since the first election in 1965, is composed primarily of well-to-do cattle ranchers, and those who aspire to join them. The BDP has maintained an open, capitalist economy which has enticed numerous multinational enterprises. Although this attitude is most indicative of the need for caution in order not to alienate the RSA, such an analysis is somewhat simplistic.[20] This approach has been highly profitable for the ruling class since the time of colonisation and is becoming ever more so as mounting government revenues are legislated for use in improving the conditions of the already well-off.[21]

Despite the recent economic improvements, Botswana's dependent nature is highly evident in many spheres of life. Most transportation links still go through South Africa, and recent hopes for routing some traffic through Zimbabwe and Mozambique have been dashed by South African-backed sabotage in Mozambique. Whereas exports are being somewhat diversified in content and direction, imports are increasingly concentrated in their source. In 1979 the percentage of imports coming from the RSA reached 85 per cent, up from 67 per cent in 1966.[22]

The reason for this dependence on South Africa is Botswana's membership in the South African Customs Union.[23] This Union between South Africa and the three former High Commission Territories dates back to 1910, with renegotiations in 1969 and 1976. It involves a complicated formula by which revenues are transferred to the BLS countries from a revenue pool in which the duty charges from annual imports and sales duties are amassed. The money is divided on the basis of each country's consumption of dutiable goods, be they imported or produced locally.[24] Revenues are collected and duties set by South Africa. Botswana is forced to buy South African products even if shopping elsewhere might be less expensive. It is virtually impossible for Botswana to create domestic import-substituting industries, as they could not possibly compete with established South African firms.[25] In this way, employment opportunities, so desperately needed in Botswana, are not generated.

Whereas in the past wage labour in South Africa compensated for the lack of jobs in Botswana, recruitment of Batswana has declined in recent years. While 40,400 Batswana were employed in South African mines in 1976, by 1979 that figure had dropped to 19,000.[26] South Africa has set the target of 1985 for ending the employment of Batswana miners in order to ease its domestic employment shortage. In previous years the remittance of part of the miners' wages had constituted an important part of Botswana's revenue. Not only has this revenue decreased as South African recruitment declined, but the employment problem has increased correspondingly within Botswana.[27]

While unemployment has worsened the plight of many Batswana, goverment coffers have been swelling at a very rapid rate. Total domestic revenue soared from P6.2 million (Pula) in 1966–67 to P264.2 million in 1980–81 at current prices.[28] A 1980 World Bank report ranked Botswana seventh out of 39 sub-Saharan African countries in measured per capita income. Such data would appear to indicate that the government has been very astute in fulfilling at least the first of its four planning objectives: rapid economic growth, social justice, economic independence, and sustained development.[29] It is necessary to ascertain the source of such growth as well as its impact upon the society as a whole, however, in order to evaluate the extent to which progress is being made in attaining social justice and sustained development in addition to growth.

Botswana's economy is now based on two exports — minerals and beef — with the production of cattle only recently becoming secondary to mining in magnitude. In 1970 diamonds were found at Orapa. Copper and nickel were later found at Selebi-Pikwe and coal at Morupule. Mining operations in all three areas were set up by South African-based, American, British- and South African-owned multinationals. With the help of the World Bank and other donors, the Botswana government provided much of the infrastructure to get the projects under way.[30] Most of the country has now undergone a geological survey, and unofficial estimates suggest that Botswana is expected to possess about double the natural resources of neighbouring Namibia. Already in 1976–77 mining was estimated to constitute 63 per cent of the total exports, and this figure is expected to grow to over 70 per cent by 1986–87.[31]

The Ministry of Finance and Development Planning has described the effects of such heavy dependence upon one commodity:

> The value of Botswana's diamond exports more than doubled between 1978 and 1979, and then increased by 25% more in 1980. In 1981 diamond exports fell by P88 million – a drop of 37%. The mineral sector's contribution to GDP fell by 17% in 1980/81 and a further 38% in 1981/82. In 1981/82 the mineral sector contributed to toal GDP only slightly more than half of what it had contributed in 1979/80. Given the importance of minerals, this was sufficient to halt real GDP growth entirely in 1980/81 and to cause a 5.3% decline in total GDP in 1981/82.[32]

The international diamond market continues to be depressed, yet production and stockpiling are continuing in Botswana. The government predicts that the real GDP of the mining sector will increase by 18 per cent per annum from 1982–83 to 1985–86, and the mineral exports at constant prices will increase by 13 per cent per annum on average.[33]

It is important to view critically the effect of mineral extraction upon Botswana as a whole. First and foremost, mining is very capital-intensive and mining technology is becoming increasingly more sophisticated. Botswana does not have the capital or the technology to undertake mineral development alone; therefore it must rely upon private and public foreign investment and expertise. In effect, it must woo investors and donors by providing attractive returns and incentives. The government appears to be willing to go to considerable expense to ensure the future of the few jobs which mining provides for Batswana. This expense has included tight control of unions involved in the mining sector.[34]

The government appears to be quite aware of the difficulties of becoming a mining economy and of the vulnerabilities which will be compounded. Its National Development Plan states: Much depends on regional politics, and on international economic trends that Botswana is powerless to influence. Botswana can create a suitable environment for investment, but it cannot compel such investment.[35] The basic conservative stance of the present government can be seen to reflect in part the creation of that 'suitable' environment in a period of international recession.

Whereas Botswana's new prime industry is foreign-dominated and capital-intensive, it meets few of the population's needs, so that there is minimal positive impact. This can be considered an inherent characteristic of mining, yet it is compounded by the way multinationals choose to operate within the countries where they have subsidiaries. Botswana is a country where the annual population growth rate is estimated at 3.3 per cent, and where only 20 per cent of the labour force has formal sector employment.[36] The proposed strategy for Botswana's sixth National Development Plan is to capture more completely the benefits of past and future mining developments by raising the share of expenditures that are directed to products and services produced domestically.[37]

Manufacturing accounted for merely 6 per cent of GDP in 1980–81, and employed only 6.5 per cent of the labour force.[38] The limitations on a manufacturing industry, apart from free trade within the Customs Union, are a very small domestic market and the lack of a skilled labour force. The development of an industrial sector would also require a large outlay of capital, something previously not readily available to Botswana. In 1982 a Financial Assistance Policy (FAP) was introduced with the purpose of channelling public funds into new ventures and expansions in the private sector.[39] Over 6 million Pula were made available for FAP in its first year, but administrative and managerial bottlenecks proved to be major constraints. Whereas it will be some time yet before such a venture could be fairly judged, one can predict that few of the new manufacturing enterprises will be able to ease Botswana's dependence on imports, particularly those needed by the mining sector.

The move toward increasing employment opportunities in manufacturing is timely given the sad state of Botswana's agricultural base. A combination of natural and human-made problems have caused severe problems in rural areas. The most significant division in rural Botswana society has been between those families which have ownership of or access to cattle and those which do not. A household which owns no cattle has neither a productive investment nor, more importantly, does it have ready access to cattle for ploughing and tilling the land. Even if cattle can be borrowed or rented in exchange for either money or labour, much of the half-month long planting season is lost waiting for the availability of the animals. This loss often results in a smaller harvest for the already poorer households. It has been estimated that 65.5 per cent of Batswana own 10 or fewer cattle, and 45 per cent do not own any.[40] Those figures were deduced before the beginning of the 1981–82 drought, during which tens of thousands of head of cattle died, most of them belonging to smallholders. It would seem that each successive year of drought is driving more people into the category of permanently without cattle.

Government programmes and policies are being directed increasingly toward the rural sector. The 1979–85 National Development Plan has earmarked P79 million for rural development, as compared with P12.1 million for the 1976–81 plan period.[41] However, it is difficult to see much being done other than some increase in government infrastructure in rural areas without a corresponding increase in either quality of services or in raising rural incomes.[42]

While the average annual growth rate of agricultural production has been dropping steadily since 1969, government programmes have been assisting cattle owners.[43] Such assistance does little for the 45 per cent of rural households which own no cattle, but it is of great assistance to the 0.2 per cent of rural homes which own over 400 head of cattle.[44] They are the ones who have benefited from policies of land control and grazing such as the Tribal Grazing Lands Policy, which was introduced in 1975 and which threatens to turn large parts of tribal land over to large-scale private cattle ranching.[45]

Many of the rural development policies appear to be widening the gap between the very poor and the well-off. It is clear that Parliament, which is full of cattle ranchers, is helping itself to a wealthier life. While opportunities are being extended to successful small farmers who wish to become more prosperous, it is becoming increasingly difficult for the poor to escape the grip of abject poverty. Without capital, which they cannot obtain, they cannot acquire cattle for investment. Whereas in the past there were numerous opportunities for wage labour in South Africa, recruitment for such work has dropped significantly as black unemployment in South Africa has risen. Not only are Botswana's poor not gaining ground; they seem to be losing it.

In looking back over 17 years of independence, it is clear that remarkable growth has been achieved in Botswana, but that high growth rate has not been translated into increased equity. The picture which emerges is that of an open, highly dualistic, heavily dependent economy. It is necessary to look at Botswana's place in the region and the world in order to get a more complete picture of her political economy.

The relationship between political economy and foreign policy

From the start of the colonial period the Bechuanaland Protectorate was designed to serve as an appendage of South Africa. Its only economic importance was as a reserve for cheap labour and as a market for South African products. Such has been Botswana's role for the past century; even the mineral discoveries of the past decade have not lessened Botswana's dependence on its neighbour to the south.

Botswana is so heavily integrated into the Southern African economic system that it is impossible to separate foreign and domestic policy. In undertaking both domestic initiatives and in interacting with her neighbours and the world, Botswana always has to consider the impact of such actions upon the bilateral relationship with the Pretoria regime. The threat from South Africa is real. 'Unfriendly' comments or actions have resulted in sudden shortages of rolling stock vital for importing products into Botswana and of refrigerated boxcars for exporting Botswana's beef, and sudden dramatic cuts in the availability of oil. It is not necessary for such power to be exercised frequently before such incidents are prevented by self-control of the dependent partner. Such self-control by Botswana has been evident on the political scene and in her role as a Front Line State in the Zimbabwean liberation struggle.

The conservative BDP had already won Botswana's first national election in March 1965 before Rhodesia's UDI in November of that year. The liberation struggle in Zimbabwe did not remain outside Botswana's borders for very long. Refugees poured into the country in huge numbers. The unguarded frontier was crossed at will by Rhodesian and South African military personnel and police, as well as by freedom fighters. There were bombings, murders, kidnappings, and wanton destruction within Botswana's boundaries, but out of her control.

Attempts were made to decrease Botswana's dependence upon her racialist neighbours in terms of air travel and energy needs. In mid-1977 the Botswana Defence Force was established. The cost was estimated at P26.5 million (US$32 million) over four years — more than 12 times the amount allocated for security in the original 1976—81 National Plan.[46] Plans were made for nationalising the stretch of Rhodesian Railways which runs through Botswana. Although to Rhodesia that rail line was quite vital, being one of two rail links with South Africa, for Botswana it was absolutely essential — the only rail link available. Open to sabotage at any time by the forces of any ideological persuasion, the fate of that route was considered very carefully, and a process was undertaken which has resulted in the formation of Botswana Railways.

The Botswana government was very concerned about another effect of the war. Thousands of refugees have entered Botswana in the past two decades. Most of them have been young and politicised toward radical change. The two most militant groups — the Zimbabweans and South Africans — were settled around the two major urban centres — Francistown and Gaborone. There they joined the large numbers of Batswana young urban unemployed, who are classic targets for radical-isation. A traditionalist and nationalist government had a difficult time dealing with increasing class consciousnes both among the unemployed and among university students. Those refugees who did not hold jobs were shipped to a large refugee camp in a rural area. After a disturbance at the University of Botswana in 1979 President Seretse Khama warned students that they should not expect their years of study to be years of 'devotion to the study of nihilist philosophies and destructive dogmas which have no relevance to the circumstances prevailing in their countries.'[47] Although Khama's assessment of the situation was historically inaccurate, it does give an insight into his own conservative philosophy and into his attitude toward change in Southern Africa.

Botswana tended to side with Zambia (see Chapter 12) on many issues concerning Zimbabwe. Zambia gave its support to Joshua Nkomo and ZAPU, the less radical of the liberation groups. While giving support to ZAPU, Zambia still made every attempt in the early 1970s to find any and every avenue for a peaceful settlement in Zimbabwe. 'Indeed, the Front Line association grew out of an attempt by the OAU to curb Zambian collaboration with South Africa's detente strategy in late 1974 and early 1975.'[48] Seretse Khama was included as a Front Line State (FLS) President by the OAU, just as he had been included in trying to achieve detente with Zambia and South Africa.

After the Portuguese coup in 1974 Botswana welcomed signs of a detente between South Africa and independent African countries. At the opening of Parliament in 1974 President Khama confirmed that he would play an active role in trying to bring about peaceful change in Southern Africa. Colin Legum asserts that Khama pushed detente and dialogue as far as possible and for as long as possible on all fronts.[49] Foreign Minister Archie Mogwe stated that 'Botswana is ready to serve as a go-between, if required, between militant black South Africans abroad and Pretoria.'[50]

By early 1976 the FLS had decided that 'peaceful negotiations had failed, and that the issue of majority rule for Rhodesia would be resolved not at diplomatic tables, but on the battlefield.'[51] That decision was not reached easily, yet the majority decision was accepted. Tony Hodges states:

> Reluctantly, the Botswana government has been cast in the role of a 'front line state', and it now voices support for an armed struggle against the Salisbury regime. It does so from a conservative standpoint, hoping that swift action to bring down the regime will check the present drift toward regional destabilisation and radicalisation and will help to safeguard the status quo in Botswana.[52]

Hesitancy about a military solution was further evidenced by Botswana's interest in any and all negotiable solutions. She supported the Washington-sponsored settlement in Namibia, and she seemed inclined to support the 'interim government' in Rhodesia, if not quite openly.[53] The interim government has been and gone, and Botswana now has a delicate relationship with its first nominally 'Marxist' neighbour.

The rocky road since Zimbabwe's independence in 1980 has had many profound effects upon Botswana. There was great joy in Botswana in April 1980, but the relationship with the new state of Zimbabwe has been a complex one. Geographical proximity and kinship have resulted in considerable unfamiliarity with the new ZANU regime, as Mashonaland and its people are much less familiar to Batswana than are the Matebele and Kalanga of Western Zimbabwe.

Trade links between the two countries, though of considerable interest to both economies as a means of lessening dependence upon South Africa, are severely hampered by the intricacies of the Southern African Customs Union and by Zimbabwe's severe foreign exchange shortage.

Relations deteriorated sharply in late 1982 and early 1983 as the internal security situation in Zimbabwe started spilling over into Botswana once again. Thousands of people crossed the border illegally, seeking refuge in Botswana. A sharp difference of opinion still persists as to whether such people were armed dissidents or genuine refugees.[54] Joshua Nkomo's arrival in Botswana in March 1983 sparked a major diplomatic crisis, which was resolved temporarily through the meetings of the respective Heads of Government.

Clearly it is in the interest of both governments to resolve any disputes as quickly and as smoothly as possible, not only in their individual interest, but also because of an all-important common variable. That common variable, which not only relishes but also nurtures rivalry and dissent in the whole region, is the Republic of South Africa.

Botswana and the region

In 1979 the Southern African Development Coordination Conference (SADCC) was formed. Currently its members are: Botswana, Mozambique, Zimbabwe, Tanzania, Angola, Malawi, Zambia, Lesotho and Swaziland. An offspring of the FLS, its objectives are:

- Reduction of economic dependence on South Africa.
- Forging links to create genuine and equitable regional integration.
- Mobilisation of resources to promote the implementation of

national, interstate and regional policies.

— Concerted action to secure international cooperation within the framework of economic liberation.[55]

The secretariat for SADCC was set up in Botswana in mid-1982.

It is not the purpose of this chapter to explore the potential of SADCC. At the same time, it is difficult to refrain from speculating on the future of such a large, disparate grouping of states. As a group, SADCC possesses huge material and human resources. However, the political and economic differences between the various states cover a large part of the politico-economic spectrum, and each country is, in its own way, highly vulnerable to interference from outside.

There have not been many successes in the history of African integration schemes. SADCC appears to be making a good start by focusing first on transportation and communication links, as they are both of pressing urgency and are perhaps more simple to implement than economic programmes.

South Africa's quiet response to the formation of SADCC is perhaps the most pragmatic approach it can take, as each of the member countries of SADCC are so greatly dependent upon it that much progress can be undone on a national rather than a regional basis.

Botswana's leadership role in SADCC may come as a surprise in the light of the history of Botswana—South African relations. In most ways, that history remains unchanged. Botswana's dependence on South Africa may have altered in format, but not in substance. Instead of tens of thousands of Batswana migrating south to work there, corporations are increasingly moving north and utilising Botswana's capital and labour to set up subsidiaries. They are assisted by tax concessions, subsidies, and the skills of a growing comprador class of Batswana, who generally move from government positions into directorships and the management of South African or global multi-national subsidiaries.

Botswana's dependent relationship *vis-à-vis* South Africa is further cemented by her own increasing wealth. It is Botswana's importance as a market for South African goods and services which will make certain that the ties between the two states will not weaken significantly or be broken. Recent figures have shown that Botswana's contribution to the South African economy both in terms of GDP and in the number of jobs sustained is considerable.[56] South Africa rewards such 'development assistance' by giving Botswana a higher cut from the Customs Union revenue pool (17—23 per cent instead of the correct 15—16 per cent) with the end result that more capital is available for use by South Africa in Botswana.

Botswana's relationship with the international capitalist system is merely an extension of her dependent position in the region. Both of Botswana's sources of revenue — minerals and beef — are commodities for which both demand and prices fluctuate considerably. For as long as DeBeer's Central Selling Organisation maintains its monopoly over the international diamond market Botswana's economic security should be assured. However, fluctuations do occur, as is evidenced by the stockpiling which has been undertaken by Botswana since 1981 because of the 'softness' of the diamond market.

As has already been mentioned, before the rapid rise of mining, beef had long been the mainstay of the country's economy. Markets were found and developed in South Africa and in the EEC, but once again, environmental and external forces tend to be the powerful determinants controlling the industry. In 1978 beef production came to a standstill due to an outbreak of foot and mouth disease. While stringent controls within the country were effective in containing the disease within Botswana, the smuggling of infected cattle from Zimbabwe during the liberation struggle seriously compounded the problem. In the 1980s drought may be the main culprit in undermining the sector which has a much more direct impact on the rural economy.

Tariffs in Europe have at times set barriers against Botswana beef. The Lomé Convention of 1975 removed the barriers, but imposed instead a variable import levy, which Botswana was able to reduce by 90 per cent. The 12-month quota system imposed by the EEC, while an improvement over the previous 6-month quota, does not allow for much planning on the part of producers such as Botswana. Exports to neighbouring countries such as Zambia and South Africa are limited by economic conditions within those countries.

Botswana's relationship with international donors has been another crucial aspect of her foreign policy. Because of her unenviable geopolitical position and the poverty in which she gained independence, Botswana was a major beneficiary of Western aid, and is still high on the list of favoured recipients. However, the flow of aid money is slowing down as Botswana's revenues increase and as donors recognise that not much headway is being made in tackling basic problems in rural areas. In this case it is the people of Botswana who are dependent, but domestic funds are often not being fed into projects for which external funding has ended.[57] Once again, the indivisibility of foreign and domestic affairs for a dependent economy is demonstrated. What then does the future hold for Botswana and her people?

The future of Botswana's foreign policy

Given the foreign policy and development policy imponderables,

Botswana's future is uncertain at present. Certainly the key variable will be the nature and speed of change in South Africa. Should there be gradual change in South Africa with little disruption of the economic status quo, the ruling class in Botswana can look forward to increased security and prosperity. As the independence of Namibia becomes more inevitable, Botswana's hopes will turn westward and an attempt will be made to make the trans-Kgalagadi railway to Walvis Bay a reality. If SADCC manages to implement even part of its proposed targets, then collective dependence upon South Africa could be lessened to a degree. Yet that would be a very slow process at best, and one that South Africa would not allow to proceed unopposed.

Botswana's mineral wealth should continue to increase government and multinational revenues, particularly once the exploitation of her coal reserves, soda ash and known hydro-carbons begins in earnest.[58]

An attempt has been made in this chapter to show that in many ways Botswana's place both in the region and in the global economy was set soon after it was colonised. Also, class structure in Botswana has been largely determined by people's ability to deal with changes to the traditional economy caused by the advent of colonial settlers and traders. Many of the problems which arose then are still those which plague Botswana and its people today.

Compared to other less developed countries Botswana's lot at present may appear to be an enviable one. Certainly the statistics concerning growth (if not development) are highly favourable. The gap between the rich and the poor is widening. To date the poor have had to rely on their own hard work and on whatever 'trickle-down' and foreign-funded projects have reached them. Even though diamond prices are low and the country is hard-hit by drought, there are indications that expectations are being raised within the country, particularly among the young and the literate. The next few years will show whether conservative forces will be able to continue to weave their magic spell over their people and international donors.

The composition of the ruling class is altering with time. President Quett Masire took over in 1980 after the death of Sir Seretse Khama, and he is not nearly as popular as his predecessor. His BDP is ever rumoured to be splitting, with the non-cattled and white-collar class seeking a more distinct articulation of their own interests. As a national election approaches in 1984 it is difficult to foretell how significant opposition will be handled in this virtually untested multi-party democracy. There is no guarantee of how the ever-expanding Botswana Defence Force would respond to any serious threat to the status quo. Speculation mounts as to the Defence Force's exact role, as it is almost impossible to imagine Botswana daring to get involved in any sort of military encounter with any of its neighbours.

It is difficult to assess the potential that Botswana has for altering its present course in any significant way. One thing is certain — the future of Botswana is tied up squarely within the parameters of the nature of change within South Africa as the dominant regional power. Until that time Botswana may well be faced with growth without development, and quiet without peace.

Notes

1 Richard Dale, *The Racial Component of Botswana's Foreign Policy* (Denver: University of Denver, 1979), pp. 18–19.
2 See Christopher Colclough and Stephen McCarthy, *The Political Economy of Botswana* (London: Oxford University Press, 1980).
3 This diamond boom inspired the production of such investment guides as P. Hartland-Thunberg, *Botswana: an African growth economy* (Boulder: Westview, 1978).
4 Ann and Neva Seidman, *South Africa and U.S. Multinational Corporations* (Westport: Lawrence Hill, 1977), pp. 180–187.
5 See Percy Selwyn, *Industries in the South African Periphery* (London: Croom Helm, 1975).
6 Jack Parson, 'Botswana in the Southern African Periphery: the limits of capitalist transformation in a "labour reserve"' *IDS Bulletin*, vol. 11, no. 4, September 1980, pp. 45–52.
7 *Ibid.*, p. 51.
8 Colclough and McCarthy, *The Political Economy of Botswana* (note 2), p. 7.
9 The proportion would have risen from 13 per cent to well over 40 per cent.
10 Botswana's claim to a border with Zambia in the middle of the Zambezi River was disputed by the Rhodesian regime. At present a small pontoon ferry crosses between the two countries. There is still talk about building a bridge across.
11 Colclough and McCarthy, *The Political Economy of Botswana* (note 2), p. 13.
12 A table showing colonial expenditure in this century is found in *ibid.*, p. 29.
13 *Ibid.*, p. 19.
14 Jack Halpern, *South Africa's Hostages* (London: Penguin, 1965), p. 111.
15 Colclough and McCarthy, *The Political Economy of Botswana* (note 2), p. 27.
16 *Ibid.*, p. 153.
17 *Ibid.*, p. 154.

18 See Hartland-Thunberg, *Botswana* (note 3).

19 An assessment of Botswana's mineral wealth is presented in 'Making jobs out of diamonds', *World Business Weekly*, 25 August 1980, pp. 23–24.

20 There is a growing literature on Botswana as a subordinate state. See for example, Parson 'Botswana in the Southern African Periphery' (note 6).

21 While it is not implied that the government could successfully reorient its international relations, it is necessary to recognise that Botswana's present situation helps a few people in Botswana become very wealthy and powerful.

22 *World Business Weekly*, 25 August 1980, p. 24. See also Botswana, *National Development Plan 1976–1981* (Gaborone: Ministry of Finance and Development Planning, 1977), p. 75.

23 For a detailed history of the Customs Union see Colclough and McCarthy, *The Political Economy of Botswana* (note 2), pp. 76–81.

24 *Ibid.*, p. 79.

25 *Ibid.*, p. 79.

26 *World Business Weekly*, 25 August 1980, p. 24.

27 Botswana, *National Development Plan 1976–1981* (note 22), pp. 40–45.

28 Figures derived from the Annual Accounts of Botswana.

29 Botswana, *National Development Plan 1976–1981* (note 22), p. 15.

30 Seidman and Seidman, *South Africa and U.S. Multinational Corporations* (note 4), pp. 180–187.

31 See Botswana, *National Development Plan 1978–81* (note 22), p. 184, *World Business Weekly*, 25 August 1980, p. 23 and Botswana, 'The Mid-term Review of NDP V' (Gaborone: Ministry of Finance and Development Planning, unpublished document, July 1983), p. 84.

32 Botswana, 'The Mid-term Review of NDP V', pp. 12–13.

33 *Ibid.*, p. 14.

34 The government has kept a lid on the unions since the strike at the Shashe Complex in 1975. In mid-1981 members of the opposition Botswana National Front were elected to key positions in the Botswana Federation of Trade Unions. That election was declared invalid because of the number of bureaucratic technicalities.

35 Botswana, *Nnational Development Plan 1976–81* (note 22), p. 62.

36 Botswana, 'Mid-term Review of NDP V', (note 31), pp. 91–92, p. 95.

37 *Ibid.*, p. 7.

38 *Ibid.*, pp. 77 and 95.

76

39   *Ibid.*, p. 53.
40   Jack Parson, 'Political Culture in Rural Botswana,' *Journal of Modern African Studies*, vol. 15, no. 4, December 1977, p. 642.
41   'Minister Kwele Reports to Constituents on Rural Development,' *Botswana Newsletter*, vol. 5, 14 August—4 September 1980, p. 3 and *National Development Plan 1976—81*, p. 48.
42   Botswana, 'Mid-term Review of NDP V' (note 31), p. 3.
43   Ravi Gulhati, *Eastern and Southern Africa: Past Trends and Future Prospects* (Washington: World Bank Staff Working Paper 413, August 1980), p. 4.
     Agricultural production's annual growth rate dropped from 3.5 per cent in 1969—73 to 1.6 per cent in 1973—77, and despite attempts within the Ministry of Agriculture to improve the arable agriculture picture, the growth rate has been arrested of late because of drought.
44   See Appendices in Donald Kowet, *Land, Labour Migration and Politics in Southern Africa* (Uppsala: Scandinavian Institute of African Studies, 1978) for a breakdown of cattle ownership in Botswana.
45   The TGLP, heralded as a land reform which would increase responsibility for land by those who use it, was intended to lessen the pressures on communal land by moving large cattle owners and groups of aspiring ranchers onto land which had been designated commercial. For a good critical analysis of the programme see Solomon Bekure and Neville Dyson-Hudson, *The Operation and Viability of the Second Livestock Development Project (1497-BT): Selected Issues* (Gaborone: Ministry of Agriculture, 1982).
46   Hartland-Thunberg, *Botswana* (note 3), pp. 70—7.
47   *Africa*, no. 90, February 1979, p. 57.
48   'Difficult Times Test Front-Line Unity', *Southern Africa*, January 1979, p. 24.
49   'Botswana' in Colin Legum (ed.), *Africa Contemporary Record, annual survey of events and documents, Volume 7: 1974—75*, (London: Rex Collings, 1975), p. B363.
50   'Botswana' in Legum (ed.), *Africa Contemporary Record, Volume 8: 1975—76*, p. B532.
51   Robert Hull, 'Rhodesia and her Neighbours', *Current History*, vol. 73, no. 432, December 1977.
52   Tony Hodges, 'External Threats and Internal Pressures', *Africa Report*, vol. 22, no. 6, November—December 1977, p. 42.
53   'Difficult Times Test Front-Line Unity' (note 48), p. 27.
54   The author was working in Francistown, in the northeast, at that time. Whereas it was clear that most people who crossed the border were genuine refugees, there were instances of dissidents

burying arms in Botswana as they had during the liberation struggle. Whereas it would have tu be obvious to Botswana that this was being done, there was no way that the government could stop such actions on the part of a very small number of people.

55 'President opens "sell the SADCC seminar"' *Daily News* (Gaborone), p. 202, 27 October 1981.

56 Figures compiled by Earl L. McFarland indicated that Botswana's imports contributed 24,000 jobs to the South African manufacturing sector, 38,000 to other sectors of the economy, and over 8 per cent of the total increase in manufacturing GDP from 1970–79. A paper on this topic is included in a forthcoming publication which is the result of a symposium on Botswana's economy held in Gaborone in September 1981.

57 As an example, funding was cut by USAID in 1982–83 for a major wildlife programme because no results were shown over a period of two years. The programme would have benefited thousands of remote area dwellers, but it had problems getting off the ground because of a shortage of wildlife specialists in Botswana and, more importantly, because major programmes often take longer than two years. The government will be hard-pressed to replace USAID funds with Domestic Development Funds in this instance.

58 Feasibility studies are nearing completion on the Kgaswe Coal Project and the Sua Pan soda ash project. In addition, it does appear quite certain that Botswana has oil, but the government and Esso are not pushing ahead with development at this time.

3 Ethiopia

Christopher Clapham

Historical incorporation and inheritance

For Ethiopia, as for other African states, foreign policy is the product of and response to the interactions between domestic state structure and the external linkages created by incorporation into the global economy. In this case it is essential to recognise, however, that both the structure of the state, and the consequent pattern of external linkage, differ substantially from the characteristic African experience, with the result that foreign policy also must be seen in a rather different light. Whereas most African territories, created as political units by an external colonialism, have gained independent statehood with an existing structure of economic production already geared to external markets, in Ethiopia statehood preceded incorporation. Though incorporation was eventually enforced on Ethiopia by the requirements of national and regime survival, it was thus mediated by an established indigenous government which was itself derived from a particular class and ethnic section.

The indigenous political economy contrasted a core area, comprising the Amhara–Tigrean plateau which stretches north from Addis Ababa to the area around Asmara in Eritrea, with the surrounding periphery.

Within the core, a grain-growing arable economy produced a surplus sufficient to sustain a hierarchical society with differentiated political and religious institutions which — provided that too close a comparison with medieval Europe is not read into the term — may broadly be described as feudal. At its apex, the emperor maintained a degree of authority which varied not only with his ability to control his vassals within the core, but also with his ability to extract tribute from the periphery. For as far back as records reach — at least 500 years — control of the local periphery has been, in its own view, the historic mission or manifest destiny of the Ethiopian state. The power of the central government within the core has indeed varied directly in proportion to its control of the periphery. The surplus produced within the core could only with great difficulty be extracted for the emperor's use; it was much more readily available to local rulers seeking to establish their own autonomous fiefdoms. Peripheral production, on the other hand, came much more directly under imperial control, especially important being the trade in slaves, gold and ivory from the south-west, and in salt from the north-east, as well as access via the Red Sea to Arabia and Egypt. The economic structure of the Ethiopian state has thus continuously depended on the control of trade from the periphery, which in turn, more than anything else, provides the dynamic which has impelled successive Ethiopian rulers to engage in relations with the outside world.[1]

Late nineteenth century colonialism, with its imposition of fixed territorial boundaries, both strengthened and weakened this national control. On the one hand Ethiopia, itself a beneficiary of the scramble, incorporated within its territory virtually all that part of present-day Ethiopia which lies south of Addis Ababa, including the south-eastern provinces of Harar, Bale and Arusi, the south-western ones of Sidamo, Gamu-Gofa, Kaffa, Illubabor and Wallega, and a strip of territory all the way up the western border with Sudan. These have since become overwhelmingly the most important areas for the production of the cash crops on the export of which the Ethiopian state depends. The reasons for this are political quite as much as geographical. It is not just that coffee — by far the most important crop — requires the forest ecology of the south-west for its cultivation, but also that the conquered provinces could be organised for centrally controlled production (through the alienation of land to central government nominees, and the conversion of the local peasantry into share-croppers or estate labourers) in a way that was politically impossible among the land-holding peasantries of the core. On the other hand, European colonialism excluded Ethiopia from direct access to the sea, and hence to the international market. From 1890 onwards Ethiopia depended on the French colonial port of Djibouti (from which a railway to Addis Ababa was completed in 1916), Massawa and Assab in Italian Eritrea, and to a lesser extent the Sudan. Italian invasions were launched from Eritrea in 1895 and 1935 — the first defeated, the second successful — and left Ethiopia with an intense concern for the control of the Red Sea coast for security as well as economic reasons.

The creation of a modern state, based on the export of cash crops, dates more specifically from Haile-Selassie's accession to power as Regent in 1916. He became Emperor in 1930. He swiftly realised, as Marcus has argued,[2] that Ethiopia's independence required the reorganisation of the armed forces, the fiscal system, and education, and that this in turn called for expansion of the cash economy. These measures equally, and in many ways even more importantly, implied the subordination of the provinces to the central government in Addis Ababa. Though post-revolutionary critics of the Haile-Selassie regime have frequently — and for perfectly understandable ideological and rhetorical reasons — referred to it as 'feudalist', this in fact seriously misrepresents the nature of the regime. What Haile-Selassie did was to establish a politico-economic structure comparable in many respects to that created by colonial powers elsewhere in Africa. His first priority was to destroy feudalism — seen as a system in which political power directly depends on the control of the land and its subject peasantry — and replace it by an urban-centred government which dominated its rural hinterland, and extracted from it a surplus created by the incorporation of that hinterland into a global economy.

Central to this process was a rapid increase in coffee exports, sustained by a shift from subsistence to a market economy, especially in the south-west. Coffee exports through Djibouti rose from a 1910—1920 mean of 3.4 million kilos to 12 million in 1924 and 20 million in 1932.[3] Exports through the Sudan, though accounting for only a sixth of the Djibouti total, showed a similar trend.[4] These charges were accompanied by the extension of a transport network firmly centered on Addis Ababa, and by the emergence of a small capitalist class led by Haile-Selassie himself, who invested not only in commercial agriculture but also in other trading ventures. Though these changes mirrored events elsewhere in Africa, there were important differences between the Ethiopian experience and that of neighbouring colonial territories such as Kenya, both in the scale of urbanisation and commercialisation of agriculture, and in its political effects. Both government and land ownership remained in indigenous hands, and while this enabled the domestic ruling class to maintain its position it also meant that rural resentment against exploitation and expropriation would eventually be directed against that class, rather than against European settlers and a colonial regime. Substantial elements of a peculiarly Ethiopian political economy thus remained.

Marcus has argued convincingly that it was in part the success of this process of state formation and economic growth which prompted Mussolini's invasion and conquest of Ethiopia in 1935—6.[5] The subsequent five-year occupation, nonetheless, intensified the trends of the previous two decades by extending the road network, reducing the autonomy of regional notables, and furthering the production of cash crops and the development of towns; in general binding Ethiopia more closely than before into the global economy.

The Haile-Selassie regime, 1941—1974

The same considerations of external security and control of the periphery continued to dominate Ethiopian foreign policy after the liberation of the country from Italian occupation in 1941, though the international setting in which they were pursued had drastically altered. The liberation, achieved largely by British and Commonwealth troops, raised critical problems on both counts. The British not only controlled all the territories bordering Ethiopia, save only Djibouti, but they also included Ethiopia itself, both militarily and economically, within the Middle East war zone. This had some advantages, notably in enabling Haile-Selassie to call on the Royal Air Force to quell a serious revolt in Tigre province in 1943, but these were far outweighed by the constraints. Economic relationships with the outside world were managed, until 1945, through the Middle East Supply Centre which regulated the entire zone as a single unit.[6] British advisers, until 1944, monopolised positions of expertise within the Ethiopian government. Most importantly, Britain continued to administer Eritrea and the Somali-inhabited areas of Ethiopia, and British officials expressed some sympathy for the separation from Ethiopia of the Somalis and (fleetingly, but much more dangerously) of the south-western Gallas.

The natural counterweight, in both economic and diplomatic terms, was the United States. In defiance of the Anglo—Ethiopian agreement of 1942, which gave Britain control over the employment of expatriates in the Ethiopian government, Haile-Selassie reappointed one of his prewar American advisers, John Spencer, and welcomed an American economic mission. Early in 1945 he met President Roosevelt in Egypt to cement the relationship in personal terms. Shortly afterwards, in July 1945, a new currency was introduced, backed by a United States silver loan and linked to the United States dollar rather than to sterling. The United States became by far the most important single market for Ethiopian coffee, and hence for Ethiopian exports as a whole, by 1953 taking 32 per cent of exports by value directly, in addition to further exports through Aden and Djibouti.[7] This proportion remained fairly constant over the following two decades.[8] Ethiopian imports were shared much more evenly between the United States, Britain, Italy, West Germany, and Japan.[9] In terms of aid, and loans the United States held an overwhelmingly dominant position, being owed for example 54 per cent of Ethiopia's external debt by the end of 1963, with a further 28 per cent due to international institutions which were largely financed and dominated by them.

In addition to its value in countering any threat from Britain, the United States connection strengthened central government control over the periphery in two much more specific ways. The first was in Eritrea, where the United States supported a UN resolution in 1951 that the territory be federated with Ethiopia under the sovereignty of the Ethiopian crown. Though this fell a little short of the outright union which the Ethiopians demanded, it nonetheless permitted the imperial government to increase its control over the region by the steady exercise of inducement and coercion until it was fully incorporated into Ethiopia in 1962. The direct pay-off for this support was the United States Kagnew communications base, just outside Asmara in the Eritrean highlands, which, until the advent of satellite technology, served as a vital missile-tracking and radio-monitoring station for the Middle Eastern region. The second was the Ethio—American defence assistance agreement in 1953, which provided for United States military assistance in both weapons and training for the Ethiopian army. By far the greater part of Ethiopia's military equipment was American, and by 1976 Ethiopia had received some $279m in military assistance, in addition to $350m in economic aid.[10]

The major function of the armed forces was, of course, the maintenance of central control, especially in Eritrea and the Somali-inhabited area, but also in the south-west. It would be entirely wrong, however, to see the United States connection as amounting, even in its heyday, to the neo-colonisation of Ethiopia. In contrast to the other main centre of United States involvement in black Africa during the post-war period, the Republic of Liberia, Ethiopia was never penetrated enough to be really neo-colonised. The United States had a natural alliance with a ruling group, but it had no substantial investments, and its interests in Ethiopia were much more strategic than economic.

The south-west remained the critical area for Ethiopian coffee production, which remained stagnant at below the 1930s level throughout the 1940s, but increased to over 40 million kilos a year in the early 1950s, and to 60 million kilos in the early 1960s. The alienation of coffee lands to central government notables also continued, particularly notorious in this respect being Ras Mesfin Sileshi, governor of Kaffa province in the 1940s and 1950s. The production of coffee, as of other south-western cash crops, remained almost entirely in indigenous hands, while agricultural investment by foreign multinationals was heavily concentrated in the Awash Valley area, south-east of Addis Ababa. The most important venture was the establishment of sugar plantations by a Dutch Company, H.V.A., which evidently secured high profits through a combination of low wage payments to Ethiopian labourers and monopoly access to a protected domestic market.[11]

In the commercial and industrial field, there was likewise a combination of investment by expatriate companies and the indigenous governing elite. The emperor himself, and his small coterie of senior officials, were heavily involved in these ventures. They included the Ethiopian National Corporation, set up soon after the liberation to exploit grain exports to the Middle East under the artificial conditions of wartime scarcity, which subsequently took over control of imported cotton goods;[12] and the emperor and his family also had the major stake in the country's principal brewery and road transport enterprise. Industrial investment was generally slight, despite generous tax incentives, and was concentrated both geographically, in Addis Ababa and its environs and to a lesser extent Eritrea, and sectorally, on textiles (with Indian and Japanese participation) and small-scale production of necessities — soap, matches, shoes — for the domestic market. Despite wide prospecting for oil, and largely abortive attempts at potash and copper extraction, there was no substantial production of minerals.

To summarise, the degree of external penetration of the Ethiopian economy during the three decades after the Second World War was, by the standards of most former colonial territories, comparatively slight. Though Ethiopia's trade was heavily oriented towards the OECD economies, these had neither individually nor collectively any major stake either in Ethiopian products, nor in Ethiopia as an export market. Equally, though its share of coffee exports made the United States by far Ethiopia's major trading partner, no single Western state had the level of economic involvement in the country which followed automatically from colonisation in almost every other African state. On the Ethiopian side, however, the economy came under the control of an indigenous ruling elite which had neither the anti-capitalist ideology nor the populist connections engendered by anti-colonial nationalism in other parts of the continent.

This capitalist-oriented elite tended naturally, therefore, to look towards the West. Haile-Selassie tried so far as possible to maximise his range of contacts with different Western states, despite inevitable military and economic dependence in the United States, and he was perfectly willing to establish contacts with the Soviet Union; he was adept, both in domestic and in international politics, at maintaining a balance among competing actors and seeking the advantages of divide and rule.[13] Though non-alignment in this sense is part of the inherited foreign policy wisdom of the Ethiopian state, both Haile-Selassie and the social stratum which ruled under him were firmly aligned by interest with the West, and looked to the West to protect them against both secessionist forces at the periphery and any radical attempt to upset the existing order at the centre.[14] For the government's opponents, both central and peripheral, this engendered an equally instinctive anti-Americanism, and a tendency to look both at Marxism as an ideology and to the Soviet Union as an ally. The Western states became, as in Iran, the prisoners of their connection with a crumbling political order which they maintained largely because, in an area where they needed allies, it supported them.

Ethiopia's economic relationships with her neighbours and African states as a whole were negligible, save only for Djibouti as the port which served the Addis Ababa railway. Until the late 1950s, her interest in the dramatic political developments elsewhere on the continent was equally slight. By 1963, as host to the Addis Ababa conference which founded the OAU, Haile-Selassie had established himself in a position of continental diplomatic leadership. This transformation was made possible by Ethiopia's diplomatic advantages (the status engendered by long independence, and the mediating position gained by neutrality as between former French and British colonies, between Arab north and black Africa, between Monrovia and Casablanca blocs), by the prestige and diplomatic skills of Haile-Selassie himself, and the shrewdness of his advisors. The impetus behind it, however, was, as always, the need to control the periphery.

By 1960 the Ethiopian state was, in contemporary African terms, an anachronism. It made scarcely any concession to the demands for national self-determination, one man one vote, or African socialism which guided the nationalist movements. It was particularly vulnerable to the demands for the unification of the Somali peoples under a single government which followed from the merger of British Somaliland and ex-Italian Somalia to form a single independent state in 1960. Eritrea presented a similar danger, especially through the links between its Moslem population and the radical Arab states. If the worst came to the worst, the Galla—Oromo and south-western peoples might make a push for independence too. The historical memory of the ruling core, its awareness of the cyclical ebb and flow of Ethiopia's frontiers, its perennial fear of hostile encirclement, presented this as a moment of danger.

In retrospect, the solution was a simple one: to make common cause with other African states whose own boundaries were no less artificial, and whose fear of state disintegration was equally great, thus penning both the Somalis and the Eritreans into the confines of the principle of respect for the existing inherited frontiers. At the same time, the creation of an ethic of inter-African governmental solidarity inhibited support for secession from the Moslem African states, the most important of which was Egypt. (The same pressure could not be brought on non-African states such as Syria and Iraq.) Nonetheless, the choice at the time was by no means so clear-cut, and as a diplomatic achievement it deserves recognition.

The essential structure of Haile-Selassie's political settlement survived until 1974, but even before the emperor's fall it was showing signs of strain: at the centre with the loss of support from the urban groups on which it most directly relied; at the periphery, with the deterioration of the military situation in Eritrea and the growth of local political consciousness elsewhere; externally, with the emergence of a new generation of Arab radicalism led by Libya, and the reluctance of the United States to match the rapid increase in the level of Soviet arms shipments to Somalia. The combination of these factors led to upheavals in both domestic and external political economy which could fairly be described as revolutionary.

Revolution and continuity since 1974

At one level, the period since 1974 has produced drastic changes in Ethiopian political structure and economic organisation, which have in turn produced an equally striking reversal of foreign relationships, and notably the replacement of the United States by the Soviet Union as the regime's principal external protector and source of arms. At another level, the continuities in Ethiopian foreign policy have been quite as important, and it is the argument of this section that the inherited structure of the Ethiopian state, and its economic relationships with its periphery, ultimately determine Ethiopian foreign policy and outweigh even the most revolutionary changes in the structure and policies of national government.

The political upheavals which, starting early in 1974, led to the overthrow of Haile-Selassie in September of that year, were the result of many different strains and deficiencies in the imperial regime. In the first place, there was its alienation of all the main urban classes, including notably the intelligentsia and state bureaucracy, and the small Addis Ababa proletariat. Second, the regime had failed to integrate the countryside into the political structure, even more evidently than it had failed in the towns, a weakness which, in the absence of political parties, the elected Chamber of Deputies did very little to repair. This resulted in revolts and rebellions, not only in Eritrea and the Somali-inhabited areas, but also in core Amhara provinces such as Gojjam, and in southern Oromo provinces, notably Bale. It was also indicated by the government's attempts to suppress information about the catastrophic 1973 famine in Wallo. Both these failures were reflected in the army, as a part of the state bureaucracy whose officers especially were drawn from the urban intelligentsia, and which was engaged in a continuous struggle for control in Eritrea and, more sporadically, in the south. And third, there was the impact of events in the global economy: symbolically, the two events which set off the revolution were an army mutiny in a remote southern outpost, and a strike by Addis Ababa taxi-drivers over increased petrol prices resulting from the 1973 oil price rise.

The overwhelming beneficiary of the upheavals was however the army, representative of a class which, however revolutionary in its aspirations, was nonetheless centralist and statist in origins, interests and ideology. Initially, the military regime — known as the Derg, or Committee, from its ruling body drawn from all ranks and units of the armed forces — expressed its aims in the nationalist slogan — Ethiopia First — which, not as vacuous as it sounds, indicates hostility both to foreigners (especially Westerners) and to regional or ethnic separatisms. From early 1975, however, it opted for a much more explicitly socialist — or state socialist — set of measures. Though this included the nationalisation of all major foreign companies, much more important was the nationalisation of urban and rural land, which destroyed the economic base both of cash crop landlords in the southern provinces, and (often the same individuals) of the rentier class who had invested especially in Addis Ababa property. It is on this measure, rather than on its pretensions to a Marxist—Leninist ideology, or its alliance with the Soviet Union, that the regime's revolutionary credentials rest. The uncompromising centralism of the regime has however prevented it from establishing political mechanisms through which the popularity gained — in the south at least — by returning land to peasant control could be mobilised as a permanent source of support. This in turn is related, as we shall see, not only to the regime's nationalist ideology, but also to its need to control the south for cash crop production for the international market. Though the main coffee-producing areas have remained under government control, this has intensified peripheral opposition to the Derg not only among Somalis and in Eritrea, but also in Tigre province in the north, and among many of the southern Oromo.

The need to police the periphery immediately raised the question of the relationship with the United States, already severely strained on the American side by the regime's wholesale execution of its opponents, on the Derg's by the association between the United States and Haile-Selassie, and on both by their now sharply divergent ideological stances. For a time, the two were held together, despite themselves, by the alliance of interests built up over the previous decades. The Americans both appreciated the strategic value of Ethiopia, and did not wish to be seen as too precipitately abandoning a client which had long depended on them. Ethiopia needed arms, and with the Russians at this time entrenched more strongly than ever in the Somali Republic, had nowhere else to look for them. Paradoxically, United States arms supplies to Ethiopia soared after Haile-Selassie's overthrow, though in the form of commercial sales rather than grant aid. From a mean of $11 million a year between 1969 and 1973, they reached $19 million in 1974, $35 million in 1975, and $143 million in 1976.[16] The Americans, however, were sensitive not so much to the Derg's economic policies — they had no major investments to be nationalised in Ethiopia — but to its political ruthlessness, and in May 1976 threatened to withhold arms if the Derg went ahead with a projected peasant mass assault on Eritrea. Supplies had already been suspended for three months after the execution of leading officials from the Haile-Selassie era in November 1974, and the inauguration of the Carter presidency in January 1977 offered little to a regime with one of the worst 'human rights' records on the continent. Quite apart from the question of ideological affinity, therefore, United States arms supplies were bought at an unacceptable cost to the Derg's domestic freedom of action.

The only alternative source of armaments in the quantities required was the Soviet Union, hitherto excluded from consideration by its very close military links with the Somali Republic. The Russians had indeed since 1972 been providing the Somalis with enormous quantities of arms, amounting to between a quarter and a half of the Republic's total annual imports,[17] for which there could be no other use than for an attack on Ethiopia. However, since the Soviet relationship with the Somalis, like the United States relationship with the Ethiopians, was strategic rather than economic, there was no inherent bar to a reversal of alliances if both Ethiopia and the Soviet Union felt that their interests would be better served by an alliance with one another than by that with their existing partners. For Ethiopia this was fairly clearly so, provided that the Russians did not in turn insist on a price for their support in terms of domestic political concessions to the Eritreans and Somalis. This at first they attempted to do, in the form of a plan for a regional confederation of Ethiopia, the Somali Republic, Eritrea, Djibouti and the People's Democratic Republic of Yemen, which was canvassed in March and April 1977 during visits to the region by Fidel Castro of Cuba and the Soviet President Podgorny. When this failed — essentially because any plan acceptable to the Ethiopians was unacceptable to the Somalis, and vice versa — they came down firmly on the side of the Ethiopians.

The consequences of that decision — the pre-emptive Somali attack on Ethiopia in July 1977, and the Soviet and Cuban intervention on Ethiopia's behalf, first against the Somalis and later against the

88

Eritreans — are familiar enough not to need repetition in a volume of this kind. One of the most striking facts about this period is indeed that neither the actions of the Soviet Union and its allies, nor those of the Western powers, can be explained to any appreciable extent in directly economic terms. Two articles on the international politics of the area in the principal journal dedicated to the political economy of Africa[18] are obliged to abandon any serious attempt at a Marxist analysis, and to revert to a conventional diplomatic and strategic interpretation. But if the Ethiopian switch of alliances and subsequent Soviet intervention did not — except in the very broadest and most general sense — have economic causes, it nonetheless had highly important economic consequences. The result of these, paradoxically, was to force Ethiopia more firmly back into dependence on the supply of cash crops to the Western economies, and thus to reinforce, both internally and externally, some of the developments of the Haile-Selassie era.

Ethiopia emerged from the war of 1977–8 with an arms bill to the Soviet Union variously estimated between $1 billion and $1.5 billion. The financial terms on which all this weaponry was provided have not been made public, but have been reported to have been half in the form of gifts and loans of equipment, and half in the form of a cash sale, to be repaid over ten years in hard currencies at 2 per cent interest.[19] There was no point in any kind of barter deal, since the Soviet Union has little use for the exports, notably coffee, which Ethiopia can provide. Ethiopia has received observer status with Comecon, little more than a formality from the viewpoint of actual trading relationships, and trade between the two countries has risen from its negligible base, but accounted in 1979 only for some 4.3 per cent of total Ethiopian import and export trade.[20] The Soviet Union's principal need is for hard currency to buy grain and technology from the West, and Ethiopia's economic usefulness to her — save for the use of the Red Sea coast as a source of fish — is as a provider of this currency.

Ethiopia's economic links with the developed market economies have thus come through the revolution relatively unscathed, and indeed encouraged by the Soviet Union. The trade agreement between the two countries stipulates that Ethiopia should pay for Soviet goods in convertible Western currencies.[21] In 1979, 68 per cent of Ethiopia's trade was still conducted with the Western industrial states and a further 22 per cent with other developing countries, though by comparison with the pre-revolutionary period, the United States' share has diminished at the expense of the EEC.[22] Ethiopia — unlike Angola and Mozambique — remains a signatory to the Lomé Conventions, and has used European Development Fund aid for post-war reconstruction. This, coupled with the disappointment of Ethiopian hopes for Soviet development assistance, led Ethiopia in September 1981 to open

discussions over compensation terms with Western companies nationalised late in 1974.[23]

The maintenance of trading links with the Western economies is the
most obvious, but in many ways not the most important, economic
consequence of external military dependence. At least as vital are its
implications for the organisation of production within Ethiopia itself.
In the first place, it means a shift in emphasis away from food crops for
local consumption in favour of cash crops for export, and an intensification of dependence on coffee, which accounts for about three-
quarters of total export earnings. Production of sugar and tea has also
been expanded. The national revolutionary economic development
campaign announced in 1978, and the two short-term economic plans
which followed in February and October 1979, gave the highest
priority to commercial agriculture and seem to have been presented
vigorously and on the whole successfully. As against that, Ethiopia
suffered a catastrophic famine in 1973–4, and further severe famines
in 1977, 1980 and 1983 and must now be regarded as a chronically
food-deficient area. Reports in August 1981 of a bumper coffee
harvest, while 4½ million people needed emergency food relief, put the
problem into sharp perspective.[24]

In the second place, the control of production has also had to be
changed. The land reform of 1975 shifted control over production,
especially in the southern areas where the greatest surplus was created,
from large-scale landlords to peasant families working plots of up to
10 hectares, and gathered into some 25,000 peasant associations. The
result was that peasants in productive areas were able to increase their
consumption of food crops of which, under the exploitative conditions
of pre-revolutionary land tenure, they would have been deprived. This
in turn meant that less was available for redistribution to food-short
areas, including the major cities; Addis Ababa suffered in 1977 and
1978 from severe shortages which had to be met from imported grain.
It is likely also that peasants will have shifted production from cash
crops — for which at best they were paid in cash with which there was
very little to buy — to food crops. These processes have had to be
reversed, notably by the establishment of large-scale capital-intensive
state farms, which from the peasant viewpoint are scarcely distinguish-
able from the old private plantations. This in turn has required the
extension of government control over the rural labour force, especially
since agricultural manpower had in any case been reduced by con-
scription into the peasant militias formed to fight in Eritrea and
Ogaden. Opponents of the regime claim that many thousands of people
have been rounded up in Addis Ababa and sent to agricultural labour
camps on the Sudanese border.[25] Surplus extraction has also been
increased, according to one report, by cutting the producer's share in

90

the value of coffee exports from 63 per cent in 1973—4 to 34 per cent in 1977—8,[26] though it is necessary to point out that the 1973—4 figure will presumably have included the landlord's share.

This increase in state capitalist production, though it serves the Soviet Union's immediate economic ends, thus does not result in any integration of the Ethiopian economy into that of the Soviet bloc, and Ethiopia is thus — unlike Cuba, for example — not cemented into any permanent relationship with the Soviet Union. It is indeed perfectly possible, if and when the enormous military benefits of the relationship to Ethiopia are no longer needed, that the pattern of alliances may once more be reversed. Ethiopia's debt repayments to the Soviet Union would become both a source of resentment and a brake on economic development, while the shift from military to economic needs would disadvantage the Soviet Union, which can supply the former, and favour the Western states, which are better able to supply the latter. In this context, it is worth noting that economic non-integration of Ethiopia with the Soviet bloc has so far been mirrored by political non-integration. Despite considerable Soviet prompting, the Derg has yet to form a Marxist—Leninist party through which contacts with fraternal parties could be carried out, and Soviet penetration deepened. The various political movements organised in conjunction with the regime have been disciplined or suppressed as soon as they showed signs of presenting any threat to the Derg itself. Mengistu Haile-Maryam has, since the end of the war in 1978, consistently given his nationalism precedence over his Marxism, and, in the process, maintained his own freedom of action. In him, the Russians are dealing with a radical military dictator who, like Nimairi in Sudan or Siyad Barre in the Somali Republic, retains both the political and the economic freedom to reverse his foreign alliances if it suits him to do so.

The Derg's relations with its neighbours reveal the same striking elements of continuity beneath a facade of revolutionary change. Just as Ethiopia's relations with the Somali Republic deteriorated despite the two regimes' conversion to Marxism—Leninism, so relations with stridently capitalist Kenya remained good, their common fear of Somali expansion outweighing ideological divergence. Relations with the Sudan, always the most ambivalent of Ethiopia's neighbours, have fluctuated in line with the Nimairi regime's sympathies with the Eritrean rebels, its intense suspicion of Soviet adventurism, and its fear of the destabilisation of its own precarious domestic political balance. For a more distant tier of states, global clientele systems indeed helped to determine regional alignments in the Horn; just as Egypt moved over to support the Somalis during the 1977 war, neatly combining pan-Islamic and anti-Soviet sentiments, so Soviet-backed Libya moved the other way, abandoning its previous assistance to the Eritrean guerrilla movements, ostensibly on the grounds that the Eritreans could now achieve their goals within a socialist Ethiopia. The three Soviet 'clientele' states of Libya, Ethiopia and South Yemen signed a tripartite mutual assistance treaty at Aden in August 1981. In a still broader context, though the OAU no longer held the importance for the Derg that it had done for Haile-Selassie, Ethiopia continued to support the same principles of boundary maintenance and non-interference that it had proposed under the imperial regime, and for the same reasons.

Perhaps the lesson of this is that, despite the claims for the disctinctiveness of Ethiopia made at the beginning of this chapter, it is the similarities with other African states which are, in the end, more important. Ethiopia's foreign policy, like theirs, is determined by a group or class whose overwhelmingly dominant political resource lies in its control of the state, and whose interests lead it to use the state as a mechanism to extract from the domestic economy a surplus with which to trade on the international market, and to extract from the international power structure the means with which to maintain itself at home. In saying this, I do not mean to ignore the considerable differences between states in the ways in which these interests are pursued, nor, especially, to deny that Ethiopia has passed through an experience which is in important respects revolutionary. The result of the Ethiopian revolution, like the French and the Russian, has nonetheless been to bring to power a regime which has ruthlessly pursued the same statist ambitions as the inefficient monarchy which it displaced.

Notes

1   See especially J. Markakis, *Ethiopia: Anatomy of a Traditional Polity* (Oxford: Oxford University Press, 1974) and, for the political economy of the periphery, N. Abir, *Ethiopia: The Era of the Princes* (London: Longman, 1968) for the 18th and 19th centuries, and M. Stahl, *Ethiopia: Political Contradictions in Economic Development* (Uppsala: Almqvist and Wiksell, 1974) for the modern period.

2   H. G. Marcus, 'The Infrastructure of the Italo–Ethiopian Crisis: Haile-Selassie, the Solomonic Empire and World Economy 1916–1936,' *Proceedings of the Fifth International Conference on Ethiopian Studies, Part B* (Chicago, 1979).

3   R. K. P. Pankhurst, *Economic History of Ethiopia 1800–1935* (Addis Ababa: H.S.I.U.P., 1968), p. 431.

4   *Ibid.*, p. 451.

5   Marcus, 'The Infrastructure of the Italo–Ethiopian Crisis' (note 2).

6   See M. Wilkington, *The Middle East Supply Centre* (London: University of London Press, 1972).

7   *Economic Progress of Ethiopia* (Addis Ababa: Ministry of Commerce and Industry, 1955), p. 94.

8   *Ethiopia Statistical Abstract 1964* (Addis Ababa: Central Statistical Office, 1964), pp. 61–64.

9   *Ibid.*

10   F. Halliday, 'US Policy in the Horn of Africa,' *Review of African Political Economy*, vol. 10, September–December 1977, p. 10.

11   P. Gilkes, *The Dying Lion* (London: Friedmann, 1975), pp. 150–152.

12   *Ibid.*, pp. 152–153.

13   See C. Clapham, 'Imperial Leadership in Ethiopia,' *African Affairs*, vol. 68, no. 271, April 1969, pp. 116–118.

14   Particularly intriguing in this respect was the role of the United States during the attempted coup d'etat by the Imperial Bodyguard in December 1960.

15   The best available account of the revolution and its consequences is F. Halliday and M. Molyneux, *The Ethiopian Revolution* (London: Verso, 1981).

16   Halliday, 'US Policy in the Horn of Africa' (note 10), p. 16.

17   See C. Clapham, 'The Soviet Experience in the Horn of Africa,' in E. J. Feuchtwanger and P. Nailor (eds), *The Soviet Union and the Third World* (London: Macmillan, 1981), p. 210; these figures differ from Halliday, but the trend is similar.

18   Halliday, 'US Policy in the Horn of Africa' and Roy Lyons, 'The USSR, China and the Horn of Africa,' *Review of African Political Economy*, no. 12, May–August 1978, pp. 5–30.

19   P. Gilkes, BBC, personal communication.

20   *U.N. Yearbook of International Trade Statistics (UNYITS) 1979, Volume 1*, pp. 321–322; the percentage of Ethiopian trade conducted with the Soviet Union and Eastern Europe rose from 2.3 per cent in 1970 to 8.6 per cent in 1979, but in 1979 Ethiopia's principal trading partners were still the EEC (30.7 per cent) and the United States (20.3 per cent).

21   B. Pockney, 'Soviet Trade with the Third World,' in Feuchtwanger and Nailor (eds), *The Soviet Union and the Third World* (note 17), p. 61.

22   *UNYITS, 1979, Volume 1*, p. 322.

23   *The Times* (London), 15 September 1981, and *The Guardian* (London), 2 October 1981.

24   E.P.F. agency messages, 5 August 1981 and 8 August 1981.

25   *The Times*, 15 August 1981.

26   *The Guardian*, 27 August 1980.

4 Ghana

Naomi Chazan

Two salient features mark the development of Ghana's international relations since independence. First, successive regimes have experimented with a diversity of foreign policy approaches. In the past 25 years these have run the gamut of non-alignment, an avowedly pro-Western orientation, disengagement, external supplication and purposeful isolation. During this same period a similar heterogeneity was discernible in development strategies and political economies, ranging from state socialism through free enterprise and state capitalism to economic self-reliance and the adaptation of more rudimentary survival mechanisms. Ghana's post-colonial history therefore furnishes a veritable laboratory not only for the evaluation of the effects of different foreign initiatives, but also for the analysis of the relationship between political economy and foreign policy.[1]

Second, despite these drastic fluctuations in official stances, Ghana's global position has undergone a steady decline. In 1957 it assumed, by virtue of its birthright as well as the predisposition of its founding father, the mantle of leadership on the African continent. Since then Ghana's initial pre-eminent standing has been persistently eroded, its influence internationally and regionally has waned, and its original centrality has been replaced by a marginality reflective of a process of severe and rapid external deflation. A fundamental question arises from these dual currents: why, given the many vacillations in outlooks and responses, has the direction of changes in Ghana's place in the world arena been so consistently retrogressive?

The purpose of this chapter is to attempt a response to this anomaly. In order to do so it is necessary to employ a multi-causal and historical approach. Several methodological considerations hence guide this work. The first of these relates to the units of analysis. Although the debate between state-centric and world system perspectives in the study of Africa's international politics is still rife, there appears to be a growing consensus that sub-state factors also play an important role in these interactions.[2] These include, most notably, specific historical dynamics; heterogeneous principles of social organisation and consequent social formations; multiple symbolic and normative systems; a variety of economic units, modes, and items of production and exchange; and divergent situational and ecological dimensions. This study is concerned with depicting the major interchanges between these three levels (as opposed to the more conventional two levels) of investigation. On this basis, the proper starting point of enquiry is the particular constellation of sub-state variables that are included in, and those that are specifically excluded from, the composition, structure, and orientation of ruling coalitions at any given time.[3] The determination of these factors sets in motion a dual set of processes. The first, and most obvious, highlights the links between those in power and their development strategies, subsequent political economies, foreign policies, external reactions, and the related internal repercussions unique to peculiar regimes.[4] The second concentrates on the more elusive pattern of responses to the origins and social bases of the leadership, to their domestic and international endeavours, and to their performance records.

This chapter will focus on the examination and elaboration of the dynamic trends evident in each of these processes in Ghana over time, and on their interconnection. It will then address itself anew, in a much more complex yet perhaps also more reflective manner, to the explications and implications of the paradoxical pattern of variegation and weakness that has characterised Ghana's international fortunes to date.

The main contention here is that the shifts in Ghana's global position are as much an outcome of the interaction of Ghanaians with the Ghanaian state as they are of Ghana with the world economy. The modes of adaptation of successive governing groups in Ghana to the conditions imposed by the world system created circumstances which became the subject of conditional responses from critical segments of the Ghanaian populace. While the reduction of Ghana's global options might be viewed from one perspective as the culmination of a series of external constraints brought to bear on its leaders, the severity of Ghana's position can only be explained by reference to the deflation of state power and the consequent diminution of the relevance of the state to ongoing social, economic and political exigencies. The external implications of power-related internal instability are therefore as significant in determining the alterations in Ghana's place as are more commonly conceived external and market impingements.[5]

Ghana's path, as that of many of its African neighbours, is a divergent one. The progressive constriction of the autonomy of the state[6] has exposed Ghana to the whims of external actors, increased its dependency, and made its maintenance subject to props from outside. At the same time, Ghanaians have gradually asserted their independence from the world market, disengaged from its vagaries, and designed alternative devices for survival, if not for development. This simultaneous over- and under-exploitation of Ghana will be traced and amplified in the ensuing discussion.

Political economy, foreign policy and the state: the formal process

Ghana's emergence as a sovereign entity on the international scene was not necessarily accompanied by a concomitant freedom of manoeuvrability. During the preceding two centuries Ghanaians had engaged in a series of unequal contacts with the outside world. As external incursions gave way to the institutionalisation of colonialism, portions of the Ghanaian economy were transformed to meet the requirements of partial integration into a broader market.[7] The restructuring of economic directions centred primarily, although not entirely, on cocoa production. This provided the basis for the consolidation of an import—export economy that still contained a large subsistence sector.[8] By 1957 the new state of Ghana was positioned not only on the periphery of the global nexus, but was also structurally subordinated to economic forces beyond its grasp.[9] Kwame Nkrumah was acutely cognisant of this situation, and of the conditions it imposed on the types of relations Ghana could conduct with other countries, particularly in the industrialised world.[10]

The Nkrumah inheritance: innovation and debt

The power structure of the First Republic was predicated on the creation of an ideologically rooted, model-based centre.[11] The Convention People's Party's (CPP) top leadership was drawn, much as that of its opponents during decolonisation, from a pool of upwardly mobile,

Western-educated, professionals and para-professionals that had evolved in and around the colonial state. Nkrumah and his closest cohorts differed from their counterparts in other parties not in their social base, but in their position within this emerging middle class. As the embodiment of a new generation of parvenus who could find a place neither near the colonially bound establishment nor in traditional socio-political institutions, Nkrumah strove to strike out against these two perceived impediments to change.[12] The normative referents of the CPP, later laid out in the formal party ideology of Nkrumahism therefore embraced the rejection of the specifically Ghanaian past in its many manifestations, an overriding concern with social change, an odd assertion of socialist programmes and phraseology, and an enticing image of Ghana as the centre of a vibrant union of African states.[13]

The CPP was able to attract support initially from urban-based horizontal groups, and especially from unemployed youth, ex-servicemen, and workers. It then utilised this base to construct a more delicate coalition with disaffected portions of rural peasantries, minority ethnic and smaller Akan agglomerations, and poorer regions. This constellation furnished the electoral strength necessary to launch Nkrumah's initial victories at the polls and to thwart increasingly vocal challenges to his position from those excluded from this network in subsequent pre-independence elections. Although Nkrumah's rise to power seemed to have been propelled by a populist surge, in fact access to the state was circumscribed both by the CPP mediatory mechanism, and by the paucity of resources at the disposal of its backers. The maintenance of linkages relied at first on goodwill, then on patronage exchanges, and finally on coercion. These considerations fostered an extremely centralised and authoritarian pattern of incorporation with strong personal and ideological overtones.[14]

The development strategy devised by the Nkrumah regime rested on two pillars. First, it sought to foment the rapid expansion of state intervention in the economy; and second, it underlined industrialisation as a top priority in establishing a self-generating economic foundation. After 1960, this import-substitution orientation was consolidated in an explicitly state socialist type of mixed political economy.[15]

In this context, foreign policy was an essential instrument of the major forces that had moulded the new political economy. It was vital to attract investment yet challenge capital, to improve the quality of life and to extend the meaning of change. Moreover, and perhaps to Nkrumah's mind ultimately most compelling, intense foreign activity provided an opportunity to transcend the confines and complications inhering in the Ghanaian state.[16]

The overall strategy developed by the First Republic was therefore one of counter-integration aimed at breaking Ghana's inherited dependency through maximising alternative sources of financing and levels of foreign policy interaction. Contrary to some perceptions, Nkrumah did not advocate disengagement from the world market, nor did he view foreign policy in an exclusively confrontational manner.[17] As Nkrumah himself explained: 'Success in international relations is not measured by the extent to which countries manage to isolate themselves; but by the degree to which they are able to work with other countries and hold their own.'[18]

The counter-integration approach evoked an aggressive, activist, outward-oriented, and multifaceted set of foreign initiatives, that were also suited to Nkrumah's personality. The thrust of these tendencies was reflected in the wide-ranging contents of Ghanaian foreign contacts during this period. The political foci of external relations revolved around three critical and well-known issues: African liberation, pan-Africanism, and socialism and non-alignment.[19] Economic matters were broadly conceived as well, and included efforts at elaborating trade links, encouraging foreign investments in capital-intensive projects, seducing new aid, and attracting labour from nearby states. Military matters were also at the forefront of the substantive elements of Nkrumah's policy. Foreign contacts were seen as a way of fortifying Ghana's own might and diversifying equipment and training. At the same time, the CPP regime actively engaged in military ventures elsewhere (most notably in the Congo, and in the provision of training for liberation movements).[20] These exchanges were rounded out by educational and cultural concerns.

To support the elaborate network of Ghanaian external contacts in the first part of the 1960s, Nkrumah augmented the machinery for the conduct of foreign affairs, expanded the Ministry of External Affairs, and set up a special Bureau for African Affairs.[21] More significantly, he restructured the levels and partners of Ghana's foreign interactions. The alliance network within Africa bypassed Ghana's immediate neighbours and regional associations in favour of a militant effort to work on the continental level through multilateral institutions.[22] Thus, real contacts with other non-activist African states were competitive and minimal, centring mostly on the OAU.[23] In the wider plane of Third World alliances Nkrumah did much to foster links with North Africa and the Middle East, with Asia and parts of Latin America.[24] He forged these countries into a critical mass at the UN. His most innovative and problematic moves were reserved for vertical links which were conducted mostly on a bilateral and direct basis. Without neglecting traditional ties to Western Europe, Nkrumah did associate openly and elaborately with the Soviet bloc.[25] The patterning of these alliances came to resemble an inverted pyramid, small at the Ghanaian base, and gradually fanning out to encompass a progressively wider set of partners as the distance between them and Ghana increased.

Ghana's standing within this framework remained dependent on vertical ties, but additional nuances, reciprocities and exchanges were appended. Although tension between the Ghanaian government and other African states mounted in the course of this phase, and acrimony with the West rose as well, Nkrumah had succeeded in easing some of the constraints of reliance, uncovering certain spheres for independent action and accumulating an influence which could not but be noticed.[26] The contradictions between political ends and economic needs, between the stress on investment and the challenge to foreign capital, between dreams of pan-Africanism and overt subversion of African governments and, inevitably, between foreign engagements and Ghanaian interests need not overshadow the innovativeness, unconventionality, diversity, and tactical ingenuity of Ghana's foreign concerns at this time.

The external reaction, especially in the West, to the style and substance of Nkrumah's foreign policy was not long in coming. This took the distinct form of conscious suppression. Two main tools were employed to implement this strategy. The first was the extension of credit on increasingly severe terms. The second and more drastic measure was to impose latent sanctions on the CPP government by denying access to capital and forcing the government to commit itself to high-interest supplier credits.[27] Nkrumah inevitably became caught in a trap largely of his own making. The inherent contradiction between the need for investment and the defiance of the organisation of the world system backfired and involved him in foreign debts and a dependency beyond those he had inherited at independence. These problems were compounded by the inefficient dispensation of available funds. The risks of effecting a counter-integration response precipitously were brought home harshly during the final years of Nkrumah's tenure.[28]

The accumulation of massive commitments to outside financial concerns had a disastrous effect on Ghana's state socialist political economy, which was already suffering from the effects of internal non-compliance, worker unrest, rampant bureaucratic corruption, and reduced productivity. The combination of these forces isolated the CPP's model-based centre and its leader from domestic currents and, on 24 February 1966, brought about his demise in a military coup.

After Nkrumah: reaction and retreat

The National Liberation Council (NLC), essentially in retrospect a transition government, narrowed down the terms of Ghana's international exchange, devoted much attention to easing the Nkrumah debt burden, followed International Monetary Fund (IMF) guidelines for economic stabilisation, and supervised a complex process of return to civilian rule.[29] During the brief hiatus of military government between 1966 and 1969, many of the excesses of the Nkrumah period were eliminated and the stage was set for a reorientation of political life on the eve of the 1970s.[30]

This revised direction was solidified in the aftermath of the 1969 elections, which ushered in the government of the Second Republic, led by Kofi Busia's Progress Party (PP). The structure of the centre created by the new regime was one of ethnic solidarity. The PP's leadership came overwhelmingly, albeit not exclusively, from the middle-class establishment that had been excluded from the CPP paradigm. The professional entrepreneurial-chiefly-large cocoa farmer 'triangle' of dominant forces interests at the head of the ruling coalition was concerned with establishing a congenial environment for continuity as opposed to change, for individual action and not state control, but technological pragmatism unhampered by ideological restraints.

The principles advocated stressed a combination of liberalism and platonic guidance derived from an adherence to the most prominent features of the pre-colonial Asante and British traditions. These precepts were cloaked in a strongly projected image of moral probity and intellectual superiority.[31] The PP's strength rested on the ability of younger intellectuals, traditional rulers and independent farmers (supported by the civil service and upper echelons of the military) to strike deep roots into the rural areas and to garner almost unanimous support among Akan groupings. This coalition was immensely successful at the polls, particularly since the old CPP alignment's network was blocked from presenting a common front in the elections. Busia was thrust into power on a wave of optimism fuelled by the promises of a new beginning.[32] To preserve this still amorphous set-up and to develop the agricultural and trade resources that came with it, Busia evolved an elaborate patronage web around the state. This led him to favour the establishment of a de-concentrated, ethnically slanted, circumscribed, elitist, and unbalanced organisational mode of incorporation that contained (in the guise of an outward openness) the constant threat of both exclusion and coercion.

The development strategy that emerged from this setting had to come to grips with a variety of historical, circumstantial and philosophical pressures. Busia's long years in opposition predisposed him to negating the Nkrumahist legacy. At the same time, he was compelled to deal with the economic realities of this inheritance.[33] Under a facade of minimal state intervention, he attempted to foster foreign investment and bolster Ghanaian productivity. Development planning was reoriented to highlight the needs of agriculture and rural growth. Ghanaian businesses were protected through the expulsion of (mostly

West African) aliens and the legislation of the first in a series of indigenisation decrees.[34] The political economy was consequently re-cast in an avowedly capitalist mould.

Foreign policy was an indispensable tool for the effective execution of this investment-oriented free enterprise experiment. It was also another avenue for escaping from the continuing shadow of the Nkrumah years. If the state itself had to be temporarily mortgaged to further the objectives of development, this submission, it was posited, could be excused should the necessary capital be attracted to secure the ground beneath Ghana's own incipient capitalists.[35]

The foreign policy strategy adopted by the Progress Party government was hence one of collaboration with Western interests and financial concerns. The scope of foreign engagements was scaled down accordingly: some foreign legations were closed; others saw their personnel reduced.[36] Ghana and Ghanaian concerns replaced global and continental ones; initiatives were carefully muted; a cooperative, low-key style was affected; and development issues were pushed to the fore-front of external orientations.

The collaborative stance of the Busia government was most immediately evident in the purposeful constriction of the contents of Ghana's outward endeavours at this time, which came to focus almost entirely on economic matters. A more healthy climate for foreign investment was nurtured, and a protectionist attitude was struck both to guard Ghanaian enterprises and to deal with the growing problems of unemployment.[37] Foreign aid and expertise were sought out in an effort to underwrite the costs of an ambitious rural reconstruction programme. At the same time, the Busia government, in an attempt to counter Nkrumah's stances on many issues, pulled back from non-alignment and pan-Africanism. Rather surprisingly, it also called, in the name of tolerance, for a dialogue with South Africa, thereby discarding what was clearly an internal consensus on the need to support African liberation movements.[38] This conscious curtailment of the scope and range of topics in the foreign domain was thus in keeping with the binding perception that it was inadvisable to provoke needlessly Western concerns on matters beyond those of the most immediate import to the Ghanaian situation.

Ghanaian foreign alliances were redesigned to keep in step with these substantive shifts. On the horizontal level, the Busia government was at pains to re-establish bilateral links with moderate African states that had been at odds with its civilian predecessor. Particular emphasis was placed at the onset on establishing a *modus vivendi* with the sur-rounding francophone countries of the Ivory Coast, Togo and Upper Volta. These and other overtures were however stymied after the promulgation of the Aliens' Compliance Order, which brought the PP administration into conflict with other West African states, especially Nigeria.[39] By 1970 African contacts, mostly formal and correct, were conducted with minimum fanfare through the OAU.

The most drastic structural change occurred along the vertical axis. Third World ties were neglected, East European relations mooted, and Western connections actively expanded. Besides the revival of the British link, contacts were made with other Western industrialised states, particularly France, the United States and West Germany. Many interactions at this level began to be carried out with several Western powers in concert.[40] By 1971, Nkrumah's inverted pyramid had been remoulded into a monolith lacking depth and breadth at either the base or the apex.

Ghana's global standing during Busia's civilian interregnum was therefore more acquiescently dependent than at any time since the attainment of independence. Indeed, the image of Ghana as particularly subject to neo-colonial pressures at this juncture was not far off the mark.[41] Nor was the prevailing sense of weakness in style, implementation and results. To a very great degree, Ghana's foreign policy during the limited years of the Second Republic was a reflection of a patronising concern with development in a peculiarly Western-derived entrepreneurial mould that suffered from a near obsession with reversing past trends to the detriment of any innovative conception of the future. The pattern that could be deduced from these links was one of an externally imposed logic that narrowed the terms of Ghana's international discourse.

Western reactions to the swings in the Ghanaian pendulum were understandably supportive. Ghana was granted generous terms by its creditors. New capital credits were extended, some of them without interest.[42] And there was a perceptible rise in foreign investment. The line dividing support and external interference was, however, to the government's eventual discomfort, exceedingly thin. The IMF, the World Bank, and privately contracted academic advisers attempted, in 1970–71, to introduce an economic package that would cushion the ill-effects of a government-induced spending spree following the windfall profits made in the 1969–1970 cocoa season. The December 1971 externally encouraged devaluation of the cedi was the immediate cause for the second military intervention.

In the course of its two-and-a-half-year tenure the PP administration accumulated debts equalling those that Nkrumah's had compiled in his nine years in office. The state-owned sector had expanded. The economy itself was at a virtual standstill. Internally, the administration was made to realise that 'no government can continue for long if it formulates policy primarily to satisfy external constituents.'[43] Workers and younger intellectuals had deserted the PP, ethnic affines were no longer willing to support the Asante-Brong power structure, and Busia was increasingly subjected to pressures exerted by those groups that had underwritten his rise to power. The effective embedment of the PP's centre of ethnic imbalance curtailed its ability to control ongoing activities. The National Redemption Council's coup of 13 January 1972 brought this short Ghanaian flirtation with state capitalism to an ignoble end.

Beyond Busia: variations on Nkrumahist themes

The after-effects of foreign meddling in the Ghanaian political economy were at the forefront of the concerns of the new military government, headed by Colonel I.K. Acheampong. The structure of the NRC, in its early years, was a prototype of a centre of political gravity. The narrow base of the middle echelon officers who revolted against Busia coupled with a pervasive distaste for politicians of any ideological bent led Acheampong to bypass existing party structures and alliances. Instead the new ruler settled for a working coalition between the military, the bureaucracy, and traditional political authorities. This inter-institutional incorporation was meant to de-politicise public life and to enable the functional integration of critical segments of the Ghanaian population in an application of Nkrumah's pan-African union government to the Ghanaian setting.[44] The government's role within this purportedly politically neutral administrative entity was conceived of in regulatory terms: to encourage local production, to oversee more equitable distribution, to increase efficiency, and to supervise exchange.[45] The type of incorporation projected at the outset of the NRC was hence emphatically bureaucratic, encompassing, and balanced by the indirect co-operation of key organised horizontal and ethnic social groupings.

The development strategy propagated by the NRC was based on two interlocking principles: self-reliance and regional reallocation.[46] The thrust of the programme was to achieve food self-sufficiency, expand the agricultural base of the economy, and develop allied industries. The reintroduction of an agriculturally defined import-substitution approach was viewed as a practicable means of alleviating the external debt burden and of mitigating Ghana's exposure to fluctuations on the world market. The first steps in the implementation of this plan were taken in 1972, with the launching of 'Operation Feed Yourself'; the injection of funds into the rural sector; and the restructuring of the administrative apparatus to serve local needs. The political economy, no longer encumbered by the ideological trappings of yesteryear, appeared to have undergone a process of pragmatic Africanisation.[47]

The external policy of the NRC was an inextricable part of its development strategy. The new attitude was one of disengagement and vocal self-encapsulation. As Roger Felli proclaimed: 'In Ghana, our faith in the future of the country has been reinforced by the rightness of our determination to overcome the present economic ills through a policy of self-reliance. This policy presupposes a dependence primarily on Ghana resources — both human and material — for the development and sustained growth of the economy.'[48]

The containment stance was accompanied by a new Ghanaian assertiveness, most readily apparent in the NRC's commitment to Nkrumah's notions of pan-Africanism and African liberation. In 1973 Ghana took the chair of the OAU's Liberation Committee, and continued to play an active role in continental affairs throughout the second period of military over-rule.[49] Though political topics surfaced once again in Ghana's foreign agenda, the significance of these issues paled in comparison to the energy devoted to economic matters. Upon assumption of office, Acheampong signalled his intentions by repudiating several debts incurred by Nkrumah, nationalising foreign mining and timber concerns, and minimising Ghana's reliance on foreign expertise.[50] Further efforts were made to limit imports, reduce economic dependence on outside sources, and capitalise on local ingenuity.

These economic interests carried over to the structural sphere. Alliances were cemented on the African and Third World levels, which became the main fora for Ghanaian activities between 1972 and 1975. Of greatest importance were the cooperative ties developed along the West African littoral, culminating in the establishment of the Economic Community of West African States (ECOWAS). Ghana also re-established strong links with the Third World in general and, after 1973, with the Arab world in particular.[51] At the same time, contacts with the West were confined to transactions that could not be avoided, and even these were balanced by a renewed effort to re-kindle those East European connections that had been permitted to lapse during the Busia years.[52] By 1975 the structure of Ghana's foreign partnerships had undergone a further change. The shape of Ghana's foreign contacts was reorganised into a more familiar pyramidal form, with the most intensive interactions occurring closer to home, and dwindling as the distance between potential partners and Ghana grew.

However, this pyramidal design did not attenuate Ghana's dependency and unequal posture *vis-à-vis* the industrialised world. Neither did it alter Ghana's global position. But if Ghana's standing did not change, the tenor of the NRC's external policy did have an impact on the nature of these relationships. As cooperative efforts were amplified within Africa, Ghana's links with the Northern hemisphere assumed a more strident, confrontational tone.[53] Disengagement was therefore coupled with a new militancy, and self-reliance with a quest for co-operation among equals.

These early NRC moves appeared to have finally produced a formula that would meet Ghanaian needs and reassert a positive Ghanaian presence in the African arena. Even external reactions were less hostile than could have been projected from the previous experience of Nkrumah. The World Bank extended Ghana a loan despite Acheampong's repudiation of medium-term debts. Foreign business concerns continued to express an interest in investments in Ghana. Most significantly, at a Rome meeting held in March 1974, Ghana's major creditors acceded to Ghana's demand for a moratorium on debt payments, acquiesced to the repudiation of tarnished debts, and reopened the government's credit line.[54] By 1975, then, a new phase of self-reliance and interdependence appeared imminent.

The demise of the dream: fragmentation and detachment

This pattern, however, was not pursued after 1975. In late November of that year Acheampong carried out a major reorganisation of the national power structure. The Supreme Military Council (SMC), composed of commanders of the branches of the Armed Forces superseded the NRC, all of whose founding members (except Acheampong) had either resigned or been retired by that date. The NRC itself was maintained as a subordinate advisory body.[55] The newly designed SMC created a standard, closed, exclusionary centre of coercion. The civil service and local authorities were placed under military control. Indirect co-optation of social formations was no longer entertained. An extremely centralised, personalised pattern of incorporation based on force had been rapidly consolidated.

With the change in the structure of the regime came a shift in other spheres as well. Self-reliance continued as a slogan of the SMC's economic direction, but economic policies became quixotic and haphazard. Subsidies to producers were inexplicably rescinded, government spending rose at an alarming pace, disbursements were unpredictable, industrial production waned. By mid-1976 the economy was rudderless, distribution patterns were totally disrupted, the black market was rapidly expanding, and government deficits had reached monumental proportions. The economy was truly in shambles.[56]

Foreign policy in these self-induced conditions was used as a relief from the exigencies of the Ghanaian situation and as the primary means of state survival. In short, foreign policy became Acheampong's development strategy. Unable either to direct internal events or to stem a growing civilian revolt, Acheampong turned to external sources to prop up the ailing state mechanism. He struct a stance of overt supplication. The substance of these efforts was not only totally confined to economic matters, but even within this narrow range to the fulfilment of basic needs: food supplies, working capital, essential medical goods, supplier's credit. All other considerations were supplanted in a desperate effort to avert total decay. It is not surprising that external alliances also changed at this juncture. Although the outlines of the interdependent pyramid were maintained, growing conflict between Ghana and its West African neighbours especially Nigeria and the Ivory Coast (see Chapters 5 and 8), led to greater inequalities closer to home.[57] And, because access to the industrialised world had been regularised through multilateral contacts, Ghana consequently came into a position of being both more dependent on and more removed from critical points of supply abroad.

The external reaction to these idiosyncratic moves was one of uncompromising avoidance. Hesitant to invest in a collapsing economy and uneasy about Acheampong's internal policy, most foreign governments, multinationals, and international financial organisations began to extricate themselves from Ghanaian ventures.[58] If not for a fortuitous boom in cocoa prices (the proceeds of which were rarely funnelled by Acheampong into the state coffers), it is unlikely that the SMC could have maintained even minimal control. As it was, by mid-1977 the SMC's days were numbered.

It is difficult to exaggerate the damage wrought to the Ghanaian economy and policy during the latter years of Acheampong's tenure. When he was ousted in a *putsch* led by General F.W. Akuffo in July 1978 the country was in a disarray and the power mechanism was on the verge of disintegration. The regimes that have followed that of Acheampong have all had to contend with the internal and external straitjacket inherited from their military predecessor. Under Akuffo's SMC II some effort was made to abide by an externally dictated fiscal policy. Thus, by the time of the brief civilian interregnum of the third Republic, headed by Dr Hilla Limann, political economy and foreign policy. Thus, by the time of the brief civilian interregnum of the Third close to $4 billion, a worrisome backlog of over $1 billion in debt repayments, and precious few indigenous resources on which it could draw, Ghana's situation under Hilla Limann was well-nigh indescribable.[59] In the early 1980s, as Ghana became even more exposed to external influences, its regional subordination (particularly *vis-à-vis* Nigeria) became more pronounced. An internal African dependency was added on to the external one. Ghana's global remoteness was aggravated.

When Jerry Rawlings returned to power on 31 December 1981, at the head of the Provisional National Defence Council (PNDC), he struck a posture of defiant isolationism. Fuelled partly by economic concerns and partly by the fear of an externally backed conspiracy, Rawlings opted to separate Ghana from its African neighbours and traditional partners in the hope of managing on the handouts of its most prominent ally, Libya. The adamant dissociation of Rawlings inevitably evoked an unwillingness to cooperate with his populist regime. In the West African setting Ghana's withdrawal triggered hostility with the government and impatience with its moves. Nigeria's extradition of Ghanaians in 1983 undermined the tenuous reciprocity of the ECOWAS network and left Ghana alone in a fragmented continent itself forced to contend with an unsympathetic global environment. Ghana has thus become encumbered in a morass of multiple, unequal, contentious and fundamental external obligations which afford little room for manoeuvrability.

The processes of centre construction, development strategy formulation, establishment of diverse types of political economy, foreign policy responses and subsequent reactions have followed a variety of distinct sequences in the course of Ghana's chequered post-colonial history. As these patterns evolved, however, Ghana's global leverage has tended to contract in a uniformly retrogressive manner.

The fluctuating downward spiral of relative reduction in global options occurred in two stages: at first Ghana's initially inflated international standing was lowered to one perhaps more in keeping with its size, location and resources;[60] and then Ghana underwent a further period of rapid, intense, global deflation. The end result of this dynamic was a definite political and economic recession domestically and a drastic decline in Ghana's global standing that assumed a dual character. The Ghana of the 1980s was more dependent than ever before, yet more removed; more bound and more detached; apparently a victim of market incorporation and an outstanding example of the reversal of such incorporative trends.

It is all too tempting to point to Ghana as dreary proof of the debilitating effects of global intrusions on the development of an African state. Few countries have experimented so widely with so many development and foreign strategies as Ghana has − to no avail. The ensuing fatalism and despair emanating from the knowledge of having tried virtually everything without achieving palpable results can then be underscored as the inevitable outcome of the inexorable infringement of global forces onto the Ghanaian scene. In this view Ghana has succumbed to an external logic well beyond its control.[61]

Little satisfaction may be gained from the neatness and mechanistic rationale of such an argument. Nor is it easy to apply many of its underpinnings to the specifics of the Ghanaian situation.[62] Ghana is not a poor country bereft of natural or human resources. Neither has its deterioration followed a uniform path, unconnected with the policies or frailties of its leadership.[63] There is, undoubtedly, a close correlation between the decline in Ghana's global position and the deterioration of its economy. But the direction of this link is unclear. 'There is no universal law of external dependence and internal collapse even in the world of the newly sovereign.'[64] While the strength of the global dependence theory cannot be overlooked, it would be almost as foolhardy to treat the policies of the state and capital in a political vacuum as it was a decade ago to divorce the actions of African states from the unequal global economic environment in which they operated.[65] It is vital, therefore, to press beyond the confines of market determinism and return, briefly, to an analysis of the heterogeneous Ghanaian responses to the successive power constellations that guided the state of Ghana since independence.

State and society: the process of decline

Ghana of 1957 encompassed a broad array of corporate groups, social formations, and community structures that constituted the basic units of political action within its bounds. This extremely intricate and often overlapping socio-economic and political network evolved gradually during the pre-colonial and colonial periods.[66] Broadly speaking, two main categories of interaction are identifiable. The first consists of horizontal organisations of the interest group type. Most prominent among these are occupational associations such as trade unions, professional unions, teachers' groups, farmer cooperatives. Also included in this classification are religious and ideological units, a broad range of social and leisure groups, and women's and youth associations. The second type of association is constructed on a vertical, solidarity basis and is more primary, or ascriptive, in essence. Included in this group are ethnic associations, kin groups, traditional political constellations, and geographically defined regions and local communities. As much more localised constructs, deeply entrenched in the countryside, these vertical entities frequently have an autonomous resource base (land), mechanisms for labour control, well-developed symbolic systems, and specific histories. These two interlocking voluntary, autonomous, and group-based modes of social organisation[67] furnish the essential, historically durable, frameworks within which social, political, and economic and cultural activities take place. Their changing relationships with various Ghanaian regimes have had an important impact not only on the nature of political life in the country but also on the viability of the state itself.[68]

The political significance of these social formations crystallised gradually during the First Republic. The first groups to dissent openly from the Nkrumah centre were intellectuals, professionals, chiefs and large cocoa farmers.[69] They were then joined by ethnic organisations, primarily those of Ewe, Ashanti, and Brong, by regional agglomerations, and by some religious associations.[70] In the waning years of the Nkrumah period the students, workers, and civil servants who comprised the core of the CPP coalition also moved into the ranks of the opposition. Initially, the demands raised by these agglomerations centred on the need to institute policy changes which would more readily meet specific concerns. Eventually, however, the generalised disaffection came to focus more squarely on the demand to displace the existing power structure and alter the composition of its leadership. Action instigated to further this goal, though broad in scale and high in intensity, was largely uncoordinated. The workers openly confronted Nkrumah by launching a long series of strike actions; cocoa farmers reduced production; traders and businessmen defied government directives; and local committees simply inured themselves from outside pressures.[71] The result of these diverse initiatives was to highlight the fragility of the CPP's roots in Ghanaian society and to isolate Nkrumah from the main political and economic currents present in the country at the time. The military action of the NLC junta sanctioned (although probably did not reflect), the lack of legitimacy accorded to the Nkrumah administration.[72]

The lessons of the Nkrumah experiences for state—society relations in Ghana were threefold. First, it was clear that the ability to conduct external relations was not easily translated into a similar capacity to maintain internal control. Second, despite the growth of coercive mechanisms, local responses to Nkrumah stressed the difficulties confronting the Ghanaian state's efforts to penetrate to the point of production. And third, the rapid expansion of the state apparatus was not necessarily coterminous with a parallel enhancement of state power.

This pattern of conditional allegiance was solidified during the Busia years. From the outset non-Akan groups were wary of the make-up and predilections of the Progress Party administration. The Muslim community was alienated by the Aliens' Compliance Order. Workers were unwilling to accept Busia's pronounced favouritism towards entrepreneurial interests, and students were hard pressed to reconcile themselves to Busia's outright attack on some of the fundamental tenets of modern Ghanaian nationalism.[73] Although the scale and organisation of opposition to Busia did not approximate that prevalent during the latter years of the First Republic, it did possess an intensity that could not be ignored. Busia's repudiation of supreme court decisions, his suppression of rural discontent, and his intolerance of opposition added little to his credibility. Acheampong's military intervention, somewhat in advance of the development of a broadly based demand for a change in the structure of authority, emphatically underlined the rapidity with which non-formal political action could challenge the legitimacy of any Ghanaian regime.[74] By 1972, then, a rhythm of instability had been established; one that highlighted not only the limitations placed on state power, but also its essential fluidity.

When Acheampong assumed office foci of autonomous action and potential disaffection were well in place. These came to the fore quickly not only because of the NRC–SMC's tenuous social ties, but also because of the systematic curtailment of those linkage structures which had previously constituted a key means of access to the state centre.

Reactions centred at first on the circumscribed structure of the NRC, on its self-reliance policies and on its equivocal performance. By 1975, however, a new dimension was added to this list, as serious questions were raised regarding the nature and integrity of the system as a whole.[75] The scope of opposition came to encompass, in one form or another, virtually every horizontal and vertical structure in the country, commencing with students, professionals, and urban labourers, and growing to include diverse peasantries, local communities, and ethnic agglomerations.[76] Ghana was, in the summer of 1977, experiencing a civilian uprising articulated in an elaborate set of political and economic coping strategies.

Four major types of responses to the prevailing mood of instability and underdevelopment were discernible at the time. The first, and most low-keyed, consisted of a tangible reduction in economic expectations, mild demands for policy alterations, and a resignation to the dictates of a contracting economy.[77] Largely an urban phenomenon, the suffer—manage syndrome was evident primarily among those salaried groups totally dependent on the state, who had few alternatives but to rely on its handouts. A second and much more complex response focused on efforts to beat the system. Economically this implied the careful consolidation of an informal economy in which farmers reversed production patterns and engaged in widespread smuggling; traders hoarded and sold commodities at black market prices; and bureaucrats indulged in widespread corruption.[78] Politically a coordinated effort was made to oust the Acheampong government, culminating in rampant non-compliance with government directives following the Union government referendum fiasco of March 1978. This activist pattern of reaction went beyond the urban centres, penetrating deeply into rural agricultural areas. A third kind of response, both for semi-skilled

110

workers and for educated personnel able to market their skills abroad, required an escape from the exigencies of the Ghanaian condition by finding temporary refuge elsewhere. An exodus of Ghanaians, mostly along the West African Coast to the Ivory Coast and Nigeria, reached worrisome proportions by the later 1970s.[79]

The fourth, and perhaps most significant, response revolved around devising alternatives rather than substitutes to the vagaries of the Ghanaian situation. This rejection itself took on two notable forms, the first of which consisted of sporadic attempts to redesign the normative and structural foundations of the polity. The thrust of this strategy was later picked up by Jerry Rawlings after the Armed Forces Revolutionary Council (AFRC) takeover and then during the Provisional National Defence Council (PNDC) regime.[80] Many Ghanaians, however, simply opted for a withdrawal from the state-controlled political and economic marketplace and the reconstruction of self-encapsulated local communal institutions.[81] Economically land and labour resources were redirected to achieving a self-sufficiency independent of broader currents. Politically local power bases were augmented, leadership networks expanded, and opportunities for new modes of participation opened. Disengagement techniques in this mould varied from place to place in accordance with diverse symbolic, situational, socio-structural, historical, and, of course, economic variables. The fragility of commitment to the authority of the state reflected in the widespread utilisation of these withdrawal strategies highlighted the degree to which the persistence of state authority was contingent on maintaining the allegiance of its citizenry.

The trends unleashed at this time were vividly played out during the period of fragmentation and turmoil that followed Acheampong's ouster in July 1978. The second SMC under Akuffo, though attempting to restore some semblance of economic and political order before the transfer of power to civilians in 1979, was unable to stem the disintegrative tendencies evoked by its predecessor. The reformist hiatus of AFRC rule marked a watershed in this regard. Jerry Rawlings' efforts to cleanse the government apparatus, eliminate the *kalabule* economy, and inject a moral propriety into the civic realm may have ended some of the most notorious malpractices common during the 1970s. But by dispersing the state's monopoly on the means of coercion, and by further undermining already vulnerable state institutions, Rawlings' actions in the long run did not provide a solid foundation for political rehabilitation at the state level. To the contrary, when he handed over to Hilla Limann in September 1979, not only the capacity but also the autonomy of the state was minimal, participation had reached a low ebb, and the detachment of Ghanaians from the Ghanaian entity was proceeding apace.[82] Rawlings' second coming further accentuated social cleavages. And, while the PNDC tried to reorganise the administration and reorient the economy, the four response mechanisms developed in the latter part of the 1970s had become deeply entrenched by the time Ghana celebrated its silver jubilee in March 1982.

This all too schematic survey of some elements of state—society relations in Ghana compels a rethinking of major facets of political dynamics in the country which is well beyond the purview of this analysis.[83] Even within the broad outlines sketched in the preceding pages, it seems abundantly clear, however, that changes in ideologies, policies, or for that matter in the components of leadership at the state level had had but a tangential effect on the structure of social, economic and political interactions outside the state domain. These possess a dynamic of their own that has developed, albeit within the physical boundaries of the Ghanaian state, but largely independent of its many transmutations. Thus, the tendency to highlight arguments over substance has obscured the much more essential task of tracing, with greater precision, the multiplicity of forms that relationships between specific, institutionalised social groupings (particularly in the rural portions of the country) and the state have taken in recent years.[84] These have followed a pattern not dissimilar to that observable in Ghana's external relations. It is possible to map out interactions ranging from total dependency and collaboration (primarily in urban settings); through confrontation, and counter-integration in a non-formal economy and polity; to disengagement, isolation, and withdrawal.[85]

The ostensible consequence of these changing relations has been to impede the ability of Ghanaian regimes to acquire a modicum of legitimacy; to accelerate the demise of state power and to redistribute it to subordinate groups; and to threaten the relevance of the Ghanaian state for all but a narrow middle-class segment of the Ghanaian population. 'The picture that now builds up is one that has coherence on a central point: it reveals an institutional failure which is profound, present everywhere, and beyond the remedial power of any mere modification of reform.'[86] The process of social involution that is taking place through the persistence and refinement of the stable indigenous moral economy has removed many Ghanaians from the pressures of the world market and permitted the exploration of alternative courses for growth.[87] At the same time the state, detached from its social base and divested of its ability to influence patterns of production, has become more inextricably subjected to external domination for its very survival.

112

Ghanaian futures: some preliminary prospectives

If this analysis contains some validity, it is as plausible to suggest that internal collapse has wrought external dependence as it is to maintain that foreign interests have brought about domestic economic decline. It appears, too, that just as global actors have not been able indiscriminately to affect Ghanaian reactions to global intrusions, so too has the Ghanaian state been impeded in the internal autonomy of its spheres of action.[88] The two propositions are intertwined and complementary. In order to achieve even a minimal understanding of the complexity of the specific pattern of Ghana's global recession it is therefore necessary to incorporate explications emanating from a careful scrutiny of the two distinct processes generated by the heterogeneous forces at work in the Ghanaian environment. Ghana's interaction with the world economy is intimately related to the scope and role of the state apparatus in Ghanaian society.

These findings have several implications for Ghanaian futures and for the comprehension of similar processes elsewhere. On the Ghanaian front, the advisability of employing certain prescriptions advocated in the literature would seem to be of only limited value. Thus, the improvement of policy-making procedures, the adoption of sound fiscal measures, the enhancement of administrative efficiency, can only have an impact on those areas still subject to government supervision and control.[89] In the same vein, the suggestions forwarded by those who uphold global interpretations merely scratch the surface of the Ghanaian condition. The now fashionable proposals to augment self-reliance through dissociation from the world market would, at least in the Ghanaian instance, probably result in the total atomisation of the Ghanaian state.[90] Even the more reassuring prospect that Ghana's dependency itself will force external interests to back Ghana's economic rehabilitation cannot be viewed with equanimity: the desire of these concerns to recuperate some of the $4 billion loaned to Ghana must be balanced against the risks of incurring further losses.

The core difficulty remains the intractable one of changing the bases of interaction between Ghanaians and their state. The possibility of state disintegration is not conducive to capital accumulation, the development of an economy of scale, or more equitable distribution. Whether Ghanaians are willing to apply their ingenuity and resourcefulness in pursuit of this quest for a more suitable and locally appropriate model of the place and functions of the state will have a direct bearing on the shape of Ghanaian society and its well-being in the years to come.[91] At least from this perspective Ghanaians have an important role to play in the moulding of their own destiny in the last two decades of this century. In the interim, it is not unreasonable to assume that the present dynamic of detached dependency will persist regardless of further shifts in development strategies and foreign policies.

Ghana's story cannot be treated in isolation. The Ghanaian experience is symptomatic of similar trends in other parts of the African continent, in the Southern hemisphere, and possibly also in sections of the industrialised world. Perhaps the refinement of the still very rudimentary multilevel, multiprocess, and multicausal method employed in these pages can assist in shedding some further light on the specific presentations of these complex issues in divergent settings.[92] Further explorations of this sort may add to a fuller understanding of differences among states, and, on this basis, possibly also to a more subtle comprehension of the divergencies in forms and mutability of interactions taking place in the global arena.

Notes

1 On this point see Timothy M. Shaw and Olajide Aluko, 'Introduction: towards a political economy of African foreign policy,' in this collection.

2 On the significance of these sub-structural variables see Timothy M. Shaw and Orobola Fasehun, 'Nigeria in the World System: Alternative Approaches, Explanations and Projections,' *Journal of Modern African Studies,* vol. 18, no. 4, December 1980, pp. 551– 573. These points were amplified substantially in their recent 'Varieties of Neo-Colonialism in Africa: Uneven Dependence and Underdevelopment,' *Canadian Association of African Studies,* Calgary, May 1981. The argument between internal autonomy and external contraints is thrashed out in the essays in Kenneth Ingham (ed.), *Foreign Relations of African States* (London: Butterworth, 1974).

3 Richard Sklar, 'The Nature of Class Domination in Africa,' *Journal of Modern African Studies,* vol. 17, no. 4, December 1979, pp. 531–552, articulately highlights the centrality of understanding the state through an examination of the social origins and bases of ruling classes.

4 These are the topics suggested in Shaw and Aluko 'Introduction: towards a political economy of African foreign policy,' this collection.

5 The possibility of the relationship between these factors was raised, though not explicitly, by John Dunn, 'Introduction,' in John Dunn (ed.), *West African States* (London: Cambridge University Press, 1978), p. 15.

6   The notion of the autonomy of the state is lucidly expounded in Theda Skocpol, *States and Social Revolutions* (London: Cambridge University Press, 1979).

7   This theme is presented in an extremely simplistic fashion in Rhoda Howard, *Colonialism and Underdevelopment in Ghana* (London: Croom Helm, 1979). A more sophisticated exposition may be found in Ann Seidman, *Ghana's Development Experience* (Nairobi: East Africa Publishing House, 1978).

8   Perhaps the best work yet on the transformation of the Ghanaian colonial economy is Robert Szereszewski, *Structural Changes in the Economy of Ghana, 1891–1911* (London: Oxford University Press, 1965). Polly Hill's work on the cocoa farmers is monumental. See, especially, *The Migrant Cocoa Farmers of Southern Ghana* (London: Cambridge University Press, 1963).

9   This is now generally conceded even by the most severe critics of dependency theory. For an interesting analysis see Ali A. Mazrui, *The African Condition* (London: Heinemann, 1980)

10 Possibly Kwame Nkrumah's best articulation may be found in his *Neo-Colonialism: The Last Stage of Imperialism* (London: Panaf, 1965).

11 This typology is borrowed from Naomi Chazan, 'The Africanization of Political Change: Some Aspects of the Dynamics of Political Cultures in Ghana and Nigeria,' *African Studies Review,* vol. 21, no. 2, September 1978, pp. 29–32.

12 A veritable industry has developed around the study of this period. The best study continues to be Dennis Austin, *Politics in Ghana, 1946–1960* (London: Oxford University Press, 1964). Less satisfying is David Apter, *Ghana in Transition* (New York: Atheneum, 1966). Bob Fitch and Mary Oppenheimer, *Ghana: End of an Illusion* (New York: Monthly Review Press, 1966), provide another perspective.

13 These strands are summarised in: the editors' foreword to *The Spark, Some Essential Features of Nkrumaism* (Accra: Spark Publications, 1964). Also see Naomi Chazan, 'Nkrumaism: Ghana's Experiment with African Socialism,' in S.N. Eisenstadt and Yael Azmon (eds), *Socialism and Tradition* (New York: Humanities Press, 1975), pp. 173–192.

14 Basil Davidson, *Black Star: A View of the Life and Times of Kwame Nkrumah* (London: Penguin, 1973) exhibits an excellent understanding of this incorporative style.

15 Two good studies are Tony Killick, *Development Economics in Action: A Study of Economic Policies in Ghana* (London: Heinemann, 1978); and Roger Genoud, *Nationalism and Economic Development in Ghana* (New York: Praeger, 1969).

16 This is set forth most lucidly in *The Spark, Some Essential Features of Nkrumaism* (note 13), p. 12. W. Scott Thompson, *Ghana's Foreign Policy, 1957–1966* (Princeton: Princeton University Press, 1969), p. 417 also perceived this point well, although other portions of this major study are more problematic.

17 These views have been suggested retrospectively in several works. See Trevor Jones, *Ghana's First Republic, 1960–1966: The Pursuit of the Political Kingdom* (London: Methuen, 1976).

18 *Ghana Public Servant*, no. 1 (March 1957), p. 13.

19 Kwame Nkrumah, 'African Prospect,' *Foreign Affairs,* vol. 37 no. 1, 1958, pp. 45–53. Also his *Africa Must Unite* (London: 1963). Thompson, *Ghana's Foreign Policy*, gives precise details on these initiatives.

20 A.A. Afrifa, *The Ghana Coup* (London: Frank Cass, 1967) and H.T. Alexander, *African Tightrope* (New York: Praeger, 1966) provide insights from a military perspective.

21 Michael Dei-Anang, *The Administration of Ghana's Foreign Policy* (London: Athlone, 1976).

22 On Nkrumah's relations with his neighbours Olajide Aluko, *Ghana and Nigeria: A Study in Inter-African Discord* (London: Rex Collings, 1976).

23 Nkrumah's role in the construction of the OAU is discussed in Zdenek Cervenka, *The Organization of African Unity* (London: Africa, 1969).

24 Thompson, *Ghana's Foreign Policy* (note 16).

25 Robert Legvold, *Soviet Policy in West Africa* (Cambridge: Harvard University Press, 1970). A critical evaluation of these moves may be found in Chris Stevens, 'In Search of the Economic Kingdom,' *Journal of Developing Areas*, vol. 9, no. 1, pp. 3–26.

26 Even Nkrumah's severest critiques acknowledge his influence in this regard. See Jones, *Ghana's First Republic* (note 17) and Henry Bretton, *The Rise and Fall of Kwame Nkrumah* (London: Pall Mall, 1966). A more sympathetic view is held by Geoffrey Bing, *Reap the Whirlwind: An Account of Kwame Nkrumah's Ghana from 1950 to 1966* (London: McGibbon and Kee, 1968).

27 F. Akin Olaluko, 'The External Debt Problem of the Developing Countries: The Case of Ghana,' *Third World Review*, vol. 3 no. 2, 1977 pp. 133–142.

28 Rolf Hanisch, *Ghana and the Cocoa World Market* (Hamburg: SSIP Occasional Papers no. 2, 1976), p. 52.

29 For summaries of foreign policy during this period see Olajide Aluko, 'Ghana's Foreign Policy Under the National Liberation Council,' *Africa Quarterly*, vol. 10, no. 4, pp. 312–329; and W. Scott Thompson, 'Foreign Policy Under the National Liber-

ation Council,' *Africa Report* (May 1969). The stabilisation programme is covered well in Thomas K. Morrison and Jerome M. Wolgin, 'Prospects for Economic Stabilization in Ghana,' *African Studies Association*, Philadelphia, October 1980.

30   A factual overview of this period is provided by Robert Pinkney, *Ghana Under Military Rule* (London: Methuen, 1972).

31   John Dunn, 'Politics in Asunafo' in Dennis Austin and Robin Luckham (eds), *Politicians and Soldiers in Ghana, 1966–1972* (London: Frank Cass, 1975). Other essays in this volume are also valuable.

32   Yaw Twumasi, 'The 1969 Elections', *ibid*.

33   Aluko, *Ghana and Nigeria* (note 22), pp. 73–78.

34   The effects of the Aliens' Compliance Order are described in Margaret Peil, 'The Expulsion of West African Aliens,' *Journal of Modern African Studies*, vol. 9 no. 2, 1971, pp. 205–229.

35   Busia's affinity to Felix Houphouet-Boigny was demonstrated in Busia's selection of the Ivory Coast as the target of his first trip outside Ghana after assuming office. Ghanaian–Ivorian links are discussed in Jon Woronoff, *West African Wager* (Metuchen, N.J.: Scarecrow Press, 1972). Also see Philip Foster and Aristide Zolberg (eds), *Ghana and the Ivory Coast* (Chicago: University of Chicago Press, 1971).

36   Olajide Aluko, 'After Nkrumah: Continuity and Change in Ghana's Foreign Policy,' *Issue*, vol. 5, no. 1, 1975, pp. 55–62.

37   'Alien Exodus Goes On,' *West Africa*, no. 2740 (13 December 1969), p. 1526.

38   'Busia on South Africa,' *West Africa*, no. 2737 (15 November 1969), p. 1386.

39   Olajide Aluko, 'Ghana and the Nigerian Civil War,' *Nigerian Journal of Economic and Social Sciences*, vol. 12, no. 3, 1970, pp. 341–360.

40   Relations with the Soviet Union at this time are discussed in Valerie Plave Bennett, 'Soviet Bloc–Ghanaian Relations Since the Downfall of Nkrumah,' in Warren Weinstein (ed.), *Chinese and Soviet Aid to Africa* (New York: Praeger, 1975).

41   David Goldsworthy, 'Ghana's Second Republic: A Post Mortem,' *African Affairs*, vol. 75, no. 280, 1973, pp. 8–25.

42   Akin Olaluko, 'Easing the Burden,' *Afriscope*, vol. 5 no. 9, 1975, pp. 28–31.

43   Ronald T. Libby, 'External Cooptation of a LDC Policy-Making: The Case of Ghana 1969–1972,' *World Politics*, vol. 29, no. 1, 1976, p. 89 and *passim*. Also see J. Clark Leith, *Foreign Trade Regimes and Economic Development in Ghana* (New York: Columbia University Press, 1974).

44 This solution is defended in Maxwell Owusu, 'Politics Without Parties: Reflections on the Union Government Proposals,' *African Studies Review*, vol. 22, no. 1, 1979.

45 Good overviews of this period are very sparse indeed. Some essays include: Barbara Harrell-Bond, 'Politics in Ghana, 1978,' American Universities Field Staff Reports, no. 49, 1978; and Jon Kraus, 'Ghana: The Crisis Continues,' *African Report*, vol. 23, no. 4, 1978, pp. 14–21. Michel Prouzet's work is most perceptive, 'Vie Politique et Institutions Publiques Ghanéennes,' *Revue Française d'Etudes Politiques Africaines*, no. 145, 1978, pp. 51–85.

46 One of the best assessments of this policy to appear to date is Donald Rothchild, 'Military Regime Performance: An Appraisal of the Ghana Experience, 1972–1978,' *Comparative Politics*, vol. 12, no. 4, 1980, pp. 459–479. Also Maxwell Owusu, 'Economic Nationalism, Pan-Africanism, and the Military: Ghana's National Redemption Council,' *Africa Today*, vol. 22, no. 1, 1975, pp. 31–52.

47 An interim evaluation appears in 'Ups and Downs of Economic Growth,' *Afriscope*, vol. 5, no. 2, 1975, pp. 26–29.

48 R.J.A. Felli, 'Principles and Current Aspects of Ghana's Foreign Policy,' *Vierjahrber*, no. 69, 1977, pp. 161–166.

49 Aluko, 'After Nkrumah' (note 36) and 'Acheampong's African Policy,' *Afriscope*, vol. 3, no. 9, 1973, pp. 32–33.

50 'Ghana's Debt Settlement: Ambiguity Sanctified,' *West Africa*, no. 2967, 1974, pp. 485–489.

51 Interview with Roger Felli, Accra, 18 July 1977.

52 A lament of sort may be found in 'Ghana 1976: La Présence Française et les Echanges Franco-Ghanéens,' *Marchés Tropicaux et Mediterranées*, no. 1588, 1976, pp. 1012–1014.

53 Felli, 'Principles and Current Aspects' (note 48), p. 161, also consult 'Colonel Felli on Ghana's Foreign Policy,' *West Africa*, no. 3101, 6 December 1976, pp. 1840–1841.

54 'Ghana's Debt Settlement' (note 50). For the Soviet position in these negotiations see Bennett, 'Soviet Bloc–Ghanaian Relations' (note 40).

55 This turning point is inadequately dealt with in the literature. The exception is Diddy R.H. Hitchins, 'Towards Political Stability in Ghana: A Rejoinder in the Union Government Debate,' *African Studies Review*, vol. 20, no. 1, 1979, pp. 171–176. Some of the economic difficulties are explained in 'Ghana's Imported Problems,' *West Africa*, no. 3057, 2 February 1976, p. 133.

56 Morrison and Wolgin, 'Prospects for Economic Stabilization' (note 29).

57 Many of these problems centred on labour migration and labour

problems. For a fuller discussion of inter-African inequalities, see Timothy M. Shaw, 'Discontinuities and Inequalities in African International Politics,' *International Journal,* vol. 30 no. 3, Summer 1975, pp. 369–390.

58 An attack on this approach is voiced by Harrell-Bond, 'Politics in Ghana, 1978' (note 45), p. 4. A counter-view is presented in Judith Marshall, 'The State of Ambivalence: Right and Left Options in Ghana,' *Review of African Political Economy*, no. 5, 1976, pp. 49–62.

59 Donald Rothchild, 'Ghana's Economy: An African Test Case for Political Democracy: President Limann's Economic Alternatives' in Colin Legum (ed.), *Africa Contemporary Record Volume 1979 –1980* (New York: Africana 1981), pp. A137–145.

60 This is Aluko's main contention in 'Continuity and Change in Ghana's Foreign Policy' (note 36).

61 A prominent, although far from convincing, exponent is Howard, *Colonialism and Underdevelopment in Ghana* (note 7), p. 229.

62 This theory may have been more successfully applied to the Nkrumah years. There is a paucity of research on these issues for the 1970s.

63 These problems of analysis are accentuated in Dunn, *West African States*, and particularly in his 'Introduction' (note 5).

64 Dennis Austin, *Ghana Observed* (Manchester: Manchester University Press, 1976), p. 1.

65 Some lucid critiques in this mode, although not applied specifically to Ghana, have been published recently: Tony Smith, 'The Underdevelopment of Development Literature: The Case of Dependency Theory,' *World Politics*, vol. 31, no. 2, 1979, pp. 247–288; Martin Staniland, 'The Underdevelopment of Political Economy,' UCLA: Center for International Strategic Studies, Working paper no. 32, April 1981.

66 On the development of these organisations see Immanuel Wallerstein, *The Road to Independence: Ghana and the Ivory Coast* (The Hague: Mouton, 1964).

67 R.E. McKown and David J. Finlay, 'Ghana's Status System,' *Journal of Asian and African Studies*, vol. 11, nos 3–4, 1976, pp. 166–179. Austin's perceptive sketch in his introduction to Austin and Luckham, *Politicians and Soldiers* is of great interest. For a specific treatment of the bureaucracy, see Robert Price, *Society and Bureaucracy in Contemporary Ghana* (Berkeley: University of California Press, 1976).

68 For a similar point, stressing how West African societies make their own history, see Dunn, *West African States* (note 5), p. 16.

69 Some of the local manipulations are discussed in Maxwell Owusu,

Uses and Abuses of Political Power (Chicago: University of Chicago Press, 1970). The growing opposition to Nkrumah is well-documented in T. Peter Omari, *Kwame Nkrumah: The Anatomy of An African Dictatorship* (Accra: Muxon Publications, 1970).

70   These responses have been traced for the north in a series of works: Martin Staniland, *The Lions of Dagbon* (London: Cambridge University Press, 1973); Yakubu Saaka, *Local Government and Political Change in Northern Ghana* (Washington: University Press of America, 1978); and Paul André Ladouceur, *Chiefs and Politicians: The Politics of Regionalism in Northern Ghana* (London: Longman, 1979).

71   The responses of railway workers have been dealt with superbly in Richard Jeffries, *Class, Power and Ideology in Ghana* (London: Cambridge University Press, 1978); those of cocoa farmers in Bjorn Beckman, *Organizing the Farmers: Cocoa Politics and National Development in Ghana* (Uppsala: Scandinavian Institute of African Studies, 1976); local reactions in John Dunn and A.F. Robertson, *Dependence and Opportunity: Political Change in Ahafo* (London: Cambridge University Press, 1973).

72   The background to the 1966 coup is described in A.K. Ocran, *A Myth is Broken* (London: Longmans, 1968), and Afrifa, *The Ghana Coup* (note 20).

73   For details on student responses see Naomi Chazan, 'The Manipulation of Youth Politics in Ghana and the Ivory Coast,' *Génève–Afrique*, vol. 15, no. 2, 1976.

74   Valerie Plave Bennett, 'The Non-Politicians Take Over,' *Africa Report*, vol. 17, no. 4, 1972, pp. 19–22.

75   These dynamics are set out in Naomi Chazan, 'The New Politics of Participation in Tropical Africa,' *Comparative Politics*, vol. 14, no. 2, 1983, pp. 169–189.

76   Naomi Chazan and Victor T. LeVine, 'Politices in a "Non-Political" System: The March 30, 1978 Referendum in Ghana,' *African Studies Review*, vol. 22, no. 1, 1979, pp. 177–207.

77   Fred M. Hayward, 'Perceptions of Well-Being in Ghana: 1970 and 1975,' *African Studies Review*, vol. 22, no. 1, 1979, pp. 109–126.

78   The outlines are discussed fully in Morrison and Wolgin, 'Prospects for Economic Stabilization' (note 29). Also see Jon Kraus, 'The Political Economy of Conflict in Ghana,' *Africa Report*, vol. 25, no. 1, 1980, pp. 9–16; Ashok Kumar, 'Smuggling in Ghana: Its Magnitude and Economic Effects', *Universitas*, vol. 2, no. 3, 1973.

79   Some of the problems of this group are retold in K. Opoku-Acheampong, 'The Road to Agege,' *West Africa*, no. 3291, 18 August 1980, pp. 1547–1548. The January 1983 expulsion of aliens from Nigeria indicated the massive proportions which this

strategy had assumed in recent years.

80 Cameron Duodu, 'The Rawlings Story,' *Statesmen*, 15 June, 1979; and Emmanuel Hansen and Paul Collins, 'The Army, the State, and the Rawlings Revolution in Ghana,' *African Affairs*, vol. 79, no. 314, January 1980, pp. 3–23.

81 The most detailed description was published by Merrick Posnansky, 'How Ghana's Crisis Affects a Village,' *West Africa*, no. 3306, 1 December 1980, pp. 2418–2420.

82 On the 1979 elections, see Richard Jeffries, 'The Ghanaian Elections of 1979,' *African Affairs*, vol. 79, no. 316, 1980, pp. 397–414 and Donald Rothchild and E. Gyimah-Boadi, 'Ghana's Return to Civilian Rule,' *Africa Today*, vol. 28, no. 1, 1981, pp. 1–16.

83 Some of these points are raised in Richard Rathbone, 'Ghana,' in Dunn (ed.), *West African States* (note 5), esp. pp. 32–36.

84 This view was emphasised in Chazan, 'The Africanization of Political Change' (note 11), p. 31.

85 Processes of rural class formation are now being studied by several scholars at the University of Ghana. One preliminary paper is Kwame Ninsin, 'Corruption in Ghana,' Lecture delivered at the University of Ghana, Spring 1980 (mimeo).

86 Basil Davidson, *Can Africa Survive? Arguments Against Growth Without Development* (Boston: Little, Brown, 1974), p. 14.

87 Rathbone, 'Ghana' (note 83), pp. 34–35.

88 Dunn, 'Introduction,' *West African States* (note 5), p. 16.

89 This realised by James Pickett, 'Development Planning in Ghana,' *Economic Bulletin for Africa*, vol. 12, no. 1, 1976, pp. 16–18.

90 Hanisch, *Ghana and the Cocoa World Market* (note 28), pp. 51–52, is extremely perceptive in this regard.

91 Basil Davidson, *Africa in Modern History: The Search for a New Society* (Harmondsworth: Pelican, 1978), p. 300.

92 John Nellis, 'Algerian Socialism and its Critics,' *Canadian Journal of Political Science*, vol. 13, no. 3, 1980, pp. 481–507, advocates a similar approach for Algeria.

5   Ivory Coast

Cyril Kofie Daddieh

> To win and proclaim a nation's independence but keep its old structures is to plow a field but not sow it with grain for harvest.
> — Sékou Touré, President of the Republic of Guinea.[1]

> To decolonise a state means essentially to dismantle the political, administrative, cultural, financial, economic, educational, juridical, and other systems which, as an integral part of the colonial state, were solely designed to impose foreign domination and the will of the exploiters on the masses.
> — Samora Machel, President of Mozambique.[2]

Judged against the standard of decolonisation proffered by President Machel, the Ivory Coast appears to epitomise a state that has yet to be decolonised. It has maintained perhaps the closest links of any of the African states with the former metropole. In fact, the French presence and influence have increased considerably: not only are the French more conspicuous than they ever were but they are also more strategically positioned in all key ministries, institutions and sectors of the Ivorian state. They are well represented among the officer class of the armed forces and in the powerful Ministry of Planning and Finance; and even the President's personal secretary, the Director of the Cabinet and the Secretary-General of the government are all French.[3] In all, some 50,000 French citizens currently live in the Ivory Coast, a five-fold increase since independence. This phenomenal growth in the French expatriate population is not hard to understand. After all, as one correspondent has observed:

> Life is pleasant for the French. At Christmas time, evergreens and Beaujolais are flown into the capital. Even in the smaller provincial towns the expatriate community will gather at a local inn and linger in long discussions with the French *patronne* over the relative ripeness of the Brie and Camembert. . .[4]

Moreover, for the avid skater, Abidjan's Hotel Ivoire is equipped with an ice-skating rink for his/her enjoyment. All these symbols of 'modernity' have earned Abidjan, the Ivorian capital, such flattering depictions as 'the African Riviera' and the 'Miami Beach' of Africa.

As the country's reputation as a comfortable tropical haven where even the telephones work far better than in Paris has spread, foreign capital has been extended to the country on a liberal scale, while agricultural workers from within and outside the country flocked to it. Branches and offices of transnational companies and financial institutions have made the Ivory Coast a regional sub-centre. Yet even with the old structures still essentially intact or at best only partially reformed rather than radically transformed or altered, the granting of independence to the Ivory Coast in August 1960 — reluctantly accepted by the leadership of the *Parti Démocratique de la Côte d'Ivoire* (PDCI) — has made possible the enjoyment of a bountiful harvest for close to two decades. The array of new 'grains' that have been sown and harvested since 1960 has been most impressive, ranging from bananas and pineapples to rubber, oil palm, cotton, and timber.

To be sure, the extroverted character of the country's political economy has made it possible for high growth rates to be realised and for surpluses extracted largely from the Ivorian peasantry and agricultural workers through the *caisse de stabilisation* to be used to initiate development projects, co-opt dissident politicians, reward trusted friends and to placate discontent more generally. This, in a nutshell, is how the Ivorian regime has enhanced its longevity.

There have been essentially two sharply contrasting perspectives on the Ivorian political economy.[5] One — orthodox conservative as well as optimistic — focuses largely on overall rates of economic growth and shorter-term projections and bureaucratic adaptations or managerial efficiency; the other — more radical as well as pessimistic — situates its analysis within longer-term structural relationships and limitations. It tends to draw attention, for instance, to the nature of the structural linkages existing within the national economy, to the corrosive financial effects and political repercussions resulting from the firm control foreign capitalist interests exercise over the national economy; the latter also points to the problematic balance between cash crop production for export and production for domestic consumption and argues that, indeed, the possibilities for achieving a take-off into self-sustaining growth are limited. Yet even radical critics of the Ivorian political economy have had to admit that it does represent a successful example, if only a short-term one, of the capitalist solution to the 'developmental' crisis of West African states (as Kenya's did in East Africa). It is thus an influential source of intellectual and developmental attraction that simultaneously poses a challenge to the search for new developmental models as well as theories capable of explaining the industrialisation of the peripheral social formations of Africa and the Third World. Samir Amin, the leading critic of the Ivorian political economy, has remarked that: 'Nobody who is interested in the future of the continent has the right to ignore this experience even if he is of socialist conviction and, because of this conviction, the capitalist path of development appears regrettable to him.'[6]

These two contrasting perspectives contain important foreign policy assumptions although these are hardly made explicit; nor have they elicited foreign policy debates thus far. Indeed, the lack of academic debate on the country's foreign policy must rank among the most serious limitations of the otherwise growing sub-field of African foreign policy. This limitation is made all the more perplexing given the Ivory Coast's popularity in the West, and its sub-imperial role and influence in Africa. Although its foreign policy is neglected in academic circles, the Ivory Coast has continued to be active and a trouble-shooter in Africa. It has been controversial in its recognition of Biafra, its advocacy of 'dialogue' with South Africa and its own continued maintenance of trading and diplomatic links with the apartheid state. It tabled the motion in 1973 for Africa to sever diplomatic relations with Israel but the commercial links between the two states continue to be strong. It has been dogmatically anti-communist, taking issue with and attempting to undermine any African states that flirted with the Soviet Union and China in the 1960s, while facilitating French military and economic activities and Western influence more generally in Africa. It has openly welcomed ECOWAS in contrast to the OAU while holding in reserve the 'francophone' associations in which it wields the effective power. Most senior Ivorian leaders, including the President and his Ministers of Foreign Affairs and Finance and Economic Planning, were on a whirlwind tour of North America and Europe on the day the critical twentieth anniversary OAU meeting finally reconvened in Nairobi; though speaking to Washington reporters, the President said he wished the OAU success.

Recently, however, the Ivory Coast has been openly critical of the speculation in African raw materials on United States and Euro-commodity markets which the state insists is responsible for the current *'conjoncture'* in the Ivory Coast.[7]

These apparent discrepancies have had the unfortunate consequence of clouding the explanation of Ivorian foreign policy in the few cases where this has been attempted. The conservative orthodoxy — dominant approach to Ivorian and African foreign policy — subsumes all of this under the Ivorian leadership's realism and pragmatism; even more uncritically, it attributes everything to one man — Houphouet-Boigny. For Nicole Delorme, 'it is impossible to study Ivorian foreign policy without speaking of the politician who has led the destiny of the Ivory Coast for nearly thirty years.'[8] This view is echoed by John Barratt who, writing in relation to South Africa, argues that:

> In discussing the political and economic development of the Ivory Coast and its place in Africa, one can do no better than to start with the President himself: Félix Houphouet-Boigny. . .

> For South Africans, President Houphouet-Boigny has particular significance because it is he who launched a movement for dialogue with the South African Government, arguing that the problems of apartheid in South Africa cannot be overcome by means of isolation, force, boycott, etc.[9]

The most recent exposition of this view argues that:

> Like Machiavelli's Prince and personal rulers in general, the Ivorian ruler has treated foreign policy as his personal domain. The independence of mind that Houphouet-Boigny has demonstrated in his domestic policy of unbridled capitalism has been equally evident in a foreign policy of cautious and quiet 'realism'.[10]

A lot of confusion might very well be cleared up in Third World foreign policy analysis if, as in all political systems, we regard the President or Head of State as the ultimate 'decision taker'.[11] For decision making in Africa and the Third World has rarely been the sole preserve of any one person. And, particularly in the Ivory Coast where the inter-relatedness of economic growth and political acquiescence at home places such a high premium on input, advice and cooperation of both foreign and domestic interests and institutions, the decision-making process necessarily involves consultations, anticipation of socio-economic and political reactions and pressures. There is thus the need to go beyond the stage-managed public announcements of weighty policy decisions by the President as 'decision taker' to examine actual decision-making processes. If the field is to advance we must attempt to relate resources or economic fortunes and needs of particular states to their policy orientations and results (implementation). In this connection, any analysis of the political economy of Ivorian foreign policy must start with Houphouet, but in the context of the objective position of the Ivorian state in the international jockeying to capture profits, growth, power and influence and in relation to the various interests, ideologies and alliances that are thrown up and animate the process as well as mediate the decisions Houphouet takes *vis-à-vis* other international actors.

The evolution of the Ivorian state: surplus extraction, accumulation and production

The nature and role of the state in the processes of profit-making, growth and production is important to an understanding of the evolution of the political economy of the Ivory Coast and the influence it has on the country's foreign policy. Ultimately, however, these processes can be understood only within the context of the particular form which the anti-colonial struggle took and the negotiated compromises that were struck before the PDCI could assume the mantle of power.

At the risk of over-simplifying complex issues and processes, it may be recalled that French colonial authorities in the Ivory Coast had intended to exploit the colony through French settlers. They pursued this objective by enacting some of the harshest taxation and forced labour laws, leading to forced emigrations to South-Western Ghana. They imposed capital tax in 1903 and labour conscriptions continued to be enforced until the 1940s. Both were designed to compel the African population to work on the plantations of French expatriates. However, the harshness of French rule and attempts to make profits proved to be a volatile mix: the process of 'pacification' was not completed until the late 1920s and even 1930s in some areas, a fact which explains the recent Ivorian economic miracle. In the meantime, the clear preference for settler plantations was coupled with the strategy of encouraging indigenous production, albeit under various labour constraints ' and discriminatory pricing policies. By the later 1930s indigenous planters had begun to play a major role in cocoa and coffee production and their farms were expanding rapidly. This emerging planter bourgeoisie comprised the privileged classes of the existing social formations of Southern Ivory Coast.

It was the growing disenchantment among these planters with the preferential treatment given to French planters in the recruitment of farm labour that led to the formation of the *Syndicat Agricole Africain*

126

(SAA) in 1944 by Houphouet-Boigny, already a wealthy planter and doctor, and some of his colleagues. The 20,000 members that comprised the SAA were already planters of importance as acreage cultivated was a criterion for joining the *Syndicat*; the majority of them were also Baoule. From its inception, then, the SAA was reformist in its objectives, Southern-oriented and predominantly ethnic in composition. It was converted into the PDCI a year later. After a brief flirtation with the French Communist Party (PCF), the party renounced its links with the PCF in 1950 and repudiated any 'radical' tendencies or associations it may have had. From then on it began to redefine as well as reinforce the central 'bourgeois' tenets that have guided its policies to the present: it decided to cooperate with 'mother France' in all fields, to follow the path of gradualism and to deny the existence of classes in the Ivory Coast and, concomitantly, to reject the ideology of class struggle as a means of resolving the outstanding contradictions in the emerging post-colony. On the one hand, it opted for unrestricted reliance on foreign and indigenous private initiative to help improve its economic prospects and consolidate its sovereignty while resisting any attempts to form larger African groupings.[12]

Quite clearly, the economic and political interest of the planter class mediated its orientation to the national economy and its relation with the outside world, especially France; they led to 'methods and techniques that are both singular and with significant social and political effects.'[13] First, there was the tactical alliance with the PCF which could only have been designed to demonstrate the PDCI's resolve to achieve the desired reforms and also organisational support and respectability. When it looked as if the PCF was going to stay in the political wilderness for longer than anticipated it was time to shift allegiance. This, too, was consistent with the class character of the party and the leadership's interest in private accumulation which could be usefully advanced by a political power-sharing arrangement with the metropole. Furthermore, the party leader, Houphouet, was an important architect of the provisions in the 1958 French Republican Constitution that sought to link the ex-colonies with France as 'associates' rather than as independent states. Whilst only Guinea voted for independence and was made by De Gaulle to pay a high price for it, even the Ivory Coast could not stay aloof from the winds of change that were blowing.

In 1960 the country became independent but not before it had signed, like the other French colonies, privileged agreements in all fields with France. A generous investment code under which priority firms were exempted from duties on imported raw materials and other intermediate goods was instituted just before independence. Moreover, the facility with which profits and incomes could be patriated added to the attraction of the Ivory Coast for French personnel and capital. The Ivorian state's interest in this arrangement was recently reiterated by its spokesman, President Houphouet: it consists in the creation and multiplication of wealth at the behest of the state. The state intended to stimulate export-led primary commodity production, while depoliticising the political economy. As one dissident has remarked, 'the President's theme has been: get rich and let me take care of politics.'[14] The *laissez-faire* policy and concomitant dependence on critical foreign inputs had, indeed, paid off handsomely, leading to consistently high growth rates. Amin has even calculated that the economy grew at the rate of 7 to 8 per cent during 1950–1960 and 11 to 12 per cent during 1960–1965.[15]

Since the 1960s an array of light import-substitution industries (flour milling, oil refining, canning, brewing, cigarettes, textiles, plastic products, saw-mills, vehicle assembly plants, etc.) have been established, displacing imports that used to come from Dakar. These import-substitution industries led to a reduction of the share of agriculture from more than half of the GDP in 1950 to a third in 1965. Industrial processing improved the sectoral distribution of economic activity in the country.

Even within the agricultural sector a successful diversification of crops to include oil palm, coconut, pineapple, cotton, rubber, rice, etc. has taken place. Together with the industrial processing, these postponed the balance of payment deficits that would have soon followed the transfer abroad of 'invisibles' such as *coopérant* salaries, consultancy fees and company profits. As long as the economy was booming transfers abroad were tolerated and political protests were muted. This relatively 'stable, supportive' and quiescent political climate, regime continuity coupled with the government guarantees of virtually unrestrained remittances of profits and capital and labour unions that had been 'tamed' by being made institutionalised organs of the party all enhanced the prestige of the Ivorian state abroad, 'a prerequisite for obtaining know-how, capital and technical and managerial skills to alleviate local constraints.'[16] It is these very favourable sets of factors that United States companies like Union Carbide, Caterpillar, Goodyear, General Electric and Price Waterhouse either actually manufacture in Abidjan or have set up their regional headquarters for West Africa here.

United States-based banks including Morgan Guaranty Trust, Chase Manhattan, and Bank of America are also doing lucrative business in Abidjan. Some have even acquired shares in Ivorian-owned banks. Citibank is reportedly so delighted in the success of the Ivory Coast as a capitalist show-case that it led a 29-country consortium in providing a $140 million loan — the largest credit ever to a black African country

— to the Ivory Coast in 1976.[17]

An important adjunct of the national growth-oriented strategy was the decision to remain in the franc zone (which guaranteed convertibility of the Ivorian CFA on a 2:1 ratio) and to participate in the West African Monetary Union (UMOA). Among other things, it made it easier for unskilled and semi-skilled labour to be imported or attracted from neighbouring countries. By 1974 over 80 per cent of the workers in the Ivorian agricultural sector and a third of the workers in industry were foreign Africans. By 1977 it was estimated that of the total population of 7.3 million, 2 million originated from elsewhere in Africa.[18] It can be concluded that: 'These memberships created outlets for Ivorian manufactured goods and gave the country continued access to surplus of unskilled labor in neighboring countries without which the rapid economic development (sic) experienced during the past twenty-five years would not have been possible.'[19]

On the other hand, the Americans have been welcomed because they presumably bring big capital which the French lack and use French firms and experts for the execution of contracts. The result has been a trade-partner diversification to include the United States (currently the most important partner after France) and the EEC. On the other hand, the United States inroads into the Ivorian political economy have yet to weaken the stranglehold of the French, particularly the 'old-timers' such as Blohorn who exert considerable political influence and subtle pressures on the Ivorian leadership. These 'old-timers' act against new French capital and socialist-oriented technocrats as well as against the British and Israeli 'foreigners'. They often frustrate the ambitions of newcomers with their technical queries.[20]

Meanwhile, in spite of a clear preference for private investment and growth the state has been compelled to intervene increasingly in the economy. This has been necessary for three reasons. First, the indigenous bourgeoisie is not sufficiently large to take control of capitalist development. As the Minister of Finance indicated when opening the Abidjan Stock Exchange: 'The problem of the Ivory Coast is simple. The ownership of the means of production in industry, commerce and transport is concentrated in foreign hands. If national savings are accumulated, they can be used to obtain the capital held by the foreigners.'[21] Second, foreign capital has been increasingly difficult to come by because of increased competition. Meanwhile, the net outflow of profits and salaries and debt servicing costs have been mounting and creating balance of payments difficulties. Hence the importance attached to the *Centre Ivoirien pour le Commerce Extérieure* (CICE). State participation in industrial investment which at the end of 1975 stood at just below 40 per cent increased to 54.6 per cent at the end of September 1977. A third reason is readily revealed by the political management of these state capitalist enterprises. They are managed by leading members of the government, often deputies to the National Assembly. In other words, state capitalism is one form of political patronage. Other forms of patronage take place via appointments to the regional secretaries-general or membership of the Political Bureau. Michael A. Cohen has observed that:

> The growth of state capitalism, through the many *sociétés d'état* and departments of government, provided opportunities for economic activity to complement what had previously been only political and administrative roles. A study of Ivorian membership of the *conseils d'administration* of 88 enterprises and economic associations show that 129 individuals hold the 287 seats involved.[22]

Furthermore, 62 per cent of the positions in 88 Ivorian enterprises are held by members of the government. This group represents the elite corps of the one party, PDCI.[23]

The agricultural strategy is also evolving in the direction of larger plantations — *blocs industriels* — and outgrower schemes which, reflecting the need to intensify yield per acre, are nonetheless turning large numbers of the rural population into landless proletarians. Smallholding property is likely to continue to decline while the concentration on the progressive (wealthy) farmers will benefit and entrench the planter bourgeoisie. In any case, the intention has clearly been to compensate the rural bourgeoisie for the worsening town—country terms of trade and to mitigate the urban biases in government expenditures.[24] Equally beneficial to this class has been its exemption from the payment of a minimum wage by the state. If the planter bourgeoisie as a group has consolidated its wealth and influence, there has also occurred a concentration of economic and political power within a small group of Ivorians through the intermediation of the party and the state.[25] In all likelihood the PDCI would have ended up a consolidational rather than a mobilisational party,[26] but the deliberate depoliticisation of the Ivorian political economy while all sorts of accumulation, profit, power and conspicuous consumption take place under its auspices recalls Frantz Fanon's poignant characterisation of the single party as 'the modern form of the dictatorship of the bourgeoisie, unmasked, untainted, unscrupulous, and cynical'.[27]

The crisis of peripheral capitalism: inequalities, recession, and forms of social conflict

To be sure, the permissiveness of the state towards foreign capital, economic growth, profit, the *embourgeoisement* of the urban class and the longevity of the regime itself are interrelated and mutually reinforcing. But this strategy has also allowed social class differentiation, however compatible it might be with the state's ideology of accumulation rather than redistribution. There are now growing indications of the degree to which economic growth has been purchased at considerable socio-economic and political cost. This awareness has stimulated economic cooperation in the sub-region and 'defensive radicalism' abroad.

First, economic growth has been highly uneven. The inequities of incomes and opportunities may be more glaring between North and South, between rural and urban areas, but there are also major differences between different rural zones as well as occupational and educational groups. The rhetorical promises of the mid-1960s regarding Northern equality with their Southern brothers and the eradication of slums and huts by 1975 have been abandoned in favour of more sober reflections.[28] It has been suggested that the underdevelopment of the North is partly because the growth strategy was predicated on a critical sectors approach since it is these sectors that were most likely to return a sure and quick profit to the investor. Moreover, the capital required for the development effort is closely linked to the European presence which for historical reasons happens to be heavily concentrated in Abidjan and several secondary towns in the South. The unwillingness of foreign capital to locate in the North should have called for new and original tactics. But these would have involved political mobilisation which the state was bent on forestalling.[29]

In any event, some of that population was needed to do valuable work on Southern plantations. But the state is now becoming alarmed over the heavy influx of rural youth from the North to the South, especially Abidjan, in seach of a piece of the Ivorian dream. The pressure on Abidjan, with a population of about 1 million in 1975 or some 50 per cent of the total urban population, is suffocating. Meanwhile, the cost of living has risen dramatically in recent years and urban wages have not kept pace with the cost of living index. Moreover, the recession has adversely affected the employment situation notwithstanding the growth in vitality of the communications sector. But the state finds it increasingly difficult to keep up the construction of costly urban infrastructure including low-cost housing so that urban slums are sprawling in Koumassi, Adjame and other places, alongside high-priced, high-class apartment complexes on the 'right bank' or plateau.

An additional source of irritation is the discrepancies in relative wages and salaries. It has been estimated that in the private sector in 1974 the lowest 40 per cent received 13.8 per cent of the total salary payments, while the middle 40 and top 20 per cent earned 32.7 and

53.8 per cent respectively. Income distribution is even more skewed *vis-à-vis* the expatriates who 'usually cost, in money terms, two to three times as much as Africans in the same job classification.'[30] The unevenness of growth, the skewed income distribution and the current *conjuncture* have contributed to social class differentiation and stimulated various forms of social conflict.

Social conflict has developed gradually in the Ivory Coast and taken different forms. It has been reflected in the increasingly strident demands for increased Ivorianisation to which the state finally gave in with the setting up of a Ministry of State for Ivorianisation. Whilst some progress has been made, the pace and direction of the exercise have hardly assuaged the discontent of young Ivorian cadres.

The state has endured a number of political crises since independence, notably the 1963 conspiracy charges, the demonstrations and riots of 1968 and 1969, and the 1974 revolt in the Bete region and the subsequent arrests of twelve officers ostensibly for plotting a coup. But as the recession in the national economy has continued unabated the political shocks have become more virulent as well as successive. In spite of a major cabinet shake-up in 1977,[31] dissidents disrupted the Independence Day festivities in December 1978. They distributed pamphlets in the streets and cafés of Abidjan and Bouaké that predicted a 'bloodbath' on that day and demanded that the French be ousted. There were concomitant acts of 'banditry' in Abidjan's plush residential districts. The jolted expatriate community threatened work stoppage. Paratroops had to be flown in on the night before Independence Day to augment the already substantial regular French military presence near the airport at Port Bouet. The French deserted the streets on the holiday itself. This incident was a 'disquieting demonstration of the tension between the groups on whose compromise of interests the Ivory Coast's economic success is based.'[32]

Of course, with decreasing state revenues and the state's attempts to maximise profits so as to sustain its investment programme, it is the peasants and migrant labourers who have borne the brunt of the commodity-based political economy. However, it is the students, professionals and a 'few' maverick politicians who have provided the catalyst for political opposition.[33] And the refusal of the state or the party to broach the issues of succession to the aging President has exacerbated tensions. But it cannot be inferred from these crises that a revolutionary transformation is imminent. As Richard Joseph reminds us: 'With the political and social hegemony exercised by the local ruling class, and the depoliticisation and repression of the masses and of radical organisations, only an as yet unforeseen conjuncture could lead to the sweeping away of this dismal legacy.'[34]

Ivorian diplomatic initiatives

Relations with France and the West versus the East

Amin has always maintained that an extroverted development is accompanied inevitably by a permanent budgetary and balance of payments crisis. But he recognises, as does the Ivorian state, that external 'solidarities' can mediate the appearance of these problems.[35] This recognition explains the unflinching support the Ivorian state had always given to the initiatives in Africa of France in particular and the West more generally. Unguarded criticisms have been carefully eschewed. In relation to the West, the Ivory Coast pursues a foreign policy of compromise and complicity.

Over the years, whilst other African states have protested against French nuclear tests in the Sahara and some have been strident in their denunciation of French military interventions in Chad, Zaire (ie, Shaba I and II), Gabon, Biafra and elsewhere, the Ivory Coast has been known to welcome and encourage some of these French initiatives.[36]

By contrast, the Ivorian state has remained as intensely anti-communist as it is unrepentantly pro-capitalist West. The state sees international relations as a zero-sum game in which 'two worlds' — the East and the West (rather than North–South?) — compete for power and it surmises that the probable 'loss of Africa' to the West if Europe should fail to 'get a grip of itself' will be a gain for the East.[37] The Ivorian state intends, then, to make Africa safe for capitalist exploitation, not to prevent it. Its policy toward the West may be shifting from *status quo* to *reformism* given its concern with the faltering growth prospects; under the current leadership it cannot be anything other than reformist.

Thus, the links the Ivory Coast has with the Eastern bloc countries are few and far between. It has diplomatic links with Yugoslavia and Rumania, presumably because they are renegade members of the socialist camp, but it is suspicious of them all, especially the Soviet Union and China. Hard economic times may yet force a diplomatic opening to the latter as Ivorian cocoa has recently sold well there. But for now at least, diplomatic relations have not been restored between Moscow and Abidjan since 31 May 1969 when the Soviet Ambassador was expelled from Abidjan and the Ivorian Ambassador recalled from Moscow over alleged indoctrination of students at Abidjan University by the Russians.[38]

The dilemma facing the Ivorian state is simple but genuine. Any diplomatic overtures to the communist bloc open up possibilities for contact, exchange of goods and ideas, the evaluation of different development paths and, who knows, perhaps even the posing of pertinent ethical and moral questions relating to particular modes and relations of production. Obviously, rather than participate in any give-and-take between East and West, the regime of pragmatism has opted to let sleeping dogs lie by neglecting to cultivate close ties with the East.

Meanwhile, the global recession and the subsequent deterioration in Ivorian terms of trade have forced the state to engage in 'defensive radicalism.'[39] President Houphouet-Boigny now insists that the West is about to 'lose Africa' because of the shabby treatment it is giving to its friends like the Ivory Coast. In particular, he has deplored the falling price for raw materials from 'friendly countries' which are 'attached' to the West by culture, language and liberal economies'.[40] In his most recent trip to Western capitals the Ivorian President returned to the same theme, wondering rhetorically how the price of a cup of coffee or a bar of chocolate can be increasing constantly while the price paid to producers is falling. In London he lamented the capriciousness of brokers and speculators who 'will bet on anything these days – some even on snail races or cock-fights' and asked whether they 'realise that when they play with cocoa and coffee prices, they are playing with the lives of a young people?'[41]

The Ivorian President clearly aspires to be the conscience of the capitalist West in Africa. But he also recognises that capitalism can display a national face or character. Thus he has been careful to distinguish between France and the rest of the West. If the Ivorian state is growing increasingly impatient with and critical of the West's insensitivity to the needs of the Ivory Coasts of the Third World, its support for France in Africa does not appear to have diminished even with the Socialists in office.[42]

It is instructive that when Houphouet attacked the 'dishonesty of some companies' in contributing to cost-overruns in the construction of sugar processing plants in the North (they apparently overcharged to the tune of 34 billion CFA francs), he delineated that the only unit that proved cost-effective was the one constructed by the French at Borotou.[43] On the whole, however, these criticisms must be understood within the context of genuine fears that the downturn in economic growth in the Ivory Coast and Africa will lead to political protests that will provide opportunities for communist expansionism – the worst of all possible scenarios for the Ivorian state.

Relations with anglophone West Africa

In relation to West Africa where the bulk of Ivorian diplomatic initiatives are concentrated, the record has been rather chequered. Already estranged from each other by their divergent views on decolonisation and belonging to opposite ideological camps during the balance of power period of African international relations (1960–1963),[44] relations with Ghana (then militant) deteriorated further as a result of Ghana's support for the separatist aspirations of the Sanwi. A shared hostility toward Nkrumah, a preference for the West and *laissez-faire* capitalism coupled with Busia's endorsement of dialogue with apartheid made the restoration of close bilateral relations compelling after Nkrumah's overthrow. This new relationship was enhanced by the signing of the Ghana–Ivory Coast Friendship Treaty in 1970.

In general, however, relations with Ghana have never really been secure, mediated as they are by the ideological bent of the particular regime in power there. Thus, the recent political changes in Ghana and Upper Volta, i.e., the Rawlings and Sankara coups, the radicalisation of their political processes and their perceived alliance with Guaddaffi will revive old insecurities and put relations on edge for some time to come. The Ivorian state is likely to continue its policy of granting asylum to political dissidents as it had done in the case of Ojukwu, Bokassa and Guinean exiles. But it is also likely to insist that it will not tolerate adventurous operations from its territory especially if radical neighbouring regimes are not perceived to pose a threat. In any case, informal economic relations continue across the porous borders irrespective of the state of political relations between the two countries, as evidenced by the continued cocoa smuggling and the constant movement of people in spite of Ghana's closure of its border with the Ivory Coast since October 1982.

Similarly, relations with Nigeria which were perhaps never too cordial to begin with had to be broken as a result of Ivorian recognition of Ojukwu's Biafra on 15 May 1968. Houphouet insists that he came round to this 'revisionist' policy because Biafra represented 'a human problem, a human tragedy'.[45] He committed his country to advancing the cause of Biafra in the international arena and began, quite naturally, by bringing De Gaulle on Biafra's side.[46] The Ivorian role went well beyond diplomatic recognition and the provision of homes for refugee children. There is reason to believe that French and later South African and/or Portuguese arms were funnelled through the Ivory Coast and Gabon.

The overwhelming size of Nigeria posed a potential threat to the sub-imperial interests of the Ivorian state, with strong implications for Ivorian growth prospects. A reunited and resurgent Nigeria was likely to serve as a powerful magnet for investments and labour, thereby exerting economic and political influence on the smaller francophone countries of the sub-region. But Ivorian prosperity depended very much on cheap migrant labour and foreign (still mainly French) capital which could not withstand competition from Nigeria. An independent Biafra with strong links to the Ivory Coast would undoubtedly scale Nigeria down

135

to a manageable size, so the thinking went. If such links could be sweetened with a concessionary sulphur-free oil deal, so much more meaningful would have been Ivory Coast's 'revisionist' policy. However, there is as yet no evidence to suggest that any such deal was struck. In any event, the Ivorian state had an additional reason for its unflinching support for Biafra: Nigeria's flirtation with the Soviets caused grave concern. It was feared that the Soviets would use Nigeria as a base for exporting their revolution in Africa. Having got rid of Nkrumah and the communist influence next door, the Ivorian leadership was in no mood to tolerate the apparent new friendliness between Moscow and Lagos.

Since October 1971, however, Lagos and Abidjan have achieved a *rapprochement*. The active participation of Abidjan in the formation of ECOWAS has permitted the forging of close ties. Ivorian participation is predicated on a desire to find an outlet for its manufactures in order to sustain its growth prospects. Continued commitment to ECOWAS, then, will depend on the performance of the Ivorian economy, the degree to which access to the Nigerian market through ECOWAS promotes economic growth and the amount of political power still enjoyed over francophone matters despite the drift of smaller states towards Lagos.

Relations with white Southern Africa

The Ivorian state has been a persistently strong advocate of 'dialogue' with the white minority regimes of Southern Africa since the early 1970s. It may well be the case that France has been instrumental in finding black friends (in the Ivory Coast, Gabon, Senegal, etc.) for South Africa. France itself has been a recognised sanction-buster from the start and has cultivated commercial and military links with apartheid.[47] However, the predisposition of the Ivory Coast to deal with Pretoria stems as much from self-interest as from any constraints imposed by the network of relations between Paris and Abidjan or from automatic support for French initiatives.[48]

These self-interests extend far beyond the Ivorian state's perception that South Africa is a comrade in arms against a more formidable menace: '. . . the real danger is communist expansion. . .it is China. . . Against this danger there is no better rampart today than South Africa with its military power and its technical capacity.'[49] They encompass the trading and technical contracts that, it is hoped in Abidjan, will keep the Ivorian miracle aglow. Indeed, since 1971 trading and diplomatic contacts have been established and are growing. The former Prime Minister Vorster is even reported to have held discussions with Ivorian leaders at Yamoussoukro, Houphouet's ultra-modern home 'village' that is slated to become the capital of the Ivory Coast.[50]

Needless to say, Ivorian support for the liberation struggle has been negligible. In a study to determine the degree of commitment of African states to the struggle between 1966 and 1971 the Ivory Coast ranked seventh from the bottom, compared to Senegal's tenth position from the top. Although economic capabilities and support were strongly correlated for the continent as a whole, one of the more economically sound countries in Africa has remained disinterested in the liberation struggle.[51] But dialogue was elusive and doomed to failure from the start because it was being constructed not only between unequal parties but it lacked in reciprocity. As Bernard Charles has suggested, the African states lacked the economic or technical clout to pressure the minority regimes 'by offering them something sufficiently attractive to bargain — or squeeze — appreciable concessions from them'.[52]

Relations with francophone Africa

The Ivory Coast has shown no such disinterest or reticence in using its resources to promote francophone regional organisations in such a way as to enhance Ivorian economic growth, prestige and influence. Such promotive foreign policies have sometimes been pursued in opposition to other potentially more powerful integrations to be led by Senegal or some other rival state. Prominent among these federations is the *Conseil de l'Entente*, which is a loosely integrative federation founded in May 1959 and headquartered in Abidjan, linking Togo, Niger (see Chapter 7), Upper Volta and Dahomey and intended to 'harmonise relations among member states on the basis of friendship, brotherhood, and solidarity.'[53] However, as *de facto* leader of the *Entente* the Ivory Coast has insisted more on uniformity of political behaviour among member states, i.e., on harmonisation, than on brotherhood. This is clearly shown in the economic pressures brought to bear on Voltaic leaders to induce more conformity in their political attitudes. 'To this end, the Finance Minister. . ., who was himself French, refused in early 1961 to pay customs rebates to the Voltaic government as had been agreed in the previous year.'[54]

The *Entente* also facilitates multilateral foreign aid and guarantees loans for a few regional development projects. Its solidarity fund — *Fonds de Solidarité* — to which the Ivory Coast is by far the leading contributor is a source of political leverage. As P-Kiven Tunteng observed, 'with a preponderant proportion of the total coming from the Ivory Coast, the latter's ability to manipulate and dominate the politics of the other member states cannot be doubted. This conclusion need not be surprising, for the Entente exists only because of the Ivory Coast.'[55]

9 September 1961 witnessed the creation of yet another, but this time broader, political federation, *l'Union Africaine et Malgache* (UAM) with French blessing. It was linked to *l'Organisation Africaine et Malgache de Coopération Economique* (OAMCE), a rather functionally diffuse association founded the previous March. Togo and Rwanda were to join in 1963, following the signing of cooperation agreements with France, as did Mauritius in 1969. Under pressure from the OAU to disband all inter-state political blocs, the UAM was transformed first into the UAMCE and then into OCAM. It is a measure of its 'sub-imperial' status and influence that the Ivory Coast has been able to win support for and sustain these organisations for as long as it has.

As suggested earlier, it is in the area of monetary institutions such as UMOA, CEAO and BCEAO and monetary policy formulation that the interaction among francophone Africa and between the latter and France have been most fruitful. These institutions have integrated French Africa more closely into the French economy and facilitated patriation of profits, dividends, wages etc. They have also insured that interaction between the Ivory Coast and its underdeveloped neighbours would benefit the former. The convertibility of the currency has been an important factor in encouraging Voltaic peasants to migrate to work in the Ivory Coast.[56]

Although the structural context within which interactions among francophone African states occur is these regional integrative federations where Ivorian influence is no doubt felt, the Ivory Coast has hardly enjoyed unmitigated policy success there. The refusal of the *Entente* states to go along with its recognition of Biafra or to endorse dialogue in Nairobi, at least not so blatantly, are cases in point. Moreover, since 1975 there has been a simmering feud between Abidjan and some of the francophone capitals over Ivorian refusal to compensate them for what they perceive as their subsidisation of the Ivorian economic miracle through the export of cheap migrant labour. The resulting slowdown in the flow of migrant labour may be hurting Ivorian growth prospects and the petty bourgeois fractions and aspirants. It has certainly had an impact on bilateral relations with Upper Volta[57] which are likely to be stressed even further by the new 'radical' Sankara regime.

These differences have been minor compared with the difficult bilateral relation with Guinea. Their divergent responses to decolonisation and continental unity, the arrogant hostility of De Gaulle's France, the latter's privileged relation with the Ivory Coast coupled with Touré's own very closed friendship with Nkrumah exacerbated tensions between the two francophone countries. After a decade of mutual accusations of plots to overthrow each other's government, a process of reconciliation was set in motion in 1971 which culminated in the famous 'Summit of Reconciliation' in March 1978 in Monrovia. The two countries thereafter decided to exchange Ambassadors.[58]

It can be argued that on the whole the beginning of the second decade of Ivorian foreign policy was quite promising. Although the desired reconciliation with Guinea was not to be achieved in 1971 there were signs even back then that attitudes might soften. To be sure, Abidjan encountered problems in OCAM: the withdrawal of Cameroon from Air Afrique was a heavy blow. Moreover, the crisis with the *Entente* attendant upon the expulsion of about 500 students from member states and Mali from Abidjan University remained unresolved in 1971, but it was reconciled with Lagos. Furthermore, President Senghor paid a ten-day visit to Abidjan, his first since independence. This trip confirmed what observers already knew, which was that after a decade Senghor had conceded the leadership of francophone Africa to the economically prospering Ivory Coast.

Conclusion

The particular political economy of the Ivory Coast which is marked by unbridled state and private capitalism in close collaboration with external associates has allowed exploitation of the country's natural resources with the help of cheap migrant labour from underdeveloped neighbouring countries. Some classes within the Ivorian state intend to keep this migrant labour as cheap as possible.

Meanwhile, external 'solidarities' and cheap labour have created opportunities for growth, surplus wealth and the *embourgeoisement* of the planter-politician class, the bureaucratic elites and many shop-keepers. As long as the state capitalist strategy involving export-led primary production and parastatals stimulated economic growth, the ruling class was left to carry on largely unchallenged. Under those circumstances the state, too, was quite content to pursue a domestic policy of accommodation (dialogue) and a foreign policy of collaboration and reaction — collaboration with France, the West and conservative associates on the continent, and reaction to the perceived communist expansionism and those African countries that facilitate it.

As the current global recession and inflation and the devaluations of the French franc have reverberated through the Ivorian political economy, they have brought the contradictions of dependent growth and concomitant conflicts to the open. Faced with a deteriorating revenue base and open skirmishes, the state has intensified its overtures to the West, has engaged in occasional defensive radicalism and has also opened up to a supranational regional organisation, ECOWAS, in which it did not hold the major trump card, as a way of reviving the flagging economy and political influence.[59] In spite of itself the Ivorian state may be becoming reformist. The degree ιo which this more positive participation in sub-regional functional arrangements can be sustained remains to be seen. But the downturn in economic growth and the increasingly strident demands for 'profound' changes in political and economic relations promise to make the future of the Ivory Coast quite an eventful one, with implications for more creative adaptations in the country's foreign policy initiatives and responses.

Notes

1 Sékou Touré, 'Africa's Future and the World', *Foreign Affairs*, vol. 41, no. 1, October 1962, p. 147.

2 Cited in Richard Joseph, 'The Gaullist Legacy: patterns of French neo-colonialism', *Review of African Political Economy*, vol. 6, May–August 1976, p. 12.

3 See 'Ivory Coast: Houphouet's critic', *West Africa*, no. 3431, 16 May 1983, pp. 1164–1165.

4 See 'The Ivory Coast: Le folklore, la prospérité', *The Atlantic*, vol. 244, no. 6, December 1979.

5 One can contrast Elliot J. Berg, 'Structural Transformation Versus Gradualism: Recent Economic Development in Ghana and the Ivory Coast' with Reginald H. Green, 'Reflections on Economic Strategy, Structure, Implementation and Necessity: Ghana and the Ivory Coast', both in Philip Foster and Aristide Zolberg (eds), *Ghana and the Ivory Coast: perspectives on modernisation* (Chicago: The University of Chicago Press, 1971). Other contrasts include Alex G. Rondos, 'The Price of Development', *Africa Report*, vol. 24, no. 2, March–April 1979, pp. 4–9 and Jon Woronoff, 'The Value of Development', *Africa Report*, vol. 24, no. 4, July–August 1979, pp. 13–19; Samir Amin, *Neo-colonialism in West Africa* (New York: Monthly Review, 1973) and also his 'Capitalism and Development in the Ivory Coast', pp. 277–288 in J.L. Markowitz (ed.), *African Politics and Society* (New York: Free Press, 1970); Bonnie Campbell, 'The Ivory Coast,' pp. 66–116 in John Dunn (ed.), *West African Studies: failure and promise: a study in comparative politics* (Cambridge: Cambridge University Press, 1978) and World Bank, *Ivory Coast: the challenge of success* (Baltimore: the Johns Hopkins University Press, 1978).

6 Amin, 'Capitalism and Development' (note 5), p. 278.

7 See Mark Doyle, 'Ivory Coast: the crisis behind *la conjoncture*', *West Africa*, no. 3418, 14 February 1983, pp. 381–382. 'Con-

joncture' has become a popular synonym for the current hard economic times and a small businessman in Abidjan has opened a new marquis nicknamed 'Tonton Conjoncture'.

8   Nicole Delorme, 'The Foreign Policy of the Ivory Coast' in Olajide Aluko (ed.), *The Foreign Policies of African States* (London: Hodder and Stoughton, 1977), p. 118. See also Alain Faujas, 'M. Houphouet-Boigny et la diplomatie ivoirienne', *Revue Française d'Etudes Politiques Africaines*, August 1971, pp. 23–36.

9   John Barratt, 'The Ivory Coast: a general profile and policy towards South Africa', *SAIIA Newsletter*, vol. 8, no. 1, April 1976, p. 12.

10 Robert H. Jackson and Carl G. Rosberg, *Personal Rule in Black Africa: prince, autocrat, prophet, tyrant* (Berkeley: University of California Press, 1982), p. 151.

11 I am grateful to Baghat Korany for drawing my attention to this important distinction. This chapter also benefited from comments by the Chairman, Douglas G. Anglin, and contributions from the participants at the Canadian Political Science Association Conference at Dalhousie University, May 1981, where it was first presented.

12 Amin, *Neo-colonialism in West Africa* (note 5), pp. 50–51.

13 Rondos, 'The Price of Development' (note 5), p. 6.

14 'Ivory Coast: Houphouet's Critic', *West Africa*, no. 3431, p. 1165.

15 Amin, 'Capitalism and Development' (note 5), p. 279.

16 World Bank, *Ivory Coast* (note 5), p. 9.

17 'The Ivory Coast: le folklore, la prospérité' (note 4). More than 60 US firms are reported to be operating in the country.

18 On the historical origins of Voltaic migration to the Ivory Coast and its implications for Upper Volta, see Joel W. Gregory, 'Underdevelopment, Dependence and Migration in Upper Volta', in Timothy M. Shaw and Kenneth A. Heard (eds), *The Politics of Africa: dependence and development* (New York: Africana 1979). On the role of migrants in the political economy of the Ivory Coast, see Eddy Lee, 'Export-led Rural Development: the Ivory Coast', *Development and Change*, vol. 11, no. 4, October 1980, pp. 607–642. See also Amin, *Neo-colonialism in West Africa* (note 5).

19 World Bank, *Ivory Coast* (note 5), pp. 9–10. See also Joseph, 'The Gaullist Legacy' (note 2).

20 *Africa Contemporary Record, Volume 4 (1971–72)*, pp. B591–B592.

21 Cited in Rondos, 'The Price of Development' (note 5), p. 5.

22 Michael A. Cohen, *Urban Policy and Political Conflict in Africa:*

a study of the Ivory Coast (Chicago, 1974), p. 62.

23   *Ibid.*, p. 62.
24   Bonnie Campbell, 'Social Change and Class Formation in a French West African State', *Canadian Journal of African Studies*, vol. 8, no. 2, 1974, p. 306.
25   Rondos, 'The Price of Development' (note 5), p. 8.
26   For conceptual equivalents, see Dennis L. Cohen, 'The Convention People's Party of Ghana: representational or solidarity party?' *Canadian Journal of African Studies*, vol. 4, no. 2, Spring 1970, pp. 173–194.
27   Frantz Fanon, *The Wretched of the Earth* (New York: Grove Press, 1963), p. 165.
28   Richard E. Stryker, 'A Local Perspective on Developmental Strategy in the Ivory Coast', p. 130, in Michael F. Lofchie (ed.), *The State of the Nations: contraints on development in independent Africa* (Berkeley: University of California Press, 1971).
29   *Ibid.*, p. 132.
30   World Bank, *Ivory Coast* (note 5), pp. 129 and 133.
31   Robert Hecht, 'Ivory Coast', in *New African Yearbook, 1980* (London: I.C. Magazines, 1980), p. 168. See also Barratt, 'The Ivory Coast' (note 9), p. 18 and 'The Ivory Coast: introductory survey', in *The Europa Yearbook, 1980: a world survey. Volume 2* (London: Europa Publications, 1980), p. 592.
32   'The Ivory Coast: le folklore, la prospérité (note 4).
33   See my 'Crisis Management in an African State: the case of Houphouet-Boigny versus Ivorian students'. Paper presented at the Centre for African Studies, Dalhousie University, February 1983. See also Robert Mortimer, 'Succession and Recession', *Africa Report*, January–February 1983, p. 4–7.
34   Joseph, 'The Gaullist Legacy' (note 2), p. 13.
35   Amin, *Neo-colonialism* (note 5), p. xviii.
36   Daniel Bon and Karen Mingst, 'French Intervention in Africa: dependency or decolonisation', *Africa Today*, vol. 27, no. 2, 1980, pp. 5–20. See also Joseph, 'The Gaullist Legacy' (note 2).
37   *West Africa*, no. 3293, 1 September 1980, p. 1646.
38   See *Europa Yearbook 1980* (note 31), p. 600. See also Faujas, 'M. Houphouet-Boigny' (note 8), pp. 28–29.
39   See Claude Ake, *Revolutionary Pressures in Africa* (London: Zed, 1978).
40   'Houphouet on "How to Lose Africa"', *West Africa*, no. 3293, 1 September 1980.
41   *West Africa*, no. 3443, 8 August 1983, p. 1850. See also *West Africa*, no. 3293.
42   The Ivorian president was the first African leader to visit Paris

142

after Mitterrand came to power in 1981. After the visit the President announced he and Mitterrand shared similar views on Eur-African relations.

43 *West Africa*, no. 3293, 1 September 1980, p. 1646.
44 On this period of alliance formation in African international relations, see I. William Zartman, 'Africa as a Subordinate State System in International Relations', *International Organization*, vol. 21, no. 3, Summer 1967, pp. 545–564; and his 'Africa', in James N. Rosenau and Kenneth W. Thompson (eds), *World Politics: an introduction* (New York: Free Press, 1976).
45 Houphouet-Boigny, 'Biafra: a human problem, a human tragedy', *The African Scholar*, vol. 1, no. 1, August 31–November 30, 1968, pp. 10–13. It has been suggested that the need to consult widely with other government and party notables delayed Houphouet's announcement of recognition. Similarly, on the dialogue controversy there was apparently no small measure of opposition by several senior ministers to the president's plan. See Ross Baker, 'The Role of the Ivory Coast in the Nigeria–Biafra War', *The African Scholar*, vol. 1, no. 4, 1970, pp. 5–8. See also Colin Legum, 'Dialogue: the great debate', *Africa Contemporary Record, Volume 4 (1971–72)*, p. A71.
46 Daniel Bach, 'Le Général de Gaulle et la Guerre Civil au Nigeria', *Canadian Journal of African Studies*, vol. 14, no. 2, 1980, pp. 259–272. See also Baker, 'The Role of the Ivory Coast' (note 45).
47 Bon and Mingst, 'French Intervention in Africa' (note 36), p. 15.
48 See Bernard Charles, 'The Impossible Dialogue with "White" Southern Africa: francophone approaches', *International Perspectives*, July–August 1976, p. 13.
49 *Africa Contemporary Record, Volume 4 (1971–72)*, p. B584.
50 Legum, 'Dialogue: the great debate', p. A81. See also Charles, 'The Impossible Dialogue' (note 48), p. 14; Jackson and Rosberg, *Personal Rule in Black Africa* (note 10), p. 151; and Barratt, 'The Ivory Coast' (note 9), pp. 22–23.
51 Vincent B. Khapoya, 'Determinants of African Support for African Liberation Movements: a comparative analysis', *Journal of African Studies*, vol. 3, no. 4, Winter 1976/77, pp. 469–489. See also R.A. Akindele, 'Reflections on the Preoccupation and Conduct of African Diplomacy', *Journal of Modern African Studies*, vol. 14, no. 4, December 1976, pp. 557–576.
52 Charles, 'The Impossible Dialogue' (note 48), p. 15.
53 P-Kiven Tunteng, 'External Influences and Subimperialism in Francophone West Africa', p. 224 in Peter C.W. Gutkind and I. Wallerstein (eds), *The Political Economy of Contemporary Africa* (Beverly Hills: Sage, 1976). For more on these regional groupings,

see Lynn K. Mytelka, 'A Genealocy of Francophone West and Equatorial African Regional Organisations', *Journal of Modern African Studies*, vol. 12, no. 2, June 1974, pp. 297–320.

54 Tunteng, 'External Influences and Subimperialism', p. 224.

55 *Ibid.*, p. 225.

56 *Ibid.*, especially pp. 216–221.

57 *Ibid.* See also Rondos, 'The Price of Development' (note 5), p. 6, and Lee, 'Export-Led Rural Development' (note 18).

58 In the same month the Ivorian state sent about one hundred of its medical personnel to assist a capitalist and reactionary ally, Zaire, following the outbreak of hostilities in Shaba province but were later withdrawn.

59 The Ivorian motives in joining ECOWAS bear remarkable resemblance to those of Nigeria. See J.B. Olatunde Ojo, 'Nigeria and the Formation of ECOWAS', *International Organization*, vol. 34, no. 4, Autumn 1980, pp. 571–604.

6 Kenya

Vincent B. Khapoya*

A great deal has been written about Kenya's economy and politics in the relatively short 20 years since Kenya was granted independence by Britain. The Western world has long regarded Kenya as a showcase of economic development and political stability,[1] a view that was rudely shattered by the painful disturbances of an attempted coup on 1 August 1982, by young air force officers,[2] coming only a few years after the mantle of leadership passed from Jomo Kenyatta to Daniel arap Moi. Despite the coup attempt, and perhaps because of it, Kenya continues to be firmly in the Western camp in its political ideals and economic development strategies. Much of the Third World and the socialist camp, on the other hand, have stressed Kenya's explicit capitalist orientation and characterised it as a perfect example of a neo-colonial state.[3] As a result, much of the literature on Kenya, with very few exceptions, has tended to focus on the relationship between the

* The author wishes to acknowledge his debt of thanks and appreciation to: Brian W. Coyer and Roger H. Marz for their comments and suggestions made on an earlier version of this chapter that was presented as a paper at the annual meeting of the African Studies Association, Bloomington, Indiana, October 1981; to Tim Shaw, for encouragement and intellectural stimulation, without which this chapter would probably not have seen the light of day; and to Izzy Khapoya for shouldering a greater part of chores on the home front while I frantically struggled to see this chapter to completion.

development strategy and class formations within the country,[4] the evolution of the bourgeoisie and their relationship with the workers and peasants of the country,[5] and the economic behaviour of multinational corporations and the extent to which the political system has facilitated their entrenchment in the country's economy.[6] While all this is important to our comprehensive understanding of what is happening in Kenya, an equally significant dimension has been missing from the extensive analysis: namely, the foreign policy dimension in which the state is perhaps much more of a principal actor than in other facets of the country's national life.[7]

This chapter, therefore, probes Kenya's foreign policy by analysing its relationship with the West, particularly the United States, and by trying to determine the extent to which that relationship has mediated Kenya's foreign policy behaviour. In a sense, this task should be easy if only because Kenya has been one of the most consistent African states in its foreign policy behaviour right from the time of its independence. Her founding president, Jomo Kenyatta, and his colleagues were committed from the very beginning to simply building Kenya upon the institutions, structures, and political values inherited from the British. The development strategy adopted was the one advised by the British. It conformed to capitalist values and ideas. All kinds of aid were sought from Western countries, and relations with the West strengthened. Even domestic power struggles in the early years of independence took on the form of proxy battles between the West and East.[8] To protect Kenyatta's image, carefully cultivated as an African nationalist with strong roots among the peasants and the masses of Kenya, it became necessary to cloak the government's economic development strategy with the rhetoric of African socialism. A government document entitled *African Socialism and Its Application to Planning in Kenya*, published in 1965, became the basis of much of the economic and political discussion, both in and outside parliament in Kenya. The content was neither African nor socialist, but that did not matter.[9] Many African countries were employing such meaningless nationalist rhetoric and Kenyan leaders were determined to be in on the action. How that capitalist development strategy mediated Kenya's foreign policy in a number of issues is the central inquiry of this chapter. First, however, a few words on the key theoretical concepts used are in order.

Political economy and foreign policy: theoretical concepts

As every student of international affairs knows, there is a fundamental, almost organic, relationship between resources and the pursuit of goals and interests in the international system. Power, made up of resources both tangible and intangible, is significant in the ability of any country to interact with others in the international system and to pursue, with any reasonable degree of success, goals that it has set for itself. Even small countries whose main objectives simply may be to have representation in the capitals of the larger states find that it costs money to field representatives abroad. So 'normal' diplomacy for smaller states may be much more a function of resources than may appear to larger states. Hans Morgenthau's fame as a 'Grand Theorist' was based largely on his valiant attempt to reduce the complexities of international relations to the concept of 'power'.[10] Power, as Morgenthau would argue over and over again, is both the short-term and long-term objective of countries. Briefly, then, the concept of power or the concept of means and ends in foreign policy runs through much of the literature. The precise ingredients constituting power may vary, but the salience of power rarely does.

In recent decades, theoretical approaches have extended the parameters and variables believed to relate to foreign policy behaviour and tried to impart a needed coherence to the way foreign policy has traditionally been conceptualised and analysed. Naturally, the specific approach one takes tends to be determined by the kinds of questions one asks and the answers one seeks. There is little doubt, as the editors also assert, that analysis of foreign policy, in the light of all these approaches, and from the perspective of both case studies and comparative studies, has improved.[11] Description is much clearer and more precise; explanation is more enlightened; and, in time, prediction and projection may become more reliable.

The term 'political economy' refers to a phenomenon that has long been discussed obtrusively in the political science literature. In Marxian terms, political economy refers to social relations (broadly defined) in the process of production, namely, the political relationships that emerge out of different modes of economic production in a given state or collectivity. Applied to a state, this approach calls for the study of social classes and their relationship to the distribution of power or authority in that state.

At the international level, political economy refers to the interplay between economic relationships that exist between countries and how these relationships determine prestige and status in the world community[12] and what a given country can or cannot, may or may not want to, pursue in the international community. The utilisation of this approach does not presuppose dependence or underdevelopment, as this attribute is dynamic rather than static, changes over time, acquiring a distinct character at each stage. For instance, when Shaw asserts, as he does in a number of works, that Kenya and South Africa are sub-imperial states, he is saying, in effect, that the development of capitalism in those two countries has reached a stage where the countries may be, or are being, used as facilitators in the capitalist conquest or capitalist incorporation of the contiguous states.[13]

A final comment on concepts concerns the term 'foreign policy.' James Rosenau points out three common conceptualisations of 'foreign policy' as: a cluster of orientations, a set of commitments to and plans for actions, and as a form of behaviour.[14] Each of these conceptualisations, according to Rosenau, 'is one phase of the sequences whereby officials link their states to events and situations abroad.'[15]

What follows, then, is a sketch of the Kenyan economy, of the over-arching relationships between that economy and external factors and of the ways in which those relationships mediate both the domestic behaviour and the international behaviour (foreign policy) of Kenya.

The Kenya economy

As stated earlier, Kenya leaders began governing an independent Kenya by simply building a new system upon the infrastructure of the old. Their notion of economic development included, among other things, continuing the cash crop economy so as to maintain the large modern agricultural sector the British left. The deal worked out with Britain to buy out white farmers using loans made available by the British government was meant to preserve the agricultural sector very much as it was, while at the same time accelerating the growth of a national bourgeoisie. Limited land distribution was carried out to appease some landless peasants, but essentially only those Kenyans economically well situated were able to acquire the choice and well developed land from the departing European farmers. As Claude Ake says:

> The land transfer scheme was a rather brilliant stroke of colonial policy. In effect, farmland was being bought from European farmers and sold to Africans. But the settlers got good, and some-times, inflated prices for land they had taken illegally in the first place, and had developed by crassly exploiting African labor and by taking advantage of extension services supported by the African taxpayers. . . The Africans who got the land were grate-ful for a real opportunity to become prosperous; they were getting rather easy loans to buy out well-established farmers. In the mean-time, the loans and grants the Kenya government got from abroad for this transaction ensured neo-colonial dependence. The Africans who took over the European farms had a vested interest in the dependence.[16]

It is precisely the commercialisation of agriculture by Kenyans who had the capital to acquire some of these farms in the first place that has contributed to the process of class formation in the country and led to the emergence of a very strong and competitive petty bourgeoisie. The process continues as more rural Kenyans, hard pressed for money to educate their children or to meet a whole host of obligations, surrender their land to satisfy the thirst of the burgeoning bourgeoisie.[17]

Industrially, the same strategy was adopted by the government, which began to move into manufacturing, particularly the kind designed for import substitution.[18] To do this, Kenyan leaders went out of their way to attract investments from abroad. As early as 1964, the Kenya government enacted the Foreign Investment Protection Act, which, in effect, guaranteed foreign firms investing in Kenya the repatriation of all their profits if they wished to do so, the payment of interest and loan capital secured abroad with earnings from Kenya, generous depreciation allowances for equipment and machinery, and the protection of the domestic market against any products from abroad which might compete with what the foreign firms were producing.[19] As Western business interests came pouring in, ideological and policy fights within the leadership ranks were won by those whose interests were being well served by Western capital.[20] Not only Western investments but aid as well was eagerly sought. And aid, in personnel, money and goods, was generally offered and continues to come in primarily from Western countries and the United States-controlled World Bank whose economic advice Kenya has accepted over the years. By 1971, according to government data,[21] 60 per cent of all expatriate personnel in Kenya were from Britain, 13 per cent from the United States and Canada, and 11 per cent from Nordic countries (Denmark, Sweden, Norway, and Finland). East European countries (only the Soviet Union and Czechoslovakia are represented) accounted for one-half of one per cent of expatriates working in Kenya either as volunteers or highly paid experts advising government ministers. It has been noted that by 1970, nearly all the commercial and industrial expansion in Kenya was controlled by Western corporations. Colin Leys declares that by that time, 'a harmony of interests between foreign capital, the local auxiliary bourgeoisie and the various politically powerful petty-bourgeoisie strata,'[22] was clearly discernible.

The Africanisation of the Kenyan economy, designed to effect the transfer of the economy to Africans and mentioned prominently as a vital national goal in the famous government manifesto, *Sessional Paper No. 10: African Socialism and Its Applications to Planning in Kenya* (1965), meant simply the replacement of expatriate or European workers with Africans as the latter obtained requisite skills. The pace was deliberately slow and seemed designed to stretch out the Africanisation process for as long as possible.[23] National debates on

Africanisation in the private and public sector in terms of whether the policy was being implemented in good time or fast enough pitted those individuals in the government identified with foreign capital against the trade unions who felt that a foreign-managed (and controlled) private sector was quite insensitive and resistant to African workers' demands.[24] Time and time again, government responses to workers' complaints were designed to discourage actions that might disrupt the economy, even if they were the only means the workers had to force employers to deal fairly with them. Inducements, co-optation and detention were methods used often by the authorities to keep militant workers in line.[26]

At any rate, as a result of the development strategy adopted during the past 20 years, the Kenyan economy came to be characterised by considerable penetration of cash crops for the export trade; by the emergence of tourism as one of the top earners of foreign exchange (with its concomitant cultural impact on the Kenyan population); by the growth in manufactures leading to a significant trade advantage for Kenya in the East African region; and, finally, by a modest rise, in the aggregate sense, of per capita incomes. The transformation of the Kenyan economy occurred hand-in-hand with an appreciable development of an indigenous bourgeoisie which was given a boost by the state apparatuses through the parastatal agencies such as the Industrial and Commercial Development Corporation, Kenya Tea Development Authority, Kenya Tourist Development Authority, and the Agricultural Finance Corporation, etc. The land settlement programme and a poor balance of payments situation, which heightened the push to attract multinational firms into the country, served to entrench the indigenous bourgeoisie. A study by Rafael Kaplinsky of large manufacturing and tourist firms operating in Kenya showed unquestionably that between 1966 and 1976 about 60 per cent of issued capital was foreign-owned. The proportion increased to 70 per cent foreign-owned when the total amount of issued capital exceeded one million Kenya pounds (K£). The larger the firms, the greater the share owned by foreigners.[26]

It should be mentioned also that as the Kenyan economy grew at rates considered impressive by Western countries, the disparities between the rich and the poor became much larger. For instance, a survey of household incomes in Kenya in 1972 shows that the top 20 per cent of Kenyan households account for 70 per cent of the income.[27] The same survey, contained in the 1972 International Labour Organisation (ILO) report on *Employment, Incomes and Equality in Kenya* stated that only 1.3 per cent of Kenyan households made K£ 1,001 (approximately $2,500 at 1972 rate of exchange) or more a year.[28] It is worth stressing that members of the national bourgeoisie in Kenya, unlike those in other countries, are pretty sure that the development strategy chosen is the correct one. They believe that it is more sensible to pursue a policy of capital accumulation first which supposedly leads to wealth creation which translates into jobs before embarking on a policy of income distribution. They anticipate capital accumulation within the country growing to the point where local capital will become a credible competitor with international capital.[29] After all, they will ask you, is 'competition' not at the core of free enterprise? Kenya is determined that this 'competition' should spill over into contiguous areas as she seeks outlets for the export of her manufactures to earn foreign exchange.

What is relevant to our discussion of foreign policy is that the economy of Kenya exhibits attributes of dependency: it has been gradually incorporated in the international capitalist system to the extent that questions can be raised as to whether or not Kenyan leaders can act independently in foreign policy matters or in any way that might be seen to jeopardise the interests of the Western powers with whom the country is strongly allied. Moreover, the national bourgeoisie has become quite strong and entrenched to the point where the international firms are beginning to feel that these individuals no longer have to be doubted in their support of the interests of the firms.[30] There is some competition between international capital and local Kenyan capital. Local capital has very strong backing of the state through the parastatal agencies as already mentioned,[31] but that competition does not really obscure the convergence of the interests of the two types of capital. Their relationship to the other classes in Kenya is substantially similar.[32]

Kenyans and their foreign policy

At the beginning of this chapter, reference was made to the three concepts of foreign policy: as a set of pronouncements of policy preferences and positions on issues, as a set of specific commitments, and finally as concrete actions involving a commitment of resources taken in pursuit of a national goal in the international system. Kenya, as any state, was to be expected to employ its foreign policy to attain certain internal and external objectives. The discussion to date shows that in pursuit of economic development, the Kenyan leadership saw foreign policy as an avenue for attracting resources from the international environment, primarily the West. Indeed, one can say that Kenyans expected that, with the British ostensibly gone, the new government was going to vindicate the bitter struggle for independence by improving earning capacities of Kenyans, raising their living standards, and promoting peace and harmony in the country. The second objective was to secure and consolidate her national borders. With these two objectives taken care of, Kenya could then grow and prosper and take her proper place as a respectable and reliable member of the African and world community of states.

Non-alignment, enunciated soon after independence by the Kenyan government as a foreign policy, was in fact nothing more than a statement designed to serve as a guideline for the country's international behaviour. Kenya wanted to let it be known that she was not going to take sides in the cold war, then at its zenith, between the Soviets and the Americans; that her position on issues was going to be governed by her own interests rather than other countries' and determined by the merits of the issues themselves. In practice this policy would have allowed Kenya to maintain acceptable contacts with both the East and West. The policy helped to assure the departing British that their interests would probably be well looked after since the country was not going socialist or radical. In practice, it became difficult for Kenya to remain non-aligned as the domestic debates and quarrels increasingly reflected proxy conflicts. The matter was resolved by the suppression of domestic forces referred to as radical or socialist and by the ascendancy of individuals whose preference for ties with the West were unashamed and unequivocal.[33]

In the same vein, during the 1960s, African socialism was touted as the cornerstone of the economic system the government wanted to build. Seeking technology and capital from wherever they were available was made a part of the strategy to build a socialist system. It was not clear from the government's own *Sessional Paper on African Socialism* how the West, with whom Kenya was already allied in a number of important ways, could become a willing partner in an economic experiment designed to lessen the West's dominance in the existing economy. But again, the declaration of socialism did help Kenya to remain apparently in the mainstream of ideological thinking in Africa at the time.

As it became clear that it was not socialism Kenyans were building or promoting, a new twist was added to the idea, namely, self-help schemes promoted vigorously by the government with the slogan: *Harambee*! (Let's pull together!) What could be more African than that! Although intrinsically a clever idea contrived to exhort Kenyans in the poor rural areas to pool their limited resources together in trying to meet their needs in health care and to provide for the education of their children, the slogan spawned an unbelievable plethora of extensive and frequent fund-raising rallies which soon became institutionalised as a way to tax the poor in return for many unfinished and badly-run projects.[34] *Harambee* activities were elevated to a national culture of charity in which politicians and other members of the bourgeoisie could travel around the country, in gross displays of generosity and care for the poor and the needy, donating sums of money that far exceeded the donors' known means of income. Donating money thus became a major activity for anyone with leadership aspirations.[35] Accumulating wealth as fast as possible was a prerequisite to launching a successful legislative career.[36] The economic system in Kenya facilitated such acquisition of wealth and went quite a distance in reinforcing the dependency orientation of the national economy.

No one familiar with Kenya ever believed that Kenya was non-aligned. One only had to look at economic relations between Kenya and other countries to realise that more than 90 per cent of Kenya's import and export trade was with Western countries, principally the United Kingdom, the United States, and West Germany.[37] Over 99 per cent of technical assistance in the form of financial aid and expatriate personnel came from the West.[38] It is significant also that most of Kenya's students were being trained in the West.[39]

Kenya's actual foreign policy behaviour throughout much of the 1960s and early 1970s has been referred to accurately as 'quiet diplomacy.'[40] This is very much in keeping with her emphasis on economic development and most probably a consequence of her dependence on Western capital. She could not afford to be activist and frighten away international capital. Indeed, when it came to issues of some significance to African countries, Kenya acted moderately and properly. Kenya consistently voted at the UN and other international forums against South Africa and for the liberation struggle.[41] She met her financial obligations (which, of course, is a reflection of her relatively greater ability to pay). But the kind of activism that might displease her traditional friends or in any way disrupt economic activities in Kenya or place undue hardship on Kenya was assiduously eschewed. Examples of such patterns of behaviour are provided by her verbal support for freedom fighters in Southern Africa while at the same time refusing to allow the presence of guerillas in Kenya or even to permit the liberation leaders to open offices in Nairobi for the purpose of canvassing for help as they have done in Tanzania, Zambia, Algeria and elsewhere. Kenya has supported some form of international sanctions against South Africa but allowed planes destined for South Africa to refuel at Nairobi and Mombasa contrary to OAU resolutions.[42]

In the Eastern African region, Kenya's increasing prosperity soon saw her become a dominant force. Arguably, international capital saw her as a possible centre for manufacturing for the Eastern African market. The infrastructure that was inherited by Kenya, Uganda and Tanzania, which had enabled Britain to consolidate certain services for the region under the East African High Commission, actually served

Kenya very well. While her neighbours — Uganda and Tanzania — became increasingly nervous at the concentration of capital and facilities in Kenya and anxious that Kenya had become exploitative, Kenya, on the other hand, grew increasingly restless over the collectivisation of the economy of Tanzania and the radicalisation of the political rhetoric in both Tanzania and Uganda. If Kenya was interested in preserving the East African market which had become essential to her continued industrialisation, it was certainly not evident in the hostility and virulence directed at her two neighbours. Kenya became arrogant to the point where she bragged about feeding Tanzania.[42]

The war of words between Tanzania and Kenya, which led to the closure by Tanzania of the border between the two countries, and the Kenyan government's ambivalent attitude towards atrocities in Uganda under Idi Amin, revealed ideological schisms in the Kenyan establishment.[44] The attorney-general was openly hostile to Tanzania and wanted an end to the East African Community.[45] The vice-president, perhaps more mindful of Kenyan dependency on the East African market, wanted the community to continue. In any case, Kenya was not too successful in mediating the quandary she found herself in, being threatened on the one hand with developments in her neighbours while, on the other hand, trying to maintain contacts with the neighbours to assure herself access either to the routes through those countries or to the markets in them.

Kenya's concern with border security arises from Somalia's claims for the North Eastern Province (formerly called the Northern Frontier District, NFD). This is the region of Kenya inhabited by Kenyans of Somali origin. The desire on the part of political leaders in the neighbouring Republic of Somalia to unite all Somali people living in Ethiopia, Djibouti and Kenya under one flag goes back a very long time to the beginning of Somali nationalism during the colonial era.[46] After a great deal of hesitation and equivocation, the British, who had even conducted a referendum in the NFD to determine the wishes of the residents there, decided instead to leave the problem to Jomo Kenyatta, the new prime minister of Kenya. Kenyatta, who had triumphantly contributed to the dissolution of the British Empire in Kenya, was not prepared to preside over the dismantling of what he saw as Kenyan territory. Kenyatta successfully prosecuted the so-called *shifta* war that was already under way when he assumed the leadership of the country.

The Somali claims continued to be a major irritant and certainly a factor in the forging of close military and security arrangements with Ethiopia, then under the late Emperor Haile-Selassie. Both countries shared the view, prevalent among African countries even today, and ensconced as the fifth principle in the charter of the OAU,[47] that

African borders inherited at the time of independence were inviolable and could not be redrawn.[48] It made ample sense for Kenyatta to forge this security arrangement and to continue it even after Haile-Selassie was overthrown and replaced with an avowedly Marxist government under Colonel Mengistu Haile Mariam. The threat posed to Kenya by Somalia's territorial claim was far more serious than the ideological orientation of the Ethiopian regime. Not surprisingly, the Ethiopian regime had no qualms about renewing the security arrangement with capitalist Kenya either. Samuel Makinda is correct in suggesting that the treaty with Ethiopia allowed Kenya to continue to concentrate on economic issues and to avoid a costly arms build-up that might have been expected for a country faced with such a serious threat.[49]

Although the Somali threat has abated somewhat and several contacts have successfully been initiated between the Somali president and the Kenyan president (the former has reportedly even said that Somalia has no territorial designs on Kenya), Somalia has not ruled out the possibility of coming to the aid of Somali Kenyans who may try to secede. Indeed, in the confrontations that have occurred between Somalia and Ethiopia and during the *shifta* war in Kenya, the Somali government claimed only to be aiding their brethren who were fighting for self-determination.[50] Recent developments, such as the attempted coup in Kenya in 1982, which resulted in President Moi disbanding the air force, would suggest that despite the thawing in Somali–Kenyan relations, the Kenyan government can be expected to continue to maintain the treaty with Ethiopia as it is in the national interest of both countries to remain militarily close.

Kenya's foreign policy under Moi

Moi's ascendancy to power in Kenya marks a new period in Kenya's foreign policy behaviour. Before Kenyatta died in 1978, a number of things were already happening that were bound to change the way Kenya had grown to treat her neighbours. Her relations with Uganda were already shaky due to the erratic and provocative behaviour of Idi Amin.[51] The Ugandan dictator had upset Kenyans by claiming the Western half of the country as Uganda's. Kenyans reacted swiftly and threatened to seal the border, thereby denying Uganda any outlet to the sea. Amin retreated, but the incident left lingering anxieties and uncertainties. A number of Kenyans — students and business people — had come to grief while in Uganda without an adequate explanation as to what had happened to them. Kenyan reactions to these incidents had been limited to verbal denunciations. Trade with Uganda, such as there was, continued and even the ban against smuggling of Ugandan coffee in 1976–78 was limited to Kenyan government statements.[52] Everyone was getting rich.[53]

However, the border with Tanzania was closed in February 1977 creating serious problems in Kenya. The tourist industry, which had relied heavily on the beautifully maintained Tanzania game parks, was hit severely. Trade with Malawi and Zambia, which passed through Tanzania, plummeted.[54] Kenya felt and was isolated. As a result of this isolation, Kenya began to court the Arab world more actively as possible markets for her exports (especially in agricultural and dairy products). An Arab–Kenya Friendship Society was revived to promote cultural and trade exchanges between Kenya and a number of Arab countries. Contacts with her northern neighbours were strengthened. In 1982 she signed a commercial treaty making her a member of the Preferential Trade Area that links together the Comoro Island, Djibouti, Ethiopia, Malawi, Mauritius, Somalia, Uganda and Zambia. That Tanzania did not sign the treaty is an indication that she wants any past grievances she may still hold against Kenya resolved bilaterally before she can reopen the border or allow the transit of Kenyan goods to the countries to the South.

In terms of relations with the major powers, Kenya, under Moi, became much more vociferous in defence of Western interest and positions. It is fair to say that this new visibility or activism may have been due to a difference of style incident to a new president who, in trying to fill the shoes of Kenyatta, definitely was not his predecessor's equal in the eyes of the people; a president who was trying to establish his position, to demonstrate that he was in command, and to assure Kenyans and international business that they had nothing to fear. An appropriate motto – *Nyayo* (meaning footsteps) – was devised to affirm a continuation of past policies, a determination to follow Kenyatta's successful road to political stability and economic development.[55]

As well, Moi took over the government at a time when the United States was having difficulties in Iran, what with the fall of the Shah and the subsequent painful hostage crisis. President Carter was casting around for another arrangement or machinery that would allow the United States to respond to such crises better next time. It was natural for the United States to approach Kenya for help as a country that had been a reliable ally in the past. And while this was going on, the Soviet Union invaded Afghanistan. President Carter became shrill in his condemnation of the Soviet Union and determined to forge a new network of facilities that would stem what was being regarded widely as Soviet expansionism. Kenya responded swiftly to these events.[56] Moi did not need any arm twisting to join the boycott of the Olympic games in Moscow in 1980.[57] He signed agreements in 1980 granting the

United States access to Mombasa as part of the Rapid Deployment Force.

It is difficult to make the case some analysts have that Kenyan leaders saw themselves as crusaders against the Soviet menace.[58] After all, Soviet assistance to Ethiopia during the Ethiopian–Somali war helped subdue a common adversary. Indeed, the Somali army suffered devastating defeats and astronomical losses of equipment that will take a while to replenish. In simple power calculations, Soviet involvement in Ethiopia redounded to Kenya's advantage. The Soviet and Cuban involvement in Angola, on the other hand, was prompted by imminent defeat of the MPLA forces by South Africans. President Kenyatta, as an elder African statesman, had been involved in mediation of the three liberation movements in Angola. He knew the dynamics of the struggle there well enough not to have interpreted the Cuban actions there as part of the global Soviet strategy to destabilise Africa. Instead, the Kenyan response is best understood in terms of the change in the leadership in Kenya which brought into the inner circle of the new president individuals who wanted Kenya to be much closer to the United States than before, who wanted to seize the opportunity provided by the crises occurring elsewhere and who felt that Kenya had the obligation to respond positively to requests of a country that was regarded as a long-standing ally. Moreover, the United States had offered badly needed economic and military aid.[59]

Disturbances of last August 1982 are a proof that even a very close relationship with a major power like the United States cannot completely insulate a government from internal turmoil. Ethiopia's intimate ties with the United States did not prevent Mengistu from coming to power. Nicaragua, Iran and other countries are examples that dissent that arises from within cannot be totally stifled successfully. In retrospect, Kenya has lost the image that she had carefully cultivated of a non-aligned country, moderate, rational, pro-West but not a satellite. Now she has to contend with the perception among her neighbours that she is an appendage of the United States. Given the thawing of relations with Somalia, if perceived to be instigated by the United States to form a sort of anti-Soviet alliance to serve American interests, may turn out to be short-lived.

Conclusions

A picture that emerges from the foregoing discussion is of a country that has certainly been consistent in its economic development strategy as well as in its foreign behaviour. This consistency has made the task of relating the two much easier than might have been the case for a country with more diversified activities. Ideological pronouncements in the early years of independence meant to pay lip service to socialism were abandoned for a more candid declaration that free enterprise or capitalism was a preferred strategy and that it was working to the satisfaction of the elite. On issues close to the African states' heart, such as the liberation of South Africa, Kenya has acted conservatively, making appropriate speeches, meeting financial obligations assessed at the OAU and the UN, and in the main, cultivating a favourable image of a pragmatic and moderate country. It is a fair assessment that at governmental level, Kenya has few enemies even among African states. This image has enabled Kenya to participate in OAU peace-keeping efforts in Chad as well as monitoring activities in the transition period in Zimbabwe. Moreover, the OAU meeting in Nairobi in 1981 was one of the largest assembly of African Heads of States on record.

It is always a problem in an effort such as this one to draw a direct cause–effect relationship between the economy and foreign policy. However, there is enough to warrant conclusions to the effect that heavy reliance on Western capital and expertise does make Kenya extremely vulnerable to pressure from the West. Decisions made in Kenya must always include serious calculations of what its 'traditional' friends are going to say or do. Ironically, the activism shown by President Moi in taking positions at the behest of the United States or in being included in the strategy of the Rapid Deployment Force – instituted by the Americans to deal with the Soviet threat, real or imagined, in the Middle East and the Gulf area – is likely to create new problems in Kenya as people begin to feel that the country is being used as a satellite by the United States in exchange for economic support and military aid.

If problems should arise because of this new emphasis on 'friendship' with the West, Moi could find himself using increasingly repressive measures against domestic opposition in order to present a facade of stability which is necessary to persuade the multinational firms to stay in the country. Due to the worldwide economic recession and the accession of Ronald Reagan to the presidency of the United States, who seems determined to tell the Third World that the answer to their economic ills lies in the free enterprise system, Moi's timing to assert Kenya's pro-Western loyalty may not have been a propitious one. Given President Reagan's emphasis on the use of force in dealing with the Soviet threat, Kenya may stand to receive increased military rather than economic aid which she needs more. If this happens, one can envisage greater distrust among the East African countries leading to increased militarisation and conflict in the region at the expense of interstate harmony, development and cooperation.[60]

Notes

1 See M. Tamarkin, 'The Roots of Political Stability in Kenya,' *African Affairs*, vol. 77, no. 308, July 1978, pp. 297–320.

2 See 'The Coup That Failed,' *Weekly Review* (Nairobi), 6 August 1982, pp. 3–17.

3 Representative of this kind of writing are, of course, Colin Leys' *Underdevelopment in Kenya: the political economy of neocolonialism* (Berkeley: University of California Press, 1974); and Nicola Swainson, *The Development of Corporate Capitalism in Kenya* (Berkeley: University of California Press, 1980).

4 Gavin Kitching, *Class and Economic Change in Kenya the making of an African petite-bourgeoisie, 1905–1979* (New Haven, Conn.: Yale University Press, 1980), Leys, *Underdevelopment in Kenya*, and Alan B. Amey and David K. Leonard, 'Public Policy, Class and Inequality in Kenya and Tanzania.' *Africa Today*, vol. 26, no. 4, 1979, pp. 3–41.

5 *Ibid*.

6 Steve Langdon, *Multinational Corporations in the Political Economy of Kenya* (London: Macmillan, 1980).

7 Even the realisation that a state qua state was a pivotal factor in fostering capitalist development via internal accumulation such as that occurring in Kenya emerged gradually and is now only beginning to be recognised. As a result, Colin Leys has begun to revise his conclusions drawn from his earlier analyses of Kenya. See Bjorn Beckman, 'Debate on Kenya Capitalism,' *Review of African Political Economy*, no. 19, September–December 1980, pp. 48.

8 The classic battles between Tom Mboya and Odinga Odinga are well known and have been amply analysed and documented elsewhere. See Cherry Gertzel, *The Politics of Independent Kenya* (Evanston, Ill.: Northwestern University Press).

9 For a detailed critique of the Kenyan variety of socialism, see Ahmed Mohiddin, *African Socialism in Two Countries* (Totowa, N.J.: Barnes and Noble, 1981).

10 See his *Politics Among Nations* (New York: Knopf, 1960 3rd Edition).

11 'Introduction: towards a political economy of African foreign policy,' this volume, p. 10–17.

12 Maurice A. East, 'Status Discrepancy and Violence in the International System: an empirical analysis,' in J.N. Rosenau, V. Davis, and M.A. East (eds), *The Analysis of International Politics* (New York: Free Press, 1972).

13 Timothy M. Shaw, 'Kenya and South Africa: "Sub-imperialist"

States,' *Orbis*, vol. 21, no. 2, Summer 1977, pp. 375—394.

14 James N. Rosenau, 'The Study of Foreign Policy,' in James N. Rosenau, Kenneth W. Thompson, and Gavin Boyd (eds), *World Politics: An Introduction* (New York: Free Press, 1976), p. 16.

15 *Ibid.*

16 Claude Ake, 'Ideology and Objective Conditions,' in Joel D. Barkan with J. J. Okumu (eds), *Politics and Public Policy in Kenya and Tanzania* (New York: 1979), pp. 124—125.

17 This is the central theme of Gavin Kitching, *Class and Economic Change in Kenya* (note 4). Attempts in the Kenyan Parliament either to limit the amount of land one person could own or to place a ceiling on land prices have repeatedly been defeated. See, for example, *Weekly Review* 10 April 1981, p. 8.

18 Import-substitution is a common strategy for rapid industrialisation in the Third World. It involves placing prohibitively high tariffs on manufactured imports in order to induce domestic firms or domestic subsidiaries and branches of foreign firms to begin producing the same products as those imported. By doing this, the developing country hopes to save on foreign exchange which is spent on foreign imports. Kenya, like many other countries, has discovered that this strategy does not solve the problem of technology and needed skills which must still be obtained abroad at exorbitant expense. At least the expected saving of foreign reserves has not occurred in Kenya. In fact, the problem has become worse. For an interesting and enlightened case study of import-substitution as it was applied in Canada, see Glen Williams, 'The National Policy Tariffs: Industrial Development Through Imports Substitution,' *Canadian Journal of Political Science*, vol. 12, no. 2, June 1979, pp. 338—368.

19 John J. Okumu, 'Foreign Relations: Dilemmas of Independence and Development,' in Barkan with Okumu (eds), *Politics and Public Policy in Kenya and Tanzania* (note 16), p. 240.

20 Needless to say, the colonial experience was significant in the acculturation of the elite that assumed power in Kenya. Moreover, by 1963, there were those among Africans who stood to benefit handsomely from continuing the same economic policies begun by the British. See Swainson, *The Development of Corporate Capitalism in Kenya*, Part IIB, 'African Trade and Business, Pastoralism and Labour,' pp. 159—279.

21 Ministry of Finance and Planning, Kenya, 'Technical Assistance Personnel Working in Kenya as of 31st March, 1971,' unpublished compilation of expatriate personnel in Kenya (Table 1).

22 Leys, *Underdevelopment in Kenya* (note 3), p. 118.

23 Charles Njonjo, who was attorney-general from 1963 to 1980, was

publicly opposed to any acceleration in the Africanisation pro-gramme on grounds that certain 'standards' of efficiency must be maintained. See 'Kenya's Outspoken Attorney-General,' *Weekly Review*, no. 146, 28 November 1977, p. 6. See also Vincent B. Khapoya, 'Interdependency or Underdevelopment: The Role of Expatriates in Kenya,' *Western Association of Africanists*, Colorado Springs, March 1981.

24   See Hilary Ng'weno, 'Kenya Does Not Need Expatriates – But It Needs Standards,' *Weekly Review*, 19 September 1977, pp. 5–11.

25   An excellent study of the trade unions in Kenya can be found in R. Sandbrook, *Proletarians and African Capitalism: the Kenyan case, 1960–1972* (Cambridge: Cambridge University Press, 1975). See also 'Cotu Gets Ready For Election Show-down,' *Weekly Review*, 15 February 1980, pp. 24–25. Cotu is an acronym for the Central Organisation of Trade Unions (COTU).

26   A great deal of data on import trade, the share of manufactures in GDP, the balance of payments situation (1966–1978), foreign ownership of large manufacturing companies and tourist firms which confirm the summarisation of the Kenyan economy can be found in Rafael Kaplinsky, 'Capitalist Accumulation in the Periphery – the Kenyan case re-examined,' *Review of African Economy*, no. 17, January–April, 1980, pp. 38–105. See also the data in Nicola Swainson, 'The Rise of a National Bourgeoisie in Kenya,' *Review of African Political Economy*, no. 8, January–April, 1977, pp. 39–55. An analysis of the Kenyan economy by the World Bank can be found in *Kenya: into the second decade; report of a mission sent to Kenya by the World Bank* (Baltimore: The Johns Hopkins University Press, for World Bank, 1975).

27   An economist, noted for his strong sympathy with Kenya's developmental strategy, is alarmed at the depressing figures cited by the ILO report and appears determined to explain away the disparities. This is his reaction:

> According to. . .the ILO report, 1,140,000 households have an annual income of between £20 and £60, while 330,000 have *not more* than £20. These are pretty startling figures – but can they be taken at their face value? The data ask us to believe that there is some meaning to saying, as a measure of the inequality within *this* group there must be many thousands who receive much less than £20 a year per *house-hold*. And this, remember, is total not just money income. Are such figures plausible? Can they conceivably indicate a reality they purport to reflect? Surely not.

See Arthur Hazelwood, 'Kenya: income distribution and poverty

161

— an unfashionable view,' *Journal of Modern African Studies*, vol. 16, no. 1, 1978, p. 87.

The Kenyan government was not alarmed at the findings of the ILO team. If they were, they certainly did not tell anyone about it. As mentioned earlier, Kenya's parliament has refused to limit the amount of land that could be acquired by rich Kenyans. The government has also been lukewarm towards the problem of income distribution saying that social justice cannot be pursued at the expense of individual freedom. See *Weekly Review*, 12 December 1977, p. 11.

28   Hazelwood, 'Kenya: income distribution and poverty,' p. 86. Recent research shows that the gap between the haves and the have-nots will widen over the years if Kenya continues to pursue a policy of growth without distribution. Projections to the year 2000 show that the proportion of Kenyans living under poverty will increase to 57.1 per cent if GNP and population increase at 5.5 per cent and 3.5 per cent, respectively. See M. S. Ahluwalia, N.G. Carter, and H.B. Chenery, 'Growth and Poverty in Developing Countries,' *Journal of Development Economics*, no. 6, pp. 229–341.

29   This assertion is inferred from the war of words between Kenya and Tanzania, particularly during the 1976–1978 period. Kenyans continually bragged about their 'successful' development strategy and the 'bankruptcy' of Tanzania's *ujamaa*. The closure of the border between the two countries was in part Tanzania's response to Kenya's arrogance and a lack of respect for a trading partner that Tanzania in fact was, rather than simply a beneficiary of Kenya's largesse. Kenya's losses in business to Zambia and Malawi and in tourism were substantial. See *Weekly Review*, issues of 13 December 1976; 14 February 1977; 21 February 1977; 23 May 1977; and 31 October 1977.

30   Martin Godfrey and Steven Langdon, 'Partners in Underdevelopment? The transnationalization thesis in a Kenyan context,' *Journal of Commonwealth and Comparative Politics*, vol. 15, no. 1, March 1976, pp. 56–57.

31   For some information on one major parastatal organisation, the Industrial and Commercial Development Corporation (ICDC), see 'ICDC Shares Raise Too Much Money,' *Weekly Review*, 16 January 1978, pp. 27–31.

32   *Ibid.*, p. 49. See also the series of debates on Kenyan capitalism, Rafael Kaplinsky, 'Capitalist Accumulation in the Periphery — the Kenyan case re-examined,' *Review of African Political Economy*, no. 17, 1980, pp. 83–105; and Colin Leys, 'Kenya: what does dependency explain?,' *ibid.*, pp. 108–113.

33 See Samuel M. Makinda, 'From Quiet Diplomacy to Cold War Politics: Kenya's foreign policy,' *Third World Quarterly*, vol. 5, no. 2, April 1983, pp. 303–304.

34 *Weekly Review*, 2 October 1981, pp. 5–6.

35 *Weekly Review*, issues of 11, 18, and 25 September 1981.

36 Indeed, the recently concluded general elections in Kenya saw some of the wealthiest individuals in the country gain seats in parliament, e.g., Matu Wamae, who used to run the ICDC: John Michuki, former chairman of the Kenya Commercial Bank; and Francis Thuo, the former head of the Nairobi Stock Exchange. See *Weekly Review*, 7 October 1983, pp. 6–8.

37 Culled from tables in *Kenya: into the second decade* (note 26), pp. 522–524.

38 Khapoya, 'Interdependency or Underdevelopment,' (note 23), p. 9.

39 This is what Marshall Singer had to say in discussing the impact on elites of education acquired abroad:

> A person learns more than merely 'science' or 'humanities' when he goes off to study; he learns a way of life as well. At Oxford and Cambridge, above all else, one learns the definition of being an educated gentleman. At the Sorbonne, he learns the glory of a French education. At Harvard or Yale, he learns more than mathematics or poetry. He learns, subtly and rather effectively, an upper class, egalitarian way of life. At Moscow, he learns not only the accomplishments of Russian space science, but a view of the way the 'good life' is to be ordered. To be sure, there are individual exceptions in each case, but by and large, at each school in every country, one learns a preferred value system, world view and way of life. That aspect of one's education is as important, if not more important, than the facts or ideas he learns in class.
>
> Thus, what is implicitly and explicitly taught at the schools attended by various segments of a country's elite becomes crucially important in understanding the perceptions, values, attitudes, and modes of behaviour of these elites. To the degree that they hold values and perceptions espoused at the schools of a country other than their own, they are perceptually tied to that country. To the degree that they feel they must look to developments and innovations taking place primarily in the country in which they have studied in order to remain in the forefront of their field, they are tied perceptually to that country.

163

Marshall R. Singer, *Weak States in a World of Powers: the dynamics of international relationships* (New York: Free Press, 1972), pp. 150–151.

40   John Okumu, 'Kenya's Foreign Policy,' in Olajide Aluko (ed.), *The Foreign Policies of African States* (London: Hodder and Stoughton, 1977), p. 136.

41   See *Weekly Review*, 9 October 1981, pp. 13 and 17, for a speech by President Moi at the 1981 Commonwealth meeting in Australia in which he called for sanctions against South Africa.

42   *Ibid.*

43   *Weekly Review*, 14 February 1977, pp. 5–8.

44   *Ibid.*

45   *Weekly Review* 28 November 1977, p. 5.

46   Christian P. Potholm, *The Theory and Practice of African Politics* (Englewood Cliffs, N.J.: Prentice-Hall, 1979), p. 216.

47   Leslie Rubin and Brian Weinstein, *Introduction to African Politics: A Continental Approach* (New York: Praeger, 1977 2nd Edition), p. 247.

48   Given the high number of ethnic/national groups in Kenya that are divided, the OAU is correct in not wanting to open a Pandora's box by trying to rectify the boundary issue. The best analysis of this issue in Africa is probably Saadia Touval, *The Boundary Politics of Independent Africa* (Cambridge, Mass.: Harvard University Press, 1972), especially pp. 82–98.

49   Makinda, 'From Quiet Diplomacy to Cold War Politics' (note 33), p. 307.

50   Indeed, there was evidence to suggest that the Somali government directly controlled the *shifta* bands in both Kenya and Ethiopia. See Touval, *The Boundary Politics of Independent Africa* (note 48), p. 101.

51   *Weekly Review*, 23 May 1977, pp. 5–10.

52   *Weekly Review*, 22 August 1977, p. 17.

53   *Ibid.*, p. 15.

54   *Weekly Review*, 21 February 1977, pp. 18–21.

55   *Weekly Review*, 23 May 1977, pp. 5–10.

56   See 'Moi's New Stand in Foreign Policy', *Weekly Review*, 8 February 1980, pp. 15–17.

57   Moi's Statement on the Olympic Games,' *ibid.*, p. 16.

58   See Makinda, 'From Quiet Diplomacy to Cold War Politics' (note 33), pp. 312–313.

59   *Weekly Review*, 9 October 1981, p. 11.

60   The impact of United States military aid to Kenya is explored in Vincent B. Khapoya, 'The Cold War and Regional Politics in East Africa,' *8th Annual Third World Conference*, March 1982.

7 Niger*

Richard A. Higgott

This case study uses the introduction as a general guideline. My first priority will be to establish the nature of 'structural' historical, environmental and economic constraints before consideration can be given to the 'superstructural' contingencies of Niger's foreign policy. The central argument of this chapter will be that despite the overwhelming nature of the inherited set of structural constraints facing Niger, its foreign policy in the first two decades of the post-colonial era has demonstrated a greater degree of change at the level of contingency than might be assumed at first glance. Such an assertion is not to deny the underlying threads and continuities of Niger's foreign relations; rather it is to alert the reader to the very real variety of conflicting tendencies and the range of changes to be examined.

The aim here will be twofold in as much as I attempt to contribute to the growing body of literature on the political economy of international relations as well as adding to the historical analysis of Niger. At a theoretical level, therefore, I confront the issue of the potential for

* This chapter was written in 1982 while the author was a Fulbright Fellow and Post-Doctoral Research Fellow in the John F. Kennedy School of Government at Harvard. Thanks are due to both the American–Australian Educational Foundation and the Kennedy School for financial support and facilities.

foreign policy makers in weak developing nations to exercise some kind of independent policy-making initiative in the conduct of their international relations. Consideration of this specific issue has tended, during the latter part of the 1970s, to be largely ignored by the theoretical literature — subsumed beneath what at times have seemed like an interminable debate between what we might call *dependencia* and Marxist approaches to the political economy of development and underdevelopment. This debate centred around competing caricatures of the state and the ruling class in the Third World as being respectively dependent and comprador in their relationship with the international environment on the one hand or as the main weapon in the armoury of a nascent indigenous bourgeoisie in its assault on international capital.[1] Both approaches, as I shall suggest by illustration in this chapter, tend to miss the complexity of given historical situations. A particularly important variable that is often overlooked in such generalised theory building is the *degree* of incorporation of a particular state within, as Shaw suggests, '... a general and common situation of external subordination'.[2]

It is if we concern ourselves with the aforementioned variable of *degree* that this study of Niger becomes of particular interest. Niger is the only former francophone land-locked state considered in this volume. While the issue of land-lockedness has been paid greater consideration over the last few years,[3] less attention has been given to comparative analysis of the impact of differing colonial experiences on this particular structural condition and especially the impact of the francophone colonial legacy on the international politics of land-locked states. The work to date on the political economy of foreign policy of former anglophone land-locked states, such as Zambia for example, has been both qualitatively and quantitively superior to that on the former francophone states.[4]

Given space constraints, it is possible here only to assert that Niger's post-independence international relationships have been heavily constrained by the historical legacies of colonialism.[5] Rather, it is intended, working from this assertion, to examine the specifics of foreign policy in the period of the two political regimes which have governed Niger to date: namely the period between 1960 and 1974, during which time Niger was governed by Hamani Diori and the *Parti Progressiste Nigérien* (PPN), and the period from 1974 during which time Niger has been governed by the military junta led by Seyni Kountché. The first section will discuss the continuities and constraints in Niger's foreign policy emanating from its achievement of independence as one of the weakest political and economic entities of former francophone West Africa. The central foreign policy goals in the early days after independence were securing the integrity of the new state, learning to conduct foreign relations and holding on to the 'familiar' in a new international environment.[6] While the Kountché period, examined in the second section, obviously exhibits similar concerns they are much less acute. This period, more interestingly, highlights the way in which changes in the political economy — in this instance the vast inflow of funds from the export of Niger's uranium — can bring about significant changes in the foreign policy environment and process. It should also be noted that exactly the opposite influences can occur: that is, changes in the international environment can have a very significant impact on the political economy of a particular state.

Following the approach adopted in the introduction I shall endeavour to demonstrate that while the inheritance of dependence cannot be ignored, neither should a country's foreign policy options be considered as entirely predetermined. Even for the weakest of states in world affairs, of which Niger is clearly one, the direction of foreign policy is open to moulding and shaping to some degree. In such a context, several broad themes have dominated post-colonial foreign policy in Niger. It is *how* the two governments have attempted to deal with these themes which provides the 'contingent' element in foreign policy. The three major themes that will be threaded through the ensuing discussion are, then:

1   The concern of Niger's governments to ensure the *security and stability* of their regimes from disruption, be it internally or externally generated. Foreign policy has been an integral part of the process of regime maintenance under both Diori and, albeit to a lesser extent, Kountché.
2   The need to respond to the inherited set of problems that specifically face *land-locked* developing countries.
3   The desire to pursue a *developmental strategy* geared to alleviating — as far as possible — Niger's immense poverty. The domestic component of developmental strategy, namely the formulation and implementation of Niger's development plans, is beyond my purview. Rather I will restrict myself to discussion of the 'external component' of development strategy, namely the way in which government raises funds to finance a particular process of national development.

The foreign relations of Niger: 1960–1974

Politics, security and regional organisation in the first decade

The immediate post-independence period saw Niger conforming to a fairly standard pattern in which the ruling PPN elite, through its

167

inherited control of the post-colonial state, became engaged in a trans-national relationship with, primarily French, external values. Indeed, preserving the 'French connection' in areas of technical, political, economic and educational support was to be the major aim of international relations for the new government. While amenable to a diversification of partners, foreign policy making in the first decade was to be primarily an exercise to improve and strengthen the inherited set of relationships. Such a policy was perceived, somewhat paradoxically, as the surest way to establish the sovereignty of the new state or, perhaps more accurately, the surest way to preserve the security of the *regime*. Perhaps the best way to demonstrate such an assertion is to make the somewhat arbitrary distinction between political and economic spheres of activity within the foreign policy process.

Niger's foreign policy makers, to wit Hamani Diori and a close coterie of supporters,[7] like most francophone leaders, had a strong desire 'to belong'. They were the political leaders of new states in search of a role, required for the first time to formulate and implement foreign policy. For Hamani Diori, as for many of the other former members of the *Rassemblement Democratique Africaine* (RDA), such as Houphouet-Boigny, one of the best ways to do this was within regional organisations that allowed them to preserve their familiar pre-independence links. The *Conseil de l'Entente* and the *Union Africaine et Malgache* (UAM) provided the perfect forums for these new leaders of francophone Africa to join together in a process of mutual reassurance. The general history of the origins and early activities of these organisations is now well documented in the secondary literature. Suffice it here to say that while such organisations were meant to demonstrate the new-found independence of their members, in many quarters they were in fact seen as a manifestation of continuing dependence on the former colonial power.[8]

More important for this chapter is the specific role these organisations were to play in bolstering a shakey PPN government against the exiled Sawaba opposition headed by Djibo Bakary.[9] After his expulsion and the outlawing of his organisation, Bakary had gone into exile in Ghana from where Nkrumah was to fund, albeit in meagre fashion, his efforts to undermine the PPN government in the first half of the 1960s.[10] Efforts to deal with the activities of Sawaba were to represent one of Diori's major foreign policy concerns in this period. The essence of his policy was, with the help of Houphouet-Boigny, to secure the implementation of diplomatic pressure to persuade (force?) Nkrumah to withdraw his support for Sawaba. The vehicle for this pressure was to be UAM and its successor, the *Organisation Commune Africaine et Malgache* (OCAM). Not the least significant factor in the creation of OCAM in 1965 was a desire on the part of Houphouet-Boigny and

Diori to found an organisation more willing than the OAU to tackle the issue of Ghanaian support for dissident groups such as the Sanwi movement in Ivory Coast and Sawaba in Niger.[11] This desire was one facet of a more general position which represented the ascendency of the 'political' school of thought in francophone African regional cooperation, at the expense of a more limited 'economic' approach that had held sway in that brief honeymoon period immediately after the creation of the OAU.

The close cooperation between Hamani Diori and Houphouet-Boigny stems from their shared experiences as members of the RDA during the pre-independence period. Houphouet's unswerving support for his Niger colleague in the face of Sawaba subversion was reciprocated by Diori in his support for Houphouet-Boigny's conception of a minimum form of economic cooperation in regional organisation. This conception was epitomised in the *Conseil de l'Entente*. While Diori, as the leader of a land-locked state, might have preferred a greater economic role for the francophone regional organisations (akin to that of Leopold Senhor's) he was in fact cognisant of the strictly limited potential of such organisations as a major source of economic assistance to Niger. While the *Conseil*, through its Guarantee Fund, did provide for the transfer of small amounts of funds from the Ivory Coast to its poorer partners in the organisation,[12] its political functions, especially as a 'core' group capable of putting backbone into the larger organisation — be it UAM or OCAM — were always paramount. The chief *raison d'être* of the francophone groupings was at all times to consolidate political sovereignty and elite maintenance at the state level, not undermine it by any movement towards supranational organisation that might require a surrender of sovereignty — no matter how slight. There can be no doubt that in the period up to the overthrow of Nkrumah in 1966 these organisations played a very important defensive role for the ruling PPN in Niger.

Although the overthrow of Nkrumah did not put an end to Sawaba it did emasculate the organisation as a source of major concern to Diori's government with the consequence that his conception of the role that OCAM might play in Niger's foreign policy changed. In his role as president of the organisation from 1966 to 1968 Diori used the kudos that accrued to him as francophone statesman and 'broker' to pursue a much more assertive foreign policy.[13] Particularly, Diori used his role as the negotiator for the francophone states in the renewal of the Yaoundé convention to enhance his own image and to foster Niger's interests abroad.[14] The *Conseil* and UAM/OCAM were not the only organisations to which Niger belonged, but they were certainly the most important for organising Niger's continental environment in the first decade after independence. They filled a role for Hamani Diori that the OAU was never deemed capable of occupying. As an out-growth of the French colonial experience, especially the common political heritage of the first generation of francophone leaders, OCAM and the *Entente* provided the natural avenue for meeting the needs of these new, and somewhat overawed, actors in international relations.

Land-lockedness and relations with Nigeria

The problem of being land-locked was the second major international issue with which the government had to cope on the attainment of independence. Whilst Niger's position at the periphery of AOF had been a serious factor inhibiting its economic development during the colonial period,[15] the achievement of independence as a single territorial entity added further problems. The securing of routes for its imports and exports was now an international legal issue as well as a practical and logistic problem. There is now a sufficient body of literature on these kinds of problems for their general discussion not to be warranted here.[16] I shall simply restrict this section to the implications for Niger's foreign policy of the two historical events that have highlighted its vulnerability as a land-locked state to date.

Niger's two routes to the ocean are via Cotonou in Dahomey and Lagos in Nigeria. At independence, the route via Dahomey was the most institutionalised, consolidated by the existence of the *Organis-ation Commune Dahomey–Niger* (OCDN) created in the last years of French colonial rule for the purpose of evacuating Niger's groundnut crop.[17] The link with Dahomey was also strengthened in a less formal manner by the close political affiliations of Hamani Diori and Dahomey's first president and former RDA colleague, Hubert Maga. This route was, however, the less important and less efficient of the two. The bulk of Niger's groundnut crop was exported via Nigeria given the closer proximity of Niger's major groundnut-producing areas to the Kano railhead.[18] Both routes have been subject to dislocation during the post-independence period. The first time was during 1964 when the border between Niger and Dahomey was closed as a result of the dispute over the Isle of Leté — or so the official government documents suggest. More important as a factor in the dispute, however, was Diori's distress at the overthrow of Maga and the belief, held in Niger government circles, that Sawaba was being given assistance to operate through Dahomey. Traffic on OCDN was dislocated during the period of the dispute and it took almost a year to restore things to normal.[19]

The second, and more serious, disruption to Niger's transit trade came during the Nigerian civil war.[20] Both disruptions brought home to the Diori government the need for a land-locked state to have an *alternative* artery to the ocean, no matter how costly or under-utilised such a route might be. An alternative route provides insurance against technical breakdowns, natural disasters, labour disputes, political upheavals, international conflicts and the tendency towards monopolistic practices on the part of a transit state. The possession of a second transit route may not prevent such factors having an immediate effect but it does offer some form of insurance against medium- and long-term disruption. For example, in this case, the Nigerian civil war coincided with Niger's largest ever groundnut crop in 1966–67. While the Nigerian government did the best it could by its northern neighbour in trying to guarantee the shipment of the crop, the war made it impossible to take as much as necessary. Through a variety of emergency measures the OCDN was able to triple its tonnage in the 1966–67 season and take nearly half the crop in contrast to the average annual share of just over 20 per cent that it had taken from independence until 1966.[21] The impact of the export of the 1966–67 groundnut crop convinced the Niger government of the need to upgrade the route via Dahomey. Even though it would in many instances be considerably under-utilised, it was anticipated that this route would come more into its own in the 1970s when Niger's uranium exports were expected to come on line.[22]

Niger's land-locked position is not, it can be argued, the worst in Africa. It does not have to operate in the hostile political environment in which some of the land-locked states of Southern Africa find themselves (see Chapter 2 on Botswana). In the main, Nigeria has proved itself to be a good littoral partner. There are, however, intangible aspects of land-lockedness that affect foreign policy formulation. It is not possible to quantify the psychological feelings of dependence and the potential susceptibility to disruption from unforseen circumstances. Consequently, a state such as Niger, existing in a grossly asymmetrical relationship with Nigeria, has to ensure the best possible link with its neighbour at all times — as a brief examination of the bilateral relationship will reveal (see also Chapter 7).

Contrary to what might reasonably be expected, the inherited colonial boundary between the two countries has acted as much as a conduit as it has a barrier.[23] Shared Hausa culture and thousands of bush tracks make the border very permeable.[24] Indeed, John Collins in a fascinating study has shown how Diori's government manipulated border trade in groundnuts to its economic advantage.[25] By fixing a higher buying price for nuts Nigerian produce could be drawn north across the border, bought and then resold to international buyers; this was especially the case up to 1967 when French price support encouraged Niger to sell as large a quantity as possible. That the policy was successful was due in no small part to the willingness of the Nigerian government to turn a blind eye to the practice of its northern neighbour. The practice had a relatively minor impact on the Nigerian economy, attesting to the asymmetry of the relationship. The war was only to demonstrate this asymmetry even further. Throughout its total course, Diori gave unswerving support to the federal cause.[26] While there is every reason to assume that this is the course of action he would have chosen had there been no constraints on him, two factors need to be noted. First, it would have been untenable to think of Niger giving even verbal support to a secession movement within Niger's major littoral partner; the asymmetry of need on Niger's part would always militate against such a course of action. And second, Niger's actions, for the first time since independence, put it in sharp conflict with its major international partners – France and Ivory Coast.[27]

This conflict of loyalties revealed for the first time the paradox of Niger's international position and is, as much as anything can be, a pointer to the future position of Niger in the regional political framework. When the Diori government was confronted by the competing pulls of an artificial colonial heritage (and to call it such is not to minimise its strength) and a compelling geographical loyalty, then the pull of Nigeria won over that of France and francophone Africa. This ambiguity in Niger's position was further highlighted in Diori's changing attitude towards regional organisation during the last years of his regime.

Niger and regional organisation:1970–1974

Regional organisation in West Africa in this period was characterised by the demise (if not actual death) of OCAM, the birth of a rather sickly *Communauté Economique Afrique Occidentale* (CEAO) and the conception of a potentially much more robust Economic Community of West Africa (ECOWAS).[28] While OCAM's problems were a blow to Diori – having sunk so much of his own personal capital into it – his objections to the creation of CEAO were much more than its being an acknowledgement of OCAM's weakness. At the creation of the CEAO in Bamako in 1971 Diori was the fiercest critic of the establishment of another purely francophone grouping – again in sharp conflict with the views of France and Ivory Coast. In contrast to Diori, who saw the creation of any regional organisation in West Africa without the presence of Nigeria as an anachronism, Houphouet-Boigny (and from a distance, Pompidou) saw CEAO as a counter to Nigeria's growing influence on the regional politics of West Africa in that assertive period of post-war reconstruction of the early 1970s.

Diori's recognition of the changes taking place in the regional environment was not, unfortunately, matched by an accompanying ability to adjust to them. He could not but join CEAO despite its 'unrealistic' nature.[29] He was too much a product of that French socialisation experience of the post-1945 era to permit him to opt out of his traditional French and Ivory Coast relationships. It is perhaps perfect testimony to the influence of the francophone connection that in the last analysis Diori – despite his growing relationship with Nigeria[30] – was prepared to join an organisation for which he had little sympathy and which he thought had little future.

Diori's policy was not entirely consistent during this period. The other major factor in the changing regional environment to which he was not so keen to adjust was the prospect of an extension of the EEC relationship to include anglophone Africa. Not only would Nigerian participation in the negotiation process eclipse his own personal role – as indeed it did[31] – but also he feared Nigerian participation in the Eurafrican relationship might dilute the trade and aid preferences with the EEC that had become an increasingly important part of Niger's economic relations over the first decade of independence.[32] Anglophone participation in the negotiation of the Lomé convention undermined the status of OCAM. Lomé I was much more radical in intent, influenced by the radicalisation of the international environment in the wake of OPEC's success and by the increasingly vociferous demands for a reshaping of the international order. The actual signing of the Lomé convention, as with the inauguration of ECOWAS, was to take place after Diori had been removed from office by military coup in 1974. While the negotiations were taking place before his overthrow, Diori was too preoccupied with the issues to play much of a role: at a domestic level he was concerned primarily with the impact of the Sahelian drought on the economy and his own precarious political position;[33] and at the international level he was preoccupied with the bilateral relationship with France, which was perceived as being of greater importance for the future of his regime.

Niger and France:1960–1974

Niger's need, but inability, to generate capital resources on a sustained basis meant that the search for external finances from a variety of sources was central to foreign policy in the post-independence period. Regional organisation was not a source of meaningful economic support and the reality for Hamani Diori, as for all African leaders, was that capital had to be sought outside Africa and primarily on a bilateral basis. The search for finance helps explain the importance of the relationship with the former colonial power. There was no other comparable source of financial support. Niger, like most of the poorer francophone states, was dependent on France in the first decade after independence, not only for public investment, but also for recurrent budgetary support – occasionally to the tune of 40 per cent of total bilateral disbursements from France.[34] These funds went towards the costs of basic administrative and infrastructural services which had, before 1959, been covered by subsidies to Niger from the wider federation of AOF.[35]

Recognition of this financial dependence on France naturally saw Niger keen to diversify as much as possible its sources of funding. To diversify did not mean to secure *less* from France, but *more* from elsewhere. To this end a very elaborate, albeit modest in scope, series of development plans were initiated in order to attract international financial support. In similar fashion the government created a variety of *Société d'Economie Mixte* (SEM) as a way of attracting international involvement in joint sponsored ventures that it believed were unlikely to attract support without governmental underwriting in some form of parastatal organisation.

These SEMs represented one of the major bonds between the dominant group of political and economic leaders within the PPN and the former colonial power. Of Niger's thirteen largest parastatals in 1969, six had members of the PPN Politburo as president or director-general while five had Frenchmen in similar positions. The boards of these organisations were dominated by a combination of Frenchmen and senior PPN officials. One man – Boubou Hama – was not only president of the PPN, the overall controller of Niger's media, but also president of the *Banque de Développement*, the *Caisse National de Credit et de Coopération* and several other organisations. Politburo members were also presidents of the *Société National des Transports Nigériens* and the *Société Nigérienne de Commercialisation des Arachides*. These organisations formed the backbone of Niger's economic infrastructure and were capitalised almost exclusively by the Niger government and the former colonial power. It was not until the creation of the uranium extraction corporation, SOMAIR, in 1968 that Niger attracted any non-French investment of note.[36]

It was envisaged that all but 10 per cent of Niger's funding for its development plans up to 1974 would come from public sources; further, no self-generated funds were envisaged at all until some surplus revenue became available with the export of uranium in 1971. Indeed, throughout the 1960s budgetary support from France still accounted for approximately 30 per cent of total French aid. While budgetary support for recurrent expenditure in Niger officially ended in 1969 it was in effect replaced by the French contribution to Niger's *Fonds National d'Investissement* created in the same year.

Having painted such a gloomy picture of the first decade of independence we should not make the mistake, common in some of the earlier, more pietistic, literature of the dependency genre, of assuming that such dependence was somehow immutable and allowing of little or no initiative for the dependent state.[37] As I want to suggest throughout the rest of this chapter, while Niger's dependence might not have diminished with the passing of the two decades since independence it has certainly changed. If we broaden our discussion of Niger's search for public finance to cover foreign aid other than that from France we can see a positive trend in the first decade away from a dependency on the former colonial power towards a multilateral dependency within the wider European context. While France provided over 76 per cent of Niger's bilateral aid and nearly 50 per cent of total aid (bilateral and contribution to multilateral aid) during the first decade, the major characteristic of the period was not this preponderance — which was to be expected in the immediate post-colonial period — but the growing role of the European Development Fund (EDF). Not only did it account for 27 per cent of Niger's aid in absolute terms but it played an increasing role throughout the first decade. By 1970 the EDF (49 per cent) had replaced France (46 per cent) as the major source of *investment* finance in Niger.[38] By the end of the 1960s Canada was also playing a growing role as an aid donor to Niger.

As with aid, similarly with trade: by the early 1970s, although France was still the primary international partner for Niger, an undeniable diversification was taking place within the wider Eurafrican context. While this was a general francophone African phenomenon of the 1960s, Niger's pattern of trading did not fit uniformly within this general pattern. In the first decade after independence, for example, French West African exports grew by 185 per cent and imports by 141 per cent, but with a decrease in the role of France as the major trader with the area; exports declining from 59 to 39 per cent and imports from 64 to 52 per cent while francophone imports and exports to the rest of the EEC grew from 8 to 20 per cent and 14 to 28 per cent respectively.[39] As the *Bulletin de l'Afrique Noire* pointed out, these overall figures were skewed, due above all to the fact that:

> La Cote d'Ivoire, le Gabon, la Mauritanie connaissent des taux de croissance brilliants, voire exceptionnels, les economies moins riches en réssources naturelles ou handicapée par leur situation géographique (RCA, Haute Volta, Niger, Tchad, Mali) enregistrent des évolutions moins remarquables.[40]

> (The Ivory Coast, Gabon and Mauritania have exceptionally high growth rates [whereas] those economies less well endowed with natural resources or handicapped by their geographical position (Central African Republic, Upper Volta, Niger, Chad and Mali) are much less impressive.)

Niger's trade underwent diversification during the same period, but not of the same magnitude as the region as a whole. France's share of Niger's imports demonstrated a marked decline, dropping to 43 per cent in 1971 but still accounting for over half of all Niger's imports in the first decade of independence. The decrease in France's stake was more than offset by the increase in that of the EEC as a whole (excluding France) from 6 to 17 per cent by 1971. Niger registered a decline in its regional West African imports. Diversification has been away from France but to other European partners.[41] France still took the lion's share of Niger's exports, varying from a high of 77 per cent in 1960 to a low of 46 per cent in 1970 and averaging 60 per cent for the decade. Niger's other major partner was its southern neighbour Nigeria, which took a fifth of Niger's exports during the same period.[42]

Niger's post-independence exports to France did not decline as fast as the regional norm. The states which demonstrated the greatest ability to diversify were the powerful states (regionally speaking) such as Ivory Coast which registered 61 per cent of its exports in 1971 *outside* of the franc zone compared with Niger's 40 per cent; and states such as Mauritania with valuable minerals which registered 71 per cent. Mali and Upper Volta, as other land-locked states, also had low non-franc zone export patterns. Niger's trade figures during the first decade indicate that it was more successful in diversifying its sources of imports than achieving new markets for its exports and, despite the multilateralisation of the European relationship, France remained, overwhelmingly, Niger's dominant partner. Further, only in 1970 did the relationship with France not register a deficit on trading for Niger. As the last section of this chapter will demonstrate, however, the growth of Niger's uranium exports in the 1970s was to alter considerably these last two tendencies.

Other aspects of Niger's foreign relations gave further support to the notion of diversification away from the former colonial power. Several factors, other than conflicting attitudes to the Nigerian civil war and the nature of regional organisation already discussed, brought about a deterioration in the relationship between France and Niger in the last years of Diori's administration. At the general level there was, of course, a serious questioning on both sides of the Franco—African partnership of the notion of *coopération* and the future direction it should take[43] — especially after France's unilateral and secret devaluation of the French franc in 1969.

At the specific level the first thing to note was the impact of Niger's growing relationship with Canada, certain aspects of which irritated the French intensely. Neither de Gaulle in his last days, nor Pompidou in his early days, took kindly to Niger's role in advancing the Canadian conception of *la francophonie* at the expense of the more limited

French conception, or to Niger's adoption as one of Canada's *pays de concentration*.[44]

The growing relationship with Canada, albeit as a pawn in Franco–Canadian rivalry, was used by Diori to demonstrate to the increasingly hostile political constituency at home that he was not merely a French puppet. The intimacy of Diori's ties were, however, very difficult to hide in as small a community as Niamey and especially given the highly visible nature of that 'Corsican Mafia'[45] of advisers with which he surrounded himself throughout the course of his time in office. Not a little ironically, Diori attributed much of the discontent amongst Niger's student population to what he believed were the activities of 'radical' *coopérants* from France. This situation boiled over following Pompidou's somewhat less than successful visit to Niger and the now celebrated 'Affaire Rostain'. Both incidents are well documented.[46] Their significance for this chapter lies not with details, but with the implications for Franco–Niger relations. They precipitated the first rift of the post-independence era between the new state and the former colonial power. Diori's tough stand resulted in the French using a series of technical arguments to stop the flow of aid to Niger. The incident did not, of course, take on the dimensions of the earlier rift between Guinea and France – Hamani Diori was not Sekou Touré. For the whole gamut of reasons outlined in this chapter Diori was in a 'no win' situation. He was clearly too much a product of his own historical, political and economic experience to make the kind of break with France that would have satisfied his critics at home. Indeed his closest international confidant, Houphouet-Boigny, ridiculed any such notion and publicly chided Diori for getting himself into such a confrontationist position with France. It was inevitable that Diori would back down – as he did later in 1972. The face-saver for Diori was an 'agreement in principle' from France that the two countries should renegotiate the outdated components of the *Accords de Coopération* which had governed relations since independence.[47] The importance of this agreement is minimised when put in context; France had by that time reached a similar agreement with numerous other francophone states.

While the spur to Diori's request for renegotiation was clearly domestic political pressure, there were of course strong practical reasons that both parties to the *Accords* recognised. Many facets of the agreements were in fact redundant but two areas specifically were under pressure for reform: France's role in Niger's educational system and the agreement governing the exploitation of Niger's uranium. Pressures for change in the educational system came from that section of Niger's youth that suffered most from the gap between the expectation that education brings and the disillusion that invariably follows in Africa.[48] Lacking an appreciation of French culture of the previous generation of Niger educated, this group expressed the strong desire to establish some kind of 'affirmation de la personnalité culturelle nigèrienne'. In keeping with the times the main essence of this tradition was a stronger commitment to the reassertion of Islamic values. Numbered in hundreds rather than thousands this group of mostly secondary school students were the most vitriolic opponents of Niger's ruling francophile PPN elite.

More pressing still for Diori was the need to renegotiate a more favourable uranium agreement with France. This was the major foreign policy concern of his last years in office. The process of negotiation has been discussed in detail elsewhere[49] but certain aspects of the process are germane to this chapter. When we contrast Diori's lack of success in this enterprise with the success of the military regime it illustrates very well the impact of a changing international environment on foreign policy making in a state such as Niger.

In 1972 the French Atomic Energy Commission announced a unilateral reduction in its uranium commitment to Niger. As France effectively controlled the exploitation of Niger's reserves, through article 5 of the Defence Agreement of 1961 which reserved to France 'par priorité. . . des matières premières et produits stratégiques',[50] this was a serious problem for Diori. Niger's chances of exploiting the resource without French assistance, or the prospect of securing an alternative major source of help elsewhere, were at that stage not good. The 1973 energy crisis changed the picture. The French government rushed through a rapid nuclear energy programme which ensured that Niger's uranium receipts would grow substantially. The issue for Diori was whether, in that period in which the Sahelian drought was at its most severe, such receipts would grow substantially enough, and quickly enough, to alleviate the problems faced by his government. Diori was convinced that the changing international environment would guarantee a better deal for Niger than the one to which it was currently committed. Such a deal would not only alleviate the economic distress but improve his political position by appearing to minimise the patron—client nature of his relationship with France. Unfortunately for Diori, he was overthrown by a military coup only five days before he was due to meet with French officials to renegotiate the deal.

The foreign relations of Niger since 1974

While the mix is somewhat different, the themes pursued in this last section follow on from the previous period. The major variable which distinguishes the two periods in Niger's recent history is the vast inflow

178

of funds that became available in the post-1974 period. This very important change in the political economy of Niger has enabled the military junta (Supreme Military Council — SMC) of Seyni Kountché to smoothe out some of its potential domestic political problems in a fashion that was not open to his predecessor. Diori did not have the funds at his disposal to buy off potential (and actual) pockets of opposition unlike the Kountché administration which has been able to quell much of the unrest amongst Niger's educated minority by providing funds to develop the National Islamic University in Niamey, making a substantial amount of scholarships available and allowing for a considerable expansion of the bureaucracy to provide new job opportunities, as well as increasing public service salaries. The bureaucracy grew from 15,500 in 1974 to 18,500 in 1979[51] — a substantial growth in a country the size of Niger. The uranium bonanza has also enabled the government to abolish the general tax which had been levied in the past on the whole population irrespective of income.[52] This was a measure which gave it considerable mileage with the poorer sections of the Niger peasantry that had come to dread this annual imposition.

That Kountché was able to act quite swiftly in a number of these measures was due, somewhat ironically, to the groundwork which had been laid for him by his predecessor. The renegotiation of the uranium agreement was completed within less than a year of the overthrow of the Diori regime. The changes to Niger's political economy that resulted from the new producer price for uranium were quite dramatic. Whereas groundnut production had accounted for 65 per cent of Niger's very feeble external revenue during the first decade after independence, as of 1976 uranium accounted for the same share of external revenue — but as part of a much larger absolute volume. In the heady days after 1974, uranium exports tripled and prices quintupled. Niger's GNP grew by 20 per cent in 1976; between 1971 and 1978 Niger's annual budget quadrupled from 12.5 billion CFA francs to 56.8 billion CFA francs. Such changes in the availability of economic resources did, of course, have implications way beyond the ability of the government to engage in a fairly successful process of 'pork-barrelling'. As Henry Bretton has pointed out, there is a fairly strong correlation between access to regular and recurrent capital resources and the pursuit of more independent courses of policy action in the international as well as the domestic arena.[53] Even Diori's government had managed to diversify its sources of funding with the growing support of bilateral actors such as Canada and, more importantly, multilateral actors such as the European Development Fund. The major component of the diversification under Kountché has, however, been of a different order. Over the last decade, Niger has been able to shift quite dramatically the balance between public and private investment in its enterprises.

Before the extraction of uranium, Niger was a very unattractive proposition for private investment: figures for 1967 show it ranking twelfth out of thirteen francophone states with only 150 million French francs worth of private capital investment compared with Gabon (14,200 million) and Mauritania (18,950 million), the major recipients thanks to their extractive industries. Indeed, extractive industries accounted for 53 per cent of all private investment in francophone Africa in the first decade after independence.[54] Uranium extraction, it goes without saying, is by far the largest capital project in Niger. (Over 70 per cent of all public and private investment in Niger in 1970 was in SOMAIR.) The position since 1970 has been even further consolidated and indicators of the rate of change in this area are worth looking at in comparative perspective. To this end a brief examination of the funding for Niger's post-independence development plans follows.

Niger's first major development plan (after a series of minor pilot projects) was to cover the ten-year period 1965—1974. This plan envisaged an outlay of just 97 million CFA francs of which 72 per cent has to come from public sources — particularly bilateral French and multilateral EDF aid. Only 20 per cent was to come from private or commercially generated funds.[55] In quite striking contrast, the latest development plan for the five-year period 1979—1983 envisages an outlay of 730 billion CFA francs, predicted on an annual growth rate of 9.5 per cent and of which nearly 50 per cent of the funds will come from commercial sources.[56]

Most of this vast increase in funding is *from* and *for* the continued development of Niger's uranium industry. Whilst the benefits of such forms of extractive development would be contested in some quarters, there can be no question that the uranium has changed dramatically the nature of Niger's dependence. Whatever else might be said, it is difficult not to argue that Niger is better off dependent on a high value-to-weight ratio product such as uranium rather than a low value-to-weight ratio product such as groundnuts, production of which is subject to all the vicissitudes of the Sahelian climate. While uranium prices are clearly subject to the fluctuations of the world market, the fluctuations for this mineral in years to come are likely to be less erratic than for those of a product, such as groundnuts, that is more and more the victim of substitution.

The end of the mining boom has in fact posed problems for the Niger government. The growth in its GNP has fallen steadily from its 20 per cent high in 1976 to 8 per cent in 1979 and the plan has had to be revised to take into account the shortfall brought about by the falling price of uranium on the world market as developed countries have scaled back their commitments to nuclear power.[57] Apart from its uranium reserves, steadily being revised upwards so that they are currently estimated in excess of 200,000 tons of high-grade ore,[58] Niger also has enough coal to reduce its dependence on import oil. Perhaps more importantly Niger has, over the years of the Kountché regime, managed to achieve a much greater level of food production. The increased revenue from uranium has lessened Niger's dependence on groundnuts as its major source of revenue and also allowed a substantial restructuring of agriculture towards food staples. Groundnut production has dropped from a high of 260,000 tons in 1973 to 74,000 in 1979 while cereal production has risen from 1,159,000 to 1,484,000 during the same period. 1979 saw a surplus of 20 per cent over the country's cereal needs.[59] While Niger is still importing rice at the rate of about 30,000 tons a year, one of the priorities of the five-year plan is to eliminate the rice deficit by the end of the plan. For the purposes of this chapter, the very ability of the government even to *contemplate* such a policy is more important than its success.

In a similar vein, uranium resources mean that the rail link between Niamey and Parakou in northern Dahomey — mooted since the days of colonial rule — at long last becomes a realistic proposition and other important infrastructural projects long dreamed about by the Diori government have now become questions of immediate policy concern.[60] Uranium funds have changed considerably the nature of Niger's dependence. While less reliant on financial inputs from overseas it is still, of course, extremely reliant on technological and administrative know-how. Most of this still comes from France, who is Niger's major partner in the uranium industry and will continue to be so for the foreseeable future despite the growing involvement of other industrialised countries such as Japan, West Germany and Italy. France also purchases the lion's share of the industries product — on average about 60 per cent of the total output.[61]

Niger also still relies heavily on France for support in other areas. There were, for example, 400 French *coopérants* in Niger in 1979 — more than there were just after independence.[62] Kountché's attitude to the relationship with France is less personal than that of his predecessor but still extremely pragmatic about the magnitude of Niger's continuing dependence on the former colonial power. Nowhere is this pragmatism more apparent than in the issue of Niger's security concerns. Despite the fact that his first action on coming to office after the coup in 1974 was to request the removal of the French military contingent in Niger and abrogate the defence component of the Cooperation Agreements, Kountché makes no bones about the fact that he would not hesitate to call on French military support in the instance of any threat to Niger's territorial integrity should, for example, Libya's expansionist posture in the Saharan regions become more explicit.[63]

Niger's relationship with its northern neighbour presents several paradoxes and poses several problems for Niger's foreign policy managers. As the francophone colonial heritage has receded over the first two decades of independence Niger has begun to 'float back' somewhat into a 'north of the Sahara' regional orbit. That this should be the case is not surprising given that the natural historical role of the Sahara has been that of a bridge rather than a barrier[64] and that Ghaddaffi has gone to great lengths to push the Islamic culture revival in the neighbouring states to the south. The closeness of the relationship between Niger and Libya ebbs and flows. Several factors have caused the relationship to deteriorate somewhat of late: after the very warm relationship that had existed in the last days of Diori's regime when the two countries, much to the annoyance of the unconsulted Niger officer corps, signed a defence pact. Libyan involvement in the civil war in Chad has angered considerably the military government in Niamey, who see Ghaddaffi's actions as a trial run for further Saharan expansion. Of greater concern, however, has been Libyan support for the domestic opponents of the Kountché regime. While Niger's population is predominantly Muslim it is also predominantly sub-Saharan in origin and sedantry. Niger's government has taken exception to Ghaddaffi's self-appointed role as protector of 'light skinned minorities in Sahel states governed by black regimes'.[65] In the Niger context this means the semi-nomadic Tuareg and Toubou in the north and east of the country whom Ghaddaffi also provided with financial and material inducements to join his Islamic Legion. Such policies and the behaviour of Libya's 'embassy turned People's Bureau' in Niamey are a nuisance rather than an actual threat to the security of the military regime; but they do make management of what is an important economic relationship with Libya very difficult.

Niger has two powerful weapons of its own with which to balance its relationship with Libya. First there is Niger's very close links with Algeria, Nigeria and France. For the first two states Niger plays an important geographical and cross-cultural bridging role and for the third it is, of course, the provider of nearly 50 per cent of future uranium requirements. Both factors would ensure Niger substantial support against any Libyan attempts to infringe Niger's sovereignty. More important, however, Niger has been the major provider of Libya's own uranium 'requirements'. Niger sold Libya 258, 150 and 180 tons of ore in 1978, 1979 and 1980 respectively before announcing that it would cease sales as a reprisal against the activities of the People's Bureau in Niamey in early 1981.[66] That year, however, saw Niger — as the world's fifth largest uranium producer — with a record 4,500 tons of ore. France, West Germany, Italy, Spain, the United States and Japan took most of this but Niger still had 800 tons plus of uranium ore unsold. Niger subsequently sold 1,212 tons to Libya.[67] Despite Kountché's desire to demonstrate his opposition to his neighbour's interference in Niger's internal affairs by withholding supplies, the lure of Libya's money, in a year when uranium prices were considerably down on the world market, proved too great. It must not be lost sight of, uranium bonanza notwithstanding, that Niger is still one of the world's poorest countries. Despite Kountché's pronouncements about uranium providing Niger with the opportunity for leverage in international affairs[68] it will be a long time before politics will be allowed to take precedence over economic necessity.

Similarly south of Niger, the economic realities of Niger's more 'natural' relationship with Nigeria continue to grow at the expense of the manufactured political legacy of colonialism. The bonds formed between Niamey and Lagos during the civil war have flourished. Fears of support from Sawaba from Nigeria's northern Hausa are a thing of the past and Kountché and President Shagari, himself a northerner, are known to be strong friends. The last decade has also seen a substantial amount of economic cooperation between the two countries.[69] While Ivory Coast may no longer have as great an influence over Niger as in the days when Diori and Houphouet-Boigny were close confidants, the relationship is still strong; and to say that the political legacies of a shared francophone experience may be diminishing is not the same as saying they have disappeared. Indeed, and not a little ironically, the CEAO is probably stronger now in a political sense than at its inception. There is strong evidence that it operates as a pressure group within ECOWAS to counter the influence of Nigeria. Ralph Onwuka has suggested that it was CEAO opposition that forced Nigeria to terminate its peacekeeping activities in Chad in 1979[70] − such is the enduring impact of colonialism.

Conclusion

This chapter has emphasised that, despite the vast continuity between the colonial and post-colonial eras, decolonisation − the granting of formal political independence − has made a difference to Niger's position in the global political economy. At the level of contingency, as the colonial era receded, a diversification in Niger's foreign relations and the potentiality for some kind of semi-independent policy initiative on the part of Niger's two regimes to date has emerged − albeit within the structural situation, the rules of which were established with the institutionalisation of the former colonial territory as the post-independence state. At the specific level I have tried to show how difficult it was for the first generation political rulers of Niger to alter *substantially* their relationship with the former colonial power, equipped as they were with the paraphernalia of the socialisation processes of French colonialism. While still strong, such socialisational processes weighed less heavily on the members of the military regime which replaced Hamani Diori and the PPN. The attitude of the military government to the former colonial power in the period under review was guided more by pragmatic considerations and less by emotional ones. Despite what we might call the 'two steps forward, one step back' flavour of the diminishing of these ties it would seem not unfair, on the basis of our examination of the first two decades of post-independence foreign policy in Niger, to expect a continuance of this diversification process in the third.

Notes

1 Colin Leys, 'Capital Accumulation, Class Formation and Dependency: The Significance of the Kenyan Case', *Socialist Register, 1978* (London: Merlin, 1978) pp. 251–253.

2 Timothy M. Shaw and Olajide Aluko, 'Introduction: towards a political economy of African foreign policy', this volume.

3 See especially Zdenek Cervenka (ed.), *Land-Locked Countries of Africa*, (Uppsala: Scandinavian Institute of African Studies, 1973) and Hendril Reisma, 'Africa's Land-Locked Countries: A Study of Dependency Relations', *Tijdschrift voor Econ. en Soc. Geographie*, vol. 71, no. 2, 1980.

4 See, for example, Douglas Anglin and Timothy Shaw, *Zambia's Foreign Policy: Studies in Diplomacy and Dependency*, (Boulder: Westview, 1979).

5 But for full justifications of this position on my part see Richard Higgott, 'Structural Dependence and Decolonisation in a West African Land-Locked State: The Case of Niger', *Review of African Political Economy*, no. 17, July–August 1980, pp.43–58 and my Ph.D. thesis, *Colonial Origins and Environmental Influences on the Foreign Relations of a West African Land-Locked State: The Case of Niger* (University of Birmingham, Centre of West African Studies, 1979).

6 The essentially 'learning experience' characteristic of early African foreign policy is discussed in William I. Zartman, *International Relations in the New Africa* (Englewood Cliffs: Prentice Hall, 1966), chapter 2.

7 On the highly personalised nature of the foreign policy-making process in Niger under Hamani Diori see Higgott, *Colonial Origins*

and Environmental Influences on the Foreign Relations of a West African Land-Locked State (note 5), pp. 226—242.

8   There is now a vast body of secondary literature on the origins and growth of francophone regional organisations in West Africa: see, F. Wodie, *Les Institutions Internationales Régionales en Afrique Occidentale et Centrale* (Paris: Librarie Général de Droit et de Jurisprudence, 1970); Pierre Biarnes, 'De L'AOF au Conseil de l'Entente', *Revue Française d'Etudes Politiques Africaines*, no. 34, October, 1969; Albert Tevoedjre, *Pan-Africanism in Action: An Account of UAM* (Cambridge: Harvard University, Centre for International Studies, 1965, Occasional Paper II) and Abdul Jalloh, *Political Integration in French Speaking West Africa* (Berkeley: Institute of International Studies, University of California, 1973).

9   For a discussion of the activities of Sawaba see, Georges Chaffard, *Les Carnets Secrets de la Decolonisation* (Paris: Calmann-Levy, 1967) pp. 269—302; Virginia Thompson, 'Niger', in G. Carter (ed.) *National Unity and Regionalism in Eight African States*, (Ithaca: Cornell University Press, 1966) and Finn Fuglestad, 'Djibo Bakary, the French and the Referendum of 1958 in Niger', *Journal of African History*, vol. 14, no. 3, 1973, pp. 131—330.

10 See J.P. Morrillon, 'La Tentative Insurrectionelle du Sawaba au Niger', *Est et Ouest*, no. 342, May 1965, p. 20; Gilbert Comte, 'Un Plan de Déstruction du Niger', *France/Eurafrique*, no. 161, April 1965, pp. 9—10 and 'Ou en est le Niger', *France/Eurafrique*, no. 175, July 1966, p. 11 and Anon 'Subversion and Sawaba' *West Africa*, 22 July 1977, p. 943.

11 Specifically on the formation of OCAM see inter alia, 'La Naissance de l'OCAM', *Afrique Contemporaine*, vol. 18, March 1965, pp. 2—9; Bernard Kalonji, 'De l'UAM a l'OCAM' *Etudes Congolaises*, July—August 1965, pp. 78—82; Victor Dubois, 'The Search for Unity in French Speaking Africa: The Birth of OCAM', *American Universities Field Staff Reports — West Africa Series*, vol. 8 no. 3, 1965, pp. 1—19 and Max Jalade, 'Nouakchott; Naissance de l'OCAM', *France/Eurafrique*, no. 160, March 1965.

12 For details of the nature of such support see *le Rapport d'Activité Pour 1971 du Fonds d'Entraide et de Garantie des Emprunts du Conseil de l'Entente* (Abidjan: Secrétariat Administratif du Fonds, 1972).

13 For a general discussion of Niger's foreign policy in this period see Alain Faujas, 'La Politique Etrangère du Niger', *Revue Française d'Etudes Politiques Africaines*, no. 72, December 1971.

14 I have discussed this issue in detail in Higgott, *Colonial Origins and Environmental Influences* (note 5), pp. 356—368. Of the numer-

ous secondary sources see inter alia, 'Hamani Diori's Progress', *West Africa*, 12 October 1968, p. 1212 and 'l'Ambassade Extraordinaire de Hamani Diori auprès des Six', *Jeune Afrique*, no. 408, 28 October 1968.

15 For general discussion of these problems see: William Foltz, *From French West Africa to the Mali Federation* (New Haven: Yale University Press, 1965) and Elliott Berg, 'The Economic Basis of Political Choice in French Speaking West Africa' in W.J. Hanna (ed.), *Independent Black Africa: the politics of freedom* (Chicago: Rand McNally, 1964).

16 *Special Problems of Land-Locked States* (UNCTAD, TD/B/308, June 1970) and *A Transport Strategy for Land-Locked Developing Countries*, (UNCTAD, TD/B/453 Add.I nd.).

17 *Organisation Commune Dahomey Niger* (Paris: COGERAF, République Française, 1960 and *Directory of Intergovernmental Organisations in Africa* (Addis Ababa, E/CN. 14/CEC/1/Rev. 1, June 1972).

18 For general discussions of these issues see the PhD thesis of John Collins, *Government and Groundnut Marketing in Rural Hausa Niger* (Baltimore: Johns Hopkins University, SAIS, 1974) and Yves Péhaut, 'L'Arachide au Niger', *Etudes d'Economie Africaine* (Bordeaux: Centre d'Etudes Africaines, 1970) pp. 15–34.

19 For the competing perspectives on the dispute see *Livre Blanc sur Les Relations du Niger et Dahomey à la Fin de 1963* (Naimey: République du Niger, 1964) and *Ce Qu'il faut Savoir sur la Crise Daho–Nigérienne* (Cotonou: République de Dahomey, December 1963). For analysis see Higgott, *Colonial Origins and Environmental Influences* (note 5), pp. 284–287.

20 The nature of the disruption is discussed in detail in official reports. See *L'Evaucation des Arachides du Niger pour la Compagne 1966–67* (Paris: Sécrétariat d'Etat des Affaires Africaine et Malgache, nd.) and *Rapport de l'Administration de SONARA* (Niamey: mimeo, 1967).

21 Higgott, *Colonial Origins and Environmental Influences* (note 5), Table 23; data compiled on the export of groundnuts from Niger by the monthly reports of the *Banque Centrale des Etats de l'Afrique Occidentale: Comptes Economique*.

22 Of the numerous studies of the improvement of transport links between Dahomey and Niger see J. Delorme and P. Trocme, *Etude de Synthèse sur le Transport au Niger* (Paris: SEDES, 1967).

23 See John Collins, 'The Clandestine Movement of Groundnuts Across the Niger–Nigeria Boundary', mimeo, 1975.

24 See Derek Thom, *The Niger–Nigerian Borderlands: a study of*

ethnic frontiers and colonial boundaries (Athens: Ohio University International Studies Centre, 1975. Africa Series no. 23) pp. 34–41.

25 Collins, 'The Clandestine Movement of Groundnuts' (note 23), pp. 8–9.

26 *Bulletin de l'Afrique Noire*, 13 November 1970, p. 11570.

27 *Africa Confidential*, vol. 12, no. 7, 2 April 1971, p. 4; for a general discussion of the varying francophone responses see G. Aforka-Nweke, 'External Intervention in African Conflicts: France and French Speaking Africa in the Nigerian Civil War', (Boston: African Studies Centre, 1976, Working Papers in African Studies, no. 2).

28 On the demise of OCAM see V.T. Dubois, 'Crisis in OCAM', *American Universities Field Staff Reports West Africa Series*, vol. 14, no. 2, 1972; Tamar Golan, 'OCAM in 1972: The Crisis in Francophone Africa's Politics', *African Contemporary Record: Volume 5, 1972–1973 A57–A64* Pierre Bernetel, 'OCAM – Et Après?', *Jeune Afrique*, 6 May 1972, pp. 14–17.

29 'Diori Speaks Out', *West Africa*, 25 December 1972, p. 1733.

30 Higgott, *Colonial Origins and Environmental Influences* (note 5), pp. 368–374 discusses the growth of this relationship.

31 On the important role of Nigeria see Isabell Gruhn, 'The Lomé Convention: Inching Towards Interdependence', *International Organisation*, vol. 30, no. 2.

32 See Nicholas Hutton, 'Sources of Strain in the Eurafrican Association', *International Studies*, vol. 4, no. 3, 1972, p. 290.

33 On the impact of the drought see Edmund Bernus, 'La Sécheresse en République du Niger', *Symposium on Drought in Africa* (University of London, School of Oriental and African Studies, July 1973, mimeo); Elliot Berg, *The Economic Impact of Drought and Inflation in the Sahel* (Michigan: Center for Research on Economic Development, University of Michigan, 1976, discussion paper no. 51). On the political impact of drought for Diori's government see Richard Higgott and Finn Fuglestad, 'The Coup d'Etat in Niger: Towards an Explanation', *Journal of Modern African Studies*, vol. 13, no. 3, September 1975, pp. 389–393.

34 'Mission Française d'Aide et de Coopération', *Niger 1971–1972: Dossier d'Information Economique* (Paris: Sécrétariat d'Etat aux Affaires Etrangères, Direction de l'Aide au Dévéloppement, October 1973), Appendix 74.

35 *Annuaire Statistique de l'Afrique Occidentale Française* (Dakar, 1955) Vol. 5, Part 3, pp. 86, 106 and ff.

36 See *Les Premières 500 Sociétés d'Afrique Noire* (Paris: La Documentation Française, 1970), pp. 291–298 for the composition of

investment and of the boards of Niger's parastatals. Information about the membership of the PPN politburo can be found in *Répértoire de l'Administration Africaine* (Paris: Ediafric, 1971), passim.

37 I have discussed this issue elsewhere. See Richard Higgott, *Political Development Theory: the contemporary debate* (New York: St Martins Press, 1983) chapter 3.

38 Obtaining an accurate picture of aid to Niger is a complicated process entailing the use of a variety of sources. The figures in the text are explained and justified in detail in Higgott, *Colonial Origins and Environmental Influences* (note 5), pp. 336–346.

39 Obtaining accurate data on trade is as complicated a process as that for aid. The basic statistical sources are the *Banque Centrale des Etats de l'Afrique Occidentale: Comptes Economiques*, the *Bulletin de l'Afrique Noire* and *Le Niger 1971–1972*, see Higgott, *Colonial Origins and Environmental Influences*.

40 *Bulletin de l'Afrique Noire*, 19 January 1972, p. 13178.

41 Higgott, *Colonial Origins and Environmental Influences*, Table 30, p. 350.

42 *Ibid*., Table 31, p. 351.

43 See 'Le Rapport Gorse', *Revue Française d'Etudes Politiques Africaines*, no. 104, August 1974.

44 For general discussions of the relationship see R.O. Matthews, 'Canada's Relations with Africa', *International Journal*, vol. 30, no. 3, Summer 1975, pp. 536–568; Louis Sabour in 'Le Canada et l'Afrique', *Revue Française d'Etudes Politiques Africaines*, no. 55, July 1970; Tamar Golan, 'Canada's Friendly Invasion', *West Africa*, 17 October 1970, p. 1217 and Philippe Cheramy, 'Les Canadiens ont des Projects Ambitieux pour le Dévéloppement du Niger', *France/Eurafrique*, no. 222, October 1970, p. 30.

45 See Chaffard, *Les Carnets Secrets de la Decolonisation* (note 9), p. 305.

46 See Tamar Golan, 'Niger – 1972: the year of the showdown', *West Africa*, 22 September 1972, p. 1249.

47 The 'accords de coopération' have never been published in full. The most detailed outline of their contents appears in a French government sponsored publication by Maurice Ligot, *Les Accords de Coopération entre la France et les Etats Africaines et Malgaches d'Expression Française* (Paris, La Documentation Française, n.d.).

48 'La Crise de Coopération Franco–Africaine', *Revue Française d'Etudes Politiques Africaines*, no. 90, June 1973, p. 102.

49 Higgott and Fuglestad, 'The Coup d'Etat in Niger' (note 33), pp. 391–392.

50 Ligot, *Les Accords de Coopération* (note 47), p. 91.

51 *Africa Contemporary Record Volume 12, 1979/80*, B573–574.
52 *West Africa*, 9 July 1979, p. 1211.
53 Henry Bretton, *Power and Politics in Africa* (London: Longman, 1973), p. 20.
54 *Bulletin de l'Afrique Noire*, 13 November 1969, p. 11586.
55 *Ibid.*, 8 April 1970, p. 11994.
56 *West Africa*, 28 April 1981, p. 731.
57 *Ibid.*, 5 January 1981, p. 11.
58 *Ibid.*, 9 July 1979, p. 1211.
59 *Le Monde*, 10 January 1981, p. 5.
60 *West Africa*, 28 April 1981, p. 731.
61 *Africa Contemporary Record Volume 12, 1979/80*, B578–579.
62 *Ibid.* B576 and Higgott *Colonial Origins and Environmental Influences*, p. 338.
63 *West Africa*, 9 February 1981, p. 270.
64 See William Zartman, 'The Sahara: Bridge or Barrier?' *International Conciliation*, January 1963.
65 Phillipe Decreane, 'Niger and its Neighbours: countering Ghaddaffi's influence', *The Guardian Weekly,* 1 February 1981, p. 12.
66 *West Africa*, 9 February 1981, p. 270.
67 *Christian Science Monitor*, 2 December 1981, p. 12.
68 *West Africa*, 9 July 1979, p. 1210.
69 *Africa Contemporary Record, Volume 12, 1979/80* B576 and M.R. Ofeogbu, 'Nigeria and its Neighbours', 12 July 1979, p. 6.
70 Ralph Onwuka, 'The ECOWAS Treaty: inching towards interdependence', *The World Today*, vol. 36, no. 2, February 1980, p. 57.

8 Nigeria

Olatunde J. B. Ojo

Two salient and apparently contradictory features have marked Nigeria's external relations since its independence in 1960: continuity and change. First, despite several changes in regime-leadership and regime-type – the latest swing being from President Shagari's democratic re-election and subsequent forceable overthrow at the end of 1983 – there has been an amazing continuity in the substance of foreign policy. True, most analysts find the performance of each succeeding regime to be so much more dynamic than its predecessor's as to constitute a 'new foreign policy'.[1] But differences in dynamism reflect only changes of a cosmetic nature; they are merely changes of style. Fundamentally, Nigeria's external relations have remained *status quo* in orientation. Relations with transnational and international interests; both public and private, have continued unchanged except in degree and even this appears to follow a natural progression; to this extent, 1984 is not so different from either 1974 or 1964.

Similar continuity (in substance) and change (of degree) have been discernible in both political economy and strategies of development. There have been changes in the size, composition and structure of the ruling class, in the rate of growth and development of the economy, and in the mode and style of development planning. But along with these changes are persistent and unchanging social relations of production, increasing salience of state capitalism and state-financed 'free' enterprise, as well as continued and expanded incorporation into the global economy. Put another way, the political economy is *status quo*-oriented, based as it is on a neo-colonial capitalist order within the parameters of which elite formation is sanctioned and sustained. Continuity in the substance of foreign policy is not unrelated to continuity in the political economy, and attempts will be made in this chapter to analyse that relationship.

The second salient feature of Nigeria's external relations has been the increasing focus on and active, often decisive, role in regional and continental affairs, despite continued and expanded incorporation into the global economy. In the early 1960s Nigeria aspired to (and indeed was expected 'to assume) the leadership of Africa which it regarded, and still regards, as its birthright on account of its size.[2] But it failed in this bid and played second fiddle to Ghana (see Chapter 4), less because of insufficient economic capabilities (important though these were) than because of intra-class and concomitant transnational linkage struggles.[3] Such class conflicts at one and the same time made the state a relatively autonomous actor (because very marginal to the process of social formations) in matters of foreign policy while deflating its power to act. Since the mid-1960s, and especially after its civil war, the 'colossus with the feet of clay' or 'the sleeping giant of Africa' as Nigeria was derisively referred to, has gained a pre-eminent standing continentally and internationally and, in contrast to its earlier marginality, has become 'the most powerful black African state',[4] the 'first major black power in modern international politics'.[5]

This increasing continental influence and global respectability may be the product, as some have argued, of Nigeria's control of valued sulphur-free petroleum which gives it strategic importance globally and of the attendant petro-dollars which enable it to surpass in GNP all the other black African states put together. If so, Nigeria's status will be as ephemeral as its petroleum and will fluctuate with the fortunes of oil in the international market. All the same, continental influence and global respect in the face of a deepening incorporation into and dependence on the global capitalist economy represents an anomaly. For while oil revenues have led to great affluence, deepening incorporation and dependency have increased underdevelopment, conjointly producing what one scholar aptly calls 'affluence and underdevelopment'.[6] That such an economy should be accorded 'greatness' in international politics is a contradiction in terms unless of course we are dealing with an illusion of greatness. Why this anomaly?

This chapter attempts to answer this question and relate it to the nature of continuity and change in political economy and foreign policy. It begins with the premise that structural conditions arising from the incorporation of Nigeria into the global capitalist system have given rise to dependent social formations which provide the historical dynamic in the evolution of the Nigerian state and political economy and, therefore, in external relations too. The process of social formation had, over time, called into existence regional, transnational and national—nationalistic bourgeoisies each with its conflicting occupational interest groups, bureaucratic, commercial/industrial, and technical/worker elements. The origins of these social formations, the initial instrumental role of international interests and later of the state in their development as well as the pattern of their interactions all determine the composition, structure and politico-economic orientation of those who exercise state power; therefore they are of interest in this analysis. Arising from this, I am interested in the links between those in power and their development objectives and strategies; in the impact of the latter on foreign policy; and in the consequences of such policy both for developmental objectives as well as for domestic politics.

My argument is that continuity in the substance and change in the style of foreign relations and political economy are the product of interactions both between the global economy and the Nigerian state and between the latter and domestic social formations. Because the global economy has presented the same conditions and restraints to successive governing groups, who eschew fundamental change in the political economy but rather share the same basic approach, objectives and strategy of development,[6] the responses have been the same: continuity in the search for 'multiple entry visas' into the global economy rather than 'exit visas'.[7] In practical terms this has meant pragmatism, restraint, and a cautious foreign policy of non-confrontation with major powers except over emotionally-charged matters such as colonialism and apartheid.

On the other hand because each succeeding governing group has had different kinds of relationships with domestic socio-economic formations, there have been differences in tactics and style which individual personalities and the opportunities available to the leaders serve only to exacerbate. Where the social formations were inchoate (as in the colonial era) or looked to state (regional) governments for the protection of their economic interests (as in the terminal and immediate post-colonial years) the powers of the Nigerian state (central 'federal' government) were circumscribed (*vis-à-vis* the regional governments) especially in economic matters. The national state merely pretended to act as a referee of economic life while the groups most 'conscious of their distinct interests and better organised to advance them' — the regional governments — regulated the politico-economic scene and thus politicised economic life.[8] There was little to be lost, therefore, in leaving the national state with a relatively free hand to pursue unfettered, if inconsequential, foreign policy (subject only to global constraints). This explains why it was possible in the early post-colonial years that 'external economic influences [should] profoundly affect the Nigerian domestic economy [but] their impact in Nigerian foreign policy [was] a better clue to an understanding of Nigerian foreign policy than crude economic determinism'.[9]

But as the Nigerian state becomes adolescent and increasingly more powerful *vis-à-vis* regional governments, as tends to happen in all federal states, there is a shift in focus towards the national government in social groups' competition for benevolence. In consequence, the national state is further strengthened. It is thus able to use social formations for its own end rather than the other way round. As the fortunes of businesses, communities and households come to hinge on its favour, the national state is able to play one social group against the other and against agents of international forces who count on its benevolence. It can thus exercise a higher degree of tactical and stylistic flexibility in foreign policy. Because the national state now is critically relevant to ongoing socio-economic formations its power becomes, as it were, inflated. This explains the fierce competition described by Terisa Turner[10] among the citizens — both national and transnational elements — as well as those international groups seeking access to the national economy or otherwise seeking to buy official goodwill. The state, in turn, tends to behave in accordance with its inflated power. There is occasional tough talking, militant style and illusions of grandeur; as, for example, the concern about developing military technology including nuclear weapons to match the capabilities of 'our country's main enemy on the African continent'.[11]

The shift in power and in the relevant social groups' focus on the federal level soon leads to the creation of a national (as opposed to regional) bourgeoisie. This process of 'nationalisation of the Nigerian political class',[12] however, excludes elements of the state-based and state-oriented (regional) bourgeoisie in addition to the transnational and international socio-economic group. As these social formations come into their own, competition among them for state benevolence changes into a fierce struggle to *control* the state apparatus itself. The previous roles are thus reversed and the state truly becomes the classic agent (rather than the creator) of the dominant social group.

Nigeria appears to be entering this stage as it moves from the periphery of the global capitalist system into the semi-periphery. But the deeper incorporation into the global system and the consequent initial shift in the struggle for control of state power in favour of trans-national *vis-à-vis* national socio-economic groups begins at this point to impose greater external constraints on foreign policy. The previous inflation of state power is revealed in its stark nakedness. Style becomes congruent with substance and with realism. This development, of course, incenses the national bourgeoisie all the more; it makes them even more nationalistic and gears them to seek control of state power by all means, thus increasing the chances of political instability.[13] These historical and emergent phases of Nigeria's political economy and foreign policy will now be discussed in detail.

The colonial inheritance

By the time of its political independence in 1960 Nigeria had had nearly 120 years of differential contact with and incorporation into the global economy. At different times, by different agencies and through different instruments the North, the East and the West were acquired, administered and transformed 'from an almost entirely subsistence economy to a predominantly money economy', geared towards exports. Each area became monocultural – the North with groundnuts, the East with palm products and the West with cocoa. Around these commodities grew new elites (commercial, administrative/clerical and professional), a new 'civilisation' called 'modernity', and a new 'nationalism' (regionalism).[14]

In spite of the 1914 amalgamation which created Nigeria, in spite of the colonial government's economic and fiscal policies aimed at maintaining unity in order to further British economic interests, and in spite of other attempts to create 'Nigerians' out of a motley crowd of tribal 'kingdoms', Nigeria emerged at independence as a federation of North, East and West regions (states), each being a veritable nation-state. It is significant in this context that the East and West became self-governing in 1957, a status acquired by the North in 1959 and by Nigeria itself only a year later.

Thus by accident of historical acquisition and the changing imperative of administrative convenience, an elite class was created; but it was internally divided on regional/ethnic lines. Fiercely competitive within each other for the development, control and share of their region's resources, and engaged in bitter struggles between each other for the lion's share of federal resources for their regions, this bourgeoisie – itself already incorporated into the global system by education, occupation and employment (often without the benefit of colonial state intervention) – sought regional administrative apparatuses which they could eventually control.[15]

For the Nigerian state, which already had the problem of not only being on the periphery of the global economic nexus but also of being subordinated to external economic forces which it could not control,

194

the regional apparatuses and the tremendous economic resources available to them[16] were formidable additional sources and symbols of weakness. The slogan of the time is instructive: 'East for the Easterners, West for the Westerners, North for the Northerners and Nigeria for nobody.' In that slogan the place of the regions as the key centres of political, administrative and financial power is underscored, the national state playing second fiddle to them:

> the regions were so large and powerful as to consider themselves self-sufficient and almost entirely independent. The Federal Government which ought to give lead to the whole country was relegated to the background. The people were not made to realise that the Federal Government was the real government of Nigeria.[17]

However, Sir Abubakar Tafawa Balewa, the first Prime Minister, understood the implications of this situation for the type of relations Nigeria could conduct with the external world.

The Balewa era

The structure of power under Balewa (1960–1966) was based on an uneasy coalition of two political parties. One – the NPC – represented the Northern aristocracy, was organised on a patron–client basis, and utilised the philosophy of 'One North, One People, One Destiny' to amass its electoral strength. The other – the NCNC – led by highly educated, upwardly mobile professionals and paraprofessionals, was truly a mass party; but basically it represented the interests of the Eastern elite, although it had a mass following in the West. Left out of the coalition was the Action Group, conglomerate of wealthy cocoa farmers, merchants and professionals and paraprofessionals who successfully intimidated chiefly authorities in the West into an uncanny alliance, using them to establish linkages with the rural peasantries. It thus basically represented the Western elite but it capitalised on minority ethnic sentiments to establish footholds in parts of the North and the East.[18]

Given this configuration of elites and structures of power, Balewa perceived the major task as state- and nation-building.[19] He had an appropriate reverence for the democratic political process and the personality – one 'calculated (more) to placate than to provoke' as well as the 'knack for compromises'[20] – to enable him to succeed. His conception of leadership – a legacy of his own experience of upward mobility in the highly ascription-oriented North – was a 'professional or bureaucratic (one), based on demonstrated ability and objective achievement, a belief in. . .meritocracy'. But he was also captivated by the traditional Northern quality of personalism and allegiance (which gave him the opportunity for education and upward mobility in the first place) and by deference to a traditional aristocratic conception of leadership.[21] Thus he was 'conservative' by upbringing and 'radical' by training, experience and conviction. This dichotomy expressed itself in a world-view that spelled gradualism, pragmatism and an insatiable belief in broad-based government, which affected his political style. Ultimately this dichotomy helped to thwart his effectiveness as it led, in the critical later years, to *laissez-faire* policy.

Meanwhile, Balewa's development strategy had to take into account not only the need for state- and nation-building but also the educational backwardness of the region that provided the senior coalition partner and the need to catch up fast in this area with the East and the West. Balewa's approach was dual: forge unity of the regional elites politically and within this induced framework of unity to work out and propel industrialisation at a pace that was optional for all the regions.

Thus foreign policy was not only an instrument of Balewa's for state- and nation-building but also an essential instrument for moulding a new political economy out of inter-elite forces. The interests which the NCNC and the Action Group represented needed to attract foreign capital and investment and yet they also loathed it for its potential to deepen their dependence.[22] This dilemma arises from the nature and the objective of the middle class which they represented. As Ukpabi Asika rightly observed, this middle class, unlike its classic counterpart, is a dependent, non-autonomous and derived class that does not own the means of production and is merely managerial rather than entrepreneuril in its activity. Yet it is this class that finds itself suddenly endowed with the function of governing. Not unnaturally it finds its status 'structurally contradictory' and determines to redress it by transforming itself from a governing into a ruling class:

> they deplore their derived and dependent status and as Africans they identify with the masses, their poverty and over-exploitation by alien-capitalists, and thus they evince some structural honesty and favour economic nationalism. As a class dependent on foreign capitalists for the maintenance and expansion of their class, they actively solicit foreign exploitation of their country. Frightened and dazzled by the scale and power of the alien-capitalists, they are forced to espouse socialism; but frightened, no less, by the precariousness of their status they seek to use their control of state power to consolidate and reinforce their position, to promote the growth of their classes as indigenous capitalists.[23]

The Northern counterparts, for their part, also needed foreign capital and investment along with modern education to enable them to catch up with the other regions; and yet they were hostile to it for its consequences on the feudal system of their region.

For Balewa, the dilemma between economic nationalism and the need for foreign investment to spur industrialisation entailed minimum foreign activity beyond that of direct concern to developmental objectives. The overall strategy therefore was a mixture of balanced dependence and state capitalism. The former was aimed at reducing Nigeria's inherited dependence on Britain through diversification of financial, trade and technical links with the EEC, North America, Eastern Europe and the countries of the Third World along with maximum use of United Nations agencies and the World Bank group.[24] On the one hand, it was hoped that this range of linkages would allow the new state some leverage and a feeling of 'independence'. State capitalism, on the other hand, aimed at not only providing infra- structures but also investment seedlings for 'nurture capitalism' in the form of infant industries which could be turned over to private entre- preneurs after a gestation period.

Balewa's balanced dependence-cum-state capitalism, however, entailed a rather active, pragmatic, inward-looking and limited set of foreign initiatives that tended to fit his personality. Politically, foreign policy revolved around non-alignment, pan-African leadership struggle and the issues of colonialism and racism. Nigeria's continental role was the critical concern. This was because Nigeria's leadership in Africa would in part reinforce foreign confidence in Nigeria's ability and capability, so attracting needed economic aid and investment, and in part instil confidence in Nigerians themselves about their state, thus helping in the task of effective state- and nation-building.

Economically, initiatives were directed at developing new trade links, encouraging foreign investments in import-substitution industries and in agriculture, attracting new economic and technical assistance, and giving economic, political and technical assistance to needy African countries, especially those fighting colonialism and apartheid. Militarily efforts were directed to diversifying sources of weapons and training. One major initiative – the Anglo-Nigerian Defence Pact – was aimed at forging political unity among elite groups as we shall presently see.

The limited range of foreign policy content and the limited scope of its strategy entailed minimal expansion in the machinery for the con- duct of external relations; but several reorganisations for greater efficiency were undertaken[25] and commercial representation was strengthened.[26] Similarly, minimal restructuring of either levels or partners in Nigeria's foreign interactions was effected. In terms of vertical links with the industrialised world, Balewa strengthened links with continental Western Europe at the expense of Britain though the latter was not neglected especially in the context of the Commonwealth which Balewa consistently sought to strengthen.[27] Links were also established with the Soviet bloc.

On the local plane, Nigeria's coalition network centred on its immediate and other West African neighbours[28] and on regional associations such as the Monrovia group; and it was directed at a functional approach to the realisation and institutionalisation of pan-Africanism. This meant that real contacts with the other more militant African states led by Ghana were intensely competitive, culminating in the formation and subsequent politics of the OAU.[29] Little effort was directed at fostering links with other non-aligned groups aside from the Middle East and Commonwealth countries and except within the United Nations forum.

Within this framework, Nigeria clearly remained independent on vertical ties. While this led to widespread criticism[30] and created domestic problems, it helped Balewa to accumulate continental and extra-continental influence which enabled him successfully to surmount the acrimonious Ghana—Nigeria rivalry and to deflate Nkrumah's claim to African leadership.[31] But the pay-off in terms of Nigeria's political economy was dismal. Vertical ties resulted in minimal external public aid, although Balewa had counted on those ties for about half of the £654 million public expenditures envisaged in the 1962–68 National Development Plan. At the end of Balewa's regime only £168 million had been offered and £140 million actually disbursed from these sources with another £63 million coming from international financial institutions (the World Bank, the IDA and the IFC) and the United Nations Special Fund.[32] External private investment, however, flowed in massively as Nigeria then appeared a model country for stability, moderation and liberal democracy. Thus whereas the first Development Plan had anticipated that just over 50 per cent of the planned £389.5 million private investment would come from external sources, by 1968 and despite the civil war foreign private investment in depreciated fixed assets, it had reached £350 million![33]

The inflow of foreign private capital meant deeper incorporation of the economy into global capitalism. The multinationals shifted their activities into mining, construction and manufacturing. New subsidiaries sprang up in the rush to help Nigeria bring about the miracle of industrial development.[34] Although Nigerians themselves were active — increasing their ownership in the manufacturing sector which was virtually nil in 1960 to 30 per cent in 1967[35] — foreigners dominated the coveted import-substitution industries and, indeed, commerce as a whole. And the shortfall in external public aid meant that the state could not fully assist citizens in realising their dreams of indigenisation and Nigerianisation as was being done in the Public Service.

The consequences of this for the political economy were far-reaching. First, the contradictions between domestic political ends and economic needs and strategy, and between stress on foreign investment and hostility towards foreign capital, widened increasingly.

Second, the national state, despite shortfalls in the implementation of its strategy, was much better off than the regions and waxed ever stronger. For one thing it was expected to account for roughly 61 per cent of the planned expenditure of the Development Plan, excluding grants and loans to the regions. Its own shortfall therefore hit the regions even harder, especially as the effect of the downswing in the terms of trade of primary commodities which began around 1954 was now beginning to result in sharp declines of regional revenue and, therefore, in budgetary deficits. And yet the authority to raise external as well as internal loans was vested in the national state which under the Banking Amendment Act of 1962 was also in a position to control the regional marketing boards and, through the latter, the financial policies of the regional governments.[36]

And third, as the multinationals increasingly knocked on the door to enter the Nigerian economy in a big way, alliances were struck with the national authorities which further strengthened them *vis-à-vis* the regions. From about 1962–63, therefore, large sectors of the bourgeoisie who formerly allied their interests with the fortunes of regional governments began to shift their allegiance. The shift was most conspicuous in the Action Group. It was epitomised in the Akintola–Awolowo rift which centred on whether the party should accept to be incorporated into the coalition government and enjoy 'federal booty' as Akintola wanted or should remain in the opposition in the belief that this 'would help strengthen the Action Group' as Awolowo believed.[37] This shift not only destroyed the Action Group; it also affected, as we shall presently see, Balewa's single most important defence initiative — the Anglo–Nigerian Defence Pact — and initiated the beginning of the end of Nigeria's First Republic.

The shift of interest towards the federal centre was not, however, for the latter's own sake. It was primarily to capture a 'share of the national cake' or 'federal booty' for the regional bourgeoisie and thus the contribution this could make in the intra-class but inter-regional struggles for dominance. In a struggle where one of the immediate objectives was to grab as much as possible for one's group, corruption became a valued instrument and hence rampant. The coalition government itself became ineffective. The various political and administrative heads of ministries naturally saw issues from the point of view of regional–ethnic class advantages and personal gains (especially lucrative kick-backs from lavish contract awards). The Cabinet became a forum for quarrels among its members, some of whom were hardly on speaking terms. Some ministers would support government policies in parliament but criticise them in public meetings or leak damaging information when they disagreed with a course of action.[38] This division sank deeper even to the level of civil servants and the military, which soon became politicised.

The entire political process increasingly assumed the character of tentativeness in the sense that decisions were based on a flexible coalition among diverse regional interest groups and were subject to revision any time. In the absence of routinised means of conflict resolution in policy making, policy adjustments were worked out between Balewa and individual ministers: 'Once a Minister was in agreement with the Prime Minster policy was made.'[39] Naturally there were struggles for *les beaux yeux* of the Prime Minister which gave him some measure of a free hand. Hence the general tone and direction of policy, especially foreign policy, reflected his character and personality: a rock of stability in a sea of swirling coalitions.

But foreign policy effectiveness was thwarted as ministers in the various ministries concerned with policy implementation − External Affairs, Finance, Economic Development, Education, Information, Trade and Industry, Defence, etc. − interpreted and implemented overall policy to suit their whims and purposes. Thus Balewa's strategy of balanced dependence, expressed in terms of non-alignment, was only partially implemented even in spirit. Some ministers did everything to implement the policy by establishing political, educational and trade relations with the Soviet bloc to balance similar ties with the Western world; others did not. Foreign Minister Wachuku established diplomatic ties with and removed the colonial government's restriction on travel to the Soviet bloc. Commerce and Industry Minister Zana Dipcharima also established trade ties with the East and even lifted the ban on the sale of columbite despite a warning from the United States that the latter might apply its Battle Act against Nigeria. And the Education Minister accepted Soviet scholarships for Nigerian students. But the Finance Minister, Okotie Eboh, would not accept Soviet financial and technical assitance, while Secret Intelligence sometimes arrested students officially sponsored to study in the Soviet bloc countries.[40]

Given these sad commentaries on his state-building efforts, Balewa, in desperation, played his strong card, suddenly abrogating the Anglo−Nigerian Defence Pact. Originally ratified in November 1960 amidst widespread and vehement protests, and intended to deter opposition groups from employing subversion or other irregular means to seize power, the pact soon became the rallying cry of the opposition, the *bête noire* of Chief Awolowo which hardened him against any possibility of bringing the Action Group into the coalition government. Its abrogation, Balewa, Akintola and the Sardauna (leader of the NPC)

200

seemed to surmise, could pave the way for the Action Group to join the coalition, strengthen the Prime Minister's hand to play one party against the other, and thus increase the scope of intra-elite and inter-party restraint. Accordingly on 22 January 1962, in time for the Action Group annual convention due to be held in about a fortnight, Balewa abrogated the pact and invited the Action Group to join the government.[41] But the abrogation failed to achieve this objective. Instead it helped to precipitate the Awolowo—Akintola split and triggered the political realignment of forces and a chain reaction that further hamstrung the Prime Minister.[42]

Like Nkrumah, Balewa had become caught in a trap of his own making. His faith in balanced dependence and mixed state/private capitalism had backfired: vertical linkages did not adequately sustain state capitalism but rather helped private international capital to take deeper roots. The failure of state capitalism where international private capitalism succeeded in turn presented him with an aspirant local bourgeoisie whose ambitions were frustrated. The end results were unabashed corruption, rampant strikes and uncontrollable political unrest. The desperate effort to use a politicised and disaffected military to restore control precipitated the military coup that killed him in the early hours of 15 January 1966.

The military era, 1966–1979

With the advent of military rule in the mid-1960s, attempts were made to weaken the regional bases of the political class and further strengthen the centre to which there had been a significant shift of political power. The first military regime (January—July 1966) closed regional offices abroad and stopped regions from sending economic missions overseas. Its over-zealousness in this context led to the promulgation of Decree 34 which would have made Nigeria a unitary state. The consequences of this decree, given the regions' remaining power, the tenuousness of the incipient transition to federal supremacy, and the disorientation and lack of legitimacy of the military, were the pogroms of 1966, the military coup of July that year and the subsequent civil war.[43] The only foreign policy initiative — appeal to foreign investors to continue to invest in Nigeria — was futile.[44]

With the second military regime (July 1966—July 1975) and the Civil War (May 1967—January 1970), foreign policy was initially geared towards efforts to win the war, both diplomatically and militarily. The vertical relations with the Western bloc remained intact but became cool because of what the military regarded as half-hearted support for its cause or outright meddling on the part of some (notably France) which tended to encourage the secessionists' intransigence. On the horizontal plane diplomacy was geared towards non-recognition of Biafra and political support for the federal side or at least benevolent neutralism on the part of African states and the OAU.[45]

During this period the regional bases of power were further weakened. The twelve-state structure, created in 1967 in order to placate minorities and win their support in the imminent war against the would-be secessionists, was the first strike at the roots of regionalism. It was also the first guarantee that the supremacy of the federal centre would be irreversible. In addition, in the war situation, the federal government increasingly assumed more powers at the expense of the new states, a trend which the centralist, hierarchical structure of military command naturally facilitated. These powers were not relinquished after the war; if anything more powers were assumed in the constitutional political–administrative and economic as well as financial fields.[46] These powers enabled the centre to intervene comprehensively (albeit in an unsystematic manner), to control and reorientate the economy and to adopt reform measures aimed at greater efficiency, self-sufficiency and the generation of surplus capital.[47] Finally, the centre emerged supreme in part because of the phenomenal increases in revenue accruing to it from Nigeria's increasing oil exports (from 58 per cent in 1970 to 94 per cent of export earnings in 1976), making the states dependent on the centre for virtually all their revenue (95 per cent in 1978–79).[48]

In the decade after 1970 the centre became the prime mover of an economy which entered a 'new stage of state-sponsored, but still dependent (or peripheral) industrialisation, along the capitalist road to development and within the framework of a more genuinely "national" economy'.[49] The structure of power in this emergent national economy was based on a tripartite alliance of civil–military (military elite, plus the proscribed politicians coopted to help rule), bureaucratic (higher civil servants) and big business interests. The latter comprised international business (represented by the multinationals and their subsidiaries), national business (those owned by Nigerians with no foreign affiliation), and the transnationals (those enterprises which are either *fronts* for international businesses or in partnerships with Nigerian 'lackeys'). The transnationals (as here defined) increased by leaps and bounds during and after the war and remain the dream of top Nigerians who retire from high public service posts (where typically they have used their positions to acquire wealth and to make international connections) in order to establish their own partnerships or 'manage' existing ones. The tripartite alliance was linked to labour through trade unions which the alliance sought to control by legislative measures and which eventually it centralised. It was linked to the masses via chiefly authorities and local politicians who helped to maintain public order, articulate government policies and provide feedback. However, these links were always tenuous and the military never succeeded in establishing grass-roots political support as the Agbekoya riots of 1968–69 well demonstrated.[50]

Since the members of the alliance were all aspirants for bourgeois status wishing to use state power to transform themselves into owners of the means of production, there were intra-alliance struggles. These struggles were not for the control of state power (the alliance already had that and no one member of the alliance group could do so singularly) but rather for influencing this power in order to further the course of economic development in a way perceived to be beneficial to various interests within each part of the alliance triangle. Thus there were civil service versus military struggles, resulting ultimately in the retirement of the so-called 'Super-Perm Secs' and the exclusion of that fraction from the Federal Executive Council during the third military regime (July 1975–September 1979). There were business versus civil service struggles and even military versus military struggles as Terisa Turner has demonstrated with respect to the oil auction episodes and the appointment of one Mr Ordor as the General Manager of the Nigerian National Oil Corporation; an appointment that was 'the straw that broke the camel's back', resulting in the 1975 coup.[51] There were also intra-group conflicts – civil servants versus civil servants and business versus business – as for example the indigenous capitalists versus the non-indigenous entrepreneurs. These struggles for dominant influence had consequences for economic policies and foreign policy. Nowhere is this more clearly demonstrated that in the events leading to the formulation of Nigeria's ECOWAS policy.

The political economy of ECOWAS policy

The war economy in Nigeria produced indigenous 'national' and 'transnational' emergency contractors and entrepreneurs on both sides of the conflict and vastly increased the size of the business sector. With the 'oil bonanza' after the war, and particularly after OPEC forced price increases following the Yom Kippur War, the number and size of these 'capitalists' further increased and the previous indigenous versus non-indigenous rivalry resurfaced at a higher level of intensity. Moreover the experience of the civil war clearly demonstrated that non-indigenous economic interests could be divergent from, and injurious to, Nigeria's political interests.[52] There was therefore clamorous agitation for indigenisation of foreign enterprises operating in Nigeria. It was in the milieu of this economic nationalism that the Second National Development Plan (as well as the subsequent Third Plan) was formulated.

In this context there was the question whether Nigeria's economic development policies should not be tied to the issue of West African integration. This, it was believed, would not only spur development in Nigeria itself but in the sub-region as a whole. It might also provide an institutional means for Nigeria to influence if not shape the foreign policies of its neighbours especially since the lack of such avenues of influence had enabled some countries, notably the Ivory Coast and Zinsou's Dahomey (Benin), to play a pro-Biafran role during the civil war. These two interrelated issues — indigenisation and West African economic integration — featured prominently in the formulation of the Second National Plan.

Phillip Asiodu, Permanent Secretary in the Ministry of Industry — supporting the interests of the 'transnationals', a group he was to join on his retirement from the civil service a few years later — argued against economic integration but supported indigenisation. In a paper, 'Planning for Development in Nigeria' from which his views and those of the group he favoured can be garnered, Asiodu recognised that 'an integrated West African Economic Community with harmonised industrial planning' could help stimulate Nigeria's growth and development but yet he preferred a purely domestic solution. While conceding that major constraints on development were partly 'questions of scale', Asiodu argued that the more important constraint was the tradition of multinationals' near-monopoly and the resultant high cost of local production. In addition there was a limit to which the existing import-substitution strategy could serve as a strong development factor. In his view, better planning, such as his ministry had embarked upon, accompanied by policies to stimulate internal demand and positive incentive laws, could remove the bottlenecks. Accordingly he opted for an emphasis on 'growth industries' such as agro-based and petro-chemical industries; modernisation and improvement of the impoverished agricultural sector; increased private Nigerian ownership and control (of at least 35 per cent equity) in all large-scale plants in the private sector; total private Nigerian ownership of small-scale industries; identification of feasible projects for more purposeful private investment; and the acquisition of industrial know-how by Nigerians on a massive scale.[53]

As for the expansion of West African trade the Asiodu group argued that one way to achieve this was to 'maintain non-discrimination duties' by 'removing the present reverse preferences' and the quotas accorded the EEC countries by the majority of the francophone states. The non-preferential fiscal and customs duties imposed by those states on other West African countries — but not on the EEC — should also be removed as they effectively shut out the products of the anglophone neighbours 'for reasons other than economic'. There was also concern within this group that Nigeria's oil wealth would be shared with the sub-region's partners, making Nigeria the paymaster of others' economic development and working to the advantage of foreign enterprises in those countries, thus negating the idea of wresting the African economy from foreign hands. Asiodu's group was also sceptical that Nigeria, which already accounted for about one-quarter of the total African trade with the rest of the world, could by membership in a West African Economic Community significantly add to its bargaining power in the international political economy.

Bureaucrats in the External Affairs Ministry supplied security and foreign exchange arguments to bolster the Asiodu group. They feared that under regional integration, French men and women who had acquired the nationality of francophone states might serve as spies for France while the concomitant free movement of labour and capital would permit 'foreign' nationals moving out of Nigeria to drain the country's foreign exchange![54]

By contrast, however, Professor Adebayo Adedeji, then Commissioner for Economic Development, and the bureaucrats in that ministry were in favour of both economic integration and indigenisation. A brilliant student of economic development and public affairs and a political appointee from his post as Director of the Institute of Administration which trained high-level public servants, Professor Adedeji had tremendous influence among civil servants and enjoyed Gowon's confidence. He had been concerned that because petroleum was a finite quantity Nigeria must not only maximise earnings from it but also apply these earnings in diversifying and transforming the economy — a task bound to the economic fortunes of the sub-region as a whole. Gowon was to put this concern succinctly when he said that there was 'a new Nigeria' that recognised its 'new role' in West Africa and that 'the gigantic task of economic and political regeneration in which [it was then] engaged [would] be of little avail' unless it was attuned to the requirements of the economy of the rest of Africa, 'particularly West Africa'.[55] The thrust of Adedeji's argument was that indigenisation and economic integration were necessary for the transformation of the economy and that long-term economic and political gains rather than the short-run costs and sacrifices of integration should be Nigeria's primary consideration.

Given this division within the bureaucracy, the military, under Adedeji's influence, literally had to call on the group with a special interest in the matter — the business community organised as the Nigerian Chambers of Commerce, Industry, Mines and Agriculture — to break the tie. As Adedeji later explained:

The reality of a community rests largely in the hands of what one might loosely describe as the agents of socio-economic activity — business, industrial and financial enterprises and institutions and their organised associations like the Chambers of Commerce and Industry, and professional associations. If these agents of socio-economic activity do not exist, they have. . .to be created. If they exist, they must be induced to function across national frontiers.[56]

Adedeji not only got the support of the Nigerian Chamber; he also succeeded in 'inducing it to function across national frontiers' as a regional interest group.

But this task was not easy, for the Chamber had meanwhile been divided itself along 'national' versus 'transnational' versus 'international' lines. By the end of Nigeria's civil war 'national' and 'transnational' Nigerian business interests comprised only about 25 per cent of the Chamber's membership. Even this had been achieved only because of the enlightened self-interest of the dominant 'international' business interests which recruited Nigerian members in order to remove suspicion that the Chamber was a powerful lobby for foreign interests and thus to continue to have some say at the planning stage of developmental and other policies. In any case the increasing numbers of large Nigerian enterprises — thanks to the war economy, the subsequent oil boom and the government's aid to Nigerian businesspeople — could no longer be ignored. Quite a few of the hitherto 'international' business interests became 'transnational' by entering into partnerships with indigenous entrepreneurs and making their top management Nigerian, especially in the area of personnel management. Unilever's United Africa Company (UAC), consisting of nine major industrial groups and eleven subsidiaries, for instance, went into partnership with Nigerian concerns in seven other major companies.[57]

One result of all these changes was that Nigerians soon became 'overrepresented in the Chamber's listed leadership' despite the small total number and relatively small financial size of the enterprises they represented. Thus 17 of the 30 members of the Executive Council in 1969 were Nigerians, some of whom held important posts, among them the presidency, one of the two deputy presidencies, and three of the five vice-presidencies. But the leadership of the vital standing committees and trade groups (Shipping, Imports and Exports, Industrial, Motor and Transport, Economics and Statistics, Publications) remained firmly in the hands of the multinationals, leaving the small businessman and the tourism committees to Nigerians.[58] The 'national' versus 'transnational' versus 'international' tussle began inside the Chamber too and several Nigerian businesspeople formed the rival Organisation of Nigerian Indigenous Businessmen in 1970, although its leadership was drawn from prominent Chamber members. The tussle was aggravated by the proposed indigenisation announced in the Second Development Plan. The indigenous groups saw themselves as the potential beneficiaries who would become the new masters, while the multinational groups came to feel they would be the dispossessed and the vanquished.

Given this situation, Adedeji and Henry Fajemirokun, the President of the Chamber and a leader of the 'national' business interests, utilised their personal friendship to advantage. Fajemirokun simply took a personal decision to throw the Chamber's weight behind Adedeji and afterwards secure the acquiescence of the rank-and-file. As a first-class indigenous entrepreneur who owned many industrial and commercial enterprises including the Nigerian Far East Line and the Nigerian South America Line it is not unlikely that Fajemirokun had calculated the benefits which he and similar groups could derive from indigenisation. And if he played his powerful card as President of the Chamber properly in support of Adedeji's preference for economic integration, he would additionally cement his particularistic ties to Adedeji and other powerful functionaries such as Gowon, thus ensuring greater political leverage in securing loans from banks and governmental agencies and in winning lavish governmental contracts.[59]

The proposed indigenisation, which initially exacerbated internal Chamber struggles, turned out to help the Adedeji—Fajemirokun team in securing the organisation's support. For instance, potential gains from indigenisation silenced the Nigerian business groups who, in theory, would normally oppose integration. The indigenisation policy seemed to pre-empt or allay their customary fear and reason for opposing integration; i.e., that integration might allow foreign companies to penetrate national protective policies such as restrictions on imports and investment, and thus undermine and eventually destroy local entrepreneurs.[60] For one thing, their inability to play the historical role of the capitalist class — the role of initiative, capital formation and increased production — on account of foreign competition could be reversed under indigenisation. For another, the indigenous Nigerian groups seemed to calculate that if they supported integration and got in early in working out its details they might be able to ensure inclusion of a clause in any integration agreement which would allow free trade in the common market only for those enterprises that were largely indigenously owned (such, indeed, became the case in the rule of origin clause in the protocols annexed to the ECOWAS treaty). The prospects of displacing foreigners at both the domestic and the sub-regional levels did arouse the interest of the Nigerian members of the Chamber.

For their part, the multinationals sensed that opposition to integration (especially when their indigenous counterparts supported it) would only antagonise the Nigerians even more and perhaps result in more drastic government policies to their detriment. Until the details of indigenisation had been worked out some foresaw that it might be premature to judge the issue. It was seen, for instance, that integration might provide greater opportunities for backward linkages with their parent firms at home and even greater opportunities for larger-scale industries since they were only just beginning to enter manufacturing in a big way.

It seemed, then, to be in the political interests of the Chamber as a whole as well as of indigenous and expatriate members in particular to support Adedeji's ministry, a ministry which supplied the Chairman of the Nigerian Planning Board and would be pivotal in working out the details of the evolving policies and their implementation. It was perceived that support might even yield a voice in the deliberations and negotiations for the proposed West African Economic Community. Accordingly, the Chamber threw its support behind Adedeji and thus buttressed the position of the pro-integrationists who carried the day in the bureaucratic politics of Lagos. Thereafter the Chamber embarked on an active campaign to solicit support from its counterparts throughout francophone and anglophone West Africa. In December 1973 at the Lomé Ministerial Conference on ECOWAS, Adedeji was to use the activities of the Chamber to clinch his argument with domestic and West African colleagues; namely, that if the business communities of virtually all the prospective member states view integration as beneficial and support it, the bureaucrats could not be heard to oppose it. Within 18 months after that conference ECOWAS was formally inaugurated in Lagos.[61]

Meanwhile a national indigenisation decree had been promulgated. Titled 'The Nigerian Enterprises Promotion Decree, 1972', it reserved exclusively to Nigerians the following: retail trade other than department stores and supermarkets; small factories assembling electronic and electrical appliances; or manufacturing bottled alcoholic drinks, bricks and tiles, bread and cakes, singlets and candles, jewelry and related articles; casinos, cinemas and pool betting; newspaper printing and publishing; radio and television broadcasting; advertising and public relations agencies; and other similar marginal sectors of the economy. Nigerians were to have 40 per cent participation in large enterprises having a capital of over $1.5 million. Such enterprises, numbering about 33 types, included the wholesale trade, meat processing, construction industries, furniture making, commercial farming and banking.[62] To facilitate implementation, especially in view of the doubts that Nigerians would not have the means to buy the affected enterprises, the government set up a Capital Issues Commission to regulate the prices and sales of shares. It also established the Nigerian Bank of Commerce and Industry to make available large loans (not less than $30,000!) to indigenous businessmen buying the foreign enterprises on the exclusive list and to underwrite the 40 per cent shares in the case of enterprises in which Nigerians were to have 40 per cent equity participation.

A more stringent decree was enacted by Gowon's successors in 1977. This decree still required all small-scale enterprises and, this time, retail stores with less than $3.2 million annual turnover as well as all agencies of international commercial and manufacturing firms, to be completely Nigerian-owned. It also required that banking, insurance, shipping, food processing, iron and steel and petro-chemical industries be 60 per cent Nigerian-owned while 40 per cent equity participation would be required in other high-technology industries listed in Schedule III of the decree.[63] Meanwhile the 'commanding heights of the economy' increasingly came under public control. For example, the government took 55–70 per cent equity interest in the existing oil companies, made the NNPC the sole licensee for new concessions in the exploration, production, transportation and marketing of petroleum, established the National Oil Marketing Company in which it held 60 per cent interest and insisted on at least 55 per cent equity interest in petro-chemical and fertiliser industries.[64]

In terms of the struggle between 'national', 'transnational' and 'international' business interests, the indigenisation decrees essentially rationalised the relationship of the Nigerian bourgeoisie with international capitalist interests in a way that defused the conflict between them. As Claude Ake has argued, indigenisation:

> limits the chances of conflict by a clearer demarcation of spheres. It reserves a sphere of influence for Nigeria's marginal capitalists, and international capitalism is to refrain from interfering in this sphere. Such restraint is clearly necessary to contain the potentially dangerous economic nationalism of the petty bourgeoisie. The decree integrates the Nigerian bourgeoisie with international capitalism by involving them in business partnerships to a greater degree than ever before.[65]

Indeed the authors of the decrees admit this. Gowon in 1973 opined that the idea was to attract 'more investment in sectors of the economy where Nigerians are not yet able to rely on themselves'.[66] And External Affairs Commissioner under the Mohammed–Obasanjo regime, Joe Garba, reassured indigenous and foreign capitalists that 'all we are trying to do is blend indigenous enterprise and capital with foreign capital, technology and management in such a way as to ensure fairness to foreigners and Nigerians alike'.[67]

The indigenisation exercise had two immediate consequences that became the inheritance of the post-milita. y regime, affecting the nature of politics and the exercise of state power as we shall see in the concluding section. First, for the multinational corporations it has meant 'their greater domestication and legitimisation within Nigerian society', as Richard Joseph points out.[68] Banks were able to reduce their high liquidity ratio which had been under constant criticism and to increase the level of their lending to Nigerians. In this process they supplied at least one-half of the funds spent by citizens to purchase shares in the indigenised firms. Joseph concludes in short that, 'looked at from the point of view of just the banks and these companies, indigenisation meant the arrangement of a new batch of loans from the former to the latter, but this time via Nigerian shareholders'. And precisely because of the holdings of their local shareholders, these companies have been given 'greater security in their operations without the concomitant danger of lessened control over their operations, or challenge to the earnings of their preference shareholders abroad.' The exercise has not 'in actual practice confer[red] on [the state] much more of an influence over these companies than it can exercise via available fiscal instruments or direct government participation.'

The second immediate consequence of indigenisation is equally striking. As Joseph puts it:

> For the tens of thousands of middle-class Nigerians able to obtain shares, heaven had descended to earth; they had procured a guaranteed income and substantial financial assets with negligible risks and effort [beyond using personal contacts and prestige to obtain application forms from the banks.] The balance sheets of all the companies involved show regularly high profits. The effort of the Capital Issues Commission to keep the prices of shares on offer as low as possible — in order to maximise the number of Nigerians able to participate — meant that the successful applicants realised an immediate capital gain as the prices on the stock exchange quickly moved to a higher level after the exercise. Furthermore, the imposition of a 30 per cent limit on distributed profits, and a 1.6 per cent dividend rate per share in 1976, did not stop the widening income gap, because the companies compensated local shareholders with bonus issues on the undistributed profits.[69]

In short the take-over of foreign enterprises or acquisition of equity therein, accomplished through private capital or through state capital deployed as though it were private capital, has enabled those closest to state power (and thus accessible to kick-backs from lavish contracts and state-owned lending institutions) to become the greatest beneficiaries. It is self-evident, then, that indigenisation has had profound effects on class formation. It has secured and continues to secure 'a certain position for a growing elite of private entrepreneurs whilst at the same time preserving the dominant place for foreign capital elsewhere in the industrial sector'. It is fostering an 'indigenous capitalism within a framework of continued dependence on foreign enterprise in many sectors'.[70] And it is adding a powerful social class aptly termed 'auxiliary bourgeoisie' by Paul Collins to the national bourgeoisie, powerful because tied in as satellites to alien capitalists whose interests 'the state must now protect even more' on account of the stake the local bourgeoisie has in them.[71]

Whether the new auxiliary capitalist class can overcome the obstacles which plagued their precursors' entrepreneurial capability (especially now that the state has handed to it the enterprises its members did not build up themselves) is a debatable point. The consensus is that 'there is little reason to be optimistic that the new owners will be more business-like in operating such benefactors from the State than they have been in running firms started on their own initiative with pre-indigenisation capital resources'.[72] Indeed, despite indigenisation – perhaps because of it – the economy has become increasingly more dependent on foreign private investment; on foreign construction firms, banks and mining companies, and on foreign personnel and technical skills and know-how needed to overcome a 'crisis of management'.[73]

In the initial stages of this tightening of vertical ties there was a euphoria of grandeur as the threat of 'nationalisation' became a weapon of foreign policy. It was used against Britain (via the nationalisation of BP assets) because of Mrs Thatcher's intransigence over independence for Zimbabwe under Mugabe. It extended to blackmail tactics and confrontation with the Ford Administration since the United States as early as 1978 took nearly 70 per cent of Nigeria's petroleum exports, although this constituted less than 20 per cent of American petroleum imports and the 'indigenised' companies still managed by Americans – Gulf, Mobil, Texaco and Ashland – produced nearly 30 per cent of Nigeria's daily output.[74]

As the vertical ties deepen further and foreigners more visibly dominate the economy – because their investment, technical assistance and engineering and management contracts are *sine qua non* to keeping up a minimum living standard (a drop in which might lead to a revolution against the bourgeoisie) – foreign policy is bound to become more traditional once again. In a sense this happened under the post-military regime between 1979 and the end of 1983: a brief and boisterous civilian interregum?

The civilian interlude 1979–1983

The elections of 1979 which returned Nigeria to civil rule brought the NPN to power. This party was clearly dominated by 'transnational' people — the Abiola's (of ITT fame) and Saraki's, the Shagari's (of Peugeot fame), the retired army generals and the self-styled 'men of timber and calibre'. The NPN regime under Shehu Shagari's adminis-stration had been widely acclaimed as favoured by the withdrawing military. That regime also replicated, in conformity with Gerald Heeger's hypothesis,[75] the civilian (Abubakar) regime displaced by the military. And the structure of power remained basically the same as under the military except that political parties joined chiefly authorities and local politicians to link the 'ruling class' to the masses.

Given these elements of continuity, it should not be surprising that the regime's development strategy was the same as that of its predecessors. By its own admission, its strategy — the Fourth National Development Plan — was a continuation of earlier plans but on a grander scale.[76] The inherited dependence sharpened. Loans, credits, grants (official, semi-official and private) were worth over $4.31 billion between 1970 and 1980: the cause of subsequent debt crises. Joint venture investments and contracts over the same period amounted to over $7.52 billion and private foreign investment some three years before the administration attained office stood at over $3.62 billion.[77] The regime thus appeared tailor-made to widen the scope of foreign capitalist interests. Significantly, and the ostensible reason for spurring the creation of new companies and curbing smuggling into the country, the state was frantic in its campaign for greater foreign private invest-ment and relaxed the priorities of the indigenisation decree for this purpose. Instead of the former 40 per cent maximum equity, foreigners may now hold up to 60 per cent equity shares in companies producing metal containers, fertilisers and cement as well as those engaged in sugar and other cash crop plantations and in food processing. Foreigners can now hold up to 40 per cent shares in the manufacture of jewelry and related products, in garment manufacture, rice milling and watch repairs, all of which were formerly reserved exclusively for Nigerians.[78] In sum, the Shagari regime despite lip-service to self-reliance has been in favour of more 'transnational' or indigenous/non-indigenous partner-ships than the previous military governments.

Not unnaturally there was no significant shift in foreign policy from that of Shagari's predecessors. The vertical ties continued unabated, though the horizontal ones were not neglected. However, there was a discernible 'low profile' in style, with little of the occasional exuberance of the former military regime to 'confront' big powers or to assert African leadership by taking initiatives *before* rather than *after* an

African consensus had emerged. Indeed on the African plane Foreign Minister Audu occasionally took reactionary (if realist) positions on some issues such as the Namibian question during the first Shagari period.

If the deepening of dependence, occasioned in part by the increasing size and power of the 'transnationals' has already affected foreign policy style it is likely to affect the substance of that policy in a short while as the foreign 'partners' come to co-opt the state policy-making machinery as was done with Busia's Ghana.[79] Much depended in the run-up to the mid-1983 general elections on the 'national/nationalist' bourgeoisie. The envisaged alliance of the so-called 'progressives' (of the four non-PNP parties: UPN, PRP, GNPP and NPP) never really materialised despite its base in the regular meetings of the 'progressive governors'. Thus although before the Buhari coup there was a possibility of transforming political economy and foreign policy, that is, providing some elements within the 'masses' supported the progressive alliance, neither the austerity nor the corruption generated a viable antithesis. The big question underlying the campaigns for the second elections of the Second Republic was whether the transnational' bourgeoisie with its foreign backers would respect any electoral victory of the 'national/nationalist bourgeoisie'[80] or would seek to pre-empt such an outcome with a right-wing *coup d'etat*.

In the event, the NPN electoral victory in mid-1983 was impressive and almost persuasive, symbolic of the hegemony of established, Northern comprador fractions. While the return of Shagari in the elections presaged further cautious, conservative rule appropriate to an era of post-oil boom 'austerity', his second 'technocratic' administration never had a real opportunity to 'take off'. Foreign policy under continued NPN stewardship was likely to reflect regional balance and 'federal character' along with a 'tilt' towards transnational rather than national bourgeois 'fractions': consolidation and consensus to avoid domestic difficulty and to secure external support. This rather moderate and modest external stance was to contain demands at home and to reschedule debts abroad: the issues of credibility and devaluation had become paramount. But before the seemingly reformed Shagari regime had time to effect either economic restraint or a national 'ethical revolution' it was replaced once again by military officers: the Buhari coup made 1984 a very different year in Nigeria from those in the brief civilian interregum.

Clearly not a sergeant's coup, the Supreme Military Council intended to restore order internally and confidence externally whilst maintaining Nigeria's mixed economy and moderate policy. Given the profound continuities of Nigeria's society and polity, this latest changing of the guard seemed to usher in an even more conservative period within which change would be very constrained: Buhari appeared determined to effect the austerity which had eluded Shagari even if this meant complying with IMF conditionality. Western politicians might lament the demise of democratic forms in Nigeria; yet Western bankers would happily accept repayments and advise further on how to transform Nigeria from a Newly Influential into a Newly Industrialising Country. It remains to be seen whether the latest incarnation of reformist soldiery can transform the 'problematic power'[82] of African any more than the discredited and displaced politicians.

Notes

1   On this view, see Olajide Aluko, 'The "New" Nigerian Foreign Policy', *Round Table*, October 1976, pp. 405–414 and J.N. Garba, 'The New Nigerian Foreign Policy', *Quarterly Journal of Administration*, vol. 11, no. 3, April 1977, pp. 136–146.

2   Timothy M. Shaw and Orobola Fasehun, 'Nigeria in the World System: alternative approaches, explanations and projections', *Journal of Modern African Studies*, no. 18, 4 December 1980, pp. 551–573.

3   On the Nigeria–Ghana struggle for leadership, see Olatunde J.B. Ojo, *Nigeria's Foreign Policy 1960–66: politics, economics and the struggle for African leadership* (unpublished doctoral dissertation, University of Connecticut, 1974). See also Olajide Aluko, *Ghana and Nigeria: a study in inter-African discord* (London: Rex Collings, 1976).

4   John Peter Olinger, 'The World Bank and Nigeria', *Review of African Political Economy*, no. 13, May–August, 1978, pp. 101–107.

5   Ali A. Mazrui, *Africa's International Relations* (London: Heinemann, 1977), p. 2.

6   Akin Fadahunsi, 'A Review of the Political Economy of the Industrialization Strategy of the Nigerian State 1960–80', *Political Science Departmental Seminar*, Ahmadu Bello University, Zaria, Nigeria (April, 1979).

7   On 'exit' and 'entry visas', see Ali Mazrui, 'Exit visa from the World System: Dilemmas of Cultural and Economic Disengagement', *Third World Quarterly*, vol. 3, no. 1, January 1981, pp. 62–76.

8   Douglas Rimmer, 'Elements of the Political Economy' in Keith Panter-Brick (ed.), *Soldiers and Oil: the political transformation of Nigeria* (London: Frank Cass, 1978), pp. 141–165.

9   As argued by Douglas G. Anglin, 'Nigeria: political non-alignment

and economic alignment', *Journal of Modern African Studies,* vol. 2, no. 2, June 1965, pp. 247–263.

10   Terisa Turner, 'Commercial Capitalism and the 1975 Coup' in Panter-Brick (ed.), *Soldiers and Oil* (note 8), pp. 166–197.

11   As advocated by no less an influential group than the Nigerian Society of International Affairs; see the *New Nigerian,* 23 February 1980 Special Supplement p. vi.

12   William D. Graf, 'The Nationalisation of the Nigerian Political Class and the Particularisation of the Second Republic', *Nigerian Political Science Association,* March 1980, University of Port Harcourt.

13   This parallels the theory that the economic take-off stage is the most politically unstable; cf. W.W. Rostow, *Stages of Economic Growth* (Cambridge: Cambridge University Press, 1963).

14   James S. Coleman, *Nigeria: background to nationalism* (Berkeley: University of California Press, 1958), pp. 41–60.

15   Olatunde J.B. Ojo, 'The Changing Centre–Periphery Relations' in William Graf (ed.), *Towards A Political Economy of Nigeria: critical essays* (New York: Orleander Press, and Benin: Korda Press, forthcoming).

16   These resources were impressive, but the most important were the marketing boards originally designed to stabilise the income of export-crop producers by insulating them from world market prices but later became an instrument of extracting savings for public use.

17   Yakubu Gowon's Assessment, Radio and Television Broadcast, 26 May 1968.

18   On the political parties, their structure, organisation and sources of strength, see Richard L. Sklar, *Nigerian Political Parties: power in an emergent African nation* (Princeton: Princeton University Press, 1963); and Richard L. Sklar and C. S. Whitaker Jr., 'Nigeria' in James S. Coleman and Carl S. Rosberg (eds), *Political Parties and National Integration in Tropical Africa* (Berkeley: University of California Press 1964), pp. 597–654.

19   See Ojo, *Nigeria's Foreign Policy 1960–66* (note 3) and, in general, see Robert C. Good, 'State-building as a determinant of foreign policy in the new states' in Laurence W. Martin (ed.), *Neutralism and Non-Alignment* (New York: Praeger, 1962), pp. 3–13.

20   Mahmud Tukur, *Nigeria's External Relations: the conduct of foreign policy in the United Nations* (unpublished Master's Thesis, University of Pittsburgh, 1966), p. 19.

21   See C.S. Whitaker, *The Politics of Tradition: continuity and change in Northern Nigeria 1946–1966* (Princeton: Princeton

University Press, 1970), pp. 92–107 and 339–340; quotation from p. 340.

22   David R. Mummery, *The Protection of International Private Investment: Nigeria and the world community* (New York: Praeger, 1968), especially chapters 1–3.

23   Ukpabi Asika, 'A Social Definition of the African Intellectual' in *Nigerian Opinion*, January–February, 1967; reproduced in Wilfred Cartey and Martin Kilson (eds), *The Africa Reader: independent Africa* (New York: Vintage, 1970), pp. 143–152.

24   Olasupo Ojedokun, 'The Changing Pattern of Nigeria's International Economic Relations: the decline of the colonial nexus, 1960–66', *Journal of Developing Areas*, no. 6, July 1972, pp. 536–553; and Olatunde J.B. Ojo, 'Nigeria–Soviet Relations: retrospect and prospect', *African Studies Review*, vol. 19, no. 3, December 1976, pp. 43–63.

25   Olatunde Ojo, 'The Evolution of Nigeria's Foreign Affairs Machinery' (unpublished paper, School of Social Sciences, University of Port Harcourt).

26   Olatunde Ojo 'Commercial Representation in Nigeria's Overseas Missions: its nature, functions and problems' *Nigerian Journal of International Affairs*, vol. 2, nos 1 and 2, 1976, pp. 50–66.

27   Olasupo Ojedokun, 'The Future of Nigeria's Commonwealth Relations' *Nigeria: Bulletin on Foreign Affairs*, vol. 1, no. 4, May 1972, pp. 8–17.

28   Mazi Ray Ofoegbu, 'Nigeria and its Neighbours', *ODU: a journal of West African studies*, new series, no. 12, July 1975, pp. 3–24 and *idem*, 'The Chad Basin Commission', Conference on Nigeria and the World, Nigerian Institute of International Affairs, January 1976.

29   Ojo, *Nigeria's Foreign Policy 1960–66* (note 3).

30   See Anglin, 'Nigeria' (note 9), and Claude S. Phillips, Jr., *The Development of Nigerian Foreign Policy* (Evanston: Northwestern University Press 1964).

31   Willard Scott Thompson, *Ghana's Foreign Policy 1957–1966* (Princeton: Princeton University Press, 1969).

32   Federal Republic of Nigeria, *National Development Plan: Progress Report 1964* (Lagos: Ministry of Economic Development, 1965), pp. 31–32; Edwin Dean, *Plan Implementation in Nigeria 1962–66* (Ibadan: Oxford University Press, 1972), especially Chapter 4 and Ojedokun, 'The Changing Pattern of Nigeria's International Economic Relations' (note 24).

33   Central Bank of Nigeria, *Economic and Financial Review*, vol. 9, no. 1, June 1971, Table 4.

34   For details and data on the shift see E. Osagie and K. Awosika,

'Foreign Capital Aid Flows in Nigeria', *Quarterly Journal of Administration*, vol. 9, no. 1, October 1974, pp. 61–76: Boston Research Group, *Other Side of the Nigerian Civil War* (Boston: 1979) and World Bank, *Nigeria: options for long-term development* (Baltimore: Johns Hopkins University Press, 1974), p. 220.

35 See World Bank, *Nigeria*, no. 13, p. 244 and P.C. Asiodu, 'Planning for Further Development in Nigeria' in A.A. Ayida and H.M.A. Onitiri (eds), *Reconstruction in Nigeria* (Ibadan, Oxford University Press, 1971), p. 185.

36 B.J. Dudley, 'Federalism and the Balance of Political Power in Nigeria' *Journal of Commonwealth Political Studies*, vol. 4, no. 1, March 1966, pp. 16–29.

37 Olatunde J.B. Ojo 'Personality, Elite Politics and Foreign Policy Decisions: the case of the Anglo–Nigerian Defence Pact' (unpublished paper, School of Social Sciences, University of Port Harcourt, 1981).

38 David M. Gray, *The Foreign Policy Process in the Emerging African Nation: Nigeria* (unpublished doctoral thesis, University of Pennsylvania, 1965), p. 172n, and 200n and *West Africa*, 20 January 1962, p. 75.

39 H.A. Asobie, 'Bureaucratic Politics and Foreign Policy: the Nigerian experience, 1960–1975', *Nigerian Political Science Association*, University of Port Harcourt, March 1980.

40 *Ibid*.

41 For details, see Ojo, 'Personality, Elite Politics and Foreign Policy Decisions' (note 37). An earlier interpretation by Gordon Idang did not go far enough; see his 'The Politics of Nigerian Foreign Policy: the ratification and renunciation of the Anglo-Nigerian Defence Agreement', *African Studies Review*, vol. 8, no. 2, September 1970, pp. 227–251.

42 For other incisive analyses of the rift within the Action Group and its consequences, see John P. Mackintosh et al, *Nigerian Government and Politics* (London: George Allen and Unwin, 1966), pp. 427–460 and Richard L. Sklar, 'Nigerian Politics: the ordeal of Chief Awolowo 1960–65' in Gwendolen M. Carter (ed.), *Politics in Africa* (New York: Harcourt, 1966), pp. 126–150.

43 Much has been written on the events of this period. One of the best accounts is B.J. Dudley, *Instability and Political Order: politics and crisis in Nigeria* (Ibadan: Ibadan University Press, 1973).

44 Mazi Ray Ofoegbu, 'Foreign Policy and Military Rule' in Oyeleye Oyediran (ed.), *Nigerian Government and Politics under Military Rule, 1966–79* (London: Macmillan, 1979), pp. 124–149.

45 Oye Ogunbadejo, 'Nigeria and the Great Powers: the impact of the Civil War on Nigerian foreign relations', *African Affairs*, vol. 75,

no. 298, January 1976, pp. 14–32 and Olajide Aluko 'Civil War and Nigerian Foreign Policy' in his *Essays in Nigerian Foreign Policy* (London: George Allen & Unwin, 1981), pp. 117–128.

46   Cf. 'The Federal Military Government (Supremacy and Enforcement of Powers) Decree, No. 28 of 1970.' For details see Olatunde J.B. Ojo, 'Federal-State Relations 1967–74', *Quarterly Journal of Administration*, vol. 10, no. 2, January 1976, pp. 105–124.

47   O. Aboyade and A. Ayide, 'The War Economy in Perspective', *Nigerian Journal of Economic and Social Studies*, vol. 13, no. 1, March 1971.

48   See Ojo, 'Federal–State Relations' and 'The Changing Balance of Centre–Periphery Relations' (notes 46 and 15).

49   Graf, 'The Nationalisation of the Nigerian Political Class' (note 12) p. 4.

50   Henry Bienen and Martin Fitton, 'Soldiers, Politicians and Civil Servants' in Panter-Brick (ed.), *Soliders and Oil* (note 8), pp. 27–57 and Henry Bienen, 'Military Rule and Political Process: Nigerian examples', *Comparative Politics*, vol. 10, no. 2, January 1978, pp. 205–225.

51   Turner 'Commercial Capitalism and the 1975 Coup' (note 10).

52   Graf 'The Nationalisation of the Nigerian Political Class' (note 12), and Paul Collins 'The Policy of Indigenisation: an overall view', *Quarterly Journal of Administration*, vol. 9, no. 2, January 1975, p. 141.

53   Asiodu, 'Planning for Further Development in Nigeria' (note 35). For a more detailed analysis see Olatunde Ojo, 'Nigeria and the Formation of ECOWAS', *International Organisation*, vol. 34, no. 4, Autumn 1980, pp. 571–604.

54   *Ibid*: p. 584.

55   *Africa Diary*, 9–15 December 1972, p. 6256.

56   Adebayo Adedeji, 'Collective Self-Reliance in Developing Africa: scope, prospects and problems', *International Conference on ECOWAS* (Lagos: Nigerian Institute of International Affairs, August 1976), p. 19.

57   See Ikenna Nzimiro, 'The Political and Social Implications of Multinational Corporations in Nigeria' in *Classes and Class Struggle in Nigeria* (New York: Monthly Review, forthcoming).

58   E.O. Akeredolu-Ale, *The Underdevelopment of Indigenous Entrepreneurship in Nigeria* (Ibadan: Ibadan University Press, 1975), pp. 49 and 63.

59   For an example of Fajemirokun's influence on Gowon see Panter-Brick (ed.) *Soldiers and Oil* (note 8), p. 135 note 14.

60   On this customary argument see Constantine V. Vaitsos, 'Crisis in Regional Economic Cooperation (Integration) Among Developing

Countries: a survey', *World Development*, vol. 6, no. 6, June 1978, pp. 729–736.

61 For details see Ojo, 'Nigeria and the Formation of ECOWAS' (note 53).

62 'Nigerian Enterprises Promotion Decree (no. 4, 1972)' in Federal Republic of Nigeria, *Supplement to Official Gazette Extraordinary*, no. 58, 28 February 1972.

63 'Nigerian Enterprises Promotion Decree, 1977'.

64 'The Nigerian National Oil Corporation (No. 18), 1971'; Federal Republic of Nigeria, *Third National Development Plan 1975–80* (Lagos: Federal Ministry of Economic Development, 1975), vol. 1, p. 143 and vol. II, p. 152; and S.A. Madujibeya, 'Oil and Nigeria's Economic Development', *African Affairs*, vol. 75, no. 300, July 1976, pp. 284–316.

65 Claude Ake, *Revolutionary Pressures in Africa* (London: Zed, 1978), pp. 47–49 and 53–55; quotation at 49.

66 Quoted in Collins, 'The Policy of Indigenisation' (note 52), p. 143. See Gowon's earlier remark to the same effect in *New Nigerian*, 3 October 1972.

67 Federal Ministry of Information, *Press Release*, no. 1205 quoted in Graf 'Nationalisation of the Nigerian Political Class' (note 12), p. 8.

68 Joseph, 'Affluence and Underdevelopment' *Journal of Modern African Studies*, 16(2) June 1978, pp. 229–330.

69 *Ibid*.

70 Graf, 'The Nationalisation of the Nigerian Political Class' (note 12), p. 9.

71 *Ibid*., p. 8 and Collins 'The Policy of Indigenisation' (note 52), p. 144 and 'Public Policy and the Development of Indigenous Capitalism: the Nigerian experience', *Journal of Commonwealth and Comparative Politics*, vol. 15, no. 2, July 1977, pp. 127 and 143.

72 Joseph, Affluence and Underdevelopment', (note 68) p. 230. For the disabilities of indigenous entrepreneurship, see Akeredolu-Alu, *The Underdevelopment of Indigenous Entrepreneurship in Nigeria*, pp. 313 and 101, and 'The Competitive Threshold Hypothesis and Nigeria's Industrialisation Process', *Nigerian Journal of Social and Economic Studies*, vol. 14, no. 1, March 1972, pp. 109–200 and Peter Kilby, *Industrialisation in an Open Economy: Nigeria 1945–1966* (Cambridge: Cambridge University Press, 1969), pp. 366 and 341.

73 Olahinde Ojo, 'Nigeria's Self-Reliance Strategy, the prospect for self-reliance in the contemporary international tributary system', African Studies Association, October 1981.

74 *New Nigerian*, 6 June 1979, p. 24; *New York Times*, 4 October, 1980, p. 4 and *Africa Research Bulletin* (Economic, Social and Technical Series) 15 July—14 August 1980, pp. 5611—5613.

75 Gerald Heeger, 'Politics in the Post-Military State: some reflections on the Pakistan experience', *World Politics*, no. 29, 2 January 1977, p. 249.

76 Federal Republic of Nigeria, *Guidelines for the Fourth National Development Plan, 1981—85* (Lagos: Federal Ministry of National Planning, 1980).

77 Ojo, 'Nigeria's Self-Reliance Strategy' (note 73).

78 *West Africa*, 16 February 1981, pp. 332—342.

79 Ronald T. Libby, 'External Cooptation of Less Developed Country's Policy-Making: the case of Ghana 1969—1972' *World Politics*, vol. 29, no. 1, October 1976, pp. 67—89.

80 On this and other contradictions see Timothy M. Shaw and Olajide Aluko (eds), *Nigerian Foreign Policy: alternative perceptions and projections* (London: Macmillan, 1983) especially pp. 1—34.

81 See, for instance, 'The light that failed' *Time*, vol. 123, no. 3, 16 January 1984, pp. 24—25.

82 Cf. Timothy M. Shaw 'A problematic power: the debate about Nigerian foreign policy in the 1980s' *Millennium: Journal of International Studies*, vol. 12, no. 2, Summer 1983, pp. 127—148.

9   South Africa

Roger J. Southall

Overviews of South African foreign policy in the post-war world have tended, not improperly, to focus thematically upon:

1   South Africa's loss of stature on the international stage resulting from the decline of Empire and withdrawal from the Common-wealth;
2   the strategy to subordinate (having earlier failed to incorporate) the former High Commission Territories of Botswana, Lesotho and Swaziland;
3   the Republic's[1] complex and diverse relations with Black Africa;
4   the attempt to maintain a cordon sanitaire of protective, white-ruled buffer states, culminating in South African engagement in the attempt to find an internationally acceptable settlement in Rhodesia (now Zimbabwe); and
5   South Africa's changing role *vis-à-vis* international organisations, with particular attention being paid to its continuing occupation of Namibia.[2]

However, because of the racially bifurcated nature of South African society whereby white dominates black, the common assumption of much conventional foreign policy analysis — that governments pursue an identifiably 'national interest' — has long been abandoned, with a resultant emphasis being placed upon South African foreign policy as an instrument to promote, maintain and stabilise white minority rule. Foreign policy has been viewed, as elsewhere, as emanating from the balance between domestic forces and interests and the constraints imposed by the external environment, the major focus in the South African case bearing upon the implications of the ethnic cleavage between Afrikaner and English-speaking whites internally, and the political, economic and strategic location of the Republic in relation, not only to black Africa, but also to the West externally. A general conclusion that arises from such analyses is that apartheid, an ideology and system of domination based upon legalised racial discrimination designed to entrench the white minority's monopoly of power (and thereby unacceptable to the international community in a decolonised world), is responsible for the disjunction between South Africa's increasing political isolation and its ever more extensive integration into the global capitalist economy. It will be argued below that the attempt to bridge this gap forms the substance of much of South African foreign policy.

The objective of the present chapter, rather than to pursue the conventional path of focusing upon the Republic's foreign policy as designed principally to ensure 'white survival', is to examine it as an expression of the dynamics of South African political economy throughout the post-Second World War years which, for the present purpose, will be divided into: the consolidation of state capitalism, 1948–61; state partnership with monopoly capital, 1961–76; and fissure and crisis of the apartheid state, 1976 to the present. It will be argued that this (admittedly arbitrary) characterisation corresponds to three broad phases in South African foreign policy, namely: resistance and adjustment to Africa's decolonisation; the Republic's emergence as a 'sub-imperial' power; and a transition from detente with neighbouring black Africa to its destabilisation. It is to the elaboration of this thesis that I will turn after a summary introduction to the historical basis of post-war South African political economy.

The rise of state capitalism and the response to Africa's decolonisation

The origins and development of contemporary South African political economy need to be located within the context of European colonisation, imperialism and ensuing dependence. Founded upon violent conquest and initially encouraged by imperial interests for reasons of commercial facility, strategy and economy, settler society in South Africa has been based upon the massive appropriation of African land, the ruthless exploitation of black labour, the extraction of exceptional mineral wealth and (from the mid-1920s), the adoption of policies of protectionism externally, this unique combination having led to a particularly high level of development.[3]

South African political economy has been founded upon a broad compatibility of metropolitan (or imperialist) and national (settler) capital since political independence in 1910. Within this context, however, there have been major changes within the structure of white society which have flowed from the ascendance, from subordinacy to political hegemony, of an Afrikaner bourgeoisie, whose economic origins lie in an ethnic mobilisation of capital in the inter-war years and their control of state capital since the victory of the National Party in the election of 1948. Founded in large measure upon an alliance of a still disadvantaged Afrikaner bourgeoisie (which was primarly located in agriculture and small-scale manufacturing) and the predominantly Afrikaner white working class in opposition to the United Party (which represented the interests of financial, mining, large-scale and thus 'English' capital), the NP came into office committed to the programme of apartheid which, in a more ideological manner than the UP, promised the fruits of racial dominance to its key constituents.[4] Subsequently, the core components of apartheid, as they developed over time, were increased legislative emphasis upon racial segregation in social life; the suppression of all political opposition which posed meaningful challenge to NP rule and the structure of white supremacy (climaxing with the banning of the African National Congress and the Pan-Africanist Congress in 1961); codification and extension of the system of influx control and pass laws, whereby entry of Africans into white areas was closely regulated to availability of employment; establishment of a highly coercive system of control, direction and regulation of labour by the state involving severe restrictions upon the black workforce and the maintenance and extension of the migrant labour system whereby cheap labour oscillated between employment in white areas and the reserves (and neighbouring territories); and the abolition of all African political rights in the central polity and the promotion of separate development whereby the African population was divided into eight (now ten) ethnic segments, each of which was allotted a territorial 'homeland' in the pre-existing native reserves, this aspect developing over time into a programme of quasi-decolonisation involving a constitutional progression of the 'bantustans' through successive stages of self-government culminating in eventual 'independence'.

Corresponding to the implementation of apartheid was the utilisation of the state apparatus to promote Afrikaner interests throughout the political economy. Apart from implementing an elaborate machinery for controlling African labour, the NP government was to embark in the 1950s upon an expansion of the public sector which was to do much to promote the Afrikaner economic advance. A number of parastatal corporations, such as ISCOR (iron and steel) and the Industrial Development Corporation, had been established before 1948, but thereafter direct state involvement in the economy was to increase enormously, including the creation of a wide array of agricultural control boards and public enterprises such as ESCOM (electricity), South African Railways and Harbours, Armscor (armaments), FOSKOR (fertilisers) and so on, a marked feature of such developments being their employment of Afrikaner personnel. 'State capitalism', remarks Giliomee, 'reflects the Afrikaner conception of South African economic development',[5] and throughout the post-war period has had the result of diminishing English and foreign control of the economy; it has also been instrumental in expanding secondary industry and making the country less reliant on mining. In turn, state capitalism and growth of the South African economy in the post-war years has significantly increased Afrikaner participation in the private sector, and contributed to a marked upward mobility of the Afrikaner population in the occupational sphere.

At the foreign policy level, Afrikaner control over the state involved a redefinition of South Africa's relation to the Commonwealth which revolved around the growing commitment of Britain to the decolonisation of her African dependencies. Pre-war foreign relations had been dominated by two conflicting traditions. The first, represented by Smuts, expressed a commitment to a joint South African (white) nationhood, and an active participation in international affairs as a sovereign state within the Commonwealth. The second, taken up by the Nationalists in opposition, was isolationist and interpreted Afrikaner nationhood as requiring the severing of formal political links with Britain as the former imperial power.[6] But Smuts' vision was doomed, not simply by the re-unification of Afrikanerdom which took place on account of South Africa's entry into the war on the side of Britain (which accordingly strengthened the Nationalists' commitment to republicanism), but also by the post-war transition to a multi-racial Commonwealth. The establishment of the United Nations, the early grant of independence to India (which took a particular interest in the face of South Africa's Asian population) and the subsequent commitment by Britain to the decolonisation of African states (though not without considerable prevarication concerning those with a sizeable white population) implied a commitment to formal racial equality to which the South African government could not but be opposed, whilst simultaneously making apartheid the butt of increasingly extensive international criticism.

Having achieved power, however, the NP's commitment to republicanism was initially tempered by the potential costs of isolation. The Smuts government has been a founder member, but the NP became increasingly resentful of the UN as it gradually came under the influence of the Arab and Asian states to engage in criticism of apartheid as a violation of human rights and a threat to peace. In particular, South Africa was resistant to claims that her legal right to govern South-West Africa (Namibia), the former German colony which the Union had administered since 1921 under a League of Nations Mandate, was invalidated because her racial policies contravened the UN's Charter of Rights. Although the International Court of Justice ruled in 1950 that the League's mandate was still in force (although South Africa was under no obligation to conclude a trusteeship agreement with the UN), the government refused to recognise any right of UN supervision. However, although the South-West Africa Amendment Act of 1949 granted whites there their first direct representation in the Union's legislature, South Africa was sufficiently wary of the international complications which would follow full legal incorporation of the territory not to take that final step, even though the government was fully determined to retain effective control.

In a post-war world which South Africa viewed as menaced by a widespread communist threat (which was associated in white minds with external 'agitation' of 'native unrest'), a major objective of the government was to gain admission to a Western defensive alliance, special effort being directed towards securing an agreement concerning the defence of the African continent. However, in part because South Africa declined to be party to any agreement which involved the bearing of arms by black (albeit colonial) troops, but rather more because the Western powers were dubious of the posited communist threat to the continent, no African alliance was formed. In addition, despite the South African government's urgings to the contrary, France and Britain were beginning to question the longevity of their stay as colonial powers in Africa, and were wary, too, of the international opprobrium that a formal defensive link with Pretoria would incur. As it was, the Simonstown Agreement of 1955 which gave the British Navy use of facilities on the Cape gave substance to the charge that Britain was in league with apartheid. Retention of Commonwealth membership therefore compensated, in part, for exclusion from other international groupings. Even though India's accession to republican status within the Commonwealth in 1949 opened up a similar option for the Union, declaration of a republic (even after a referendum) would have been divisive of whites, whilst outright departure from the Commonwealth would have likely reduced Pretoria's influence over Britain's Africa policy, and implied loss of imperial preference for South Africa's trade goods in a world increasingly hostile to apartheid.

Despite this diplomatic estrangement, relations with the West were strengthened throughout the 1950s by an extension of economic linkages. South Africa emerged from the war with large financial reserves, and these were considerably augmented by a large capital inflow from Britain. Nonetheless, pent-up consumer but particularly capital-goods demand resulting from the high level of investment by both private industry and the rapidly expanding parastatal sector caused acute balance of payments crises in 1954 and 1958. The consequent development of the manufacturing sector, which had received a major boost from the war, not only extended overseas linkages but also diversified South Africa's international contacts (notably with European countries and the United States). As it was, South Africa had long been the world's largest supplier of gold, but industrial growth in the advanced capitalist economies now fuelled demand for the country's enormous wealth of other minerals, i.e. chromium, platinum group metals, manganese, vanadium, asbestos, and vermiculite (of which South Africa has the world's largest known deposits), as well as iron, coal, uranium, diamonds and copper. The export of these minerals was not only instrumental in redressing the imbalance of trade in other commodities, but also in forging stronger ties with mineral-consuming countries, many of whom were in significant measure dependent upon South Africa for their supplies of scarce minerals (not a few of which had considerable strategic importance). If the decline of empire required that territories to the North be now conceded to the uncertainties of African rule, the prospect of continuing white supremacy served to increase, rather than diminish, South Africa's attraction to external investors and to guarantee the country's continuing incorporation into the capitalist orbit.

South Africa was strongly opposed to all prospect of decolonisation. Heartened by Portugal's resolve to maintain control over Angola and Mozambique, Pretoria became progressively dismayed by Britain's doubts, prevarications and eventual decision to withdraw from Africa. In early days, South African politicians deemed it inconceivable that Britain could hand over power to independent black states. Prime Minister Malan's flotation of an 'African Charter' which was committed to the protection of Africa against domination by Asians (particularly Nehru's India) and communism and to the preservation of Western civilisation was necessarily premised upon continuing colonial rule.

Yet if South Africa displayed alarm at colonial strategy, the most immediate concern was to ensure continuing white hegemony over Southern Africa. In 1953, the two Rhodesias had been joined with Nyasaland in the Central African Federation, in part to 'resist the fatal

226

southward pull of Malan's Nationalist Union',[7] whose manufacturing industries found a ready market for their goods in all three countries. If the subsequent development of nationalism in Northern Rhodesia (Zambia) and Nyasaland (Malawi) was in considerable degree a struggle against political domination by white settlers in their Southern neighbour, South Africa was steadfast in its commitment to the upholding of white rule in Southern Rhodesia as a bulwark against emergent black Africa. More pressing, during the 1950s, however, was the issue of the High Commission Territories, whose proximity and dependence upon the Union, together with their intimate historical ties, gave the Union a particular interest in their future.

The British Protectorates of Basutoland, Bechuanaland and Swaziland had not been incorporated into South Africa at the time of Union, but provision had been made for the possibility of their later transfer. Their geographical position, with Basutoland entirely surrounded by and Bechuanaland and Swaziland both bounded on three sides by South Africa, together with their acute dependence upon and linkages with their white neighbour as labour reserves and as members of common monetary and customs unions, made them extensions of the South African economy. Regarded by Nationalists as outposts of empire whose natural destiny lay with South Africa, there was also a wish to extend the Union's 'native' policy to the Protectorates lest any advantages which their inhabitants might enjoy unsettle the Union's own Africans. Accordingly, successive Union governments sought to negotiate the Protectorates' transfer to South Africa, their failure to persuade the British to hand them over being ascribed to imperial perfidy and continuing antipathy toward the Afrikaner.

The spectre of decolonisation transformed an historical anomaly into a matter of contemporary dispute. In the context of the early 1950s, the indefinite continuation of British supervision of the High Commission Territories (HCTs) seemed as unattractive as it seemed impracticable for states with such small populations and limited resources to assume politically sovereign status. Yet while imperial thinking remained far from clear as to how the future lay, it was politically necessary to honour a long given promise that the Territories would not be incorporated into the Union unless their inhabitants were consulted (and these had continuously been opposed), and it was politically impracticable for any British government to transfer them for so long as the South African government continued to implement apartheid.

More was at stake for the South African government than simply extending direct control over territories which, if ever independent, might perhaps offer a threat to security and stability, for their incorporation would mean that instead of the 13.7 per cent of the land area of the Union which the consolidated Bantu areas would compose, the addition of the HCTs would mean that some 47 per cent of the greater Southern Africa would be reserved for the African population.[8] This apart, there was considerable concern about how developments within the HCTs would affect the government's policy of separate development if they were not transferred. Although the bantustan strategy was, from the first, premised upon the segregationist notion that Africans would develop along their own lines, the NP initially rejected opposition claims that the logic of their scheme implied political independence, and argued rather that the Bantu areas would remain under white guardianship indefinitely. If, however, the HCTs were themselves advanced to political independence by the British, then the likelihood that the bantustans would themselves remain constitutionally incorporated within the Union would be correspondingly reduced; and for the majority of white politicians at this time, whether in government or opposition, the prospect of bantustan autonomy was synonymous with the certainty of communist infiltration and subversion.

As the 1950s progressed, the worst fears of the South African government were realised, with the HCTs moving cautiously but steadily towards political independence. In turn, the bantustan policy began to evolve in parallel, so that from 1959 onward, government rhetoric became increasingly redolent of the language of self-determination and decolonisation, with the ultimate aim being now declared the eventual formation of a 'South African Commonwealth' corresponding to the area of the greater Southern Africa which would have come about had the HCTs been incorporated. In the meantime, efforts previously aimed at securing the incorporation of the HCTs were now directed at circumscribing their forthcoming independence by entangling them within their web of dependence upon the white South African economy.

The accession of some 17 (mostly French) colonies to independence in 1960 highlighted the transformation of relations between governments throughout Africa. Having failed to stem the tide of decolonisation, South Africa under Premiers Strydom and Verwoerd attempted to adjust by proposing coexistence between black and white states founded upon mutual recognition of each other's rights. If this approach was in large measure founded upon the notion that South Africa, as the most advanced industrial power on the continent, could play a leadership role in technical and economic spheres, it was simultaneously premised upon an insistence that sovereign states should not interfere in the internal affairs of another. Hence relations with Ghana when that country became independent in 1957 were optimistically correct, for the Nkrumah government evinced an initial willingness to continue trading with South Africa despite its opposition to apartheid. But further cooperation never materialised, for at the very time when the decolonisation process was bringing political freedom for black nations, the increasingly repressive implementation of apartheid remained premised upon unmitigated inequality. As a result, the Union was to find itself gradually excluded from almost all continental African (and many other international) organisations, whilst South African meddling in the Congo crisis — when Pretoria lent covert succour to the secessionist Katanga regime — served only to draw a sharper line between white and newly independent black Africa. The Sharpeville massacre on 21 March 1960, when police fired on unarmed demonstrators protesting against the pass laws, provoked further mass defiance that led to the banning of the major nationalist organisations (ANC and PAC), and it seemed that South Africa was now about to reap the whirlwind of African nationalism. The NP's subsequent declaration for a republic and South Africa's transition to that status on 31 May 1961 thus seemed like an act of defiance against world opinion; and when Verwoerd's consequent re-application to join the Commonwealth as a republican state foundered on (mainly Afro-Asian) criticism of apartheid, the government was subsequently forced to make a virtue of political isolation.

Although there was a flight of capital out of South Africa after Sharpeville, the new Republic was far from isolated economically; the consolidation of state capitalism and the associated rise of an Afrikaner segment to influence within the settler bourgeoisie was accompanied by more extensive links with the metropolitan capital. If there was, nonetheless, some concern within the expanding secondary sector that the government was playing too little attention to promoting trade links with newly independent black states, events had shown that 'political questions had primacy in Africa at this time'.[9] This being the case, with prospects for political coexistence blocked, South African energies were now to be redirected into expanding relations with black Africa in the economic sphere.

State partnership with monopoly capital, 1961–1976: the Republic's emergence as a sub-imperial power

During the 1960s, the South African economy experienced one of the highest growth rates in the Western world. Underlying this was a three-fold increase in gross domestic investment (from Rands 1163 in 1961 to R3642 in 1970), and a particularly rapid growth in the manufacturing sector, whose contribution to GDP now exceeded that of agriculture and mining combined. Thus whilst the latter two sectors continued to expand, the volume and value of manufacturing output doubled between 1966 and 1973, this expansion being most particularly located in heavy industry, a development which underlined the economy's increasing capacity for achieving self-sustaining growth. Compared with the rest of Africa, therefore, where the forces of production were generally far less developed, South Africa became ever more the industrial giant of the continent.

The economic boom which South Africa experienced during the 1960s was based on low wages for black labour and high profits for capital. The African workforce, composed of an increasingly substantial urban-based black proletariat in the towns as well as a mass of migrants from the homelands and neighbouring territories, was paid at minimal levels. Even if the most highly-paid strata of urban Africans which made a steady advance into semi-skilled and skilled work areas previously reserved for whites were better off materially than the bulk of wage workers in black Africa, the 1960s nonetheless saw a widening of the overall wage gap between black and white populations to the latter's advantage.

Low African wages were enforced by the rigorous application of apartheid which constituted an efficient method of obtaining cheap labour for capital that was appropriate to the rapid pace of industrialis-ation. Influx controls, the pass laws, restrictions on unionisation, denial of the right to strike, the colour bar, and the migratory and bantustan systems all combined with the repression of political resistance to secure the reluctant acquiescence of the black workforce to its exploitation. For transnational corporations, the particular attraction was not merely that wage costs were low relative to those available in their home countries, but that the Republic also offered a political stability and ideological commitment to capitalism that did not generally obtain in black Africa. As a result, the corporate gains were consistently high. Between 1961 and 1965, for instance, the general profit rate of between 15 and 20 per cent annually was twice as high as the world average, and profits continued to rank amongst the highest in the world until the economy began to slow down in the mid-1970s.

Following the outflow of capital after Sharpeville, South African-based finance and national capital moved swiftly to invest widely in a wide range of industrial spheres. This then laid the basis for the growing interpenetration, not only of Afrikaner and 'English-speaking' capital, but of 'national' with monopoly capital, which flowed back into South Africa once the state had demonstrated its determination and capacity to crush all effective black opposition. Thus parallel to the advance of Afrikaner capital in the private sector (most notably in mining and manufacturing) came a massive inflow of foreign funds.

Between 1960 and 1970 South Africa's total foreign liabilities grew from R3024m to R5818m, whilst direct foreign investment increased from R1819m to R3943m. By the end of the decade it was officially estimated that 40 per cent of the manufacturing sector was directly controlled by foreign interests, this in part being a reflection of a shift by foreign investment towards secondary industry proportionate to mining. In the meantime, growing competition by transnational corporations to expand trade and investments in South Africa led to a continuing diversification of South Africa's trading partners and the pattern of foreign investment. Whilst British companies still provided the largest share of foreign investment and Britain remained South Africa's largest export market, transnational corporations from elsewhere (notably the United States and West Germany) substantially increased their stake in the economy. In sum, conclude Seidman and Makgetla,

> transnational firms from all the major capitalist nations contributed to the dynamism of South Africa's economy in the post-Sharpeville era. U.S. and (West German) companies, however, gradually took the lead from British investors, especially in strategic, fast-growing manufacturing industries. French firms traded and invested less, but made a special contribution to the regime's military build-up. Japanese industrial groups, prohibited from direct investment, expanded trade and licensed South African partners to produce their models. The most important role of the Swiss was in banking, particularly in the sale of gold. By competing to find new sources of profit in South Africa, transnational corporations ensured thorough attention to the requirements of the regime.[10]

These various developments underwrote increasing economic and covert political collaboration with the apartheid state. Not only did transnationals work closely with South African parastatals, but the British government, in particular, became engaged in direct investment, through its nationalised corporations such as British Steel and British Leyland, in South African industry, especially in iron and steel, chemicals, oil refining and transport. Meanwhile, despite the adoption of a voluntary UN embargo on the sale of arms in 1963, the Western powers continued to supply South Africa with sophisticated weaponry. While France and Italy openly flouted the embargo, the United States and Britain continued to provide spare parts for earlier sales; and as South Africa began to move towards self-sufficiency in the production of arms, an 'invisible' arms trade involving many governments (but most notably the United States and Britain) developed whereby the Republic built up the most powerful military force on the continent. Furthermore, despite denial by Pretoria that it is involved in any such an undertaking, acquisition of technology from Western sources has been vital in enabling South Africa to develop nuclear weapons capability.

In the context of a changing international division of labour (involving, *inter alia*, the merging of international monopoly capital and a proportionate shift of productive investment away from metropolitan core to 'semi-peripheral' countries with lower wage costs), South Africa emerged as a 'sub-imperial' power. In sum, the major features of this sub-imperialism were:

1   the partnership between national and metropolitan capital (as elaborated above) which was integrally related to South Africa's domination of neighbouring countries as the regional centre for investment, services, technology and industry;

2   control of the state apparatus by the national bourgeoisie, not only to repress the black population (the major source of productive labour), but to organise the accumulation of capital so as to strengthen the relative power and autonomy of the South African economy in the global system;

3   the development of the industrial base, not so much to meet the material needs of the mass as to satisfy the wants of the settler population; and

4   the consequent existence of a skewed market which, because of the severely limited purchasing power of blacks (who constitute some 70 per cent of the South African population), led to an accumulation of excess productive capacity particularly in the manufacturing sphere, which therefore required outlets in neighbouring territories for its capital and goods.

The outward policy

The most immediate manifestation of South Africa's sub-imperial role was its so-called 'outward' policy, the systematic expansion of the Republic's relations with white-controlled and any black-ruled states that were prepared to swallow their distaste for apartheid in return for perceived material or political advantage.[11] The way forward on the 'Great North Road' was cleared by Verwoerd's renunciation in 1964 of South African ambition to incorporate the HCTs now that it had become clear that these Territories were irrevocably destined for independence. Acceptance of the need to treat them formally as sovereign equals signified South Africa's adjustment to decolonisation and eased the diplomatic recognition of other black African states. Meanwhile, the devolution of 'self-government' to the Transkei in 1963 invited comparison with decolonisation, the bantustans being projected, not simply as the key to the resolution of domestic racial conflict, but also as bridging the gap between white and black Africa, and providing a foundation for schemes of regional cooperation with other states. Yet visions of 'co-prosperity' or of a Southern African 'commonwealth' remained idealised figments of foreign policy rhetoric, for prospective harmony inevitably foundered upon the fundamentally unequal relation between an overbearing and dominant South Africa and economically dependent, but racially sensitive neighbouring states.

The outward movement had major political—diplomatic and military—strategic objectives but had an underlying material basis in the requirement of South African-based capital for increased resources, larger markets, expanding spheres for investment and maintenance of the existing supply of foreign migrant labour. By deliberately maintaining a reserve army of employable labour, South African-based capital was enabled to minimise labour shortages and undercut wage demands by the black workforce. The largest employer of foreign labour was the Chamber of Mines, whose post-war recruitment structure was shaped, until the early 1970s, by the internationally fixed price of gold, which in limiting the capacity of the mining companies to transfer increases in costs to consumers in the form of price increases, perpetuated production methods which depended on the extensive use of unskilled, cheap labour. In contrast, given that it was not subject to the same price constraint, the expanding secondary sector was enabled to pay somewhat higher wages, with the result that it drew domestic labour away from the mines and encouraged the latter towards a greater dependence upon foreign sources (so that whereas in 1946 some 56 per cent of the black workforce on the mines originated from outside South Africa, by the early 1970s the proportion had risen to around 75 per cent). Consequently, the maintenance of foreign supplies of workers (from Angola, Botswana, Lesotho, Malawi, Mozambique and Swaziland) became an important policy objective, especially after post-independence bans by Tanzania and Zambia on the recruitment of their nationals for work in South Africa indicated that decolonisation meant that historical sources of labour could no longer be taken for granted.

But cheap labour was not the only resource to be drawn from neighbouring countries. In the first place, an increasing requirement for energy led the South African government to collaborate with Portuguese and transnational corporate interests in the building of the major Cabora Bassa (Mozambique) and Kunene River (Angola) hydro-electric projects with a view to the satisfaction of future needs; natural gas was piped from Southern Mozambique to the Southern Transvaal, and negotiations were started (only to be brcken off until the 1980s) for the construction of a dam in Lesotho which would supply electricity and much-needed water to South Africa's industrial heartland. Second, mining finance houses and transnational firms from the Republic became increasingly engaged in the extraction of mineral wealth from neighbouring states; for instance, the Anglo-American Corporation (together with American Metal Climax) partnered the Zambian government in the production of copper and, in the 1970s, the Botswana government in the extraction of nickel and copper from its Selebi-Pikwe mine. But the major case of South African involvement in resource extraction beyond the Republic's borders lay in Namibia where, under the auspices of the continuing occupation, transnational and South African firms (notably De Beers Consolidated Diamond Mines, the Tsumeb Corporation and – from the mid-1970s – Rio Tinto Zinc), plundered the country's wide variety of minerals (especially diamonds, copper and uranium). Despite South Africa's determination to retain direct control over Namibia, political uncertainty surrounding the future convinced the mining companies that there would likely be no more auspicious time than the present, with the result that rates of exploitation of Namibian minerals and expatriation of surpluses in the form of profits, salaries and taxes paid to the South African administration increased to a level only adequately described as asset stripping.[12]

Yet the economic dimension most ambiguously associated with the outward policy was South Africa's urgent search for new markets. Here there were three underlying, related factors. First, throughout the 1960s, the Republic's high rate of economic growth was accompanied by serious balance of payments problems. Although imbalances on current account were offset by regular surpluses on the capital account (via large sums of foreign investment), South Africa looked to increased manufacturing exports to rectify what was a structurally unstable situation. Second, because the fixed price of gold was making production of that mineral (which had for so long provided the major balancing item in South Africa's foreign trade) relatively less attractive, output was declining. And third, inherent limits were placed on the domestic consumer market by the low wages paid to the majority black population so that the secondary manufacturing sector, whose rapid growth was fuelled by large inflows of foreign funds, could only avoid stagnation by expanding exports both of goods and surplus capital. Africa, although impoverished and underdeveloped, offered a rapidly expanding and potentially lucrative market, with South Africa's geographical propinquity promising Republic-based industry a competitive advantage over other, more distant, albeit established, metropolitan suppliers.

Thus it was that South African manufacturing industry made a determined push into Africa. In 1960, the only state in Africa with which South Africa conducted a significant export trade was the

Central African Federation, but by 1970 she had displaced Britain as the main exporter to Rhodesia, and that country and Britain as the main exporter to Zambia. New trade agreements were signed with Rhodesia and the Portuguese territories, and in March 1967, with Malawi (the first with a black state), whilst the Customs Union which had bound the HCTs to South Africa since 1910 was refurbished by a new agreement in 1969 which, whilst somewhat more advantageous to the three smaller countries (especially in revenue terms), continued to bind them closely to the white economy and was protective of South African industry. Meanwhile, exports to an increasing number of black African states (including such as Zaire, the Ivory Coast and Gabon beyond the South African perimeter) were steadily, if quietly, increased, such goods often being 'laundered' by reprocessing or repackaging in third party states (such as Mauritius, which in 1970 specifically altered its law to allow for the through passage of South African exports which could appear to originate from its own territory).

Associated with South Africa's export drive was an attempt to divide and confuse the continental opponents of apartheid by establishing cooperative relations with willing black African states. During the mid-1960s, when African states were still emerging from the colonial yoke, opposition to apartheid and commitment to the liberation of Southern Africa became an article of faith which found expression in the founding charter of the Organisation of African Unity. Whilst it was freely admitted that independent Africa was as yet too weak to challenge South Africa economically and militarily, even a collection of weak states could, through united action, serve as an international pressure group for isolating the apartheid regime.

Yet this was a fragile unity and was not to last for long. The transition to independence of Zambia, Malawi, Lesotho, Botswana and Swaziland, all of whom exhibited varying degrees of dependence upon the Republic, rendered impractical any total boycott of South Africa, a strategy which, in any case, conservative leaders such as Chief Leabua Jonathan and President Hastings Banda were opposed. Ironically, too, attempts to impose sanctions against Rhodesia after Ian Smith's Unilateral Declaration of Independence (UDI) in 1965 made Zambia, in particular, more rather than less dependent on the Republic. Furthermore, the failure of African states to take a united line against British reluctance to act decisively against UDI, and later, their inability to intervene militarily against Rhodesia or to support adequately the first guerrilla forays (themselves of limited impact), served to undermine the prospects for success of any radical strategy premised upon bringing about change within South Africa through diplomatic isolation and external pressure.

The OAU's advocacy from its foundation of a trade boycott of South Africa represented a counter to the Republic's outward thrust. But the Republic's objectives were more than economic, and accompanying her exports went promises of aid, the government reducing its rather limited contributions to international schemes by providing instead for the direct channelling of low-interest loans to African countries in forms which could be clearly identified as South African. The amount of this aid was not large, but was concentrated in a few countries. In 1972, for instance, the total extent of financial assistance was R171m dispensed to Malawi, Madagascar, Swaziland, Lesotho and the Portuguese, a feature being South African preference for the creation of infrastructural projects which would integrate regional economies into the South African network. Nonetheless, the premise of aid was there, and there were those who were tempted by the prospect of receiving it.

South Africa's greatest successes were with Malawi and Madagascar. The former was to become the foremost ally of the Republic in black Africa, becoming the first (and only) independent African state to exchange diplomatic representatives with Pretoria (in 1967). This was later followed up by a visit in May 1970 of Prime Minister J.B. Vorster to Malawi; a return tour of the Republic by Banda in 1971, and the acceptance of a South African military attache in Blantyre. According to initial explanations of his policy by Banda, Malawi's foreign policy was dictated by the realities of its poverty, dependence and geographical position. However, a more likely rationale lies in the benefits of South African collaboration in securing him against his radical opponents (who fled the country in the early 1960s) and entrenching him domestically by allowing him to extend his support via the dispensation of patronage.[13] Meanwhile, South Africa's relations with Madagascar were built upon the conservative Tsirana government's design of liberating itself from overbearing French economic and cultural domination, whilst simultaneously strengthening its defences against perceived Chinese and Russian communist threats to Indian Ocean and domestic security. Although internal opposition and doubts as to the efficacy of the South African connection (even within Malagasy ruling circles) served to prevent the establishment of diplomatic ties, the political linkages that were made provided an opportunity for South Africa to penetrate further into francophone Africa.

Contemporary French policy involved closer collaboration with Pretoria, this entailing a total disregard for the 1963 UN embargo on the sales of arms. However, despite increasing criticism from Africa, it was not inconsistent that francophone states seeking to increase their standing with France should adopt a conciliatory position towards South Africa, especially if this meshed with their own conservatism.

Certainly, this was the case with President Houphouet-Boigny of the Ivory Coast, who in November 1970 declared the failure of existing strategies towards apartheid and called for an African conference to discuss an alternative of dialogue. The Ivory Coast had no apparent economic motive for leading the dialogue campaign, and it is likely that Houphouet-Boigny took up the issue on account of his close ties with Tsirana. But the timing of his call was probably influenced by the current campaign being waged by the OAU and non-aligned movement to block the newly elected Conservative government of Edward Heath in Britain from resuming the sale of arms to South Africa.

The idea of dialogue ran contrary to the position adopted in April 1969 by the Heads of State and Government in East and Central Africa in the 'Lusaka Manifesto', a document which, whilst registering something of a retreat from the OAU's uncompromising stand towards South Africa, emphasising a preference for conciliation and non-violent change in South Africa, nonetheless declared for boycott and isolation of the Republic so long as it showed no signs of abandoning apartheid. In spite of this, the idea of dialogue received some considerable support from francophone Africa (including, apart from Ivory Coast and Madagascar, the Central African Republic, Gabon, Dahomey, Togo and Niger), whilst being roundly rejected by others (notably Guinea, Senegal and the Cameroons). In anglophone Africa, meanwhile, although Kenya and Sierra Leone vacillated before finally coming down against dialogue, Houphouet-Boigny found three of his most vocal supporters in Ghana, Lesotho and Malawi. Yet such support was compromised. Kofi Busia, Prime Minister of Ghana, was a known conservative, and his support for dialogue was widely repudiated in his own country; Chief Leabua Jonathan's government in Lesotho had long been an advocate of collaborating with South Africa, and had been sustained in power by covert South African support in a disputed election earlier in 1970; and Banda had already forged his connection with the apartheid regime.

Attempts by Houphouet-Boigny to have the dialogue issue discussed by the OAU summit in 1971 was defeated. Instead, a summit of leaders of east and central African states soon moved beyond the Lusaka Manifesto to adopt a Mogadishu Declaration which endorsed armed struggle as the sole way of achieving liberation in Southern Africa and condemned African states who might presume to forge closer links with the apartheid Republic. Thereafter, although Ivory Coast, Malawi and Lesotho sought to keep it alive, the removal of the military of both the Busia and Tsirana regimes from office in their respective countries was to rob dialogue of two of its leading supporters; and soon, even Leabua Jonathan, dissatisfied with the amount of South African aid and now perceiving a need to reconcile his countrymen to his government's disputed rule, began to adopt an increasingly radical posture against apartheid which soon paid dividends in facilitating a flow of economic assistance from elsewhere and by increasing his government's stature throughout Africa. Nonetheless, although the dialogue issue thereafter died away, it had demonstrated the existence of divisions within the African community of which South Africa could seek to take advantage as the liberation struggle intensified.

Whilst South Africa was seeking friends in black Africa, it had simultaneously been consolidating ties with its neighbouring white regimes. Portuguese resistance to decolonisation was welcomed in Pretoria, for Angola and Mozambique were located strategically as buffer states. In addition, given the flow of labour from both colonies (especially Mozambique) to the mines, together with the potential market they offered when much of Africa remained closed to South African exports, there were sound economic, as well as military, reasons for strengthening collaboration with the Portuguese. Although South African trade with Angola and Mozambique during the early 1960s was not very substantial (this reflecting the determination of Portugal to maintain monopolistic control of its empire which freer trading relations would erode), this was destined to grow significantly, the balance of trade lying very markedly in the Republic's favour.

The Portuguese, claiming their colonies to be overseas extensions of the metropolis, were reluctant to isolate themselves from the international community. Accordingly, they attempted to divorce themselves from apartheid, which they argued compared unfavourably with their own policy of Lusitanian assimilation. But political distance between Pretoria and Lisbon became narrower as the colonial regime came under increasing pressure, notably from the nationalist guerrillas who waged a protracted struggle for liberation from 1961 in Angola and 1964 in Mozambique. Thereafter, the Portuguese sought to resist the decolonisation tide by encouraging the large-scale migration of white settlers from the motherland, and by opening the territories up to foreign investment. Hence it was that South African capital now flowed freely into both Angola and Mozambique, the Portuguese objective of basing colonial development on mineral and resource extraction melding neatly with the Republic's own industrial needs. Indeed, although the search for oil in Angola was dominated by Portuguese concerns and the Portuguese were successful in attracting international capital from the United States, Britain and Europe to assist in financing their various schemes, such ventures as Cabora Bassa, the Kunene River project and the construction of the natural gas pipeline from Mozambique to the Transvaal would not have been viable without South African finance, expertise and, most critically, guarantee of a future market.

As the guerrilla threat mounted and the Frente de Libertacao de Mocambique, in particular, being determined to halt construction of Cabora Bassa (associated with which was an irrigation scheme designed to attract one million settlers), South Africa became more closely involved in the defence of the Portuguese empire. However, the bulk of such assistance lay in the provision of supplies and extensive exchange of intelligence rather than in direct military involvement, for South Africa was as wary of becoming engaged in an expensive, long-running encounter as Portugal was cautious about encouraging a growth of South African influence in the determination of its colonial future. Yet even if political tensions overlaid a more fundamental imperialistic harmony, South Africa remained sensitive to Portuguese aspirations, not only because of a shared interest in the maintenance of the colonial order, but because friendship with Portugal was seen as an entree to South America via its close connections with Brazil. Here South African hopes were directed at the formation of a South Atlantic Treaty Organisation to counter the perceived communist threat. Such an organisation would not only legitimate South African military and naval expansionism, but would also serve to integrate the Republic with the North Atlantic Treaty Organisation through Portuguese joint membership. Although this project did not eventuate, it nonetheless remained an important objective, as South Africa's outward policy stretched beyond the African continent to involve bilateral economic and military linkages with a number of South American regimes.

Detente

Rhodesian UDI in November 1965 clarified South Africa's sub-imperial role, compromised the outward thrust and forged closer bonds between Lisbon, Salisbury and Pretoria. UDI was not welcomed in the sense that it introduced an enormously complicating factor into South Africa's external relations, yet in the absence of an independence settlement which would have effectively legitimated white rule, Verwoerd's long-standing opposition to decolonisation guaranteed South African support for the maintenance of racial minority rule.

Without South African (and Portuguese) assistance, Rhodesia would have been denied oil, transport linkages and vital supplies. Yet South African commitment was not unambiguous in that it eschewed recognition of the illegal regime and espoused a formal neutrality which urged a negotiated settlement between the British and Rhodesian governments. South African efforts were devoted to ensuring that British-imposed and UN-mandated sanctions against Rhodesia were rendered ineffective (in large part, to discourage the adoption of such a weapon against the Republic itself); and when British determination to end the rebellion proved irresolute, the Republic did not hesitate in 1967 to send its police to assist the Rhodesian military confront insurgents on the grounds that South African ANC guerrillas were fighting alongside ZAPU (the Zimbabwe African People's Union). Indeed, South African military support was an important factor in enabling Rhodesian forces to achieve a predominance which was, for the moment, underlined by divisions within and between the various nationalist organisations.

Confidence in the enduring strength of the white entente encouraged Prime Minister Vorster (who had succeeded Verwoerd in 1966) in promoting dialogue. Yet so long as South Africa succeeded in suborning only known conservative states, prospects for securing a major breakthrough into black Africa remained slender. Hence it was that from 1968 the South African government engaged in secret correspondence and contacts with Zambia, the black state in Southern Africa most openly identified with opposition to the various white regimes (see Chapter 12).

Since well before independence, President Kenneth Kaunda had been closely aligned with the nationalist movements opposing minority rule in Rhodesia, colonialism in Angola and Mozambique, and apartheid in South Africa. Yet inherited dependence of Zambia upon the Republic (notably domination of the copper-mining industry by the Anglo-American Corporation and reliance upon South Africa for skilled manpower, transport routes and imports) imposed the necessity of economic links with South Africa, even though the Zambian government consciously sought to disengage from the white South by extending its transport networks and trade with black Africa, whilst simultaneously offering nationalist guerrillas substantial material and political support.

Although South African collaboration with Rhodesia and Portugal intensified mutual hostility across the Zambezi, the Republic's policy towards Zambia remained one of restraint. Indeed, as far as South Africa was concerned, Zambia symbolised the great prize whose capture would crown the outward movement with lasting success, for detachment of the Kaunda government from support for pan-African strategy could simultaneously deprive nationalist guerrillas of their land base and undermine the perceived credibility of militant armed struggle against white rule in favour of more gradualist compromise founded upon 'economic realism'. For his part, Kaunda did not repudiate the South African government's covert initiatives, reasoning that he might thereby dissuade Vorster from lending the Rhodesian regime its unequivocal assistance.

Kaunda's role in promulgating the Lusaka Manifesto was consistent with his objective of avoiding a confrontation with South Africa. If it did little to endear him to Pretoria, his explicitly non-Marxist ideology of humanism and his accommodation to transnational firms (albeit within a 'state capitalist' framework) at home, marked him out as a political 'moderate' with whom South Africa could not unlikely deal. However, his accession to the chairmanship of the OAU in 1970, and his resulting prominence in campaigns against dialogue and the announcement of the recently elected British government that it intended to resume arms sales to South Africa, were now to render him an obstacle to the Republic's immediate goals. Consequently, given Kaunda's increasingly insecure domestic position (related in part to economic shortages which were relieved only by the import of maize from Rhodesia in breach of sanctions), Vorster attempted to expose Kaunda as duplicitous by revealing his secret correspondence with him. However, Vorster's breach of confidence brought condemnation even from his partners in dialogue (afraid, perhaps, of themselves being exposed as more involved with South Africa than the world was aware). And if his revelations were intended to precipitate Kaunda's overthrow, they failed, even though they succeeded in highlighting the ambiguities which Zambia's dependence imposed upon its actions in the foreign policy sphere.

South African concern with mounting guerrilla threat in Angola and Mozambique, together with a major strike by workers and increased activity by the South West African People's Organisation in Namibia, led to more extensive collaboration with Portugal. Breakthrough by Zimbabwean guerrillas from 1971 also led to a greater South African involvement in counter-insurgency alongside Rhodesian security. Consequently South African relations with Zambia continued to deteriorate, with Pretoria evincing particular concern at the strategic implications of the Chinese built Tan-Zam railway (which gave Zambia access to the sea) and expressing 'mounting impatience' with the operation of 'terrorists' from Zambian territory.[14]

Yet South African support for Rhodesia was not without its strains, one instance of which was Vorster's anger at Premier Ian Smith's unilateral closing of his border with Zambia in January 1973 in retaliation for that country's harbouring of guerrillas. Kaunda's response of making the closure permanent reinforced South African conviction that air strikes upon the guerrilla camps would have been more propitious than a move which encouraged economic disengagement. Even so, Pretoria's continuing support for the illegal regime was, for all its difficulties internationally, premised very largely on a determination to keep the guerrilla threat away from the Republic's own borders.

Regional relations were transformed by the coup d'etat of 25 April 1974 in which the Portuguese Armed Forces, disillusioned and radicalised by the colonial wars, overthrew the fascist state. Although the new military government was immediately divided between the revolutionary left (which argued for independence for the African dependencies) and the supporters of the new President, General Spinola, who favoured an explicitly neo-colonial, Lusitanian federation of the metropole with self-governing colonies, it was clear that the alliance between South Africa, Portugal and Rhodesia had now been irrevocably breached. Rhodesia and Namibia could now expect to become exposed to guerrilla pressure from once Portuguese borders that had formerly provided for their protection, whilst South Africa also had to reckon with a re-evaluation in Western capitals of those Southern African policies which had been based on the mistaken assumption of the invulnerability of white power.

Following the coup, South Africa gave immediate recognition to the new Portuguese authorities and also indicated that she would cooperate with a (self-proclaimed) Marxist—Leninist FRELIMO government in Mozambique, which it now perceived as inevitably coming to power. Pragmatic acceptance of a liberated Mozambique was based, further, not merely on optimism concerning the extent of that country's economic dependence upon South Africa, but also upon the need to secure a continuation of the flow of Mozambique workers to the mines and the supply of energy from Cabora Bassa (which was about to come on tap), as well as obtaining a guarantee that Mozambican territory would not be used as a base for guerrilla attacks upon the Republic. Accordingly, there was no South African support for an attempted putsch launched by right-wing settlers in Laurenco Marques (soon re-named Maputo) in September 1974, this bringing its reward in the form of a reciprocally pragmatic orientation towards the Republic by the incoming FRELIMO government. Importantly, however, FRELIMO made the withdrawal of South African forces from Rhodesia a pre-condition of all future negotiation.

This brought a fundamental reassessment of South African policy towards Rhodesia. White minority rule in that country was now seen as doomed, and it became the South African goal to avoid extensive military involvement, alongside Rhodesian security, in an intensifying war with nationalist guerrillas which would become increasingly costly and whose pursuit would isolate South Africa even more inter-nationally. Regional stability, seen as vital to the long-term preservation of the apartheid political economy, now became defined as convincing the Smith regime of its fateful destiny and easing a transition to a 'moderate' black (or majority-rule) government in Rhodesia which would restore peace internally, receive recognition internationally and cooperate functionally with the South African regime. But the constraints of white politics within South Africa meant that Vorster could not ditch Smith too unceremoniously, and the only way in which his government could secure its new objectives was through bringing about a negotiated settlement between the contending forces.

It was the essence of the ensuing period of detente that this aim coincided with at least some interests of its black neighbours. In the case of Zambia, for instance, whose economy was confronted by a combination of a drastic decline in the government's economic management and strategy, elements within the governing African bourgeoisie saw detente (involving a Rhodesian settlement, a re-opening of the border and increased linkages with South Africa) as leading to an inflow of foreign capital and commodities, thereby alleviating the immediate crisis. But the ruling elements of the other Front Line States — Botswana, Tanzania, Mozambique and (later) Angola (whose economies were all ailing to some considerable extent, (see Chapters 1, 2 and 10) — were also eager to achieve some measure of political accommodation with the Republic; and in consequence, the basis of the deal was that while Vorster would deliver Smith to the conference table to negotiate a transition to majority rule, the Front Line States (and notably Kaunda and Nyerere) would ensure the cooperation of the Zimbabwean liberation movements.

The substantive result of detente was the Lusaka Agreement of December 1974. Made possible by Vorster leaning upon Smith so as to secure the release of the nationalist leadership which had been imprisoned since before UDI (notably Joshua Nkomo, President of ZAPU, and Robert Mugabe and Ndabaningi Sithole of ZANU, the former having displaced the latter as leader), the agreement was further facilitated by the Front Line Presidents (Kaunda, Nyerere and Botswana's Seretse Khama) bludgeoning the nationalist movements (ZANU, ZAPU and the smaller FROLIZI) into uniting under the rubric of the African Nationalist Council, formally headed by Bishop Abel Muzorewa, in order to negotiate a settlement with Smith.

The Lusaka Agreement resulted in a ceasefire as a preliminary to constitutional negotiations. However, there were immediate disagreements about the terms of the truce. For their part, the nationalist leaders claimed that they had only agreed to suspend the armed struggle once Smith had consented to a number of preconditions (including the release of political prisoners, the lifting of the bans on ZANU and ZAPU and the permitting of free political activity). For his part, the Rhodesian Premier announced that he had received a guarantee that 'terrorist activity in Rhodesia [would] cease immediately and the proposed constitutional conference [would] take place without preconditions.'[15] Indeed, Smith's refusal to release further detainees (as had been agreed), and his insistence that the ceasefire implied the unconditional surrender and disarming of the guerrillas, signified his intent to sabotage the entire detente exercise, which he correctly perceived as inimical to the survival of his settler regime. Consequently, although something of a ceasefire came into effect on 11 December 1974, conflicting interpretations by both sides about what each had conceded led to a resumption of hostilities the following month.

With detente in danger of collapse, the Front Line Presidents and Vorster sought to cajole their respective allies back to the negotiating table. In this they succeeded in the sense that the constitutional conference agreed upon was convened on 25 August 1975 on a train parked symbolically on the Victoria Falls Bridge between Rhodesia and Zambia. To reach this stage, however, Vorster had had to exert pressure upon the minority regime to the extent of withdrawing all South African forces from Rhodesia, whilst the Front Line States had sought to contain opposition to detente within the nationalist movements. With Nkomo of ZAPU emerging as the one leader who combined the virtues of widespread legitimacy (as the father of Zimbabwean nationalism), eagerness to negotiate a settlement, and acceptability to Vorster as the potential head of a 'moderate' majority-rule regime, Kaunda had moved to suppress ZANU within his territory, whilst Tanzanian and Mozambican troops had also taken over guerrilla camps in their own countries and restricted the flow of weapons to ZANU in the field. But with the nationalists locked together in only an externally imposed unity, and with Smith determined not to give way, the talks were doomed to an early demise, despite the active personal interventions of both Kaunda and Vorster. Subsequently, however (with the continuing support of Kaunda but not of Nyerere), Nkomo pursued talks with Smith independently of the other major nationalist factions, these lasting from December 1975 through to March 1976. But by now South Africa was overwhelmingly preoccupied with the outbreak of the Angolan civil war, and these negotiations foundered, not merely upon Smith's continuing intransigence, but also as a result of the reassessment of their objectives and strategies by the major backers of the detente exercise.

At the time of the April 1974 coup, the Portuguese retained a not unfavourable position in Angola, where the nationalist forces were divided between three competing parties: the MPLA (Movimento Popular de Libertacao de Angola), whose support was located principally amongst the working masses in the greater Luanda area and which enjoyed the backing of the Soviet Union; the FNLA (Frente Nacional de Libertacao de Angola), representative mainly of ethnic Bakongo and supported by the United States-backed, neo-colonial Mobuto regime in Zaire; and UNITA (Uniao Nacional para a Independencia Total de Angola), the smallest of the three groups, led by Jonas Savimbi and based in Zambia and Eastern Zaire. As a result of this division, as well as a fragmentation of authority between contending left and right factions which supported the MPLA and FNLA respectively, the Portuguese decolonisation strategy was based on the remarkable Alvar Agreement of January 1975 which, inclusive of UNITA at the last moment in a bid to balance the two older parties, scheduled independence for 11 November 1975. In the meantime, the various parties agreed to remain within their own liberated areas, to cooperate in the building of a national army, and each to participate in the formation of a transitional government which would draw up a constitution and allow for national elections before independence.

Angola was the most valuable of Portugal's African territories: by 1974, it was the third largest oil-producing country on the continent, as well as being a significant source of coffee, diamonds and other minerals including iron ore, copper and uranium. Accordingly, when the Alvar Agreement collapsed in March 1975 (as the FNLA strove to drive the MPLA out from its Luanda base area), the conflict rapidly became internationalised. With the Portuguese army divided, indecisive and demoralised to the extent that its major concern was not in extricating itself from the country, Congo-Brazzaville and Zaire (favouring the MPLA and FNLA respectively whilst simultaneously supporting different factions of FLEC (Front for the Liberation of the Enclave of Cabinda), a secessionist splinter group), both eyed the oil-producing Cabina enclave jealously while the major Western powers and South Africa gave their clandestine backing to FNLA and UNITA; but as MPLA mobilised its support in Luanda through a network of *poder pover* (people's power) committees and rapidly took the offensive, threatening to establish control over most of the country by the date set for independence, Western assistance to their clients became more overtly forthcoming in the form of finance, weapons and mercenaries. Most crucially, however, on the understanding that it would receive concerted United States support, the South African government sent some 2–3,000 troops across the border to confront the MPLA, backing them up with an equivalent number of mechanised cavalry in December.

The South African Defence Force enjoyed rapid, early success, penetrating far into the heart of Angola, but they soon ran up against two obstacles which were fatal to their design of a quick campaign which would leave the Western-backed FNLA and UNITA in power. First, the MPLA received substantial military assistance in the form of large supplies of weapons from the Soviet Union and up to 9,000 troops from Cuba; and second, fearful of becoming embroiled in a second Vietnam-type war, the United States Congress declined to support Secretary of State Henry Kissinger's plans for more extensive involvement in the conflict. Accordingly, despite desperate attempts by some Western interests and various African leaders (notably Kaunda) to secure the formation of a new coalition government, the Cuban-backed MPLA pressed on to a victory over its rivals sufficient to gain diplomatic recognition from most African states which, outraged by the South African invasion, acknowledged it as forming the legitimate government of Angola in February 1976. In contrast, let down by the United States 'betrayal', South African troops beat a humiliating retreat in exchange for an MPLA guarantee for the security of the electricity-providing Cunene Dam.

The South African invasion had been launched in the name of detente, to which a victory of the revolutionary forces of the MPLA was represented as fatal. Indeed, it is probable that the South African action had had the active, if covert, blessing of both the Zambian and Zairean governments which supported UNITA and FNLA respectively, both preferring to see a pro-Western, non-radical government assume power in Luanda. But as continental anger at the South African involvement crystallised, no African leader could afford to be associated with the aggressive intentions of the apartheid regime. Even worse, from the South African viewpoint, was the fact that the Angolan war now shifted the initiative amongst the Front Line States to the radicals, who now favoured a resumption of the armed struggle in Rhodesia. Detente was not yet dead, but it was only with some considerable difficulty that it was now to be revived.

Fissure and crisis of the apartheid state, post-1976: from detente to destabilisation

The collapse of Portuguese authority, the consequent handover of power to FRELIMO in Mozambique, outbreak of war in Angola and the intensifying scope of the conflict in Rhodesia, caused a major reassessment by the Western powers of their short- and long-term interests in Southern Africa. No longer able to rely upon the 'triple alliance' of white regimes to protect their interests within the region, they were particularly alarmed by the perceived strategic and economic threat which was posed by growing Soviet influence (more usually termed 'intervention' after Cuban troops had arrived in Angola at the behest of the MPLA). But of greatest immediate significance was the Soweto uprising of June–September 1976 in South Africa itself, which, based initially upon the revolt of school pupils against the impositions of Bantu education reflected the growing strength of black labour and developed into a broader struggle involving widespread and sustained strikes by black workers. Signifying the growing determination of the oppressed majority to overthrow white supremacist rule, it caused a major outflow of capital which indicated foreign investors' growing doubts about South Africa's political stability.

Detente, laid to rest by the Angolan debacle, had specifically political objectives (notably an end to war and a negotiated transition to majority rule in Zimbabwe), but it had an economic basis in the asymmetric relation between the Republic's expansionism and black Africa's dependence and underdevelopment. Thus between 1966 and 1976, South African exports to other parts of Africa rose by R256m to R453m, an increase of 130 per cent; imports rose by R181m to R310m, an increase of 141 per cent, giving a healthy balance of trade surplus in South Africa's favour. Yet despite this growth in the absolute levels of trade, the Republic's outward thrust was encountering serious limitations. In the first place, the proportion of South African exports going to the rest of Africa was subject to a dramatic decline: while 19 per cent of South African exports went to Africa in 1964 holding constant until 1971 (18.6 per cent), the proportion dropped thereafter to 10 per cent by 1980. Whether this decline took place because of a re-emphasis in Africa's trading relations with Europe under the Lomé Convention, or whether simply because African countries lacked foreign exchange as a result of higher oil prices and the world recession, is not immediately clear. What is evident, however, is that the decline was not due to the supposed OAU boycott by South African goods, for by 1981 — if the South African Foreign Trade Organisation is to be believed — 47 of Africa's 51 independent states did business, directly or indirectly, with South Africa.[16]

A second major obstacle to the outward thrust in the late 1970s was that the bulk of South Africa's African trade was accounted for by the Southern African periphery, especially Zimbabwe, but also the BLS states, Mozambique, Malawi, Zambia, Zaire and, in addition, Mauritius, (which implies that any future concerted re-orientation of regional trading patterns could have disproportionate effect upon South Africa's African exports). As it is, the proportionate decline in South African exports to Africa was one contributory factor underlying the slump that afflicted the Republic's manufacturing sector during the mid-1970s. Indeed, the fact that the manufacturing sector has remained a heavy net importer of goods and services (the ratio of manufacturing imports to exports being greater than three to one in 1975) means that South Africa continues to rely on the export of primary products (and notably gold) to acquire the foreign exchange necessary to finance its continuing industrial expansion.

Equally important, however, was the major shift in trading and investment relations on the part of Western capital towards black Africa and away from South Africa. Thus whereas new investments and reinvested earnings by United States firms amounted to $9m and $73m respectively in 1976, the comparable figures for Africa as a whole were $256m and $584m. Similarly, whilst South Africa was Britain's third largest export market in 1967, buying 5 per cent of all British merchandise exports, it had fallen to sixteenth place in 1977, taking only 1.8 per cent of such exports (a trend which was reinforced by British membership of the EEC). In contrast, by 1978, Nigeria — black Africa's oil-based, economic giant — had become Britain's ninth largest trading partner, and having surpassed South Africa in total trade with the United States and in the rate of new American investment in 1973, supplied 16 per cent of total United States oil imports in 1980. But what gave Nigeria its particular importance in the Southern African context in the late 1970s was its declared intention to use its newly acquired leverage to cajole the West into extracting concessions from the white minority regimes (see Chapter 8).

Detente, phase two

The Cuban engagement in Angola had given cause for United States foreign policy under the republican administration of Gerald Ford to award greater weight to Southern Africa in order to contain 'Soviet expansionism'. Accordingly, it was signalled to Pretoria that, in return for South Africa agreeing to cajole the Smith government in Rhodesia into making the concessions necessary for a negotiated settlement, the United States would use its influence to divert international pressure away from the Republic (so long as the apartheid regime also agreed to introduce a number of convincing domestic reforms). Hence, despite the rift over Angola, yet spurred by the explosion of Soweto on 16 June, Pretoria exerted the required force upon the Smith government, the dramatic result of talks between Kissinger, Vorster and the Rhodesian premier being the announcement by Smith on 24 September 1976 of his willingness to negotiate a transition to majority rule within two years. However, the subsequent October–December 1976 constitutional conference in Geneva, summoned to negotiate a transition to majority rule, collapsed when it became clear that the ruling Rhodesian Front Party was not prepared to confer more than an appearance of political power on the African majority, being determined to retain effective control over both the government and the economy.

When the democratic administration of President Jimmy Carter assumed office in 1977, it initiated a sweeping reassessment of United States foreign policy. As far as Africa was concerned, this involved a recognition of the expanding United States material interest in black states (especially Nigeria), whilst Carter's 'human rights' stance also resulted in a more open critique of apartheid which culminated in a call by Vice-President Walter Mondale for equal participation by all citizens of South Africa in the election of their government. Furthermore, United States support was also given to the mandatory arms embargo imposed by the UN after the South African regime cracked down on black militants when it banned some 34 political organisations in October 1977.

The consequent deterioration in relations between Washington and Pretoria (Vorster called and won an election in November 1977 to counter alleged United States 'interference' in South Africa's domestic affairs), resulted in a major South African policy shift in favour of Ian Smith's concurrent efforts to find an 'internal settlement'. Propelled by the urgency of a marked escalation of the liberation war (notably by ZANU) which it became increasingly clear it could not hope to win, the rebel regime was now engaged in feverish efforts to manipulate the divisions within nationalist ranks (between and within ZANU and ZAPU, as well as internal groups) in order to forge a working alliance with 'moderate' black leaders which would leave the white power structure essentially intact. Initially, enabled by the increased scope for manoeuvre now granted him by Pretoria to reject further Anglo-American proposals for a settlement, Smith sought to come to terms with Nkomo, increasingly seen as a Kenyatta-like, pro-capitalist, potentially neo-colonialist leader. However, when this failed, Smith turned as second choice to Abel Muzorewa, now leader of the United African Nationalist Council, an internal party which enjoyed not inconsiderable domestic African support. Joined by Ndabaningi Sithole (deposed leader of ZANU who had been excluded from the 'Patriotic Front' which that movement had forged with ZAPU under pressure from the Front Line leaders) and Chief Jeremiah Chirau (who had been appointed to the Rhodesian Cabinet in 1976 to give it some semblance of African support), Muzorewa came to an agreement with Smith on 3 March 1978.

This internal settlement provided for a majority rule constitution, but within this framework involved the preservation of white seats in Parliament, white veto over further constitutional change for ten years, and effective white control over the military, internal security, the civil service and the judiciary whilst also guaranteeing existing rights of property, pensions and public employment. Furthermore, the transition government in which power was formally shared between the Rhodesian Front and the internal nationalists was effectively dominated by the former ruling elements; and although Muzorewa subsequently assumed office as Prime Minister of what was now termed Zimbabwe-Rhodesia after his UANC won 51 out of 72 African seats in an April 1979 election, his government embraced a coalition with the Rhodesian Front, and the substance of power still remained with Ian Smith.

The internal settlement was condemned by the UN, the OAU and both wings of the excluded Patriotic Front, which stepped up its guerrilla campaign, ZANU operating from Mozambique (having been driven from Zambia after Kaunda's clampdown) and ZAPU (although considerably less active) from Zambia. Although failure to end the war and confront settler power led to a steady erosion of Muzorewa's domestic support (even if this was not obvious to those who were committed to the increasingly fragile settlement), South African material and military support was vital in enabling the Zimbabwe-Rhodesian regime to survive. Indeed, Pretoria now viewed Muzorewa's government as a viable and favourable enterprise, for the prospects of its gaining international recognition seemed now to have become more propitious. Zambia, undergoing the throes of an acute foreign exchange crisis, had reopened the border with Rhodesia in October 1978 in order to clear a backlog of copper exports and was desperate for some sort of settlement, as was Mozambique (host to ZANU), whose territory was continuously being violated by Rhodesian air strikes and military raids; Pretoria's cool relations with Washington were steadily thawing out as the Carter administration became increasingly concerned with Soviet penetration of Africa (Cuban troops being used in Ethiopia as well as Angola); and in May 1979, a Conservative government under Margaret Thatcher swept to power in Britain and seemed set to recognise the Muzorewa regime.

But such recognition was not to be, for at this critical juncture, Nigeria intervened, linking nationalisation of British Petroleum, a refusal to countenance British firms' bids for federal contracts and other economic measures to British plans for legitimising the internal settlement. Not only Britain, but the United States was thus warned of the costs which a commitment to Muzorewa would entail. As a result, previous Anglo-American proposals for a settlement inclusive of the Patriotic Front were revived culminating in the convening of the Lancaster House Conference in December 1979. There, with the West and South Africa pressing Smith and Muzorewa, and with the Front Line States levering both ZAPU and a ZANU which was reluctant to make compromising concessions, agreement was reached on new elections and a new settlement.

The subsequent victory of Robert Mugabe's ZANU (which in March 1980 elections won 51 out of 80 seats in a 100-seat parliament where the remainder were reserved for whites), shattered British calculations which had been based upon an assumption that no one party could secure an absolute majority, and that ZANU (whose explicitly socialist programme was viewed as a severe threat to Western interests) would be excluded from power, hopefully via a coalition between UANC, ZAPU and even the Rhodesian Front. But the government which now took power was effectively run by ZANU, even though Joshua Nkomo and ZAPU were incorporated into a coalition as subordinates. Only time would tell if the Mugabe-led ZANU would turn out to be the radical force which South Africa, the West and the Rhodesian settlers had so feared.

Siege and destabilisation

South African acceptance of Lancaster House had been premised on expectation of, if not a Muzorewa victory at the polls, then at least the election of a 'moderate' coalition government which the Front Line States would be forced to recognise by their vested interest in a settlement. But South African confidence that Muzorewa enjoyed greater domestic support than the 'terrorists' was wrong, and the news of the Mugabe victory was received in Pretoria with a profound sense of shock. Nonetheless, Prime Minister P.W. Botha (who had succeeded Vorster in 1978) resisted the temptation to support a post-electoral coup by Rhodesian security forces and thereafter announced a policy of careful neutrality. Although the Mugabe regime was regarded with considerable misgiving, solace was taken in the new Zimbabwean government's strenuous efforts to forge a national reconciliation between blacks and whites and to prevent an outflow of the latter from the country, the ready moderation of its socialist programme, its pragmatic acceptance of capitalist enterprise, and its declared intention of courting foreign investment. Mugabe's immediate post-independence emphasis upon the need for coexistence with South Africa founded upon the recognition of Zimbabwe's acute dependence upon its trade and transport links with the Republic), was therefore cautiously reciprocated.

Confirmation of these linkages with Zimbabwe was mirrored by South Africa's ties with other neighbouring states. Mozambique, for instance, continued to supply migrant workers to the mines, whilst South Africa made considerable use of Mozambican railways and harbours, and continued to receive electrical power from the Cabora Bassa Dam; Zambia, meanwhile, had increased both its imports and exports with the Republic. Inevitably, however, the settlement in Zimbabwe meant that South Africa was more isolated than ever before, notwithstanding its forging of closer links with other 'pariah' states such as Taiwan, Israel and Argentina. Thus although the immediate attentions of the international community were now to be directed at securing an independence settlement for Namibia, no one could doubt that this would form but a prelude to an increasingly determined assault by the force of liberation upon the apartheid regime itself.

The apartheid state had now encountered a period of acute crisis whose most dramatic manifestation was open fissure within the white ruling bloc. Conflict was (and remains) principally centred around the extent to which the government should rationalise apartheid, adjusting the instruments of labour repression and control to the requirements of the modernising economy, whilst simultaneously making it more stable politically. Largely associated with Premier Botha's 'total strategy' (designed to counter a 'communist-inspired total onslaught'), the new reformism includes a complex of political and economic measures. These include: the absorption of key segments of the coloured and Indian populations into the central polity (via a tripartite parliamentary structure ultimately controlled by whites); co-option of the small but expanding African middle class by easing African access to home ownership and participation in the business sector in urban areas; dividing the urban from the migrant black working class by trans-formation of the former into a labour aristocracy whose *relative* privilege will stem from a streamlining of influx control (granting greater permanence and greater job stability for the employed in urban areas), greater mobility into higher skilled work areas vacated by whites, and its incorporation into trade unions whose bargaining potential will be contained and controlled by state supervision. Com-bined with a relaxation of petty apartheid, a clamping down on black radicals, and increased defence spending, Botha reformism is designed to shore up the crumbling foundations of white power. However, although it has been welcomed by foreign and national large-scale capital, it nonetheless offends entrenched interests within the white bloc (notably petty bourgeois and working-class elements threatened by the spectre of black upward mobility). This has resulted in severe con-flict within the ruling party, although the 1981 breakaway of a far right, *verkrampte* wing under former Cabinet Minister and Transvaal Party Leader Andries Treurnicht also reflects ideological tensions and factional stresses stemming from the changing class composition (reflecting the *embourgeoisement* of the Afrikaner community) of the NP after more than 30 years in office.

Botha's reform strategy has been implemented only because of severe pressure. Internally, the regime now faces an assertive black majority whose strength derives from an increasingly militant, mobilised and self-confident working class. Externally, it faces guerrilla struggle by the South West African People's Organisation and increasingly, also, by the ANC, together with mounting (if spasmodic) diplomatic pressure to come to a settlement in Namibia.

Against the background of a major strike by African contract workers on the mines in 1971, the Portuguese coup provided a major turning point in the Republic's strategy towards Namibia. Although black political activity was to remain episodic until 1978, the South African government recognised the need for some accommodation to the forces of change. Initally, however, the coup seemed to have strengthened South African commitment to separate development within the territory. But subsequently, following Western prompting via the UN Security Council, the South African government convened the so-called 'Turnhalle' Conference of representatives of diverse ethnic groups (and thus exclusive of SWAPO) to draw up a blueprint for the territory's future. Extending through September 1975—August 1976, the negotiations culminated in a basic change in South African policy, setting a date for independence for Namibia (31 December 1978) and laying to rest a favoured notion of giving Ovamboland (the most populous ethnic homeland) a separate independence. However, later constitutional progress was hampered by the determination of the white delegation not to depart from the basic structures of apartheid. Western impatience thus led to Vorster's suspending Turnhalle's constitutional role, and (as part of the wider detente exercise), appointing a transitional administration which would work in tandem with the UN towards the holding of a general election for a constituent assembly which would prepare for independence. Following further diplomatic initiatives, both the South African government and SWAPO were then induced to accept a plan for a peace settlement which was then endorsed by the UN Security Council in its Resolution 435 of (June) 1978. Its essence was that a UN administrative and military force should share responsibility with South Africa during an interim administration leading up to elections for a constituent assembly (which unlike the Turnhalle version, of course, would be inclusive of SWAPO), before which a ceasefire would be implemented, SWAPO and South African forces restricted to specified camps, and discriminatory and restrictive laws repealed.

Resolution 435 provided the framework for the Geneva conference between South Africa, SWAPO, the 'Contact Group' of five Western powers[17] and the five African Front Line States in November 1979. But no agreement was reached, the deadlock having been foreshadowed by earlier South African reluctance to implement vital aspects of the proposed plan. In particular, Pretoria declined to contemplate a reduction of its military forces in Namibia to 1,500, to accept a proposed 7,500-man UN supervisory force, to trust UN monitoring of SWAPO guerrilla bases in Angola during the transition period, or to allow SWAPO to establish military bases within Namibia after a ceasefire took effect. South African intransigence, upheld amongst other things by the victory of Republican presidential candidate Ronald Reagan in the November 1979 United States election, was thus to be converted into a covert repudiation of the UN plan and a decision to back the Democratic Turnhalle Alliance (DTA) as the vehicle for an internal settlement along the lines of the model then currently being implemented in Rhodesia.

Vorster's suspension of the Turnhalle negotiations in 1977 on account of the slow progress being made had resulted in a rift within the South West African National Party between a reformist group, which broke away to form a Republic Party, and hardline Nationalists, who regrouped as Aktur. Supported strongly by Pretoria, the Republic Party liaised with various black ethnic groups to form the DTA dedicated to building upon the basis of Turnhalle according to confederal principles, wherein 'group' interests would be protected by a two-tiered structure of government whose multi-ethnic central level would somehow operate on a consensual basis, while the lower, local level (based on homeland and white territorial structures) would retain important powers. Within this framework, the role of the DTA was to forge a coalition of accommodative whites and conservative black ethnic leaders which would work to exclude SWAPO from the political process. A territory-wide election in December 1978 carried out under South African auspices to implement this scheme (and which was therefore boycotted by SWAPO's internal wing) resulted in a handsome victory for the DTA (this being reflective of South African pressures upon voters). Subsequently, the DTA was instrumental in ending an array of discriminatory practices. However, whilst this resulted in loss of its rather tentative white support for going too far, it correspondingly involved a reduction of its limited black support for not going far enough.

Yet prospects for a viable internal settlement in Namibia were dashed by the rapid pace of events concerning Rhodesia and increased SWAPO guerrilla activity from bases within Angola. Accordingly, considerable efforts to revive the UN plan were made throughout 1980 to 1982, with South Africa moving from intransigence to somewhat doubtful cooperation with the Contact Group. Latterly, however, these efforts have been undermined by United States diplomacy which, under the Reagan administration, has subordinated the issue of Namibia independence *per se* to securing a withdrawal of Cuban troops from Angola. In consequence, Western pressure upon the Republic to come to a settlement has diminished and – at the time of writing – there is again talk of South Africa opting for an internal administration, even if this will require an alternative instrument to the DTA, whose evident loss of support led to the dismissal in January 1983 of the National Assembly in Windhoek and the resumption of direct rule from Pretoria.

The Contact Group's objective in Namibia is to reach a neo-colonial settlement, inclusive of more groups than SWAPO, whereby the West retains access to the territory's rich mineral wealth. In addition, as stated, the current United States administration is obsessed with obtaining a Cuban withdrawal. Meanwhile, South Africa has different concerns. First, SWAPO is perceived not as a legitimate nationalist movement which would come to a pragmatic accommodation with its white neighbour, but as a revolutionary movement spearheading the international communist onslaught against South Africa itself. In consequence, second, the possibility of a SWAPO regime in Windhoek is seen as representing a major threat to the Republic's security and material interests, whilst also providing a major boost to the confidence of black radicals at home. And third, major concessions offered to SWAPO would be strongly resisted by settlers in Namibia and would likely provoke a serious backlash amongst the electorate which would be exploited by the government's right-wing opponents.

Against this, the Republic has to weigh the fact that the OAU, the Front Line States and Nigeria, frustrated by continuous South African stalling, have begun to link failure to make progress towards a settlement along the lines of the UN proposal to the imposition of sanctions. In acknowledgement of this, the Contact Group made major efforts throughout 1981 in order to entice South Africa back to the conference table. Yet Pretoria remains to this day reasonably confident that the West will veto sanctions, which in any case the Front Line and other Southern African states could probably not afford to implement. Stunned by the victory of Mugabe's ZANU (the most radical group on offer) in the Zimbabwean election in 1980 (and which most observers feel serves as a pointer to a similar victory for SWAPO in any free and fair electoral context in Namibia), the South African policy remains devoted to breathing life into a confederal constitutional framework.

But closely linked to this continuing prevarication are South Africa's extensive military operations in Angola which are designed both to physically smash SWAPO and to weaken the Angolan government to the extent that it feels compelled to withdraw its support from the liberation struggle (see Chapter 1). A report made to the MPLA Congress in December 1980 claimed that South African aggression had resulted in 1,800 casualties and 3,000 wounded. According to Luanda, South African forces violated the Angolan frontier 529 times in the first six months of 1980; and since that time, there have been major South African incursions in 1981, 1982 and 1983. South Africa is thus effectively engaged in a full-scale, if low-intensity, war, and reliable reports indicate that attacks are launched systematically not merely against SWAPO, but also against Angolan targets.

Such aggressive tactics threaten to bring an escalation and internationalisation of the conflict in their wake. Doubtless this would be resisted by the Western powers who wish to see no excuse given for further Soviet involvement. Yet the South African strategy is simultaneously linked to attempts to destabilise surrounding states. In Angola, apart from invasion, South Africa is lending support to UNITA, which continues to be active in the southern half of the country. Similarly, South Africa supplies and trains the *Resistancia Nacional Mocambicana*, an anti-FRELIMO group formerly trained by the Rhodesian special branch; and in January 1981, South African commandos made an assault on an ANC base at Matola in the same country. Meanwhile, it would seem that South Africa has also given passive, if not active, support to the Lesotho Liberation Army (the military wing of the exile faction of the Opposition Basotho Congress Party) in retaliation for Chief Jonathan's hosting of ANC refugees; and in December 1982 South Africa supplemented this with a direct military raid upon Maseru which resulted in the slaughter of some 12 Basotho civilians as well as 31 black South African refugees and visitors. Furthermore, recruitment of white Rhodesian soldiers for the SADF as well as Shona members of Bishop Muzorewa's former militarised auxiliaries suggests preparation of a South African-sponsored Zimbabwean force to destabilise the Mugabe government, already troubled by strife between its dominant ZANU and junior ZAPU components. The inclusion in 1983 by Pretoria of Botswana in the category of countries it claims are supporting the ANC suggests that that country too will soon become a target of South African military aggression.

The destabilisation strategy is designed principally to heighten the costs to regional governments of support for guerrilla activity by the ANC. Yet in so doing it contradicts another major plank of current South African foreign policy. In November 1979, Prime Minister Botha voiced ambition to establish a 'constellation of states', an initiative which though never systematically spelt out, revived Verwoerdian aspirations for a formalisation of South African hegemony. At one level, it was suggestive of increased political cooperation between the Republic and its dependent neighbours, these latter to include those bantustans (Transkei, 1976; Bophuthatswana, 1977; Venda, 1979; and Ciskei, 1981) whose collaborative leaderships have accepted formal (albeit internationally unrecognised) 'independence' from the NP government; but at another, arguably more basic level, the principal thrust of the constellation idea was to provide a regional economic framework in which South Africa could increase its exports of both capital and goods. In short, the constellation would have provided a solidified basis for South Africa's now declining sub-imperialism.

Yet the constellation idea has made little headway. In the first place, by seeking to include the 'independent' bantustans as partners on equal terms with Southern African states, Botha has been seeking covert recognition of the apartheid framework of a South African white core state and ethnicised peripheries. Second, and more critically, the ZANU victory in Zimbabwe more or less killed constellation by providing the momentum for a counter-strategy. Indeed, in contrast to the constellation, the Southern African Development Coordination Conference, launched initially in Arusha in July 1979 but later being expanded by the addition of Zimbabwe, Swaziland, Lesotho and even Malawi to the Front Line States in order to foster a reduction of dependence upon South Africa shattered whatever prospect there was that the Republic might seriously assume regional leadership.

Although, for the moment, SADCC is committed primarily to coordination of material economic action for development rather than economic action against South Africa, it is quite overtly part and parcel of the broader liberation struggle, as is indicated by the fact that member states have also begun to lay the basis for regional military (as well as economic) security. In addition, to the extent that it succeeds in promoting disengagement of regional state economies from their dependence upon the Republic (even if this can by no means be completely achieved), it may yet provide the muscle enabling Southern African states to move towards implementing sanctions. Such a remarkable achievement as yet remains a long way off, but that it today constitutes a realistic potentiality suggests the foreseeable demise of the apartheid regime — barring South African nuclear assault upon the forces of liberation whose very possibility renders the eventual defeat of apartheid the intimate concern of humanity as a whole, and not simply of those who are directly oppressed.

Conclusion

A few comments are in order in conclusion. First, it is clear that, in the present era, white South Africa now stands more exposed, more vulnerable and more isolated than at any time before. On the one hand, South Africa is isolated politically from the West. To be sure, this is not to say that ruling circles in Western states are overtly hostile to the Republic, or even unsympathetic, but rather that they appreciate the costs of supporting South Africa openly. Whatever the heinous sins perpetrated upon their peoples by other governments (and, heaven knows, there are many which have engaged in quantitatively far greater slaughter of the innocents than South Africa), it is almost unanimously accepted that the racially motivated doctrine of apartheid — however refurbished ideologically — is morally unacceptable in a post-Nazi, decolonised world. That at least is one major gain of the second half of the twentieth century. Hence even those external forces which are broadly supportive of the *status quo* in South Africa must necessarily simultaneously proclaim their commitment towards racial and political equality, however slow and intricate their preferred process of change might be.

On the other hand, if — in this context — we discount Namibia as a separate entity, South Africa now stands isolated in Africa as the only remaining state ruled by a white majority. With its buffer hinterland of Portuguese colonialism and settler Rhodesia gone, South Africa now faces the prospect of mounting external pressure in the form of guerrilla challenge, diplomatic squeeze by friend and foe, and possibly, even economic sanctions at some future date. Despite continuing divisions within the OAU, and despite whatever linkages which South Africa manages to forge with black states, rejection of apartheid continues to provide an emotional bond behind which the rest of the continent can unite. Thus as the struggle in Southern Africa becomes more polarised, it may be expected that continental solidarity will harden around the need for a majority rule settlement in South Africa. If this will not exclude different political alternatives (and different ideological and material interests of the various African and especially Front Line States may imply that they seek varied solutions), there will nonetheless be an intensifying demand for South African whites to concede their monopoly of power. It follows from all this that the conflict over South Africa's future will likely become increasingly internationalised. But even if greater Soviet support were to be lent to the forces of liberation, the moral bankruptcy of apartheid will render South African attempts to identify continuance of white power with an anti-communist crusade ultimately futile.

In contrast to its political isolation, however, the Republic is now much more closely integrated into the global capitalist economy, just as the Southern African peripheral states continue to exhibit a critical level of dependence upon South Africa. Yet the purport of this chapter is that these linkages are not determinate. Despite the rise in the price of gold in the late 1970s which has given major support to the South African economy, the Republic continues to remain dependent upon inflows of capital goods, investment and technology from Western countries. Correlatively, although Western countries undoubtedly place a high value on South African mineral and raw material wealth, the increasing importance of the West's economic ties with black Africa will feed an appreciation that any successor to the existent regime in Pretoria will also need to market its supplies globally. Indeed, cold war scenarios which predict restriction of South African strategic produce to the Soviet Union overlook the fact that, not only is there considerable overlap between the variety of minerals produced by South Africa and the Soviet Union, but also make an unwarranted assumption that a majority rule regime would necessarily be Soviet-inclined. Hence Western efforts will be devoted to securing a non-racial settlement which will continue to foster the interests of international capital, whatever its overt political complexion.

Meanwhile, it appears likely that, although neighbouring African states will inevitably continue to remain economically subordinate and dependent upon the Republic, there will be a concerted attempt to disengage. There will doubtless be many contradictions, and this trend will not exclude a contrary extension of some economic linkages; for instance, land-locked Lesotho, although a member of SADCC, is currently negotiating terms for the construction of the major Malimabatso hydro-electric scheme to provide water and electricity to the Transvaal. However, current South African aggression against the Front Line States designed to suffocate their utility as guerrilla bases is likely to have the major consequence of hastening disengagement rather than inducing further dependence, polarisation between black and white Africa being underlined by South Africa's own declining need (given a contemporary surfeit of black labour at home) for foreign migrant labour.

In conclusion, therefore, it is suggested that Pretoria's foreign policy will prove inadequate to the task of bridging the gap between the Republic's political isolation and its increasing incorporation into the global capitalist economy. The Western powers, accepting that the writing is on the wall for continuing racial domination, are likely to become more interventionist in South African concerns with a view to moulding an eventual settlement which is favourable to their own needs. They also have global concerns that go well beyond Southern Africa, and certainly beyond the immediate interests of the present rulers of the Republic. Accordingly as the costs of supporting the apartheid regime rise — and there can be no doubt that they will — Western interests will come to see unmitigated white rule in South Africa as increasingly dispensable. This is not to suggest either that Western influence will be the major determining factor in any future settlement, or that the South Africa white ruling bloc will give up its monopoly of power without a long and bitter struggle, for they will not. But what it does suggest is that South African foreign policy will fail in any bid to link the *ultimate* survival of the apartheid regime with Western perception of Western long-term interests. The policy's primary function in future years would therefore seem to be to gain greater scope, manoeuvrability and time for the present rulers to adjust to an eventual fate of conceding majority rule; hence the continual shifting in the balance between destabilisation and detente in Southern Africa, symbolised by South Africa's incursions into, and subsequent negotiations with Lesotho, Angola and Mozambique in late 1983 and early 1984.

Notes

1   For the purpose of the present chapter, the term 'the Republic' will refer exclusively to South Africa.

2   Because of the summary nature of the present chapter, and the fact that it is dependent solely upon secondary sources, I have attempted to keep footnotes to an absolute minimum. Consequently, much of the analysis and data which follows is not specifically acknowledged. However, the author has relied extensively on the following works: J.E. Spence, *Republic Under Pressure: a Study of South African Foreign Policy* (London: Oxford University Press, 1965); and 'South African and the Modern World' in Monica Wilson and Leonard Thompson, (eds), *The Oxford History of South Africa, Vol. II, South Africa 1870–1966* (London: Oxford University Press, 1975), pp. 477–523; James Barber, *South Africa's Foreign Policy 1945–1970* (London: Oxford University Press, 1973); Amry Vandenbosch, *South Africa and the World: The Foreign Policy of Apartheid* (Lexington: University Press of Kentucky, 1970); Kenneth Grundy, *Confrontation and Accommodation in Southern Africa* (Berkeley: University of California Press, 1973); and especially Sam C. Nolutshungu, *South Africa in Africa: a study in ideology and foreign policy* (Manchester: Manchester University Press, 1975). Overviews of the post-1976 period are less numerous, but the following have proved most useful: Alex Callanicos and John Rogers, *Southern Africa after Soweto* (London: Pluto Press, 1977); Alex Callanicos, *Southern Africa after Zimbabwe* (London: Pluto Press, 1981); R.W. Johnson, *How Long Will South Africa Survive?* (London: Macmillan, 1977); and John Seiler (ed.), *Southern Africa after the Portuguese Coup* (Boulder: Westview, 1980). For a reasonably up-to-date and comprehensive bibliography, see Gail Lynda Rogaly, *South Africa's Foreign Relations, 1961–1979* (Johannesburg: South African Institute of International Affairs, 1980). On international economic linkages see especially Ruth First, Jonathan Steele, and Christabel Gurney, *The South African Connection: Western Investment in Apartheid* (Harmondsworth: Penguin, 1973); Ann and Neva Seidman, *US Multinationals in Southern Africa* (Dar es Salaam: Tanzania Publishing House, 1977); and Ann Seidman and Neva Seidman Makgetla, *Outposts of Monopoly Capitalism: Southern Africa in the changing global economy* (Wesport: Lawrence Hill, 1980). On military linkages, see J.E. Spence, *The Political and Military Framework* (London: Africa Publications Trust, 1975), and Western Massachusetts Association of Concerned African Scholars,

US Military Involvement in Southern Africa (Boston: South End Press, 1978).

3   For a recent introductory review of the important debate on South African political economy between 'liberals' and neo-Marxists, see Frederick Johnstone, ' "Most Painful to our Hearts": South Africa through the eyes of the New School', *Canadian Journal of African Studies*, vol. 16, no. 1, 1982, pp. 5–26.

4   Which is not to say, of course, that NP and UP policy would have been much different in practice. On this, see Martin Legassick, 'Legislation, Ideology and Economy in Post-1948 South Africa', *Journal of Southern African Studies*, vol. 1, no. 1, 1974, pp. 5–35.

5   Heribert Adam and Hermann Giliomee, *Ethnic Power Mobilized: can South Africa change?* (New Haven: Yale University Press, 1979) p. 164.

6   The UP was born in 1933 from the 'fusion' of the then ruling NP (under Prime Minister Hertzog) and the opposition South African Party (under General Smuts) as a result of a crisis created by the government's initial decision not to follow Britain's abandonment of the gold standard. However, portraying fusion as having sold out to imperialist interests, the Purified Nationalists under D.F. Malan split from Hertzog and remained in opposition. Subsequently, Hertzog and his remaining supporters (who favoured neutrality) themselves left the government when the House of Assembly voted to enter the Second World War on the side of Britain, and after Hertzog's death his rump Afrikaner Party (under N.C. Havenga) entered an electoral coalition with the NP for the 1948 election whose later success was underwritten by the predominance (57 per cent) of Afrikaners within the white population.

7   Eric A. Walker, *A History of Southern Africa* (London: Longman, 1962), p. 797.

8   *Report of the Commission of Enquiry into the Socio-Economic Development of the Bantu Areas* (Tomlinson Report, Summary) (Pretoria: Government Printer, 1955), Chapter 46, paragraph 31.

9   Nolutshungu, *South Africa in Africa* (note 2), p. 80.

10   Seidman and Makgetla, *Outposts of Monopoly Capitalism* (note 2), p. 85.

11   Robert Molteno, 'South Africa's Forward Policy in Africa; milestones on the Great North Road', *The Round Table*, no. 243, July 1971, pp. 329–345.

12   Department of Information and Publicity, SWAPO of Namibia, *To be Born a Nation: The Liberation Struggle for Namibia* (London: Zed (1981).

13   Nolutshungu, *South Africa in Africa* note 2), pp. 192–218.
14   Colin Legum, *Africa Contemporary Record, Volume 4, 1971–72,*
     p. B366. (Relevant sections of this invaluable annual survey have
     been used extensively throughout this chapter.)
15   Colin Legum, *Southern Africa: the secret diplomacy of detente;*
     South Africa at the crossroads (New York: Africana, 1975), p. 12.
16   'SA trade booms in black Africa', *The Star* (Johannesburg), 21
     March 1981.
17   Namely the United States, Britain, France, West Germany and
     Canada.

10 Tanzania

David H. Johns

More than two decades have elapsed since Tanzania's independence. If nothing else, Tanzania has succeeded through her domestic and foreign policies in gaining visibility and influence and in creating a marked degree of controversy which few African states can equal. Indicative of this was the presence of President Julius K. Nyerere at the 1981 North–South summit at Cancún, Mexico, when Tanzania was being characterised as 'a classic case study in third world tragedy' in a prominent Western newspaper.[1]

In many respects Tanzania is quite unchanged since colonialism. She remains poor, underdeveloped, and heavily reliant on agriculture. Despite – some would say because of – her policy of socialism at home her economy and development programmes are in serious trouble which is acknowledged by her own leadership. Further, despite her policy of self-reliance, she is more dependent upon foreign aid and, her leaders argue, more subject to the vagaries of world economic conditions.

The purpose of this chapter is, given the specific conditions confronting post-colonial Tanzania and the general changes in the international political and economic systems, to delineate some of the myriad factors which have gone into the determination of the national interest, choice among domestic and foreign policy options, and the implementation of policies. It is not to establish whether or not Tanzania's policies of socialism and self-reliance were the most appropriate ones for the 1960s and 1970s and/or whether they are the most timely for the 1980s. Similarly, to determine whether or not these policies have been successful — and the criteria for measuring partial or complete success — falls outside the scope of this analysis.

It is argued, however, that the decisions taken in response to the economy established an overall tone for domestic politics and foreign policy and set Tanzania on a seemingly irrevocable course. Also, it is pointed out that over time there has been considerable uniformity and consistency in policies and that, further, domestic and foreign policies were more or less compatible with each other.

Agriculture continues to be the mainstay of the economy. For instance, in 1980 some 88 per cent of the population lived in rural areas.[2] At approximately the same time 83 per cent of the workforce was in agriculture, 51 per cent of the gross domestic product was derived from agriculture, and primary commodities, other than minerals, provided 90 per cent of export earnings.

As elsewhere, export earnings are subject to the vagaries of supply and demand and Tanzania has experienced this phenomenon. For instance, in 1965 the price of sisal, then the largest source of foreign exchange earnings, dropped precipitously; despite a larger tonnage shipped, export earnings from this crop dropped 35 per cent.[3] This alone virtually nullified the inflow of foreign aid pledged to Tanzania's first five-year development plan. Yet Tanzania has more diversification in her agricultural exports than many developing nations. In the decade beginning in 1972, 1977 was the only year in which the two leading exports accounted for more than one-half of export earnings.[4] This diversification of crops, however, lessens the potential for dramatic positive changes in foreign exchange earnings; in most years a doubling of earnings from coffee, cotton, sisal, cashew nuts or cloves would increase total export earnings by less than 10 per cent — usually not enough to offset inflation.

For some time Tanzania has encountered severe foreign trade problems. Formerly she had a net favourable balance in trade; now she has a chronic deficit. The rising cost of petroleum is one obvious factor affecting Tanzania, which has been designated as one of the 'most seriously affected' states. In 1980, for example, even though Tanzania was importing less oil than in 1972, her petroleum import costs were ten times those of 1972[5] and the cost of petroleum imports were virtually one-half of total export earnings.[6]

Moreover, Tanzania has become a net importer of foodstuffs. As has been pointed out by Thomas Biersteker, 'the country has not been able to increase agricultural productivity, let alone achieve agricultural self-sufficiency'.[7] In the late 1970s the volume of agricultural exports declined modestly, while their value remained more or less constant. The country's trade gap widened considerably, for not only has Tanzania increased her food imports, but import costs have increased dramatically.

Hence, among other things, there has been a growth in reliance on capital transfers. In agriculture, where external funding was higher than in any other ministry, it exceeded local funding by a ratio of about six to one.[8] The extent of the country's dependency, more generally, is suggested by the fact that by the end of the 1970s Tanzania had become the leading recipient of World Bank loans and credits in sub-Saharan Africa;[9] it received more aid per capita than any other sub-Saharan African state.[10]

Essentially, Tanzania provides a striking example of the rapid deterioration of prospects for economic development in the Third World. Agricultural production and earnings have been static at best. Increased costs of imports have severely undermined the viability of the economy. Foreign reserves have dropped precipitously – especially in 1979 when the intervention in Uganda cost perhaps US $500 million before the fall of Kampala and was the prime cause of the 75 per cent drop in foreign reserves.[11] A shortage of an adequate supply of energy – particularly due to the costs of imported oil but also because of low rainfall and a shortage of spare parts – has crippled power production. Famine has threatened on several occasions. Tanzania's industries were running between 30 and 50 per cent of capacity.[12]

Domestic politics and policies

In February 1977, *Choma Cha Mapinduzi*, (CCM) the Revolutionary Party of Tanzania, was established. Its main significance was that it brought into being a single party from what had been the one mainland party, the Tanganyikan African National Union (TANU) and the single (surviving) party of Zanzibar and Pemba islands, the Afro-Shirazi Party (ASP). The Party's constitution reaffirmed the separate but intricately related principles of socialism and self-reliance. In contrast to its predecessors' concern for the struggle for independence, the emphasis was upon 'the struggle for internal liberation'.[13]

Almost from the outset Nyerere, TANU and the government of what was to become Tanzania pledged themselves 'to make socialism the basis of ... policy in every field'.[14] In 1967, with the enunciation of the Arusha Declaration[15] Tanzania moved quickly to institute socialism. The government passed legislation nationalising banks and insurance companies, large industrial concerns, and sisal estates and these firms were reconstituted as state-owned and state-controlled parastatal organisations. Policies were enacted which also lessened the possibility of an indigenous Tanzanian capitalist class emerging to replace the foreigners. The Arusha Declaration required TANU leadership and then all party members to disown the notion of private advantage; one could not earn more than one salary, hold shares or serve as a director in any privately owned enterprises, or rent houses to others. In other words, Tanzania became one of the first sub-Saharan African states both to articulate and practise a policy of socialism. 'Until the emergence of Marxist-oriented regimes in Angola, Ethiopia, Guinea-Bissau, and Mozambique in late 1974 and 1975', it has been asserted, 'Tanzania was the only country in sub-Saharan Africa, except possible Guinea, pursuing an avowedly socialist conception of development.'[16]

By 1967 a policy of self-reliance, designed to augment and support socialism, was articulated. According to one observer, 'Tanzania's reassessement [sic] of its development policies . . . began with a concern for the achievement of development through self-reliance rather than with a concern for socialist construction'.[17] One aspect of self-reliance was its call for an inward policy, rather than external orientation, with respect to development. This was ideologically acceptable for it sought to maintain sovereignty and to avoid dependency and it was politically realistic for, in the absence of outside funds, 'Tanzania was making a virtue of necessity'.[18]

Heretofore, at least officially, Tanzania had sought to encourage foreign investment. But, for whatever reasons and there were many, the expectations which Tanzanian leaders had had at independence regarding economic development and the role to be played by foreign exchange earnings and foreign investment and capital proved to be unrealistic. The first five-year development plan had envisioned external investment to provide approximately 80 per cent of the development expenditures. In point of fact, local funds provided more than three-fifths of the development revenues in 1966.[19] There was the decline in export earnings and income from export taxes was down 40 per cent from projections.[20] A shortfall in foreign assistance was the direct result of West Germany's and Britain's responses to Tanzanian foreign policies. Both states had promised substantial sums for development; both reneged on their commitments.

A second feature of self-reliance was an emphasis on agriculture. This was necessary, it was argued, to lessen the possibility of dependency on foreign capitalists, for they would be more interested in industrialisation, and, further, to avoid the exploitation of the peasantry by the urban sector, whereby the latter used monies received from the export of cash crops to purchase equipment for the cities and towns. With this orientation Tanzania moved away from the prominent view of other Third World states and became one of the first to commit herself to 'the agrarian path to socialism'.[21]

Mwongozo, the 1971 TANU guidelines,[22] marked another milestone in the evolution of domestic politics and policies. The guidelines called for more participation by the people, especially in running the parastatal organisations. To institute this goal two major decisions were announced: one for decentralisation and one for governmental reorganisation. Of greater importance, perhaps, the party decided to force the issue of villagisation. This policy made Tanzania and China 'the two most well-known attempts to create a high degree of local self-reliance based on genuine participation of the poorest strata of the society'.[23] Whereas in 1973 only 15 per cent lived in these government villages, when compulsion was added to inducement the situation changed rapidly so that by 1976 more than 90 per cent lived in these villages.[24]

Neither the policies of socialism nor self-reliance produced the hoped-for results. Accordingly, as early as the mid-1970s a number of measures were instituted which might be labelled 'economic liberalisation'.[25] These pointed toward less central control and greater reliance on individual initiative. The government backed off from imposing communal farming. Peasant-run cooperatives could be reestablished. Nyerere himself criticised the parastatal organisations for their decline in output per worker and the lack of surplus with which to finance new investment. The third development plan, 1977—82, gave absolute priority to industry and projected that more than one-half of its financing was to come from outside the country.[26] The main thrust of Tanzanian policy, however, continued to be socialism and self-reliance; the 1977 CCM constitution reaffirmed that commitment.

The gradual integration of Zanzibar with mainland Tanzania indicates the importance of economic factors in internal and foreign politics. The revolution in Zanzibar in January 1964 was essentially an internal affair, precipitated by long-standing racial and economic differences which could no longer be contained since the British had departed. However, the revolution may have served as a catalyst for those on the mainland opposed to the *status quo* which they thought was continuing after colonialism. This, together with the absence of the police who had been sent from the mainland to Zanzibar to help restore order, probably emboldened some of the officers in the Tanganyikan army to mutiny one week after the revolution.

Three months later Tanganyika and Zanzibar announced their merger. Although motives and reasons for the decision are subject to many and varying interpretations, one fairly widely-held view, denied by both parties, is that it was brought off in order for Tanganyika to prevent a destabilising, revolutionary movement from affecting the mainland while Zanzibar's leaders were fearful of losing their effective independence to Eastern European states, especially East Germany, given the rapid increase in diplomatic and political influence in Zanzibar. The interim constitution gave Zanzibar considerable autonomy for the islands were authorised to maintain their own party and government and, in effect, Zanzibar, although part of the merged state, had her own development plan, her own state marketing boards and enterprises, and accepted (or rejected) her own foreign aid. Both parties to the merger agreed not to push for close or quick integration of either political organisations and structures or economic systems. By not forcing a choice between different political and economic options on certain issues, both sides provided a measure of stability which might not have been attainable otherwise.

1974 stands out as a particularly crucial year in facilitating a series of events and decisions which brought the Republic closer to unification in substance as well as in form. Earnings from cloves, which went into Zanzibar's own account in London, were one-third those of the preceding year.[27] This caused the islands' government to utilise its foreign exchange earnings, heretofore held in reserve for development, for recurring expenditures.[28] By 1978 Zanzibar proposed her first long-term development programme, one 'integrated more closely with the rest of the Republic'.[29] By 1979 the islands had been forced to borrow from the mainland treasury.[30] At the same time, Zanzibar's President (and Tanzania's first Vice-President), Aboud Jumbe, pushed the ASP towards an acceptance of preliminary talks with TANU and then into more extensive discussions leading to the merger of the two parties. Given the dominance of the new party − i.e., choosing candidates for elections − the establishment of a single party was of tremendous significance in the integration process. Subsequent to the merger of the parties, Zanzibar agreed to the promulgation of a permanent constitution. Ironically, the very dependence of a single-crop economy, the bane of many Third World states, contributed to the consolidation of the United Republic.

Realignment and reorientation in the regional political systems

The merger of Tanganyika and Zanzibar, even if it took 15 years or so to effectuate, was clearly the most dramatic change in the region following the end of colonial rule. But Tanzania did change the pattern of her relationships with most of her neighbours. In response to her perception of political and economic realities, she turned southward

268

and away from her immediate neighbours to the North, Kenya and Uganda, with which there had often been a coordination of policy during British rule.

The League of Nations mandate and later the United Nations trusteeship helped set Tanganyika apart and affected local perceptions as to the desirability of closer cooperation. While Tanganyika was brought into the East African currency system shortly after the mandate was approved and gradually was integrated into the East African common market, Tanganyikan authorities openly expressed reservations. The 1932 report to the League, for example, advocated that Tanganyika should take steps forthwith to levy customs import duty 'on foodstuffs imported from Kenya and Uganda . . . and should cease to deplete her revenue and impoverish her citizens by protecting the products of her neighbours'.[31]

By the time of Tanganyika's independence Kenya was the administrative, economic and political capital of East Africa in substance if not in name, for Britain was able to force agreement or set a uniform policy for the three countries and Kenya benefited disproportionately from regional cooperation. Despite Kenya's hegemony, independent Tanganyika was willing to continue joint cooperation pending Uganda's and Kenya's independence. Long-term participation would continue only if realignment of the existing structure and a reversal of the relative benefits and costs were forthcoming. The combination of Zanzibar's revolution and the army mutiny in Tanganyika persuaded the Tanganyikan leadership that it had to take decisive measures to alter the country's economic condition, including in particular the relationships with Kenya and Uganda, both of which were now independent. Negotiations led to an agreement calling for the allocation of certain industries within Tanganyika and Uganda so as to reduce Kenya's relative advantage, but there were no mechanisms for forcing changes in the *status quo*. Even more decisively, before the three national assemblies approved the agreement, Tanganyika and Zanzibar announced their merger. The primacy of Kenyan, Tanganyikan, and Ugandan political – and surely economic – relationships was violated.

Although the three states negotiated a restructuring of their common services and certain modifications in the common market in the 1967 Treaty of East African Cooperation, the will to continue the relationship – let alone strengthen it – was absent. Kenya was wary of Tanzania's commitment to socialism and self-reliance which was now moving towards implementation, while Tanzania reciprocated with her concern for Kenya's capitalism and growing integration into the Western international economy (see Chapter 6). In addition, the treaty was not meeting the objective of sharing the benefits of cooperation equally. Kenya's share of intra-regional exports actually increased to more than 80 per cent while her share of intra-regional imports decreased to less than 20 per cent.[32] As the head of the Tanzanian National Bank of Commerce, Amon Nsekela, put it, 'The difficulty has always been that the benefits ... have tended to be concentrated in Kenya and so far we have been totally incapable of rectifying this ... This concentration of benefits should not, on the whole, surprise us. Regional concentration and imbalance is a characteristic of capitalist development throughout the world and one which history has showed, tends to be aggravated over time'.[33] When Idi Amin seized power in Uganda in 1971 Tanzania had a rationale for boycotting the East African Community meetings. But it was the irreconcilable nature of the Kenyan and Tanzanian approaches to development and their mutually contradictory ideologies which broke up the system. In February, 1977, the community collapsed, following Kenya's withdrawal from the East African Airways and Tanzania's closure of the Tanzanian–Kenyan border. The following year trade between the two was 10 per cent of what it had been before the collapse of the community.[34] It was much more than a coincidence that the community's demise occurred at the same time that CCM was launched.

Tanzania and Uganda had a common interest in confronting Kenya's economic hegemony within the region, but efforts to develop this proved ineffective throughout the 1960s and then impossible after Amin seized power. Nyerere refused to recognise the new regime from the outset. He even gave tacit support, in an episode comparable to the Bay of Pigs incident, to Ugandan exiles' efforts to overthrow Amin in 1972.[35] In 1978 Amin's troops invaded Tanzania. She responded by first forcing the invaders to withdraw, then pursuing them into Uganda, and, finally, in a combined and successful effort with Ugandan deserters and exiles to overthrow Amin. It is generally acknowledged that the first two post-Amin governments were forced out of office because of pressure from Tanzania. In fact, Tanzanian troops remained in Uganda until after the elections which brought Obote, someone approved by Tanzania, back into power. While there were possibilities for Tanzania and Uganda to establish close economic ties, Uganda's economy was in shambles and Tanzania's closest ties were with Mozambique, a state with a different colonial experience, a markedly later independence date, and — because of differences between Portugal and Tanzania — virtually no political or economic ties before 1975.

Tanzania had supported the liberation of Mozambique from the inception of the Frente de Libertacão de Mocambique (FRELIMO) which established its headquarters in Dar es Salaam. Both TANU and FRELIMO shared a common ideology. As the first head of state to visit independent Mozambique Nyerere signed two agreements, one to establish special and economic links which were more encompassing than those in the still existent East African Community,[36] and the other to establish a permanent commission of cooperation to explore various joint endeavours which might also be open to other states within the region. By 1978 Tanzania was importing from and exporting to Mozambique more than she was with any other African state.[37] Mozambique provided a welcome alternative to the East African Community and the relationship, taken together with the earlier development of closer ties with Zambia, marked a decided tilt to the South.

Among the former British territories and land-locked states in the region Tanzania has developed the closest ties with Zambia (see Chapter 12). Anxious to construct a railway so as to bring Zambia out of the Southern African region, Zambia and Tanzania approached international organisations and Western states and, finding them unreceptive, asked China for assistance; China agreed to finance the *uhuru* railway. After the project was completed, most of Zambia's exports were carried on the railway; by 1977 Zambian cargo accounted for 40 per cent of the traffic in Dar es Salaam harbour.[38] But there were differences and difficulties as well. Nyerere and Zambia's President, Kenneth Kaunda, supported different sides in the fighting in Angola before her independence. There were different perceptions as to the means to be used towards Zimbabwe's independence. Moreover, Zambia claimed she was unable to pay her share of costs for goods shipped through Tanzania because of her own critical balance of payments problems following the drop in copper prices on the world market. Adding to the tension was Zambia's decision to expel 1,000 Tanzanians working in Zambia in order to provide some of her own citizens with employment.

Between 1961 and 1981, then, relationships among the states with which Tanzania shares a common border underwent a basic realignment and reorientation. The connections within former British East Africa did not survive because of different conceptions of development strategy in Kenya and Tanzania in the 1960s and mutually antagonistic perceptions of security needs in Uganda and Tanzania in the 1970s. Tanzania set herself on a course leading to a more dynamic set of relationships and one more consistent with her own commitment to socialism and self-reliance. This led to a more Southern orientation, first with Zambia and then even more with Mozambique, in her quest for collective self-reliance internationally. Indeed, in addition to working together with her neighbours for the liberation of Southern Africa, the idea of regional cooperation for economic purposes was gaining acceptance again, albeit on a decidedly different basis than that which accompanied colonialism and the abortive experiment of the East African Community.

Participation and advocacy in the African political system

Tanzania has two overriding objectives within the African continental system: first, defending the sovereignty of the independent African states and pushing for the liberation of the non-independent territories; and, second, promoting African unity through collective self-reliance, whereby African states cooperate with each other in economic development endeavours and to have greater bargaining *vis-à-vis* the North. Differences with other African states arise because throughout the continent these goals have differing interpretations and the level of commitment for realising them varies. States also disagree on the means to be utilised to attain these goals.

The united republic's leadership has been prepared to speak out forcefully and, as much as possible, to take action to further the liberation of Africa. Nyerere indicated Tanganyika would not apply for membership in the Commonwealth if South Africa was given membership when reapplying as a republic – a position which directly led to South Africa withdrawing her application. The Portuguese Consul-Generalship in Dar es Salaam was closed after Tanganyika's independence because Portugal refused to acknowledge the right of her overseas territories to independence. At the founding of the Organisation of African Unity (OAU), a liberation committee was set up and, partly for geographical reasons but also at the urging of Tanganyika, its headquarters were established in Dar es Salaam. Tanganyika banned flights of South African Airways into and out of Tanganyika and refused to issue entrance visas for South Africans. Nyerere urged other OAU members, especially those not forced by geography and by economic considerations to rely on South Africa, to break their relations with that state.

As indicated, Tanzania worked closely with Zambia to assist her in breaking away from the Southern African orbit. Before Rhodesia declared her independence she also worked directly with Britain and the United States to try to persuade them to alter their policies. After Rhodesia's UDI (see Chapter 13), Tanzania was one of the few states which honoured the OAU's Council of Foreign Ministers resolution calling for the rupture of ties with Britain if the latter didn't bring Rhodesia back under her control. Tanzania and Ghana, which restored relations two months later, after Kwame Nkrumah's fall, were the two Commonwealth African countries to break relations; Tanzania was the only country with proximity to Zimbabwe to do so and the last state to restore relations with Britain.[39]

Tanzania took an increasingly active role in trying to utilise the OAU to pressure the West in its policies towards Southern Africa. Disappointed at the seeming indifference of the United States and Britain to the problems of African liberation, Tanzania rallied support for the 'Mogadishu Declaration' at the 1971 OAU heads of state meeting which accepted the necessity of violence if peaceful change towards majority rule was not possible. Then she helped bring together several states to assume special responsibility, with OAU approval, for the liberation of Zimbabwe and Namibia. By 1976 Angola and Mozambique had joined Botswana, Zambia and Tanzania in trying to negotiate for the independence of these dependencies and this group – the Front Line States – chose Nyerere as Chair. They kept the issue of independence and majority rule of Zimbabwe alive and effectively pressured Britain and the United States against recognition of the Muzorewa regime and towards a new round of constitutional talks, which led to Zimbabwe's independence.

By 1971 Tanzania began to press the OAU for greater emphasis upon the liberation of Africa, even if it undermined the unity of African states. Basically, Nyerere was beginning to question certain norms operating within the African political system. One was the sanctity of the state and non-recognition of secessionist movements or, at least, of revolutionary movements. Another was making the head of the country hosting the OAU meeting the Chairman of the Organisation for the following year. Hence, in 1975 when Uganda hosted the Summit, Idi Amin became Chair and, partly because Uganda was host and partly because Amin was Chairman, Nyerere boycotted the session. A third norm was the strict rule of non-interference in the internal affairs of other states which, in effect, meant that once a state had attained membership, OAU members would neither question the state's position on domestic or foreign policies nor challenge the credentials of its representatives attending OAU meetings. Nyerere argued that there was a double standard in the Organisation: one for independent black African states and another for South Africa. While the latter could be condemned for her policy of apartheid, the OAU refused to criticise its own members. It did not matter what a black African head of state did, Nyerere lamented: 'He could kill as many people as he liked in his country and he would still be protected by the (OAU) Charter'.[40]

Uganda's 1978 invasion of Tanzania violated the OAU norm requiring sanctity of borders and the peaceful resolution of disputes. Nyerere was furious when the OAU refused to condemn Uganda. Only Tanzania and the other Front Line States, together with Ethiopia and Malagasy, condemned Uganda; the OAU called for a ceasefire and then mediation between Tanzania and Uganda. For some Tanzania's subsequent direct intervention in Uganda was also and even more so a violation of OAU principles. Libya, which had directly supported Uganda, along with Sudan and Nigeria, raised the issue at the heads of state meeting of the OAU in 1979. But, in effect, the issue was dropped, especially as the Ugandan delegates were seated without any controversy and, indeed, arose to defend Tanzania's actions.

Tanzania consistently has taken a strong position against the use of outside force against African states. Even though she did not recognise Amin, Tanzania condemned Israel's actions at Entebbe in July 1976. Later she worked against certain proposals, especially those advanced by France, for a pan-African security force. When the issue was raised at the 1978 heads of state meeting in Khartoum, Tanzania opposed those states voicing concern about the threat of Cuban forces in Africa, pointing out that they had been invited by the respective regimes in Africa, and not as part of an all-African force. Her position was accepted, if in a compromise form, when a resolution was adopted stating 'that any initiative to establish a pan-African force should be planned and taken solely within the framework of the OAU'. Its purpose would be 'the elimination of the racist minority regimes of Southern African and the total liberation of the continent'.[41]

Surely, Tanzania chose a policy of participation and advocacy in the African political system. She was prepared to threaten the survival of the OAU by raising issues on which no consensus was possible. She was also willing to break OAU norms and to go outside the Organisation with or without its approval on certain matters that she thought necessitated action. In this sense she perhaps contributed to the subsequent demise of the Organisation as it had existed since its inception. While she saw the need for the OAU, she also regarded the Organisation as too conservative and too unwilling to confront African and North—South issues from what she regarded as the proper perspective and with what she deemed appropriate action. Accordingly, her second overriding objective within the African political system — namely collective self-reliance — would have to be pursued at the regional, rather than the continental, level or, alternatively, at the global level.

Confronting the global system

Tanzania has advocated and sought to further two broad policies in the global system; namely, non-alignment, which is more politically oriented, and collective self-reliance, which is somewhat more economically relevant. At least each has its own particular forum in the global system: the non-aligned movement and the Group of 77 within UNCTAD, respectively. From the perspective of Tanzania's leadership the two merge together indistinguishably and correspond to and complement the dual objectives of maintaining sovereignty and facilitating development.

274

At independence Tanganyika opted for non-alignment. She established diplomatic relations with the United States, the Soviet Union and China and indicated her intention to exchange and establish missions in all three states. Perhaps reflecting India's role in the non-aligned movement, the only mission established during the first year of independence, apart from one in London, was one established in New Delhi.

Tanzania had commanded favourable attention from certain states in the Third World when she refused to yield to West Germany over the issue of recognition. Her decision to accept substantial aid from China brought her additional visibility even if Tanzanian leaders were annoyed by the inference drawn in the West that she had joined the communist camp. By April 1970, when she hosted the preparatory conference for the third non-aligned movement conference, Tanzania had clearly established her non-aligned credentials.

At the meeting Nyerere advocated that the movement turn away from political and military concerns as its major focus and confront the problems of economics: 'The real and urgent threat to the independence of almost all the non-aligned states', he maintained, 'comes not from the military but from the economic power of the big states. It is poverty which constitutes our greatest danger'.[42] Although the non-aligned movement did not accept the proposal, the Tanzanian leader persisted. Nine years later Tanzania hosted the preparatory meeting for the Group of 77 at Arusha before the Manilla UNCTAD meetings. Again Nyerere called for greater cooperation; again he called for a series of institutions composed of Third World states. At this juncture the idea of self-reliance was accepted. As one commentator summarised the meeting, 'The result was "The Arusha Programme for Self-Reliance and Framework of Negotiations" . . . Most of the demands had been heard before, but the appearance of "self-reliance" in the title . . . put more slant on self-help'.[43] It might be added that the appearance of 'Arusha' in the title confirmed Tanzania's influence in the Third World and at least qualified acceptance of her local approach, articulated in TANU's Arusha Declaration of 1967, to the international economic system.

During the 1960s and 1970s Tanzania's relations with the three superpowers fell within the parameters of non-alignment as defined and interpreted by the united republic. The relationship with the United States was basically proper, but never particularly close. Partially this reflected apprehension about what she saw as an American presence in Kenya. Nonetheless, in 1978, after an hiatus of ten years the peace corps returned to Tanzania. The United States also resumed funding of various bilateral aid programmes, including several on Zanzibar.

A comparable pattern was characteristic of the relationship between Tanzania and the Soviet Union. The two had signed a 15-year treaty for economic assistance in the mid-1960s, but a number of the projects agreed upon had not yet been completed by the end of the 1970s. Tanzania had been apprehensive about the Soviet Union's involvement in Uganda between 1971 and 1978. At the 1979 non-aligned meeting in Havana, Tanzania was unwilling to accept Cuba's definition of non-alignment, namely that there was a natural alliance between it and the communist camp. Nyerere's speech at the meeting marked the death knell for Fidel Castro's proposal. On the other hand, Tanzania was not willing to take a strong stand against Soviet intervention in Afghanistan and she resisted the efforts of the United States to boycott the Olympic Games in Moscow. Surely Tanzania was not unwilling to use athletics in policy implementation; she played an important role in keeping South Africa out of the Olympics beginning in 1968 and was one of the first to withdraw from the 1976 Montreal Games.

Tanzania's relationship with China, especially when China agreed to finance the Tanzania–Zambia railway, was substantially different; rather than violating the concept of non-alignment, it reaffirmed it. In point of fact, the West agreed to finance a competing road system in Tanzania when the financing for the railway was announced.[44] Ties with China did not develop into the type of alliance which some had envisioned. Trade did increase rapidly following the loan agreement and during construction, but it also decreased decidedly with the completion of the project. China was willing to continue to extend aid, although in much more modest amounts, as indicated by the commitment to finance the new CCM headquarters in Dodoma.

Tanzania also sought to diversify economic relations within the international economy and to place greater emphasis on aid from middle-level powers and on multilateral, rather than bilateral, grants and loans. By the end of the 1960s Tanzania had succeeded to a considerable extent in diversification, although about three-quarters of her trade remained with the West.[45] Considerable progress in diversifying sources of aid was also realised. Similarly much of her goal of moving towards multilateral grants was realised.

However, this brought unanticipated problems. In 1979 Tanzania experienced a protracted and heated controversy with the IMF. The critical situation in her economy triggered the problem. The IMF proposed, among other things, a 25 per cent devaluation in addition to the previous year's 8 per cent devaluation, relaxation of foreign exchange allocation, wage freezes except for incentive salaries, and extensive cuts in public spending including education and health services. Neither the President nor the party was willing to accept these measures. In a speech to the diplomatic corps in January 1980, Nyerere blasted the IMF as 'a device by which powerful economic forces in some rich countries increase their power over the poor nations of the world'.[46]

An agreement was reached the following September. Tanzania, while she agreed to restrain public spending, conceded relatively little. Tanzania had thus managed to weather the crisis, but with limited assurance that she would be able to do so in any future showdown.

Tanzania has been successful in articulating the ideas of non-alignment and collective self-reliance and in gaining their widespread support philosophically and rhetorically from the vast majority of the Third World. Clearly considerable credit can be given to Tanzania and her spokesperson Nyerere, although a cause-and-effect relationship can only be inferred. However, the unity and power of the Third World, upon which the policies are critically dependent, have not materialised. The competition and rivalry between the superpowers and the accompanying armaments races have not been halted. Obviously the proposals for a new international economic order have not been implemented. This augurs poorly for Tanzania's efforts to successfully confront and alter the global system, let alone to develop her own impoverished and marginalised economy.

Conclusion and projection

Tanzania has many of the characteristics of the least developed states. This is particularly true with respect to internal economic conditions and Tanzania's integration into the international economy. In other words, she has attracted little foreign investment not only because of her policies but due to her lack of resources and her small population. Further, her geographical location is not strategically crucial. Yet, quite clearly, Tanzania has attracted attention and commands influence which cannot be explained by her objective economic or geographical position. Why?

Pushing for socialism — but not Marxism — in her quest for development and her domestic political and economic organisation are partially responsible. Opting for agriculture rather than for industrial development at a relatively early time is another reason. The focus on a programme of self-reliance is yet another. The Arusha Declaration and the impression of a firm commitment and principled approach to realise these objectives were major elements in Tanzanian policy. She thus carved out a niche for herself, especially in the 1960s, which was unique in Africa and quite distinctive among Third World states generally. As a consequence, she commanded interest, if not always support, from a wide variety of sources. Rivalry with Kenya and the contrasts between their development strategies also brought Tanzania further notice.

Tanzanian foreign policies attracted attention also. The decisions of Tanganyika and Zanzibar to merge to form the united republic gave Tanzania a particular status in the ideology of pan-Africanism and African unity. Because of Zanzibar's standing immediately before the merger, Tanzania received increased attention within the context of the Cold War, despite the fact that in the 1960s the international political system was moving towards detente and normalisation. The decision to say 'No' to West Germany promoted an image of non-alignment while the break with Britain provided evidence of principled determination to work for the liberation of Southern Africa. These actions partially compensated for the lack of economic and/or geographical importance. By going alone, along the path of her choice, Tanzania increased rather than diminished her influence within the regional, African and global systems.

Then, too, Tanzania became host to the OAU liberation committee. With the presence of groups and organisations within Tanzania which were speaking out for nationalist causes, other states, including the superpowers, showed a greater interest than might otherwise have been the case. When the situation in Zambia changed and then when Rhodesia declared UDI, Tanzania came to play a special role in Southern Africa. China, of course, played into this situation with her assistance for the *uhuru* railway. In other words, proximity to Southern Africa and her status as a coastal state enhanced Tanzania's role in regional, African and world politics.

With such visibility Tanzania was able to diversify sources of foreign aid and, despite the commitment of the Arusha Declaration to self-reliance, dramatically to increase the amount of foreign aid relative to other sub-Saharan African states. This not only led to additional prominence but it also made Tanzania a 'test case'. International agencies and middle-level powers continued to provide funds perhaps out of fear that their previous efforts might otherwise prove to have been ineffective. Paradoxically, as conditions have deteriorated, Tanzanian leverage has increased.

There is heated controversy as to whether or not Tanzania has gone far enough or too far on the path to socialism and whether she should have adopted a policy of self-reliance. Further, many question the utility of non-alignment and collective self-reliance. Some argue that the militant positions taken by Tanzania have been to attract attention and, hence, perhaps influence. In a sense, powerlessness has corrupted Tanzanian leadership, it might be concluded, just as power has often corrupted others, even if in very different ways.[47] Others counter that Nyerere and Tanzania have continually taken the morally correct and humanitarian position because of its own logic and integrity. Because it was a principled position, it rocked the boat. Still others maintain that

Tanzania, with such limited resources, had no other choice than to try to utilise conference diplomacy and Third World organisations and she succeeded because she was able to make issues about which she was concerned those issues discussed elsewhere.

Tanzania, then, has obtained a presence in the international system which was not foreseen at independence. This is no mean accomplishment. That she might have done things better or that she might have done them differently is clear. These things can be said about the foreign policies of any state. Whether Tanzania, had she moved differently, would have been in a much different situation than she presently finds herself in cannot be answered definitively. By certain standards Tanzania is not much better and perhaps is even worse off than in 1961. Drought and floods; costs of imports and declining terms of trade; inefficiency in the parastatals and ineptitude on the part of the peasants; corruption; loss of incentives; the colonial legacy and the reactionary forces of the West — these and other real or bogus answers may be advanced, however persuasively, to explain Tanzania's contemporary situation. It needs to be remembered, nonetheless, that the construction of a socialist society at home and the transformation of the international political economy are ambitious tasks and, in any case, require considerable time.

The future of Tanzania and her foreign policy is hard to predict. Much depends on the transition to a new generation of leadership and on the ability of that leadership to get the economy working again. Unlike many Third World states, Tanzania seems to have a more organised and effective party apparatus and the basic commitment to development through socialism and self-reliance appears to have more than a modicum of popular support. However, failures at home and dislocations caused by the international economy during the past few years have exposed weaknesses in the party and have jeopardised the sense of a basic commitment. Surely the international economic system cannot be held responsible for all of Tanzania's shortcomings.

The Nyerere regime has striven for a basic equilibrium between the domestic policy and economic policy. Foreign policy during the first two decades of independence has been utilised as development policy. Yet, however effective Tanzania has been in the use of her limited resources, these resources have not been adequate for the required tasks. The present economic situation makes the perpetuation of the *status quo* politically unacceptable. There is growing scepticism and frustration for, tragically and ironically, the policies of socialism and self-reliance may have been necessary but they may not be sufficient for continued political stability and economic development. Tanzania will probably attract less attention and command less influence in the future. Her role in international politics will decline.

Such a decline may be accelerated with the end of Nyerere's reign in Tanzania.

Notes

1 *Wall Street Journal*, 17 July 1981.
2 Statistics in this paragraph are taken from the World Bank, *World Development Report 1980* (New York: Oxford University Press, 1980).
3 International Monetary Fund, *International Financial Statistics Yearbook 1980* (New York: United Nations, 1981), p. 403.
4 *Ibid.*, pp. 402–403; and International Monetary Fund, *International Financial Statistics*, vol. 35, no. 8, August 1982, pp. 398–399.
5 *Los Angeles Times*, 2 March 1980.
6 See note 4.
7 Thomas J. Biersteker, 'Self-reliance in Theory and Practice in Tanzanian Trade Relations', *International Organization*, vol. 34, no. 2, Spring 1980, p. 245.
8 James H. Mittelman, 'International Monetary Institutions and Policies of Socialism and Self-Reliance: Are They Compatible? The Tanzanian Experience', *Social Research*, vol. 47, no. 1, Spring 1980, p. 154.
9 *Ibid.*, p. 143.
10 *Los Angeles Times*, 2 March 1980.
11 *Africa Contemporary Record, Volume 11 (1978/79)*, B 397; and *Volume 12 (1979/80)*. B 323–327.
12 *Wall Street Journal*, 28 October 1982.
13 *Daily News* (Dar es Salaam), 6 February 1977, as quoted in *Africa Contemporary Record, Volume 10 (1977/78)*, B 403.
14 Quoted from Julius K. Nyerere, *Ujamaa: Essays on Socialism* (Dar es Salaam: Oxford University Press, 1968), p. 8.
15 Reprinted in *ibid.*, pp. 13–37.
16 Joel D. Barkan, 'Comparing Politics and Public Policy in Kenya and Tanzania', in Joel D. Barkan with John J. Okumu (eds), *Politics and Public Policy in Kenya and Tanzania* (New York: Praeger, 1979), p. 9.
17 *Ibid.*, p. 7.
18 Claude Ake, 'Ideology and Objective Conditions', in Barkan with Okumu (eds), *Politics and Public Policy in Kenya and Tanzania* (note 16), p. 122.
19 *Ibid.*
20 Cranford Pratt, 'The Administration of Economic Planning in a

Newly Independent State: The Tanzanian Experience, 1963–1964', *Journal of Commonwealth Political Studies*, vol. 5, no. 1, March 1967, p. 41, cited in Okwudiba Nnoli, *Self Reliance and Foreign Policy in Tanzania: The Dynamics of the Diplomacy of a New State, 1961 to 1971* (New York: NOK Publishers, 1978), p. 99.

21 Barkan, 'Comparing Politics and Public Policy in Kenya and Tanzania' (note 16), p. 57.

22 'TANU Guidelines on Guarding, Consolidating and Advancing the Revolution of Tanzania and Africa' (Dar es Salaam: Government Printer, 1971). Interestingly, *Mwongozo* is not included in the third volume of Nyerere's writings and speeches which cover the years 1968–1973; see Julius K. Nyerere, *Freedom and Development* (London: Oxford University Press, 1973).

23 Gunnar Adler-Karlsson, 'Eliminating Absolute Poverty: An Approach to the Problem', in W. Howard Wriggins and Gunnar Adler-Karlsson, *Reducing Global Inequities* (New York: McGraw-Hill Book Company, 1979), p. 171.

24 Dean K. McHenry, Jr, 'The Struggle for Rural Socialism in Tanzania', in Carl G. Rosberg and Thomas M. Callaghy (eds), *Socialism in Sub-Saharan Africa: A New Assessment* (Berkeley: Institute of International Studies, 1979), pp. 37–60.

25 Michael F. Lofchie, 'Agrarian Crisis and Economic Liberalisation in Tanzania', *Journal of Modern African Studies*, vol. 16, no. 8, September 1978, p. 451–475.

26 Zaki Ergas, 'Why Did the Ujamaa Village Policy Fail? Towards a Global Analysis', *Journal of Modern African Studies*, vol. 18, no. 3, September 1980, p. 394.

27 United Nations, *1980 Yearbook of International Statistics*, 1 (New York: United Nations, 1981), p. 1002.

28 *Africa Contemporary Record, Volume 7 (1974/75)*, B289.

29 *Ibid., Volume 11 (1978/79)*, B399.

30 *Ibid., Volume 12 (1979/80)*, B330.

31 *Report on the Administration of Tanganyika Territory for the Year 1932*, Col. No. 81 (London: His Majesty's Stationery Office, 1932), p. 128, quoted in Thomas M. Franck, *East African Unity Through Law* (New Haven: Yale University Press, 1964), p. 23.

32 John J. Okumu, 'Foreign Relations: Dilemmas of Independence and Development', in Barkan with Okumu (eds), *Politics and Public Policy in Kenya and Tanzania* (note 16), p. 254.

33 Amon Nsekela, *African Development* (London), February 1974, EA 15, quoted in Agrippah T. Mugomba, 'Regional Organisations and African Underdevelopment: The Collapse of the East African Community', *Journal of Modern African Studies*, vol. 16, no. 2,

June 1978, p. 265.

34 *Africa Research Bulletin*, vol. 18, no. 7, 15 August 1981, p. 6104B.

35 Nnoli, *Self-Reliance and Foreign Policy in Tanzania* (note 20) pp. 269–271.

36 *Africa Contemporary Record, Volume 8 (1975/76)*, B332.

37 United Nations, *1979 Yearbook of International Trade Statistics* (New York: United Nations, 1980), p. 993.

38 *African Contemporary Record, Volume 10 (1977/78)*, B 415.

39 Susan Aurelia Gitelson, 'Why Do Small States Break Diplomatic Relations with Outside Powers? Lessons from the African Experience', *International Studies Quarterly*, vol. 18, no. 4, December 1974, pp. 472–474.

40 *Africa Contemporary Record, Volume 11 (1978/79)*, B395.

41 Zdenek Cervenka and Colin Legum, 'The Organization of African Unity in 1978; The Challenge of Foreign Intervention', in *ibid.*, A36.

42 Nyerere, *Freedom and Development* (note 22), p. 164.

43 Stephen Taylor, 'UNCTAD V: Part of a Long Haul', *The World Today*, vol. 35, no. 8, August 1979, p. 312.

44 Timothy M. Shaw, 'African States and International Stratification: The Adaptive Foreign Policy of Tanzania', in K. Ingham (ed.), *Foreign Relations of African States* (London: Butterworths, 1974), p. 221. Cf. Mittelman, 'International Monetary Institutions and Policies of Socialism and Self-Reliance' (note 8), pp. 154–155.

45 United Nations, *1980 Yearbook of International Trade Statistics*, p. 998.

46 Ken Adelman, 'The Great Black Hope', *Harper's*, vol. 263, no. 1574, July 1981, p. 18.

47 R.H. Green, 'Power and Self-interest: Reflections on the Parameters for Progress Toward Independent International Economic Systems', (sic) mimeo, 1969, 3, cited in Nnoli, *Self-Reliance and Foreign Policy in Tanzania* (note 20), p. 89.

11 Zaire

Michael G. Schatzberg

I think the Zairian Government and the Zairian economy are dependent, unless we are going to anticipate things going back to some sort of primordial state, and are going to be dependent on foreign assistance... We are not simply trying to maintain a static situation to maintain an individual in power. We are trying to support − to help to reform, to strengthen − an economy that is very important in the functioning of the Western industrial system, a large economy with large resources which we would like to stay within the Western economic system and in a friendly political relationship to us.

Richard Moose,
US Assistant Secretary of State for African Affairs [1]

Admittedly all of this is part of an intricate, but a highly articulated international system. The number of things going on out there in Zaire are vast and vastly complicated − it is not just the military, there is reform of the gendarmerie; there is reform in the customs receipts. And all of this fits into the whole.

Lannon Walker,
US Deputy Assistant Secretary of State for African Affairs [2]

In addition, our diplomacy is that of the open door and of the truth.

Mobutu Sese Seko[3]

Zaire is a polity in crisis. Although analysts of different disciplinary and ideological perspectives might disagree over the ultimate causes and long-range effects of the current situation in Zaire, few would contradict one observer's statement that 'the human costs are appalling, reflected in a pauperization which has . . . few historical parallels'.[4] The various dimensions of this crisis have been amply documented and need but brief recapitulation.[5] Mobutu Sese Seko seized power in a military coup in November 1965 and was able to initiate remarkable reforms over the next several years. The disorders of the first republic gave way to a highly centralised state and single party as the tendencies which had rent the polity were gradually controlled. Inflation was contained. economic production increased, and political order extended to the countryside for the first time since independence in 1960. Mobutu was genuinely popular during the early days of his rule and there can be no doubt that he deserves major credit for ending the Hobbesian state of nature characteristic of Zairian politics and society from 1960–1965.[6]

Favourable copper prices provided the regime with funds to implement ambitious development plans and the newly-found stability inspired a climate of confidence. Western industrialists and bankers felt at home and believed that their investments and loans would be both safe and profitable. The early 1970s thus witnessed a resurgent, sure-footed Zaire; a state fully prepared to exercise its responsibilities as one of the largest, wealthiest, and most powerful on the continent. During these years, Mobutu confidently expanded diplomatic contacts with China and North Korea, and was even secure enough to rupture relations with Israel. His aim was to assert Zaire's claim to leadership in Africa and the Third World.

During this period analysts of Zaire's foreign policy lavishly praised Mobutu's endeavours. One noted approvingly, 'In his foreign policy the President of Zaire follows a radical orientation, hoping to emerge as one of the spokesmen of the African continent'.[7] Another complimented him in these glowing terms: 'After having known how to reestablish order and economic prosperity, General Mobutu has also known how, through a diplomacy as active as it is circumspect, to make his country the leader of the African continent'.[8] The chorus of acclaim had few dissenting voices.

But by 1974 Zaire's roseate destiny had begun to dissolved. A dramatic decline in the price of copper on the world market coupled with an equally impressive increase in the price of petroleum diminished significantly the regime's financial latitude. Furthermore, many economic initiatives Mobutu introduced during the period of prosperity, such as the Zairianisation of commerce and agriculture, were egregiously mismanaged. The revenues available to the government for its development projects and ordinary needs declined, whilst loans contracted when it seemed Zaire was about to 'take off', began falling due. Zairian intervention in the Angolan civil war in late 1975 brought Mobutu's regime into open alliance with the American-backed Roberto-Savimbi forces and the Republic of South Africa. This adventure was, to be kind, ill-considered. The Zairian army demonstrated that it was inefficient, corrupt, and subject to the same strains which were becoming increasingly visible in other institutions. The closing of the Benguela railway impeded exportation of Zairian copper and constrained Zaire's ability to keep its creditors at bay. The International Monetary Fund (IMF) imposed stringent conditions on Zaire's finances as a condition for further assistance. Abysmal terms of trade, blatant corruption, and mismanagement of the nation's resources and infrastructure all contributed to a decline in economic productivity.[9]

The impact on the lives of ordinary Zairians, in both urban and rural areas, was catastrophic. Rampant inflation eroded purchasing power and real income declined precipitately. By May 1979 Kinshasa's consumer price index, based on a 1969 starting point of 100, had reached 2,507. Health care suffered and the rate of infant mortality rose to 25 per cent in some regions. Cholera epidemics were seen in the east; hunger and malnutrition became widespread. Erosion of living standards and quality of life engendered discontent throughout the country. Political repression intensified and violations of human rights increased apace.[10] The regime was teetering when rebels invaded Shaba Province in March 1977 and May 1978. The Zairian army again failed to distinguish itself against opponents who could fight back and Mobutu was forced to plead for military assistance from friendly Western powers. By this time, whatever popularity Mobutu had once enjoyed as the man who had pulled Zaire back from the brink of chaos in 1965 had long since evaporated. Life in Zaire had again become solitary, poor, nasty, brutish, and short. The *Mobutiste* Leviathan state had succeeded in reproducing the very conditions it had been created to combat. The Leviathan had sired, most paradoxically, a Hobbesian World.

This summary of the crisis and inventory of its most visible dimensions is necessary for review, but is analytically misleading. Any preoccupation with the virulent manifestations of the contemporary crisis unfortunately tends to obscure the historical and structural roots of the problem. The focus, then, should be on the disease itself, the continuing and long-term impact of the international system on the dynamics of class formation in Zaire, rather than on its more ephemeral symptoms. This may be achieved by examining the external constraints which shape Zairian foreign policy, and by exploring the ways in which the international environment contributes to the reinforcement and reproduction of the Zairian class structure. In other words, how does Zairian foreign policy interact with its environment to create a context which favours the enrichment of one class at the expense of others? And how does this dominant class use President Mobutu's 'open door' diplomacy to profit from the 'highly articulated international system' mentioned by Secretary Walker?

To accomplish these tasks and answer these questions historical background concerning the external context of the formation and evolution of Zaire's dominant politico-commercial bourgeoisie will be provided. I shall then explore the long-range and deep-seated aspects of Zaire's multiple dependencies on the international system as the major structural constraint within which Zairian foreign policy must operate. The effects of dependent status on the contemporary dynamics of social class formation will also be studied. More specifically, I shall deal with Zaire's commercial dependency on the international market; the regime's increasing reliance on private banks, multilateral lending institutions, and bilateral aid; the pernicious effects of thorough-going technological dependence on foreign personnel; and, finally, the more general, but somewhat ambiguous, political dependence which both results from these factors and, in turn, regenerates them.

Throughout the analysis, close attention will be given to the interests of Zaire's politico-commercial bourgeoisie. What are its aims and goals? How much room for manoeuvre does it have within the international system? To this end, the interplay of Zairian class interests and ambitions with those of relevant actors in the external environment will be studied. Moreover, the ways in which the international system moulds these interactions also merit elucidation.

The politico-commercial bourgeoisie: historical origins [11]

Colonialism in Zaire was by and large a profitable venture. Belgian financial interests were an integral part of the colonial enterprise — especially after the discovery of mineral deposits in Shaba. From that moment on, Belgian capital played a major role in the colonial system, but almost always in close collaboration with the colonial state. The Union Minière du Haut Katanga (UMHK) was created as a subsidiary of the Belgian trust, Société Générale, in 1906. In general, the state actively aided UMHK and other large companies in their efforts to extract and export Zaire's subterranean wealth. Initially, this was done by granting immense concessions of land and, subsequently, by encouraging and, at times, compelling people to participate in the construction of the large public works required to provide an adequate infrastructure for the mining industry. The state also mobilised large numbers of labourers to work in the mines, often through the imposition of taxes which forced peasants into the cash economy by obliging them to seek employment. The profits available to Belgian financiers were enormous, especially when compared to rates of return on investments then prevalent at home. The same land and taxation policies were applied in agriculture and Lever Brothers began operations in Zaire in 1911.[12]

The breadth and depth of colonial penetration in Zaire was probably second to none in sub-Saharan Africa. The colonial state and its large financial allies involved themselves in even the most mundane aspects of daily life. One historian has recently labelled the colonial state in Zaire, 'totalitarian'. Although this designation may be debated, there can be little doubt that the entire colonial mechanism was extractive, oppressive, and authoritarian.[13] European interests and personnel controlled nearly all economic activity and foreigners eventually monopolised industry, agriculture, mining, and commerce. Even retail commerce gradually came under the colonial thumb. This, furthermore, was not accidental, but a deliberate premise of the colonial power. Colonial economic policy explicitly favoured large mining and agro-industrial concerns and the state did everything possible to nurture them. Small traders and agriculturalists were hampered severely at every turn. An article on the economic future of Equateur Province which appeared in 1921 noted:

> Whites and blacks have . . . commercial fever. In Equateur, within two months, 1,000 trading licences have been delivered . . . These are, in general, brokers who plough through the country to buy the products that they are going to resell at large profit to traders or merchants. Monsieur Engels [the *Commissaire Général*] wishes the suppression of all these intermediaries, through the creation of direct relations between large commerce [*le grand commerce*] and the natives. . . [14]

The development of a rural agricultural and commercial petty bourgeoisie was therefore impeded.[15]

The problem was that there were few opportunities available for either social mobility or capital accumulation in the productive sectors of the economy. The needs of Belgian and other foreign capital tended to structure which avenues would be closed off or opened up to ordinary Zairians in search of a better life. Those who desired advancement were restricted — with the exception of the church — to subordinate roles as clerks in either the state or the large, foreign-owned companies. It was not until the 1950s that the Belgians tried to create something resembling a middle class. But by then they were primarily concerned with merchants and artisans in large cities. Their desire was to create a group that might be instrumental in forging a vaguely defined Belgo-Congolaise community; a group which could be used to preserve and protect Belgian domination.[16]

Independence arrived far more quickly than even the most optimistic observers had predicted. Events surrounding the decolonisation have been amply documented and need no reiteration here. Nevertheless, two points deserve emphasis. First, political decolonisation was not accompanied by any change in control of the means of production. Economic power remained firmly in the hands of Belgian and other expatriate interests. Thomas Kanza's account of the crucial Belgian–Congolese economic roundtable discussions is germane:

> The Belgian experts involved in financial discussions and negotiations gave the appearance of taking quite seriously the talks that they had with the young students who made up the Congolese delegation, talks which covered the complex of technical problems which formed the real substance of Congolese independence. The basis of their talks was a collection of working papers prepared by Belgian experts. The Congolese had not the experience to recognize the glaring omissions in them, the absence of certain vital information, just as they had no way of knowing the various secret financial and other agreements which had been made between the Belgian government and some of its allies, and between Belgian financial bodies and other European and American business concerns.[17]

The newly-independent state was not to be master of its economic patrimony.

Second, since control of the means of production was not possible, the Zairian politico-commerical bourgeoisie has been dependent on control of the state. The hurried departure of the Belgians in 1960 left an enormous political and administrative vacuum. As there was but an insignificant economic petty bourgeoisie to compete with them, the levers of state command were taken over by the erstwhile clerks and subalterns of the colonial state with only their salaries in hand. Unable to accumulate any appreciable capital under colonialism, they soon learnt how to rectify that situation by making use of the state apparatus to create their own riches. Indeed, throughout the history of independent Zaire, access to political and administrative office has been a source of wealth. State power, administrative position, and public funds have been used repeatedly to acquire private perquisites. The usual legal measures, as well as some extraordinarily creative illegal ones, have been employed. Once accumulated, the fruits of this bureau-cratic capitalism could be used to obtain economic enterprises of varying sorts such as plantations, bars, and commercial establishments.

Access to the coffers of the state has thus been a considerable and irreplaceable trump in the economic consolidation of Zaire's politico-commercial bourgeoisie. But of equal importance for our purpose here, the political consolidation of this class has enabled it, gradually and progressively, to renegotiate the rights of access to Zaire's economic infrastructure with representatives of foreign interests. In other words, those who dominate the state have asserted control of relations with foreign capital of all kinds and have used their strategic position as gatekeeper to bargain for an ever-increasing share of Zaire's great wealth, to increase their own access to domestic resources, and to maintain intact the broad outlines of the extractive colonial state. These class interests are thus being pursued at the expense of the majority of the Zairian population.[18]

Multiple dependencies

Commercial dependency

Zaire's economy is extroverted, dominated by the exportation of copper, and is therefore markedly dependent upon the price of this basic commodity on the world market. Since roughly 1950, Zaire has accounted for about 7 per cent of the non-communist world's production of this mineral. This has given UMHK and its successor parastatal organisation, Générale de Carrière et des Mines au Zaire (Gécamines), preponderant weight in the Zairian economy. The sale of copper usually furnishes some 70 per cent of Zaire's hard currency and, until the decline of copper prices in 1974, taxes levied on UMHK-Gécamines would regularly account for approximately 45–50 per cent of the state's total budgetary receipts. But since the start of the current crisis, Gécamines' contribution to the revenues of the state has fallen to an estimated low of 15 per cent in 1978. According to one projection, an increase of 1c per pound in the world market price of copper may add $10 million to Zaire's total export earnings. Because of fluctuations in the price of this basic commodity, Zaire is subject to cyclical wind-falls or severe shortfalls in government revenue which affect signifi-cantly the state's financial latitude and ability to plan. Zaire's depen-dence on the price of copper should thus be apparent.[19]

Although the history of Mobutu's relations with UMHK and the ostensible nationalisation of the firm have been treated elsewhere, the importance of copper in the economy is such that a brief account of

289

these events is in order.[20] When Mobutu seized power in 1965 he had a number of compelling needs. First, as Tshombe's successor, he wanted to reassert Zaire's independence in the eyes of the world. In addition, once in power he discovered that the coffers were nearly empty and funds would be needed to smoothe the retirement or political conversion of first republic politicians. This was all the more pressing since most economic activities had remained in the hands of expatriates. Control of the mining sector's enormous resources would therefore provide a source of remuneration and perquisites which could be distributed to build loyalty and support for the new regime.[21] Finally, there may well have been some ideological commitment to economic nationalism — to assert control over what was, by far, the national economy's most lucrative sector. This confluence of interests and desires provides the background against which the 'nationalisation' of UMHK should be understood.

The Bakajika Law, a measure reasserting the state's control over all land and mineral rights, was promulgated in 1966. In effect, territorial concessions granted to UMHK and other foreign companies under the colonial regime were ended abruptly without mention of compensation. Tensions increased when UMHK responded by unilaterally raising copper prices to align them with those of Zambia and Chile. Mobutu was profoundly angered since the Zairian government, unlike its Zambian and Chilean counterparts, had not been consulted. But the final straw was Mobutu's subsequent insistence that UMHK transfer its headquarters from Brussels to Kinshasa by the end of 1966. UMHK refused and Mobutu retaliated by nationalising the company at year's end. The official announcement indicated the expropriation of UMHK and the creation of a new Zairian parastatal to replace it beginning in 1967. The new Zairian enterprise was called Société Générale Congolaise de Minerais (Gécomin), later to be renamed Gécamines. In addition, Mobutu ordered all copper exports halted at the end of 1966 so that UMHK would have to suspend its own sales.

The nationalisation was ineffective and incomplete. Zaire's dependence upon mineral wealth for its governmental revenue was such that a threat to halt the exportation of copper lacked credibility. The temporary halt in operations caused a decline in the state's revenues and encouraged further inflation. Moreover, UMHK had been accumulating reserves outside Zaire and had enough copper stockpiled to continue its refining and sales operations for about five months. Added to this was the inescapable fact that most of UMHK's key administrative and technical personnel in Zaire were Belgian. A lengthy series of claims and counter-claims ensued, but Mobutu's bargaining position was weak because of a near absolute dependence upon revenues provided by the sale of copper. The inevitable capitulation occurred in February 1967 when Gécomin reached an agreement with the Société Générale des Minerais (SGM), another subsidiary of Société Générale. The agreement provided that although SGM would have no participation in the capital ownership of Gécomin — which was held completely by the state — it would aid in commercialisation, and in the technical management and operations of the new parastatal. In return for technical supervision and marketing, SGM would be entitled to 4.5 per cent of the value of Gécomin's total sales. Zaire had neither the cadres nor the marketing outlets to perform either function. Thus, although there had been a change in ownership of the copper industry, effective control remained outside the country.

A new convention was reached in 1969 which extended the initial agreement for 25 years. Under the new terms, SGM would receive 6 per cent of Gécomin's total sales of minerals for 15 years, after which time its share would be reduced gradually from 6 per cent to 1 per cent. Furthermore, SGM received a guarantee of continuous supplies of copper for its refining operation in Belgium. Unsurprisingly, the financial arrangements between Gécomin and SGM evolved in favour of the latter. Between 1968 and 1972 the remunerations due SGM for its marketing and management know-how accounted for a large percentage of the total profits of the Zairian parastatal. The low was 48 per cent of total profits in 1968; the high 162 per cent in 1972. In April 1974 yet another agreement was concluded and the 6 per cent compensation figure was replaced by a flat sum of $100 million.[22]

In theory, one of the benefits to be derived from the nationalisation of the industry was the Africanisation of cadres and some progress was made in this regard. In January 1967 Gécamines employed 251 Zairian white collar workers of a total of 2,166, or 11.5 per cent; by the end of 1976 Zairians held 1,309 white collar positions of a total of 2,252, or 58 per cent.[23] Whilst on one level this is indeed a step forward, too much should not be made of it. As late as 1976, the regime-imposed revolutionary steering committee of Gécamines was composed of the company's 13 top executives of whom three were Zairian, one Swedish, one French, and eight Belgian.[24] Ownership passed to the state; control remained abroad.

In sum, it is difficult to quibble with Nzongola's judgement of the 'nationalisation' of Zaire's copper industry. 'Rather than weakening the links of economic dependence *vis-à-vis* the imperialist centres of the world capitalist system, the nationalization of the copper industry strengthened them'.[25] Parenthetically, since being nationalised UMHK has been able to diversify its holdings and expand into other areas of the globe. The regime's goal has most assuredly not been to revolutionise relations of production, but rather to strengthen its own position in dealing with foreign capital.[26] It matters little to the politico-commercial bourgeoisie that effective control is in foreign hands as long as payments and benefits to itself are forthcoming. Within this general state of dependency, however, the bourgeoisie can, and does, seek a larger share of the economic pie and this may well be the ultimate meaning of the repeated renegotiations of copper conventions between Zaire and Belgian interests.

Many of these same phenomena are at play in other sectors of the economy. Although agriculture has not attracted the magnitude of investments that mining has, foreign capital is nevertheless present. Unilever, an Anglo-Dutch conglomerate, has been involved in Zairian agriculture since the early part of this century. In 1911, Unilever benefited from the pattern of concessions which had already emerged in the mining sector and received 750,000 hectares of land. The result was Huileries du Congo Belge (HCB), the principal Unilever company in Zaire. The 1911 convention granted Unilever these large tracts and extended administrative responsibilities in them, in return for, among other things, Unilever's assurance that it would care for the indigenous populations. The company was to construct schools, hospitals, and housing for its employees, in addition to staffing the new educational and medical facilities. The convention saw to it that Unilever received a good chance to profit from growing, processing, exporting, and trading natural palm oil products. The difficulty, however, was that these activities were in no way to cause any adverse consequences for the Zairians whose land was taken and labour used in the process.

Implicit in the agreement was the curious colonial notion that the happiness of the natives and the profits of the company could, and would, go hand in hand. HCB became the classic 'paternal' colonial employer in the agricultural sector.[27] But neither colony nor company spent much time worrying about the paradox of paternalism and the state helped recruit the labour necessary to exploit the new plantations. Taxes forced Zairians to seek wage labour on the HCB concessions and local chiefs designated a certain number of their able-bodied men to sign contracts with HCB for specified periods. In return for this service, the chiefs received a percentage of the workers' salaries.[28]

Believing in vertical integration, Unilever started a firm to manufacture margarine and soap (MARSAVCO), and installed branches of its commercial affiliate, SEDEC, throughout the country. Thus, in addition to its export trade, the company also produced and marketed goods for local consumption.[29] The omnipresence of SEDEC's general trading outlets also had the effect of providing extremely efficient and well-funded competition for smaller merchants and traders — be they European or Zairian. Despite financial ups and downs, Unilever-Zaire proved to be a reasonably profitable enterprise.[30]

When independence arrived, Unilever successfully accommodated itself to the new order, and HCB was renamed Plantations Lever au Congo (PLC, later changed to PLZ). Although political decolonisation resulted in constraints on the expatriation of profits and other restrictive policies, PLZ was a major earner of foreign exchange for the new state and those in power, especially after the death of Lumumba, had no desire to terminate this lucrative arrangement. The fact that the firm was not Belgian-owned and operated also played in its favour, as did a programme to Africanise cadres. Unilever rode out the troubles of the first republic by consolidating its plantations and reducing their total area under cultivation. Nonetheless, despite operational difficulties spawned by turbulent times, the firm's plantations increased production slightly up to the 1970s.

In 1975, PLZ was hit by nationalisation of the agricultural sector, but Unilever people continued to run the plantations. The experiment in nationalisation shortly came a cropper, and by 1977 the firm and its plantations had once again been returned to their original owners.[31] The trade-off has been fairly clear. PLZ has received a virtually unrestricted hand in setting the wages of its employees and in determining prices paid to independent farmers for their products. Wages are below the Zairian minimum and the company's purchases of agricultural products are occasionally two to four times below the world market price.[32] In return, the state, or rather the politico-commercial bourgeoisie, has received the benefits of foreign exchange earnings which contribute to its luxurious life-style. PLZ is an archetypal enclave.

In addition to the cooperative relationship PLZ has been able to establish with the Mobutu regime, it has also attracted support of other kinds. For example, the World Bank decided to fund a project for the expansion of palm oil production in 1978. The aim of this venture was to help the Zairian government avoid having to import palm oil, a product used for cooking in most Zairian households. Whilst the intentions of the Bank were perhaps laudable, the way in which the project was conceived speaks to the question of multinational penetration of Zaire's agricultural sector. The plan's cost is estimated at $47 million, with almost $23 million in foreign financing. The project was formulated and submitted to the World Bank by its three main beneficiaries: PLZ, Busira-Lomami, and Compagnie de Commerce et de Plantations (CCP). Belgian interests own both Busira and CCP. These three companies would implement the project and the Zairian government pledged to exempt investments in new palm trees, replantings, and new equipment from import duties under the liberal, 1969 investment code. The report also mentions that because of this infusion of funds from the international system, all three firms would be able to service their debts completely and pay increasing dividends beginning in

1983. Zaire's position, on the other hand, is not so optimistic. The state's cash flow from the project would be positive until 2002, but from the following year until 2027 it would be negative because debts incurred to international lending agencies would fall due, and the newly planted trees would by then have ceased production. In effect, Zaire is mortgaging its economic future so that three multinational firms and the Zairian government may derive immediate and short-term benefits.

One additional point needs be mentioned. During the 1973–1977 Zairianisation–radicalisation–retrocession fiasco, Mokolo acquired CCP and Engulu took over Busira. Both gentlemen have long been influential members of Mobutu's inner circle. It is possible to speculate that when these plantations reverted to their former owners, both officials might have been able to arrange retention of some form of participation in the enterprises.[33] The palm oil project indicates several things. First, foreign assistance and development aid have been channelled from the international system to multinational corporations which control about 60 per cent of Zaire's palm oil industry. Second, this project — whatever short-term benefits may accrue — will further contribute over the long term to Zaire's precarious debt position. Third, it would appear that the interests of the politico-commercial bourgeoisie are being cared for, especially given the once dominant role in two of the three relevant firms by a pair of Mobutu's closest and most trusted collaborators.

The Inga Shaba power line illustrates another series of themes and trends in the regime's attempts to manage the Zairian economy and is worthy of at least brief note. The construction of the powerful Inga dam in Lower Zaire was completed during the 1960s with foreign financial backing and is, without doubt, one of the most impressive hydro-electric complexes in Africa. In the late 1960s it appeared as though energy consumption was going to be a problem in Shaba's copper-mining areas. Sufficient power was needed to extract and process the ores. This projected energy deficit was extremely serious for it would force Gécamines to curtail its plans to expand production. The government was alerted and then commissioned a technical study of the problem. Written by a Zairian technocrat, the cost–benefit analysis showed that the best way to accommodate the copper industry's needs for more power would be to construct a new hydro-electric station at Busanga, close to the heart of Shaba's mining complex. This, observers felt, would be far preferable and much less risky than linking the Inga dam with Shaba — a decision which would require stringing 2,000 kilometres of power line. Much of this line, moreover, would have to traverse underpopulated and largely inaccessible regions of the country and an undertaking of this length had never before been attempted. The World Bank was willing to finance construction of the new Busanga station, but the project and the $65 million loan were unilaterally cancelled by the presidency, which ordered work begun on an Inga Shaba power line.

The president apparently made this decision for several reasons. First, there was a surplus of energy in Lower Zaire. Inga had been expanded in preparation for the establishment of aluminium plants in that region and when these investments failed to materialise, the area was left with a surfeit of power. Second, there is good reason to suppose that Mobutu wished to reaffirm his political mastery of Shaba. Given both Shaba's history of secession and the state's dependence upon copper for its revenues, the president might well have looked favourably upon a solution which would give him, in Kinshasa, the ability to shut down the region's hydro-electric power thereby crippling any future attempt at separation. Finally, there are indications that Mobutu wished to diversify Zaire's dependency. The creation of an Inga Shaba line could lead to competitive bidding from firms representing many industrialised nations. Indeed, the American firms of Morrison Knudsen, and Fishback and Moore International emerged as major contractors. By 1979 the cost of this line had far exceeded preliminary estimates and was being calculated at $680 million. The United States Export–Import Bank put together a consortium to finance the project, along with Swedish and Zairian funds.[34]

Several lessons emerge from this episode. In the first place, the actual cost of Inga Shaba is likely to dwarf the projected price of the cost-efficient plan to build a new hydro-electric complex at Busanga. Second, political motivations — both national and international — were probably responsible for initiating the power line. On the one hand, Mobutu wished to exert control over Shaba in a concrete and dramatic way, whilst on the other, a project of this magnitude provided for yet another infusion of foreign capital into Zaire and also permitted the regime to choose industrialists of a variety of nations. There has thus been a trend under Mobutu to end Zaire's once exclusive dependence upon the former colonial power. There have been important and consistent efforts made to attract American, French, German, and Italian investments. Diversification of dependency does not alter the basic extroverted nature of Zaire's economy, but it at least provides Mobutu a chance to play one set of interests off against another — something he has done with consummate skill. There is, then, despite Zaire's dependent status, room for manoeuvre; room to induce competition within Western capital; and, therefore, some leeway within the structure of the system to increase the benefits accruing to the politico-commercial bourgeoisie by bargaining over terms of access to Zaire's wealth. This pattern has also been evident in Mobutu's attempts to attract a wide range of international financing to the mining sector, thus decreasing Zaire's once near absolute dependence on Belgian interests.[35]

Taste transfer, the transmission of social and cultural preference from the international system to a dependent state, is one of the by-products of dependency and is, in turn, one of the factors which helps reproduce the dependent condition itself. An example of this process, one I was able to observe at first hand in the town of Lisala, concerns bottled beer. The place of beer in Zaire's political economy has been dealt with elsewhere. An examination of Lisala's beer trade indicated that this commodity was important both economically and politically. Economically, because the bar trade is both lively and profitable, and many bar owners have used the proceeds from their taverns to finance other investments. Politically, because the regime has found that it is to its own advantage to make sure that people are kept happy drinking. Political grumbling and discontent rise markedly when beer is unavailable.[36] From a national perspective, beer is politically important for much the same reason and its economic importance is reflected in the fact that from 1970–1976 investments in this industry totalled Z33,438,000, or 25 per cent of the total investment under the 1969 investment code in all Zairian manufacturing industries. During the same years, only Z29,839,000 were invested in agriculture.[37]

Beer was introduced into Zaire during the colonial period and over the years demand for it has spread amongst the entire population. Because the price of beer is relatively high, economic factors dictate that much of its consumption will be restricted to those on regular salaries. Nevertheless, beer is enjoyed and demanded by almost all strata of the population. What has occurred in this domain, both literally and figuratively, is a case of taste transfer. The economic and political consequences are sketched above, but the social aspects of this phenomenon also warrant elaboration. First, virtually all of the economic arrangements which occur around marriages in Lisala make use of beer as one of the media of exchange between families. Naturally, other financial resources also change hands, but beer is almost always included. Indeed, one school teacher was compelled by his prospective father-in-law to postpone his nuptials until the next shipment of beer so that the precise number of cases agreed upon could be transferred. Mourning ceremonies also require beer and would be inconceivable without it. In addition, gifts of beer regularly occur in bars. Such exchanges represent a means of demonstrating friendship, kinship solidarity, or political deference. Beer was so important to social life that when Lisala's supply was interrupted, night life all but came to a halt. Most men preferred to spend their evenings in bars and when taverns closed for want of beer, social interaction declined dramatically. People tended to stay at home because there was nowhere else to go.[38]

In July and August 1975 such a beer drought occurred in Lisala. During these two months the town was bone dry and not a bottle could be begged, borrowed, or stolen. Why? The problem in this instance was neither the productive capacity of the breweries nor the occasionally flighty and inefficient distributive system. It lay, rather, in the structure of the Zairian beer industry itself. Although Zaire is Africa's largest producer of beer and has had its own breweries since the 1920s, the country remains dependent upon the importation of raw materials from Europe to keep its beer industry afloat.

From 1970 to 1978, Zaire's beer industry required total imports of hops and malt worth over $146 million. The average yearly value of these commodities was roughly $15.4 million. By the summer of 1975 when Lisala suffered from beer withdrawal, the Zairian state was already in dire financial straits due to plummeting copper prices. At that particular moment, there was simply not enough money in the coffers to purchase the raw materials necessary to keep the breweries running at normal capacity. The resulting decline in production was felt more in the hinterland, in places like Lisala, than in Kinshasa for the regime's priority for distribution of resources has always been Kinshasa first, and the rest of the country later.

Beer-belly dependency is no laughing matter. The beer drought in Lisala during the summer of 1975 had serious effects on local life. There was, first, a general economic slowdown throughout the region. Those merchants who needed profits from their taverns to finance their other economic activities found themselves in difficulty. Because these profits were unavailable, workers went unpaid and stores could not be restocked. The effects were also significant politically for there was a visible increase in the level of popular discontent. Derogatory comments about the inability of local officials to assure the supply of beer were often heard, and the scepticism with which the regime was viewed probably tended to increase. Finally, the severe effect on the town's social life has already been noted.

From a national perspective, beer-belly dependency poses a dilemma for the regime in power. Zaire cannot afford to spend $15 million per year on its beer industry at a time of financial crisis. Such expenditures do nothing to end the crisis and contribute to a further evaporation of the state's precious supply of hard currency. And yet, were the state's leaders to declare that henceforth there would be no beer brewed in Zaire, the economic, political, and social effects would be devastating. Whilst in the West beer is an ordinary item, well within reach of the average worker, in Zaire it has become a luxury affordable only by wealthier elements. The problem, however, is that taste transfer has been so complete that demand for beer cuts across nearly all social strata.[39] Taste transfer has thus been effected and tends to deepen Zaire's overall state of commercial dependency.

Bread is another example of taste transfer. Although until the end of the last century bread was virtually unknown in Zaire, during the colonial period Europeans imported whatever wheat was necessary for their own bread-making needs. But for most Zairians, the staples were either manioc or maize. After independence Zairian elites continued importing wheat, bread having become a food connoting wealth and power. Wheat was relatively inexpensive in the 1960s and could be imported more easily than reorienting agricultural production. As the population of Kinshasa grew, more and more migrants to the city adopted bread as their preferred starch. It was available and inexpensive, but had progressively become associated with wealth and status in the popular consciousness. A network of bakeries appeared gradually in Kinshasa and other cities, and the luxury of wheat and flour soon became a necessity. The urban population became dependent upon bread, and thus on the international system.[40]

This increasing reliance on bread opened the way for the penetration of Zaire by the Continental Grain Company, a large, United States based multinational corporation. Continental opened a modern flour mill in Zaire in May 1973 and had difficulties from the outset. By 1974 the effects of the economic crisis were beginning to register, and the Zairian government was in debt and unable to pay Continental for its wheat. The situation was complicated further by worldwide increases in the price of wheat in 1973 and 1974.

By 1976 Continental was becoming frustrated with attempts to extract payment from an insolvent government and decided to act. It did not deliver its monthly wheat shipment to the mill, thus reducing the amount of flour produced. The results were impressive. Lengthy queues materialised at bakeries throughout Kinshasa and people began hoarding bread. The regime soon realised that the situation was potentially explosive and acceded to the firm's demands. It began repaying its outstanding debt to the tune of $1 million per month in hard currency. Moreover, the government agreed that only United States wheat would be imported in the future and Continental was granted the exclusive right to mill flour in Zaire. Continental thus became Zaire's unique importer of flour, having received a virtual monopoly. At the time, the Mobutu regime was extremely weak and in no position to extract favourable terms from the multinational. Zaire's dependence upon Continental for both wheat and processing facilities had become seriously constraining and the regime has been forced to spend an average of almost $20.4 million from 1970–1978 to keep local bakeries in flour. In addition, Zaire's reliance on external sources underscores its vulnerability to sudden price increases on the world

298

market. In 1973 Zaire imported 145,000 metric tons of wheat worth over $15 million. The following year, roughly the same quantity of wheat cost more than twice that price. Once again, the regime's precarious financial position simply cannot tolerate so serious a drain on the nation's hard currency. It can almost go without saying, moreover, that the sums spent annually on grain might better be used for development projects designed to increase local production of foodstuffs. Unfortunately, the regime now seems to be a prisoner of the process of taste transfer and of the demands of its domestic constituency which must have bread.

Other examples of the serious consequences of taste transfer abound, particularly among the politico-commercial bourgeoisie. Whilst one may suggest that the funds spent annually on beer and wheat might serve better purposes, the fact remains that demand for these products is widespread and all Zairians have come to enjoy them. No Zairian regime could long survive if these products were suddenly unavailable. Nevertheless, there remains ample room for improvement along other dimensions of the taste transfer phenomenon. The World Bank has recently calculated that in 1973 Zaire spent $200 million on 'non-essential' imports. These expenditures totalled $220 million in 1974; $140 million in 1975; and $135 million in 1976. The list of these 'non-essential' imports makes interesting reading. Included in this category are: tinned fish and meats, shell fish, cheese, breakfast cereals, fruit, jams, jellies, chocolates, alcoholic beverages, tobacco products, toys, sporting goods, linoleum, carpets, cut flowers, lace, tapestries, pottery, china, gold and silverware, household appliances, watches, photo equipment, radios, records, automobiles, jewelry, lamps, musical instruments, and central heating and plumbing equipment.[41]

The World Bank is correct in that these goods are 'non-essential' to the development of Zaire and to the overwhelming majority of the population. Such importations obviously drain the regime's dwindling supply of hard currency and cannot be tolerated in a period of financial crisis. The problem, however, is that to members of Zaire's politico-commercial bourgeoisie such goods are essential. These people wish to continue leading the 'good life' and desire a life-style comparable to that of their counterparts in the world's industrialised nations. It is more important to members of this class to have these 'non-essential' products than it is to spend the nation's money on goods likely to be of aid in rural areas. These importations also show exactly where the priorities of the dominant class in Zaire are to be found. This example of taste transfer from the international system redounds only to the advantage of the politico-commercial bourgeoisie.

Financial dependency[42]

Zaire is a debt-ridden state. Tentative indications are that by 1980

Zaire's outstanding debt to both private and public international creditors had risen to over $4,000 million. In 1977, the last year for which relatively complete figures are available, Zaire's external public debt was $3,537 million of which approximately 58 per cent was owed to private lenders (i.e., commercial banks) with the remainder due to multilateral organisations (IMF, World Bank) and individual national governments. Cumulative debt service payments in arrears reached $378 million and Zaire was behind at least another $400 million on short-term commercial notes. From 1975–1977 Zaire's external debt service totalled $938 million of which only $399 million or 42 per cent was actually repaid to creditors.[43] How did this situation arise?

It will be recalled that in the early 1970s Zaire looked like a good investment. Copper prices were high and Zaire's mining potential is impressive. It appeared, therefore, that Zaire would be able to repay any debts contracted through future sales of minerals. Moreover, after the 1973 petroleum crisis, there was much liquidity in the international financial system and banks were looking for places to park their money. In 1973–1974 private banks thus followed the bullish copper market into Zaire in a way which they probably soon came to regret. In 1973 a group of Japanese banks made a series of Eurodollar loans to Zaire with the hope that such transactions would ensure future Japanese access to Zairian raw materials. This set off an avalanche of loans as United States, British, and Belgian banks hopped on the bandwagon. Large international banks led the way in most instances, and these initial offerings were general, all-purpose budget loans. Their aim was to get a foot in the door because of Zaire's huge natural endowments and the rosy financial and developmental future which almost all predicted. These 'brownie-point loans' were not always tied to specific infrastructural projects, but were designed to create a presence in Zaire which could be exploited subsequently.[44]

Local and international greed worked in tandem. The Zairian elite wished to maintain the flow of funds from the international system to finance its grandiose development schemes such as Inga Shaba and to maintain its sumptuous life-style. The more funds which appeared from varying sources, the more could be 'appropriated', or 'lost', or 'mislaid'. One economist's estimate is that roughly 60 per cent of the ordinary funds which pass through the hands of the Zairian government are put to purposes other than those for which they were intended.[45] Think, then, of the opportunities for speculation provided by the millions being lent to the state. Corruption flourished as never before. On the other side of the equation, Western bankers were interested in relatively high rates of return on their money. From 1970–1976, average interest rates on loans made to Zaire were 6.9 per cent and included a grant element of 20.6 per cent. This was in marked contrast to the more lenient loans offered other low-income countries for which interest rates average 2.6 per cent with a grant element of 57.2 per cent.[46]

By the end of 1975 Zaire had fallen into arrears and a stabilisation agreement with the IMF was concluded in March 1976. In return for a further loan, Zaire was to devalue its currency, denationalise certain parts of its economy, restrain government spending, and reduce the budget deficit. Despite Zaire's inability to limit spending, the denationalisation and devaluation did occur and the funds were released. Throughout the late 1970s, Zaire was involved in a never-ending series of negotiations with the IMF, private banks, and the governments which had provided assistance. Details need not detain us. Suffice it to say the arrangements did not succeed and Zaire has remained both in debt, and in serious financial difficulty. By 1978 the regime had, in effect, defaulted and the IMF demanded expatriate supervisory personnel in Zaire's key financial institutions as a condition for continued assistance. Mobutu agreed to this humiliating condition and a German IMF bureaucrat was seconded to the Banque du Zaire. Despite his best efforts, the politico-commercial bourgeoisie did not cooperate with his attempt to bring things under control and he left Zaire after less than a year. Specifically, he had tried to impose severe limits on what Zaire could spend on imports and this angered Mobutu and his collaborators — many of whom ran shops which imported the 'non-essential' items mentioned earlier.[47] These efforts, and others, failed. Zaire's debts continued to spiral and it became apparent that Western finance was unwilling to write off money spent in Zaire by cutting its losses and withdrawing. By 1980 the sums involved were quite considerable.

During this period Soviet—Cuban adventurism in Angola and Ethiopia contributed to an atmosphere in which Western governments were also reluctant to see the Mobutu regime crippled financially. The United States and other members of NATO continued bilateral assistance to Zaire, albeit at a diminished rate. In this regard, the fate of the United States PL 480 programme in Zaire is instructive. Although furnished with the intent of supplying low-priced food to the neediest elements of the population, in practice the system broke down and members of the politico-commercial bourgeoisie appropriated the rice and sold it at enormous profit.[48] Hearings in the United States House of Representatives highlighted the difficulties. Approximately $1.3 million generated from the sale of PL 480 commodities was, according to the United States—Zaire agreement, to be used for development projects. The Zairian government, it turns out, 'lent' these funds to eight farmers. The loans ranged from Z99,000 to Z600,000 and, unsurprisingly, the 'farmers' in question were all either current or former high-ranking government officials.[49]

The problem is not that private banks supply loans, that the IMF tries to oversee Zaire's finances, or that individual governments furnish bilateral aid. The real difficulty is the use to which this money is put by the Mobutu regime and the members of the politico-commercial bourgeoisie who dominate it. Headline-capturing development schemes designed to increase the regime's prestige have little positive impact on the lives of ordinary Zairians. Data from the World Bank indicate that from 1970–1977 the government allocated 59.3 per cent of all loans received to large infrastructural development projects. Only 2 per cent were devoted to agriculture or livestock projects and, as already seen, multinational firms absorbed at least some of these funds.[50] In other words, few of these loans or aid projects are likely to ameliorate the lives of farmers. Money and other resources which enter the country from abroad, as well as funds generated from within, simply do not reach the rural folk who comprise close to 70 per cent of the population.[51] This was certainly true of the PL 480 monies 'lent' to 'farmers' who also just happened to be relatively wealthy officials.

Related to the failure of resources to 'trickle down', are the aims, intentions, and interests of the politico-commercial bourgeoisie. This class has made use of the fact that Zaire's commercial and financial dependencies are closely intertwined. When the bottom fell out of the copper market in 1974, its members had neither the will nor the courage to restructure their economy. To be fair, it must be said that even had these two qualities been present, they might not have had the ability to change Zaire's economic orientation significantly. Nonetheless, where revenues from the sale of minerals had once financed the expensive tastes and life-styles of this class, they soon became equally dependent upon loans and other types of foreign assistance. Rather than devoting these funds to projects which, at the very least, might have mitigated the harsher effects of the crisis on the population, they continued to spend much needed monies on luxuries obtainable all too easily from foreign sources.

Technological dependency

Closely linked to both commercial and financial dependency, technological dependency will here refer to the transfer of technical knowledge and technically skilled personnel from foreign sources, usually advanced industrial states, to other nations. This process, in its broader aspects, engenders and perpetuates Zaire's external orientation and reliance on the international system for its economic well-being.[52] Inga Shaba is a case in point. American construction crews are largely responsible for building the power line with imported equipment. Should any part of this mammoth undertaking need repair, new parts will have to come from abroad — most likely accompanied by the expatriate technicians needed to install them. It might be objected that such processes of technology transfer will ultimately redound to Zaire's long-term advantage because, eventually, many Zairians will be trained to take over the technological functions accompanying the importation of relatively advanced infrastructural material. This, in fact, *might* be the case if Zairians were being trained. They are not. A recent study based on interviews in 63 mining and manufacturing enterprises demonstrates that 'formal training programmes are rare in Zaire's industries. Less than 20% of the firms interviewed have provided formal training and instruction on a continuing basis' and Zaire depends upon foreign personnel to furnish technological know-how to keep the industries running.[53]

The educational system deepens the difficulty in training Zairians to assume technical functions in the economy. Before independence, educational opportunities were severely restricted and in 1960 the new nation had to face the world with less than a score of university graduates. After independence, the public demanded, and received, an extraordinary expansion of the nation's educational network. The pattern adopted, however, was based primarily on the classical Belgian educational system. Its emphasis was on a traditional general formation in the humanities — a type of schooling not adapted to Zaire's needs. Unfortunately, Zairian social pressure was exerted to see that it was continued. This process of educational technology transfer was encouraged further by the presence of large numbers of Belgian technical assistants. Today the educational system remains unsuited to Zairian priorities and realities; a premium is still placed on traditional, classical education at both secondary and university levels. In consequence, few secondary school or university graduates have the skills, preferences, or orientations necessary to find employment in technical spheres and foreigners must be employed to perform these tasks. This significant expatriate presence reinforces Zaire's technological dependency and propagates a foreign role model and life-style heavily reliant upon technological gadgetry and modern appliances of all kinds.[54]

So ill-suited is the educational system for the nation's technological needs that even those few firms both willing and able to train Zairian youth as technicians experience difficulty. In 1975 one industrial firm, Chanic, launched an employee training programme specifically designed for graduates of the *option scientifique* of their secondary schools. This programme came at a time when many had difficulty pursuing university-level studies because of restricted admissions. The goal was to train them as skilled labourers in the factories, but the experiment failed. The firm discovered that most trainees did not succeed because they were intent only on finishing their studies, preferred to remain unemployed rather than learn a technical trade, and were more interested in office work than in getting their hands dirty. They displayed, in other words, a repulsion for manual labour of any kind, no matter how technical or skilled.[55] This disdain continues to be communicated effectively by the hidden curriculum of most Zairian secondary schools.

Unfortunately, not all firms are interested in training Zairian replacements for their expatriate personnel. Indeed, most probably fall into this category. In Shaba, for example, there has been considerable opposition from European engineers to programmes intended to train Zairian counterparts. Even those Zairians already trained as engineers tend to encounter much hostility and intransigence from their European colleagues. The location of files is not revealed, or certain critical information withheld, until the Zairian has learnt enough to ask for it specifically.[56] Such obstacles may seem petty, but they are part of the larger problem and process of successful technology transfer and should not be discounted. More important in most regards is the fact that the presence of highly skilled European technical personnel means that Zairians rarely control their own economy. This is true in the case of Gécamines, Inga Shaba, and also holds for other industrial enterprises. Foreign interests, represented by expatriate personnel placed in important functions within the Zairian economy, are not usually interested in relinquishing effective control.

The aims and goals of Zaire's politico-commercial bourgeoisie should by this time be apparent. The members of this class are concerned primarily with maintaining the cash flow; it matters little that expatriates control the economy as long as their own benefits are not reduced. It is in this light that we must understand Mobutu's 'open door diplomacy'. Foreign participation in Zaire's economy is welcomed with open arms as long as members of the dominant class are 'associated' with it. Indeed, in his speech before the opening session of Second Ordinary Congress of the Mouvement Populaire de la Révolution (MPR), the president proclaimed 'All foreigners who love our country, who respect our laws, who wish to make their living by bringing their contribution to Zaire, are free to install themselves here without limitation on their activities'. But Mobutu went on to recommend strongly that such foreigners should be associated with Zairian partners of their own choosing.[57] A crystal ball is not necessary to predict that most of those who will ultimately be selected to 'associate' with these new foreign ventures will be members of the politico-commercial bourgeoisie. In Zaire, as anywhere else, a well-placed and politically influential business partner can work wonders in eliminating or circumventing bureaucratic impedimentia.

Political dependency

At this juncture it should be clear that control of the Zairian state, and its coffers, is a fundamental and necessary condition for the continued dominance and enrichment of the politico-commercial bourgeoisie. It is manipulation of the state apparatus which enables the ruling class both to extract resources from the population, and to bargain over terms of economic access with Western interests. Preservation of the integrity of the state and of the political supremacy of the *Mobutiste* bourgeoisie is thus a key aim of Zairian foreign policy. This concern takes precedence over all others and contributes to a political dependency of considerable magnitude. This political dependency, which is both a continuing cause and consequence of the multiple dependencies discussed above, was never more important than in March 1977 and May 1978. Within the space of 15 months Zaire was twice the victim of invasions by rebels of the Front National pour la Libération du Congo (FNLC). The first invasion, subsequently dubbed the 'War of eighty days', witnessed an attack by 1,500–2,000 rebel troops. The Zairian military again displayed its customary inefficiency and corruption and Mobutu had to solicit help from his Western friends. This episode was not especially serious in military terms. The invaders withdrew and faded across the border when confronted by Moroccan troops. The 1978 invasion, later known as the Second Shaba War, was a much deadlier affair. The invaders seized and held Kolwezi, a crucial mining town, until French Legionnaries and Belgian paratroopers could mount a rescue operation. The United States provided logistical support for the counter-offensive. The alacrity with which Western powers succoured the Mobutu regime is indicative of both the political and economic importance enjoyed by Zaire in occidental perceptions of African international events.[58]

That the West would react speedily to an invasion of Shaba should come as no surprise. Shaba is the centre of Zaire's vast mining industry and no one in Western capitals wished to see this source of copper and cobalt jeopardised. The global political context was also important for Soviet–Cuban involvement in Angola and the Horn of Africa had contributed to a considerable cooling of détente between the superpowers. Furthermore, Mobutu was extraordinarily skilful in playing on Western fears of a new Soviet–Cuban excursion in Africa's strategic heartland. In July 1977 he announced to all who would listen:

> The offensive directed against my country, as everyone knows, is a generalised offensive of the Soviets in Africa encouraged by the successful operation in Angola and the indifference that they have perceived on the part of the West. It is therefore the Russians that have made the situation today what it is.[59]

The matter is more open to question than Mobutu wished Americans and Europeans to believe. It now seems relatively certain that Cubans present in Angola had, at some point, provided training for the Shaban rebels. But from this fact it is difficult to deduce that Cubans were therefore implicated in the two attacks. Or, as one excellent account of the events has it, 'The fact that one cannot deny an important Cuban military presence in Angola does not authorise the conclusion that the Katangans must have had Cuban instructors behind them'.[60]

For most residents of the invaded areas, many of whom rallied to the banner of the invading forces, the issue was not one of Cuban presence, but of opposition to an increasingly corrupt and oppressive regime. It was primarily Mobutu who sought to link these events in the minds of policy makers in Washington, Paris, and Brussels with Soviet interests in expanding their influence in Africa and elsewhere. Mobutu manipulated successfully, and to his own advantage, Western concerns over global confrontation with the Soviets. Linkage, to use Henry Kissinger's term, is more than a two-way street and it is not always the diplomats in the United States State Department who are responsible for creating links.

The interest of Mobutu and the rest of Zaire's politico-commercial bourgeoisie in the successful outcome of the Shaba wars is apparent. If a rebel force were to conquer Shaba, then the regime would be deprived of its main source of income and those in power would probably fall. Mobutu's pre-eminent need was to retain control of the state and to assure this in both 1977 and 1978 he had to invite active Western intervention. Even a display of blatant, overt, and completely humiliating military and political dependency was preferable to the unthinkable alternatives.

Zairian foreign policy is indeed dependent on the West but one should not infer from the existence of this structural constraint that Mobutu and the class he so ably represents are in any way 'puppets' that dance when strings are pulled. Indeed, since independence, Mobutu and other Zairian leaders have displayed a notable autonomy *within* the limits of political dependency. For example, documents recently declassified indicate that although during the first republic Mobutu and the rest of the Binza Group accepted funds and counsel from the United States Central Intelligence Agency (CIA), they were in no sense blindly following American initiatives. In the words of one United States ambassador's cable to the State Department: 'I hope that the Department is not assuming from a few modest successes that the Embassy has Kasavubu, Mobutu, or any other Congolese "in the pocket". While we have consistently endeavoured through counsel and advice to guide moderate elements along a reasonable path, they rarely consult us voluntarily regarding their prospective moves'.[61]

Similarly, although there is reasonably good evidence that Mobutu's coup in 1965 was facilitated by the CIA,[62] this has not made Mobutu an unquestioning tool of United States interests. In 1973 he publicly broke diplomatic relations with Israel during a speech before the General Assembly of the United Nations. At a time of tension in the Middle East (October 1973), this can hardly be attributed to subservience to United States policy directives. Furthermore, in 1975 he loudly accused the CIA of fomenting a plot against him within the Zairian armed forces. As a result, the United States ambassador was expelled and relations between Mobutu and his friends in Washington cooled perceptibly. The charges Mobutu made in 1975 remain unsubstantiated and it seems that the CIA may merely have been a convenient whipping boy. The episode furnished an excuse to purge the army of those officers thought to be politically suspect whilst, at the same time, allowing him to score diplomatic points with more radical Afro-Asian states.

Mobutu's political autonomy in the international arena is further enhanced by skilful exploitation of divisions within the Western camp across a wide range of issues. In the economic sphere he has sought to diversify his dependence by playing one set of foreign interests off against another, and a similar dynamic is at work in the political domain. Mobutu and those who represent him in international councils are shrewd enough to know that the West rarely speaks with a unified voice and that fissures within the Western alliance may provide significant room for manoeuvre. Competition between France and Belgium has played a role here. The Belgians have long been concerned by what they consider French designs on their former colony. The French, for their part, have actively tried to entice Zaire into a closer political and economic relationship. France has recently invested in several large projects and Giscard d'Estaing treated Mobutu with great respect. In addition, French stock rose visibly amongst Mobutu and his collaborators when Giscard responded quickly to Zaire's plight in 1977 and 1978.[63]

Nonetheless, care should be exercised to avoid overstating the degree of autonomy displayed by Zairian foreign policy under Mobutu. Although not a puppet, the room for manoeuvre is indeed limited and Zaire's foreign policy might best be described by the term *dependent autonomy*. The reasons for this condition of dependent autonomy are not difficult to discern. They lie in the close complementarity of interests between Western powers and Zaire's politico-commercial bourgeoisie. Above all else, class interests predominate in the formulation of Zairian foreign policy. Mobutu is interested primarily in what will be good for himself and his class, and Zaire's 'open door' diplomacy should be understood with that in mind.

The operative goals of the politico-commercial bourgeoisie would appear to be maintenance of its hold over the extractive and oppressive post-colonial state; continued exploitation of Zaire's wealth for private purposes; and the continuation of the flow of Western finance and technology into Zaire. Given the structure of the Western industrial system, Zaire's colonial history, and the origins of its politico-commercial bourgeoisie, it becomes possible to state that, in general, the interests of the West will prove to be compatible and complementary to those of Zaire's leaders. Nzongola has argued forcefully, and correctly, that Zaire is not a puppet regime. He notes that 'reciprocity and the interpenetration of interests are the keys that explain the regime's pro-American actions'.[64]

But this is not to argue that specific differences will fail to arise, or that Zairian interests will always be compatible with those of the West. Most specifically, there have been examples of the politico-commercial bourgeoisie pushing hard to extend its own portion of the economic pie it shares with those who control Zaire's economy. If the politico-commercial bourgeoisie cannot command its economy, then at least it can muster certain resources to achieve a larger share of it. This was certainly one of the lessons of the Zairianisation–radicalisation episode. The bourgeoisie tried to eliminate foreign ownership of commerce and agriculture by expropriating mostly Belgian interests with only vague promises of compensation. The politico-commercial bourgeoisie's aim was clear: appropriate a larger share of the pie.[65] Although he probably underemphasises the role of the state, Girvan's analysis of dependent comprador bourgeoisies is relevant:

> Usually it is assumed that this bourgeoisie is an internal ally of international capital, and defends the latter; but in fact its objective position is rather one of ambivalence. Normally it is true that this class allies itself with foreign capital in order to protect its privileged position relative to the rest of the national population. But there is no reason to suppose that it is objectively satisfied with the weak, dependent and junior position it occupies in relation to international capital. On the contrary, where it perceives a configuration of international and domestic circumstances which provides the conditions for it to assert greater independence and to develop its material base internally, there is every reason for it to take advantage of such opportunities.[66]

That the Zairianisation–radicalisation effort failed this time around is irrelevant. The attempt will assuredly be made again when Zaire is economically and politically stronger.

Conclusion

Throughout this chapter I have argued that if we are to comprehend the wellsprings of Zairian foreign policy it is essential to consider constraints and opportunities provided by the structure of the international system, as well as the ways in which the international system influences the context of domestic class formation. In addition, it is crucial to uncover the operative goals and interests of the dominant class and discern its influence on the process of policy formulation — on the process, most especially, of setting the nation's foreign policy agenda.

The dynamics of contemporary Zairian foreign policy cannot be understood without reference to the past. Foreign economic penetration occurred throughout the colonial period and has affected, decisively and perhaps unalterably, the paths along which an independent Zaire may travel. Large multinational firms such as UMHK and Lever Brothers came to dominate the Zairian economy and, with the willing cooperation of the colonial state, ensured the extroverted orientation of Zaire's economy. Extraction of raw materials was stressed; the creation of broadly based manufacturing industries virtually ignored. Zairians were discouraged from engaging in commerce as foreign interests were consistently favoured as a matter of policy. In Zaire, unlike some other African states, there was no genuine indigenous agricultural or commercial petty bourgeoisie. African participation in the economy was, for the most part, limited to the status of labour reservoir, cash crop farmers, or food growers whose harvests were required to feed plantation workers and miners.

When independence came in 1960, Zairians neither owned nor controlled the means of production in their society. Political change was effected without economic change. Foreign interests remained firmly and forcefully in control of the most productive sectors of the economy. One consequence was that those who rose rapidly to assume the levers of domestic political command had spent most of their lives as clerks in either the state or the foreign companies and possessed no source of wealth other than their control of the state apparatus. Since opportunities for the accumulation of capital had been denied them under colonialism, they set about converting state office into economic wealth; a process pursued vigourously. State office was used to generate both legal and illegal funds which enabled them to obtain commercial houses, bars, and plantations. Political and administrative power thus preceded economic power, and it was only gradually that the former clerks were able to transform themselves into a politico-commercial bourgeoisie. Once the members of this class successfully consolidated their political power, they soon perceived that it remained in their interests, much as it had once been in the interests of the colonial master, to retain the oppressive and extractive structure of the state they had inherited. Any Zairian foreign policy will therefore seek to provide and maintain conditions which will permit the retention of state power.

In addition to the structure of the colonial state, this class also acquired a taste for Western-style luxury. Their former rulers had lived well, so they should be able to also. Control of the state provided the means both to acquire and indulge certain tastes present in advanced industrial societies. Bottled beer replaced banana beer and bread replaced manioc. The funds necessary to import raw materials for these, and other, products come largely from the sale of minerals on the world market. When the price of copper is high, tastes are indulged. When prices plummet, other arrangements and sources of financing have to be found. Control of the state is crucial for it affords the members of the politico-commercial bourgeoisie the opportunity to control incoming revenues and to bargain with foreign capital over rights of access to those Zairian resources it needs or desires.

Throughout Mobutu's regime, this class has consistently looked outward, to the international system, for ways of increasing its wealth. Loans were contracted, investments pursued, and other arrangements made periodically. The loans, of course, went directly into the state coffers controlled by Mobutu and his close collaborators. Investments by multinational firms and other investors have been devoted to large-scale projects designed either for the regime's prestige or the comfort of members of the dominant class. Bilateral aid channelled into Zaire by well-intentioned donors went astray — into the pockets of the politico-commercial bourgeoisie. Commercial, financial, and technological dependency have intensified.

This account is not meant to imply that Zaire's ruling class and the foreign policy it has conducted is, or should in any way be seen, as passive and reactive. On the contrary, within the limits imposed by overwhelming dependence on foreign sources, Mobutu and his associates have tried to expand and enlarge their room for manoeuvre and their access to wealth. It is in this context that the nationalisation of UMHK and the Zairianisation radicalisation episodes should be perceived. Members of the politico-commercial bourgeoisie have tried to bargain with international capital for an ever-expanding portion of the economic pie. They would like to increase their share of the wealth; if this can be done at the expense of foreign interests, so much the better.

Toward this end, in an attempt to increase the regime's latitude, Mobutu has constantly sought to diversify the sources of his dependency. Loans are accepted from many nations and organisations; joint ventures are encouraged from entrepreneurs of all nationalities;

consortia of investors are welcomed. The diversification of dependency has provided some occasions to play one set of external interests off against others. Mobutu is far too shrewd a politician to think that Western capital speaks with a single voice. The door is open – not just to one, but to all – provided that foreign investors are willing to associate Zairians with their business endeavours.

Zaire is also dependent politically, but the regime has made, especially in recent years, efforts at diversification. Aid is accepted not only from the former colonial power, but from the United States, France, West Germany, China, North Korea and other states. Mobutu is remarkably catholic in his willingness to accept political and military assistance from a wide range of nations. Zaire's foreign policy is politically dependent, but nevertheless enjoys considerable autonomy within the confines of this constraint. Dependent autonomy is real and in no way may Mobutu's foreign policy be said to be dominated by any single external state. Mobutu is neither a puppet of the United States, nor of any other major power. There is a complementarity, not a congruence, of interests. Conflicts will continue to arise between the Mobutu regime and its sponsors.

But what of the future of Zairian foreign policy? Zaire's external relations, at least in their broad outline, are conditioned on the one hand by the nation's multiple dependencies on the international system and, on the other, by the internal dynamics of social class formation. A radical change in the structure of the international system which would reduce Zaire's dependency seems remote. Equally unlikely, especially given external support for the present regime and the continuation of business as usual, would be a change in Zaire's class system. But only a complete and thorough-going social revolution can accomplish that task. A mere change in regime will be meaningless. Even if Mobutu should fall, say, after a third Shaba war or violence and revolt in the urban centres, there is simply too much at stake to permit the evolution of a new class structure. Powerful interests, both foreign and domestic, have profited from the open door of Zairian foreign policy. I strongly suspect that they will continue to do so.[67]

Notes

1 Richard Moose, 'Testimony', in US, Congress, House, Committee on Foreign Affairs, Subcommittee on Africa, *Foreign Assistance Legislation for Fiscal Year 1981 (Part 7)*, 96th Cong., 2nd session, 5 March 1980, pp. 537, 539.
2 Lannon Walker, 'Testimony', in *ibid*., p. 591.
3 Mobutu Sese Seko, 'Discours d'ouverture', 2ième Congrès Ordin-

aire du MPR, Kinshasa, November 1977, p. 9. This and all subsequent translations are mine.

4 M. Crawford Young, 'Testimony', in US, Congress, House, Committee on Foreign Affairs, Subcommittee on Africa, *Foreign Assistance Legislation for Fiscal Years 1980–81 (Part 6)*, 96th Cong., 1st session, 5 March 1979, p. 371.

5 The following several pages are based largely on: Crawford Young, 'Zaire: The Unending Crisis', *Foreign Affairs*, vol. 57, no. 1, 1978, pp. 169–185; Ghislain C. Kabwit, 'Zaire: The Roots of the Continuing Crisis', *Journal of Modern African Studies*, vol. 17, no. 3, 1979, pp. 381–407; Comité Zaire, *Zaire: le dossier de la recolonisation* (Paris and Brussels: Editions l'Harmattan and Editions Vie Ouvrière, 1978); Guy Gran (ed.), *Zaire: The Political Economy of Underdevelopment* (New York: Praeger, 1979); and World Bank, *Zaire: Current Economic Situation and Constraints* (Washington, D.C.: East Africa Regional Office, The World Bank, May 1980).

6 The Hobbesian image is taken from Young, 'Zaire: The Unending Crisis', pp. 170–171.

7 Thomas Kanza, 'Zaire's Foreign Policy', in Olajide Aluko (ed.), *The Foreign Policies of African States* (London: Hodder and Stoughton, 1977), p. 240.

8 Jeannick Odier, 'La politique étrangère de Mobutu', *Revue française de science politique africaine*, no. 120, December 1975, p. 41.

9 Most of this period is admirably related in Crawford Young, 'The Portuguese Coup and Zaire's Southern Africa Policy', in John Seiler (ed.), *Southern Africa Since the Portuguese Coup* (Boulder: Westview 1980), pp. 195–212.

10 The figures may be found in World Bank, *Zaire: Current Economic Situation and Constraints* (note 5), pp. 24 and 191. On the quality of life in the rural areas see René Lemarchand, 'The Politics of Penury in Rural Zaire: The View from Bandundu', in Gran (ed.), *Zaire: The Political Economy of Underdevelopment* (note 5), pp. 237–260; Elinor Sosne, 'Colonial Peasantization and Contemporary Underdevelopment: A View from a Kivu Village', in *ibid.*, pp. 189–210; and M. Carel *et al.*, 'Le Kivu Montagneux: Surpopulation, sous-nutrition, érosion du sol', *Cahiers du CEDAF*, nos. 2–3, 1979, pp. 2–28. On human rights see Amnesty International [AI], *Human Rights Violations in Zaire: An Amnesty International Report* (London: AI, May 1980); AI, 'Student Arrests in Zaire during the First Half of 1980', AFR 62/37/80, August 1980; AI, 'Violations of Human Rights of Refugees from the Republic of Zaire', AFR 62/44/80, September, 1980; and

Nzongola-Ntalaja, 'The Continuing Struggle for National Liberation in Zaire', *Journal of Modern African Studies*, vol. 17, no. 4, December 1979, pp. 595–614.

11 The remainder of this chapter constitutes an attempt to come to grips, however tentatively, with the international context of the political dynamics of class formation in Zaire. My earlier work concentrated on domestic factors and although the international aspects of the question are important, I was able only to allude to them. See Michael G. Schatzberg, *Politics and Class in Zaire: Bureaucracy, Business, and Beer in Lisala* (New York: Africana, 1980), pp. 177–183 and 186.

12 See Jean-Philippe Peemans, 'Imperial Hangovers: Belgium – The Economics of Decolonization', *Journal of Contemporary History*, vol. 15, no. 2, 1980, p. 261; Bogumil Jewsiewicki, 'Zaire Enters the World System: Its Colonial Incorporation as the Belgian Congo, 1885–1960', in Gran (ed.), *Zaire: The Political Economy of Underdevelopment* (note 5), pp. 29–53; and Pierre Joye and Rosine Lewin, *Les Trusts au Congo* (Brussels: Société Populaire d'Editions, 1961), p. 57. Joye and Lewin note that the average profit margins for large capital in the Congo from 1950–1960 ranged from 15–21 per cent; those obtained at home from 7–9 per cent.

13 Bogumil Jewsiewicki, 'African Peasants in the Totalitarian Colonial Society of the Belgian Congo', in Martin A. Klein (ed.), *Peasants in Africa: Historical and Contemporary Perspectives* (Beverly Hills: Sage, 1980), pp. 45–46.

14 'L'avenir économique du Vice-Gouvernement de l'Equateur', *Congo*, vol. 2, no. 1, 1921, pp. 288–289.

15 Jean-Philippe Peemans, 'The Social and Economic Development of Zaire Since Independence: An Historical Outline', *African Affairs*, vol. 74, no. 295, 1975, p. 151.

16 Schatzberg, *Politics and Class in Zaire* (note 11), pp. 16–17.

17 Thomas Kanza, *Conflict in the Congo: the rise and fall of Lumumba* (Harmondsworth: Penguin, 1972), pp. 83–84.

18 This account has been developed from a variety of sources. For the domestic evolution of this class see Schatzberg, *Politics and Class in Zaire* (note 11). Also, Jewsiewicki, 'Zaire Enters the World System' (note 12), p. 60; Peemans, 'The Social and Economic Development of Zaire' (note 12), pp. 162–165; and Daniel Van Der Steen, 'Echanges économiques extérieurs du Zaire; dépendance et développement', *Cahiers du CEDAF*, nos. 4–5, 1977, pp. 6–7. On the mechanisms of bureaucratic capital accumulation see David J. Gould, *Bureaucratic Corruption and Underdevelopment in the Third World: the case of Zaire* (New York: Pergamon,

1980), pp. 31–149.

19   Drawn from Ghifem J. Katwala, 'Export-led Growth: the copper sector', in Gran (ed.), *Zaire: The Political Economy of Under-development* (note 5), table 7.1, p. 125; Raymond F. Mikesell, 'The Copper Economy of Zaire', in Scott R. Pearson and John Crownie (eds), *Commodity Exports and Economic Development* (Lexington: Heath, 1974), p. 180; Gould, *Bureaucratic Corruption* (note 18), p. 40; Jean-Claude Willame, *Patrimonialism and Political Change in the Congo* (Stanford: Stanford University Press, 1972), p. 86; and World Bank, *Zaire: Current Economic Situation and Constraints* (note 3), pp. 29, 51–52.

20   The following account of the UMHK episode depends heavily on Willame, *Patrimonialism and Political Change in the Congo* (note 19), pp. 85–92; Gould, *Bureaucratic Corruption* (note 18), pp. 36–40; Katwala, 'Export-led Growth' (note 19), pp. 122–136; Comité Zaire, *Zaire: le dossier de la recolonisation* (note 5), pp. 104–109; Mulumba Lukoji, 'La commercialisation des minerais de la Gécamines', *Zaire-Afrique*, vol. 15, no. 94, 1975, pp. 209–220; Ilunga Ilunkamba, 'Conventions de gestion et transfert de technologie au Zaire: le cas du cuivre', *Africa Development*, vol. 2, no. 2, 1977, pp. 73–94; and Wolf Radmann, 'The Nationaliz-ation of Zaire's Copper: From Union Minière to GECAMINES', *Africa Today*, vol. 25, no. 4, 1978, pp. 25–47.

21   See Ernest J. Wilson, III, 'The Political Economy of Public Corporations in the Energy Sectors of Nigeria and Zaire', (unpublished Ph.D. dissertation, University of California, Berkeley, 1978), pp. 473–478.

22   The figures on SGM's remuneration may be found in Mulumba Lukoji, 'La commercialisation' (note 20), p. 212.

23   The percentages were calculated from data presented in Radmann, 'The Nationalization of Zaire's Copper' (note 20), p. 44.

24   David J. Gould, 'From Development Administration to Under-development Administration: a study of Zairian administration in light of the current crisis', *Cahiers du CEDAF*, no. 6, 1978, p. 27.

25   Nzongola-Ntalaja, 'The Authenticity of Neocolonialism: ideology and class struggle in Zaire', *Berkeley Journal of Sociology*, vol. 22, no. 1, 1977–1978, p. 122.

26   *Ibid.*, pp. 122–123 and Jean-Claude Willame, 'Le secteur multi-national au Zaire', *Cahiers du CEDAF*, no. 1, 1980, p. 14.

27   D.K. Fieldhouse, *Unilever Overseas: The Anatomy of a Multi-national 1895–1965* (London: Croom Helm, 1978), pp. 494–515 and Willame, 'Le secteur multinational au Zaire' (note 19), pp. 16–20. See, too, M.K.K. Kabala Kabunda, 'Multinational Corporations and the Installation of Externally-oriented Economic

314

Structures in Contemporary Africa: the example of the Unilever-Zaire Group', in Carl G. Widstrand (ed.), *Multinational Firms in Africa* (Uppsala: Scandinavian Institute of African Studies, 1975), pp. 303–322.

28 Fieldhouse, *Unilever Overseas* (note 27), pp. 512–513.

29 Willame, 'Le secteur multinational au Zaire' (note 19), p. 17.

30 Fieldhouse, *Unilever Overseas* (note 27), p. 533.

31 *Ibid.*, pp. 543–545.

32 Willame, 'Le secteur multinational au Zaire' (note 19), p. 21.

33 World Bank, 'Zaire: Appraisal of the Oil Palm Project', Report No. 1592-ZR, 29 March 1978 and, on the question of ownership of CCP and Busira, see Région de l'Equateur, Division Régionale de l'Agriculture, *Rapport Annuel 1974*, pp. 132–138.

34 This account of Inga Shaba draws extensively on the excellent work of Ernest Wilson, 'The Political Economy of Public Corporations' (note 21), pp. 590–604. See, too, Willame, 'Le secteur multinational au Zaire' (note 19), pp. 35–41.

35 On diversification in mining, see Willame, 'Le secteur multinational au Zaire' (note 19), pp. 43–48. Examples are provided concerning SMTF and SODIMIZA.

36 Schatzberg, *Politics and Class in Zaire* (note 18), pp. 83–98.

37 Banque du Zaire, *Rapport Annuel 1976* (Kinshasa: Banque du Zaire, 1977), p. 71. The Zaire currency (Z) is now worth US $0.18, but it has been progressively devalued since 1978. At the time of my study, 1974–1975, Z1 = $2.00.

38 Michael G. Schatzberg, 'Bureaucracy, Business, Beer: The Political Dynamics of Class Formation in Lisala, Zaire', (Ph. D. dissertation, University of Wisconsin-Madison, 1977), pp. 235–237.

39 In 1974 Zairian per capita beer consumption was 23.6 litres. The following year it declined to 19.1, and in 1976 it dropped again to 17.7; a trend which reflects both the specific problems evinced above and the overall crisis situation. See UN, *Statistical Yearbook, 1978*; UN, *Demographic Yearbook, 1977*; and, on the importation of hops and malt, FAO, *FAO Trade Yearbook, 1975–1978*.

40 The section on bread is based on Dan Morgen, *Merchants of Grain* (Harmondsworth: Penguin, 1980), pp. 289–304 and 325. Data on importation of wheat and wheat flour may be found in FAO, *FAO Trade Yearbook, 1975–1978*.

41 World Bank, 'The Manufacturing Sector of Zaire', Report No. 2212-ZR, 29 October 1979, p. 21.

42 The distinction made amongst commercial, financial, technological, and political dependencies is quite artificial, wholly arbitrary, and done only for convenience. The various depen-

dencies catalogued are interrelated and overlap considerably.

43   World Bank, *Zaire: Current Economic Situation and Constraints* (note 5), p. ii gives a 1979 figure of $4,160 million and Guy Gran, 'The Sociology of World System Stabilization: The IMF in Zaire 1978–1980', *African Studies Association*, Philadelphia, October 1980, p. 17a gives a 1980 figure of $4,696 million. The 1977 figures cited may be found in World Bank, *Zaire: Current Economic Situation and Constraints*, pp. 37–38.

44   P.A. Wellons, *Borrowing by Developing Countries on the Euro-Currency Market* (Paris: Development Centre of the Organisation for Economic Co-operation and Development, 1977), p. 125.

45   Peemans, 'The Social and Economic Development of Zaire since Independence' (note 15), p. 162.

46   World Bank, *Zaire: Current Economic Situation and Constraints* (note 5), p. 37.

47   Much of this account of financial dependency is based on Gran, 'The Sociology of World System Stabilization' (note 5); Guy Gran, 'Zaire 1978: The Ethical and Intellectual Bankruptcy of the World System', *Africa Today*, vol. 25, no. 4, 1978, pp. 5–24; and Jonathan David Aronson, *Money and Power: Banks and the World Monetary System* (Beverly Hills: Sage, 1977).

48   David J. Gould, 'The Problem of Seepage in International Development Assistance: why United States aid to Zaire goes astray', *Civilisations*, vol. 29, nos. 3–4, 1979, pp. 253–267.

49   US, *Foreign Assistance Legislation for Fiscal Year 1981 (Part 7)*, p. 470.

50   World Bank, *Zaire: Current Economic Situation and Constraints* (note 5), p. 39. The figures on which the percentages are based are $2,212.6 million for infrastructure and $74.5 million for agriculture.

51   There is now an array of documentation for this assertion. See *ibid.*, pp. 17, 24–25 and 84; Gould, 'The Problem of Seepage' (note 48), pp. 253–267; and Michael G. Schatzberg, 'Blockage Points in Zaire: The Flow of Budgets, Bureaucrats, and Beer', in Gran (ed.), *Zaire: The Political Economy of Underdevelopment* (note 5), pp. 161–188.

52   See Van Der Steen, 'Echanges économiques extérieurs du Zaire', (note 18), pp. 84–85; Daniel Van Der Steen, 'Le Zaire malade de sa dépendance extérieure: aperçu historique et diagnostic de la crise de l'économie zairoise en 1978', *Genève-Afrique*, vol. 17, no. 1, 1979, pp. 127–128; and Benoît Verhaegen, *L'enseignement universitaire au Zaire: De Lovanium à l'Unaza* (Paris, Brussels, Kisangani: Editions l'Harmattan, CEDAF, CRIDE, 1978).

53   Eckhard Siggel, 'Technology Transfer and the Choice of Industrial

Technologies in a Developing Country: the case of Zaire', (unpublished Ph.D. dissertation, University of Toronto, 1978), pp. 64 and 328.

54 Most of this account is drawn from Freddy Mulier, 'La coopération technique belge dans l'enseignement zairois', *Cahiers du CEDAF*, no. 1, 1979, pp. 9 and 66–69 and Van Der Steen, 'Echanges économiques extérieurs du Zaire' (note 18), p. 92.

55 Mulier, 'La coopération technique belge dans l'enseignement zairois', *ibid.*, pp. 20–21. Convincing confirmation for the argument that most educated Zairian youth prefer to seek work in offices may be found in Kasongo Ngoyi et al., 'Les étudiants et les élèves de Kisangani (1974–1975): aspirations, opinions et conditions de vie', *Cahiers du CEDAF*, nos 7–8, 1977.

56 Wilson, 'The Political Economy of Public Corporations' (note 21), pp. 622 and 624.

57 Mobutu Sese Soko, 'Discours d'ouverture' (note 3), p. 30.

58 The precise events occurring in both wars remain murky and it will probably be some time before there is an accurate account of what happened. The waters were further muddied by claims and counterclaims concerning Cuban participation. See, Peter Mangold, 'Shaba I and Shaba II', *Survival*, vol. 21, no. 3, 1979, pp. 107–115; Jean-Claude Willame, 'La seconde guerre du Shaba', *Genève-Afrique*, vol. 16, no. 1, 1977–78, pp. 10–26; and 'Contribution à l'étude des mouvements d'opposition au Zaire: le F.N.L.C.', *Cahiers du CEDAF*, no. 6, 1980.

59 *Salongo* (Kinshasa), 7 July 1977 cited in 'Contribution à l'étude des mouvements d'opposition au Zaire', p. 28.

60 Willame, 'La seconde guerre du Shaba', (note 58), p. 11. Weissman takes a stronger position and states categorically, 'there is no evidence that the anti-Mobutu Katangans were Soviet-influenced'. Stephen R. Weissman, 'The CIA and US Policy in Zaire and Angola', in René Lemarchand (ed.), *American Policy in Southern Africa: the stakes and the stance* (Washington: University Press of America, 1978), p. 423.

61 Cited in Stephen R. Weissman, 'CIA Covert Action in Zaire and Angola: patterns and consequences', *Political Science Quarterly*, vol. 95, no. 2, 1979, p. 268.

62 *Ibid.*, p. 273. Weissman's invaluable account states 'According to three informed individuals – a US official then in Washington, a Western diplomatic Congo specialist, and an American businessman who talked with the returned CIA man, Devlin – the CIA was at least "involved" in the second Mobutu *coup* of November, 25 1965'.

63 Drawn from the accounts of the Shaba wars cited above.

64 Nzongola-Ntalaja, 'The US, Zaire and Angola', in Lemarchand (ed.), *American Policy in Southern Africa* (note 60), p. 157.

65 On the general strategy see Van Der Steen, 'Echanges économiques extérieurs du Zaire' (note 52), pp. 108—109. For general information on the Zairianisation—radicalisation see Schatzberg, *Politics and Class in Zaire* (note 11), pp. 121—152 and Edward Kannyo, 'Political Power and Class Formation in Zaire: the "Zairianization measures", 1973—1975', (unpublished Ph.D. dissertation, Yale University, 1979).

66 Norman Girvan, 'Economic Nationalists v. Multinational Corporations: revolutionary or evolutionary Change?', in Widstrand, (ed.), *Multinational Firms in Africa* (note 27), p. 38.

67 I am grateful to Doreen R. Ellis, René Lemarchand, and M. Crawford Young for their probing comments and criticism of an earlier draft of this chapter. They are in no way responsible for any remaining deficiencies.

12 Zambia

Marcia M. Burdette

At independence in 1964, the new Zambian politicians and diplomats had to forge a complex and complementary set of foreign policies on two levels – the regional and global. The region incorporated several settler regimes and colonial territories with movements dedicated to their overthrow as well as various independent African-ruled countries. The most powerful states – Rhodesia and South Africa – were not well disposed towards the newly independent black-ruled regime in Zambia.[1] As the wars of liberation 'heated up' in the late 1960s and early 1970s, the Zambian people and regime were often endangered. Such crises required strong responses from the government of Zambia. Yet the ability of this government to respond was constrained by a relatively weak military establishment and an economy dependent on the white South.

For the first decade after independence Zambia paid a heavy price for its principles[2] in support of the liberation movements and in the attempt to establish greater economic autonomy. The region, thus, required the immediate attention of many of the Zambian officials. On the global level, Zambian politicians and civil servants tried to develop a coherent set of policies towards the advanced industrial states, primarily, though not exclusively, capitalist. This arena too had its set of pitfalls and problems because the interests of a raw-materials exporting nation such as Zambia rarely fit comfortably with the interests of consumer nations who are also often the source of needed manufactured goods, technology and capital.

Although distinct geographically, the global and regional levels obviously intimately affected one another and created cross-pressures on Zambian foreign policy stances. Both sets of policies have revealed puzzling kinds of inconsistencies by the Zambian government. Within the regional level, for example, as a Front Line State and a backer of the Zimbabwe African People's Union (ZAPU), the government was a major force behind the eventual settlement of the Zimbabwean war. Yet Zambia's leaders sometimes chose to curb harshly the various liberation groups in Zambia. The government even handed over some freedom fighters to their political opponents and thus to almost certain death or internment in the early 1970s.[3]

On the global level, Zambia affronted international capital by the nationalisation of mining assets located in Zambia in the late 1960s. Simultaneously politicians drafted legislation specifically framed to attract direct foreign investment in hopes of increasing ties and capturing benefits from international involvement in Zambia. Thus the government has appeared simply to lurch from one set of policies to another depending upon the exigencies of the moment — an essentially *ad hoc* foreign policy. Yet on looking at the policies carefully, at the level of trends rather than just incidents, I can detect some underlying structural features which help to explain motivations of the policies as well as to illuminate some tendencies for Zambian foreign policy in the future.

I see an intimate connection between the nature of the productive system in Zambia, local class formation and patterns of international constraints, and what one author calls 'transnational class cooperation'.[4] Zambia's mineral industry is part of an international system of production and exchange of commodities. As a consequence, its own domestic patterns of class power reflect international alliances as well as international pressures. I address the governing Zambian political class and its factions in some detail here because I argue that this is the nexus of the domestic and international influences. Specifically, I do not subscribe to the argument that Zambia's governing class is totally subservient or obeisant to the interests of foreign capital. Rather I see much contestation and dispute, demonstrated in the foreign policy arenas. Yet many objective tendencies within the international system have tended to make Zambia more dependent despite efforts by the governing class to carve out some more independent role for itself.

In the late 1960s Zambian officials initiated policies purported to lessen the state's dependence upon the colonial metropole, Britain and

320

the settler regimes of the region. By the middle of the next decade, however, this dependence was being replaced by a growing resort to the multilateral institutions of the Western capitalist system and the re-emergence of reliance on the white-controlled regimes of the region. In other words, a more *exclusive dependence* seemed to give way to a *multilateralisation of dependence*. Its effects are evident in foreign policies on the regional and global level. Specifically, after 1973, there is a growing alignment of the Zambian state with international capital which fundamentally differs from alignments in the earlier period. The choice to focus on the period after 1973 is not arbitrary. This period has contained unparallelled geopolitical upheavals, heavy strains on the health of the export-dependent economy, and heightened inter-class disputes in Zambia. After 1973 Zambian foreign policy was (and is) more visibly strained between ideological, personal and historical ties, and the objective realities of its incorporation into the Western market system and continued reliance on its Southern African neighbours.

In this chapter, then, I focus on production, class power and foreign policy. I emphasise, moreover, the sector of mining because that is the heart of the modern political economy and its welfare affects the health of the whole nation. First, I look at the background of the modern Zambian political economy. Second, I explore the nature of the dominant political class and its factions. Third, I begin to trace shifts in foreign policies from the mid-1960s. And fourth, I develop the argument about the particular character of the post-1975 period and argue class motivations for these changes.

Background to the modern Zambian political economy

Independent Zambia faced a series of hardships that derived from its colonial inheritance, relations with international resource companies operating the major mines, and contemporary vagaries of the copper market. These tendencies were (and are) exacerbated by the combination of a deep dependency upon copper and the land-locked status of the country itself. From the start in the 1920s, its mining sector was totally reliant upon certain factors of production which came from Great Britain and South Africa and export routes which were dominated by Rhodesia and South Africa. Other forms of capital, for example, settler capital, were important in the politics of the territory, particularly in the legislative council. But in the final analysis, it was mining capital which dominated the colony and set the para-meters for colonial and later independent Zambian domestic and foreign policy.

In the period of the federation (1953–1963) of Northern Rhodesia with Southern Rhodesia (now Zimbabwe) (see Chapter 13) and Nyasaland (now Malawi), the federal authorities intensified the infrastructural integration of the North and South. Some key economic decisions favoured Southern Rhodesia, such as the decision to place the major portion of the new Kariba Dam on the Southern bank of the Zambezi River although its major customer was to be the copper mines of the North. Further, financial resources of the North were paid into federal coffers in this decade. Over ten years of 'partnership', about £10 million per year went into the federal treasury.[5] This influx of capital permitted federal officials to build a manufacturing base in Southern Rhodesia and to fund the creation of a large administrative centre in Salisbury, then the federal capital. Meanwhile, the economy of the North outside the mining sphere stagnated. What capital came in did so from Europe, the United States and South Africa. Many of the white settler politicians in the North argued that Northern Rhodesia got little out of federation with Southern Rhodesia.

In the 1950s, Northern Rhodesia was one of the world's largest exporters of primary copper. The benefits of this great mineral wealth flowed unequally, with the companies taking the lion's share and the state and people of Northern Rhodesia receiving the residue.

No other economic activity in Northern Rhodesia even began to compare with the scale, capital intensity, and profitability of the mines. Transportation, manufacturing, and agriculture all served the needs of the mines. Northern Rhodesian officials were aware of that and so were careful in their dealings with the international companies despite their awareness that the state could be shortchanged. The Northern Rhodesian economy was a classical disarticulated economy in that it produced what it did not consume, and consumed what it did not produce.

In addition to this economic asymmetry, power over the formal institutions of the polity also rested exclusively in the hands of resident or foriegn whites. The elective and appointive officials of the federation were nearly all Europeans. The federation itself was dominated by Southern Rhodesia in a loose political partnership with the metropole, Britain. Africans had no effective voice within the formal institutions of the federation. The major political voice of the African people was the nationalist movement which, after a struggle, took over the government in 1962 and brought the nation to independence in 1964. The newly independent African government, then, had formal authority over the society but real power over the major engine of the economy — the mines — rested with the foreign-based companies.

Post-independence Zambia: early foreign policies

African nationalist leaders of UNIP and the ANC targeted the institutions of racism in their own society as well as those of the white settler regimes of South Africa and Rhodesia. From the start, their foreign policies carried a tone of moral indignation and promises of economic disengagement from the white South. The early militancy of the leadership, however, was soon qualified by global and regional realities. The white settler regimes of the South were main sources of manpower, trade and investment capital for Zambia. Further events in the region seemed to connive to undercut the new nation's economic stability.

In 1965, Zambia was confronted with the Unilateral Declaration of Independence (UDI) by her former federation 'partner', Southern Rhodesia. An avowedly racist party called the Rhodesian Front, which took power under the direction of Ian Smith, presented an immediate challenge to Zambia's foreign policy of anti-racialism and economic disengagement.[6] Zambia was confronted overnight with United Nations' demands for an embargo rather than a slower replacement of these trade links. Such immediacy, combined with the deep Zambian commitment to majority rule of her Southern neighbours, meant that the economy had to disconnect rapidly from the Southern Rhodesian political economy. Foreign policy advisors and politicians seemed aware of the dependence upon the white South for essential supplies, technical services, transportation facilities and communications. As they disengaged the economy from Rhodesia, they permitted continuance of many links with South Africa, particularly those which affected production in the mines. The trade network with the white South, however, continued to be vulnerable to frequent changes in political climate. Economic issues proved to be the key to foreign policy within the region.

More enduring than regional economic policies were the global ties to the international companies and consumers. Although the nationalist government had initiated formal diplomatic ties with the major industrial states by 1965, the international mining companies seemed to play the major role in economic diplomacy and negotiations. The parent companies, the Anglo-American Corporation of South Africa Ltd and AMAX and Selection Trust, controlled the sales and marketing of Zambian copper as well as the pricing agreements. Arrangements were made by the multinational headquarters and local management rarely consulting the exporting nation. Further, new financing for the mines came from heavy foreign borrowing, arranged by the international parent companies and based on their evaluations of the needs and pay-offs of the Copperbelt facilities. In making these loans, the banks had assessed the stability of the regime and the quality of the 'investment climate'. Much of this information came from the mining companies. Zambian officials seemed to be more preoccupied with the regional arena of foreign policy making. The mining companies handled much of the dealings with the advanced industrial states and the international financial institutions themselves.

The foreign policy of any state, however, reflects a mixture of objective pressures upon the state, as well as interests of the state. These derive from its relations with other political and economic entities, as well as the nature of the dominant class or classes within its geographical boundaries and, in turn, their relations with classes in other societies. Within Zambia, a new class was taking shape — a new governing class — which was creating policies which would fundamentally alter the structure of ownership of and control over the mining industry. These policies would have profound implications on the foreign policies of the state in the 1970s.

The political class in Zambia and control over the economy

The embryo of this class was the leadership of the African nationalist movement in the 1950s. The leadership of the United National Independence Party (UNIP) and the African National Congress (ANC) included businessmen and small commercial farmers, as well as individuals from the professions, civil servants and trade union officials. This group began to form itself into what I call a class after gaining control over the apparatuses of the state at independence. Over time, its interests began to diverge from its initial constituency, the peasants and urban and peri-urban workers.[7] This formative governing class was, however, at first responsive to popular pressures for social services. To pay for these, it required revenues which came from mining. Top officials were sensitive to the economic dependence of the whole economy upon the foreign mining companies as well as inherited reliance on the metropole, Britain.

As already indicated, this new governing class had been denied ownership of productive property, control over the key sectors of the economy, and the employment of large-scale labour by the peculiarities of the colonial and federal political economies. Therefore, it could not dominate the economy as a traditional bourgeoisie. Rather, it asserted its power through the mediation of the state. The degree of its pre-eminence within Zambia revolved around the extent of its control over the state. Therefore, I call it a 'political class' to emphasise that its power is mediated through control of the state rather than through its members' ownership of the means of production and property.

324

As any class, this new political class evolved in relation to other classes in society. For Zambia, this meant predominantly the workers and peasants, a middle stratum of white settlers in commercial and agricultural sectors, and a militant faction of white mineworkers. The degree of its pre-eminence was limited for the state — its power base — did not control the huge sectors of production owned by resident expatriate or foreign capital. Thus I argue, this Zambian political class was not the paramount class in the wider political economy. The true *ruling* class[8] was external and was composed of the international mineral companies, and related financial institutions, which together make up powerful elements in the bourgeoisies of their own parent states.

This governing political class was only in the process of formation in the 1960s and 1970s. Its power may prove to be temporary in the 1980s, with its pre-eminence threatened (or consolidated) by a military coup, or it may yet evolve into a more traditional bourgeoisie through its ownership of the secondary sectors of the economy. At the end of 1960s, however, this new political class challenged the external owner-ship of key sectors of the economy and sought to supplant the foreign mining companies or at least to supplement its own power through more control over the economy.

The political class in Zambia chose to expand its power by participation of the state in various businesses through partial or total nationalisation of the assets. Since many of these enterprises were owned by foreigners (most of these came from the former colonial power — Britain — or Rhodesia, South Africa and the United States), this strategy affected both global and regional foreign policies. With the significance of the mining industry to the society as a whole, access to that particular sector had to be the linchpin for any strategy. State participation in that sector was approached slowly and carefully so as not to 'kill the golden goose'.[9]

As the political class attempted to assert its influence into the primary and secondary sectors of the economy, splits emerged within it. A class holding a position between the domestic productive class (or classes) as a whole and external owners of capital who function as the *ruling* class, often is rent by intense inter- and intra-class rivalries. Such a struggle within the political class in Zambia intensified as different factions emerged, composed of 'technocrats',[10] 'entrepreneurs', 'national politicians' and 'civil servants'. Although all part of the wider political class, these factions had differing strategies and attitudes towards the takeover of foreign-owned enterprises. As a consequence, they conflicted over the direction of Zambian foreign policy for the region and globally.

The 'national politicians' are the faction most closely oriented to the

325

national economy and most reliant or local political support. They seem committed to Zambianisation of manpower and ownership. In the foreign policy arenas, this faction is less concerned with the niceties of international diplomacy with either the parent states of the multi-national corporations or the headquarters of the companies themselves. In the 1960s and 1970s it pushed for an aggressive foreign policy *vis-à-vis* the racist regimes of Southern Africa, arguing that their continued existence meant a permanent threat to the security of Zambia. Many individual members of this national politician faction also had long-standing ties to the leaders of the liberation movements of Southern Africa, particularly with ZAPU. 'Anti-racialism' was the essence of this faction's attitudes towards the minority regimes. Moral indignation flavoured the tone of much of the diplomatic and political exchanges between Zambia, South Africa, Rhodesia and Portugal in the later 1960s.[11] This faction advocated support for the liberation movements both within the wider political class in Zambia as well as on the continental and international planes, although not as selflessly or idealistically as some authors have suggested.[12] Their general policies of anti-racialism fit with the drive to capture more of the investible surpluses from the mining industry and the desire to lessen dependency upon the white South and the Portuguese colonies. State participation and more accessible transportation routes, they hoped, would lessen the stranglehold that the white-ruled regimes had over Zambia's economy.

A small faction of entrepreneurs within the political class emerged in the middle to late 1960s.[13] As a group, this faction was keen to gain personal ownership over the means of production and to evolve into an indigenous bourgeoisie. But in the 1960s it was very small indeed and had to rely on others to wrest control over small- and medium-sized enterprises from local expatriate and foreign capital. This faction was (and is) closely allied to the other factions in the political class in order to press the state to open the doors of ownership for its members. Further, individuals within this faction hoped to be rewarded with various privileges which would permit them preferential access to items such as import licences which would allow them to profit from their new businesses.

Foreign policy which would be most acceptable to these entrepreneurs would combine protectionism for their 'infant industries' with open relations towards the closest sources of supplies including South Africa and Rhodesia. Their general stance, thus, was quite pragmatic although they certainly were not (and are not), supporters of apartheid.

'Technocrat' and 'civil service' factions[14] have interests and policies which often overlap with those of the 'national politicians' and 'entre-preneurs'. Together, they are concerned with the relationship of Zambian industry and the state to the international sources of the factors of production so vital for the industrial basis of the economy. Aware of the state's dependence upon the mining sector, and in turn the industry's dependence on the foreign companies and the Western marketplace, they are quite willing to bargain for better terms with international and locally based capital, which is primarily South African, Rhodesian, British and American in origin. Yet they do not want to antagonise foreign capitalists either by aggressive economic nationalism or by militant foreign policy stances on Southern African decolonisation.

In the first decade after independence they tended to press for strategies which recognised the *symbiosis* that existed between the Zambian state and the external ruling class composed of the foreign mining companies and their allies, and then made the best out of that mutual reliance. They argued that the foreign corporations needed the backing of a strong state to maintain order and to supply services. These foreign companies could then be pressed, ran the argument, for aid and support to keep the industry alive in times of stress and help the economy obtain foreign loans. Since the state would receive revenues from the mines and the employment of a sizeable portion of the organised labour force while the foreign companies received profits this relationship could be seen as mutually beneficial.[15] Such a sensitive balance should not be disturbed by heavy-handed foreign policy behaviour which could affect such items as Zambia's credit ratings in Western financial circles. Any policies which would raise the costs of domestic inputs or imports, whatever their ideological satisfactions, should be carefully questioned.

Thus various factions of the political class had different attitudes about the appropriate kind of foreign policy for the Zambian state. At various times, under differing internal and external pressures, one faction seemed to have sway or greater power than the others concerning policies for the regional and global level. None of the factions seemed to have power for long enough to coordinate and enact a coherent and future-oriented set of policies. Instead policies seemed almost always to be in a state of flux. But the whole political class seemed to agree on certain core themes such as decolonisation, anti-racialism and economic independence. These were constantly reiterated by the Zambian government as the bases of foreign policy. Yet day-to-day behaviour diverged from a close pursuit of these goals. Occasionally, policy also underwent major changes.

Post-independence Zambian foreign policy: changes in late 1960s–early 1970s

As indicated above, domestic and foreign policies of the political class immediately following independence (1964) seemed to reflect a cautious, measured approach rather than a militant one. Policy was often set by the civil servants in alliance with some British colonial secondees. It was not until 1968 that the national politicians and embryonic entrepreneurs framed and executed a domestic strategy which deeply affected global diplomacy. This policy included participation by the state and private Zambian businessmen in sectors of the economy previously owned or controlled by resident or foreign expatriate capital. A core of politicians, led by President Kaunda, began a series of economic reforms styled as the Mulungushi Revolution.[16] New regulations (1968) permitted Zambian entrepreneurs to initiate or take over smaller-scale enterprises such as retail stores and construction industries.

The civil service and technocratic factions pressed for a lessening of the deep dependence of the economy upon a few countries and corporations. They wanted to attract other foreign investors and create new trading partnerships. This goal was moderately successful in reference to Japan, China and the East European countries. A series of diplomatic exchanges were undertaken to attract new sources of technology, capital and skills either from multinational corporations or East European parastatal organisations.[17] Taxes and mineral codes were reworded with an eye to the new investors. This attempt to attract new investment did not directly conflict with the Mulungushi reforms as these reforms affected small- and medium-scale business while the civil servants and technocrats focused upon major projects on a large scale. So the thrust of global relations was to widen the spectrum of political and economic alliances providing the state with more flexibility in trade and aid relations. This wider arena was dominated by the civil servants and technocrats with the general accord of the other factions.

Another domestic policy which deeply affected both regional and global relations was the decision in 1969 to nationalise the assets of the mining groups. These local groups had been owned by foreign international corporations based in South Africa, the United States and Britain. After an initial flurry of diplomatic and journalistic bombast, there followed an intricate set of negotiations between Zambian representatives, the companies and the 'parent' government of the head-quarters of the multinational corporations. The tenor of these talks was quite benign, probably because the Zambian government made it clear from the start that the companies would be compensated and indeed were likely to be invited to stay on as managers and minority partners in the two new mining companies, NCCM and RCM.

On the global scene, then, the formative Zambian political class handled itself quite well. It successfully used the state to extend its control over the major means of production located within the nation.

By and large, it managed to do this with little damage to its global economic reputation although foreign capital is always uneasy about nationalisations. It was the regional arena which proved to be more troublesome, although it took a number of years before the deep fissures within the political class began to manifest themselves over the conduct of regional foreign policy.

Throughout the late 1960s, policy statements towards Rhodesia, South Africa and the Portuguese colonies continued to be strongly worded. The Lusaka Manifesto of 1969 addressed the prevalence of racism in Southern Africa and called for the rapid decolonisation of the sub-continent.[18] The political class was in general agreement with these statements and rarely did physical conflict approach the level of the verbal hostility. In the case of Rhodesia, there was plenty of provocation as disputes arose around the Unilateral Declaration of Independence (UDI).[19]

The technocrat and civil service factions along with the small group of entrepreneurs were concerned that stable economic relations be maintained in the region. On the other hand, the national politicians were eager to make a clean break from economic relations with the white South. The political class was split further over whether the British could be relied upon to unravel the Rhodesian question. It took several years before the Zambian leadership acknowledged Britain's inability or unwillingness to end the rebellion of the white settlers in Rhodesia. By then (the early 1970s) the policy of reorienting the Zambian economy away from Rhodesia, including the expansion of plans for alternative routes to the sea and new sources of supply of materials, had been instituted. These actions radically lessened Zambian dependence on her former federal overlord. This in turn gave Zambian diplomats some more manoeuvrability in regional politics but domestic class evolution produced another set of problems.

With the Mulungushi reforms, new parastatal organisations were set up to oversee the nationalised companies (FINDECO, INDECO and MINDECO). Both local entrepreneurs and technocrats moved into directorial positions and in some cases into direct managerial posts. Some Zambian technocrats and civil servants who had returned home after earning higher degrees abroad assumed senior posts within these parastatals and some were infused back into ministries. The embryonic political class, therefore, began to expand its membership particularly in the technocratic and entrepreneurial factions. Some of these same individuals were then drawn into high-level political positions within the Party and civil service. But, I argue, the technocrats tended to maintain their primary identity with that faction and to act as a moderating voice in some policies suggested by the national politicians or those put forward by the small but vocal group of entrepreneurs. To the technocrats and entrepreneurs, the most rational foreign policy included some continuation of trade wiʌn Rhodesia and South Africa despite those countries' racist policies. But they found themselves pitted against the more influential national politicians who pressed for more militant behaviour in the region.

Foreign policy in the early 1970s

Events in the region posed more challenges as the new decade began. The struggle for decolonisation began to intensify in Rhodesia, Mozambique and Angola. Zambia became more and more embroiled in these wars of liberation. Efforts by the political class to construct a neutral foreign policy were overtaken by events. The population was subjected to increasing economic hardship and even military invasion. Zambia became a refuge for many peoples fleeing the wars as well as those intending to prosecute them. The Zambian government extended some humanitarian aid to the refugees. Yet the political class was reluctant to be drawn into direct military confrontation over these issues. Eventually, it had to develop a new set of policies to contend with the building pressures upon the regime and those within the political class.

Regional foreign policies in the early 1970s proved to be quite controversial. There are two general lines of argument about the motivations and actions of the political class in this period. One argument has it that the Zambian leaders were trying to bring about a 'neo-colonial solution' for the region, particularly as regards Rhodesia. To this end, they forced ZANU and ZAPU leaders to negotiate with each other and with the Smith regime; they formed ties with UNITA, the Angolan nationalist group identified closely with South Africa; and in general, they tried to insure that the African governments coming into power in neighbouring lands would not be of too radical a bent.

The other major argument emphasises the pressures upon the regime and credits Zambian politicians and diplomats with great efforts in support of the liberation movements and the refugees.[20] Such authors point frequently to the heavy price that Zambia has paid for its aid to the liberation forces − a point well supported by economic data.

Information is not conclusive on these arguments nor likely to become so. I accept the 'neo-colonial' argument as more credible but with modifications. In the long run, the tactics followed by the Zambians added to the scale of the price they paid. In the decision to back UNITA, for instance, the Zambians incurred costs for their foreign policy stance, but these scarcely could be considered the costs of a progressive stance. On the other hand, the arguments based on the 'neo-colonial' assumptions are tinged with an accusation of a moral flaw in the Zambian political leadership which was revealed in hypocritical foreign policy stances. Rather, it might be more useful to accept that the new political class had its own material interests to protect. These interests tended to direct its actions. Principled stands had little appeal as an economic noose was being tightened around Zambia.

In this period, Zambian transport routes remained vulnerable to South African and Rhodesian actions. Zambia's foreign policies, thus, were largely reactive and defensive within the region. Some would call them 'pragmatic'.[21] The political class was unified in its concern that neither the liberation groups nor the South African and Rhodesian forces interfere in its domestic politics. All the factions hoped for a constitutional resolution to the rebellion in Rhodesia but were careful to protect Zambia's own economic interests. Much of the rhetoric of Zambia's policy was directed against the Smith regime together with ritual denunciations of South Africa's apartheid. Beneath this layer of rhetoric though, various factions were eager to stabilise relations with South Africa, especially the technocrats and entrepreneurs. As early as 1968, President Kaunda and Prime Minister Vorster of South Africa had begun a correspondence that was later subject to great speculation.[22] The intention of this communication was to open a dialogue between the two nations to discuss de-escalation of tensions in the region. In October 1974, South Africa and Zambia announced openly a new era of détente. A coincidence of global and regional developments had produced a complementarity of interests between the Zambian and South African governing classes. Yet as this growing alliance was buffeted by some internal and external events, the Zambian political class was forced into more active support for the liberation movements and to bolster the military to face the almost certain onslaught of the Rhodesian forces.

In the period 1972 to 1975 areas of common interest grew between some South African and Zambian politicians. When ZANU opened a front in north-east Rhodesia in 1972, this put new pressure on the Smith regime. In 1973 Smith struck at Zambia's transport by closing the border between Rhodesia and Zambia. This action effectively shut down the Rhodesian route for Zambian imports and exports. Kaunda retaliated by sealing the border on the Zambian side; it remained closed to Zambian trade until 1978. The coup d'état in Portugal in April of 1974 brought a precipitous end to the long battles to decolonise Mozambique, Angola and Guinea-Bissau. This respite gave the Zambians hopes that these transit routes could take up much of the slack in the closure of the 'southern routes'. Soon the Zambian government was forced to choose between the contending nationalist forces in Angola — the MPLA, FNLA or UNITA? Officially the government took a neutral position; unofficially it sided with UNITA.[23] When the Benguela railway was closed (in August of 1975), the Zambians were really desperate for transport routes. The economy was slowly being strangled. Politicians, civil servants, technocrats and entrepreneurs alike had to try to locate capital, to negotiate more suppliers' credits from abroad, and try to find a way of easing the transport bottleneck without appearing to 'give in to' Rhodesian belligerence.

On the South African side, the removal of Portuguese suzerainty over Angola and Mozambique cost South Africa a set of buffer states. The South African economy was also having some troubles, exacerbated by the post-1973 increases in oil prices. South African politicians began to look more actively for economic cooperation with black Africa and détente with Zambia was a central feature of a wider 'dialogue'.[24]

No doubt the Zambian political class thought that South Africa's ostensible policy of détente would include a willingness to pressure the Smith regime to come to the bargaining table and an openness to the installation of some sort of constitutional regime. If this was the calculation, the faction was sorely mistaken. In essence, however, the ability of the Zambian politicians to prosecute détente with South Africa, to stabilise relations with Rhodesia, selectively to support certain liberation movements and to ward off external influences, rested on the power and stability of the political class. After 1973 this power and stability was threatened by a decline in the nationalised mining industry.

In 1973 the president announced a second nationalisation of the mineral industry. Kaunda demanded an end to the junior partner status of the state in the mining industry. The contracts drawn up in 1969–70 were cancelled, the outstanding debts to the foreign mining interests were to be repaid almost immediately, and the Zambian government altered the foreign exchange and taxation provisions written into the prior accords. Negotiations over the second nationalisation step lasted more than 17 months, both with the companies and with their parent states. In the end, the Zambians gained more access to the mine management and marketing. It took several more years before that access was translated into more effective control.

Domestic politics were pivotal in the decision to renationalise the mines in 1973. Various politicians and technocrats, finding themselves questioning technical, administrative and financial decisions by the minority partners, argued for an end to foreign management under these contracts. Certainly it would be far too crude to say that the Zambian government took a stronger hold over the mines because of an active fear of sabotage by the South African, British and United States managers who were seconded from the international resource companies. As tensions grew, however, the desire of the political class as a whole to entrench itself in power and to protect its control over the major industrial enterprise in the society contributed to the decision to further nationalise the mines. The loyalties of the minority partners in the mining companies were less of a concern.

There was a hidden cost in the strategy of state control over the mineral sector, however. As long as the mines remained productive and profitable, control over them and some control over the direction of the profits would imply considerable strength for the political class and large revenues for the state. Beginning in the early 1970s, however, the international terms of trade had begun to move seriously against the Zambian economy. The economic decline that followed produced more pressures upon the regime which, I argue, resulted in new foreign economic policies in the latter half of the 1970s.

The growing crisis in the Zambian political economy: 1975 onwards

As has been stated above, the economic well-being of the political class in Zambia rests heavily upon the narrow base of industrial mining. After 1973 the government slowly extended more and more control over that industry and over its direction. Yet the industry itself began to reveal serious structural difficulties. An economic crisis began in the mines and, when combined with other weaknesses in the system, spread throughout the political economy. The reasons behind the mining decline and the structural weakness of the system will be explained below.

After independence, Zambian politicians and civil servants, aided by some local and foreign advisors, began to draw up development plans for the economy. The intention was to follow a basic policy of import substitution in order to diversify the economy away from mining and to create a large manufacturing sector for the country. The plans required heavy infrastructural investments to be financed from surpluses produced by the mines. The manufacturing sector itself was envisaged as being developed by private capital, both local and foreign. Such a strategy, of course, implied a heavy import bill to pay for the initial machinery and technology not available within Zambia itself. The Second National Development Plan (1972–76) included a wider role for state-owned businesses and explicitly encouraged the establishment of manufacturing firms.

Although the Zambians borrowed the phraseology of socialism and some of its structures – the one-party state, for example – the goal of the nationalisation of various industry and in particular the mines was essentially capitalist, i.e. to realise profit in a class society. The Zambian managing directors of NCCM and RCM were expected to continue mining much as before the state takeover of top management. They were supposed to produce profits and cr ntinue employing local miners. There were no plans to change the structures of industrial hierarchy between the workers and management or to redirect the industry towards local consumption or needs. The bulk of the profits confidently expected to flow from the Copperbelt mines were to finance the other development plans of the state — specifically the expansion and diversification of the mines, an increase in capital investment in that sector as well as the development of productive and social infrastructure in previously unproductive parts of the country.[25] Further, it was hoped that state equity in the big mines would encourage more tertiary businesses through local sub-contracting and stimulate agricultural production. These tertiary businesses were to be privately owned, and this would give a wider base to the new bourgeois elements in the political class. In general, all of these expenditures as well as increased costs of government (both recurrent expenditures and capital expenditures) were to be paid for out of the copper revenues.

A fatal flaw in this strategy of import substitution and heavy export reliance appeared after 1975. The bottom began to drop out of the copper market. This meant a crucial shortage of foreign exchange to purchase the supplies vital to the import-substitution industries and also the luxury goods needed to satisfy the increasing consumer demands from the wealthier sections of society. In a short-term boom in late 1973 to early 1974, the price of copper skyrocketed and so did Zambian hopes. In late 1974 the price dropped and continued to be at a low level when the current price was corrected for inflation. The Second National Development Plan was based on the expectation of a decent profit from the sale of 900,000 tonnes of refined copper per year. By the mid-1970s it was obvious that both the production and price calculations were far off target. The spending programmes for the country, however, were tied to the estimated availability of foreign exchange from mineral sales. The increasing downturn in the Western industrial system plus the rising costs of imports (particularly oil) and the declining terms of trade for Zambian copper, meant that the Zambian economy slowly slipped into an ever-worsening recession beginning in 1975.

The ability of Zambian officials to stem this decline was limited by the fact that major forces which control the copper market are beyond their reach. The pricing of primary copper and the demand for it rests largely in the hands of international companies which form an oligopoly — a set of companies which control production and, in cooperation with brokers and marketing firms, control price and often demand. The price for Zambian copper is based on quotations from the London Metals Exchange and the United States Stock Exchange. Most of Zambia's copper and cobalt, moreover, is sold on long-term supply contracts to a limited number of buyers and prices reflect to some degree the overall supply in the market. More important, however, are the calculations of the oligopoly of what price they can expect for the copper when they sell it to fabricators. Also they want to impede the entry into the market of new investors who are not members of the oligopoly and pricing is one mechanism to meet such an oligopolistic end.

In the 1970s the supply of primary copper on the international market was slowly rising as demand was holding steady. New producers came 'on stream' which produced at lower cost than Zambia. These included Papua New Guinea, Australia, India, South Korea, Taiwan and Poland. Most of these new mines, moreover, had been developed by the very companies controlling the worldwide copper trade. Small local producers and nationally owned industries had to get their products to market as cheaply as possible in order to remain in business at all.

Zambia's ability to negotiate the price for the copper was further weakened by a chronic oversupply of copper on the market. Despite the formation of a producer cartel of copper exporters, the price continued to drop and stockpiles continued to rise. The overall efforts by CIPEC to lessen the decline were generally ineffective. Moreover, substitution materials such as aluminium and plastics competed actively for copper's use in the construction and electronic industries. A plan to develop a buffer stock of copper to 'soak up' the excess primary copper overhanging the market also came to naught. The price for copper continued at a low annual level, despite some brief upturns such as the one in 1979.

The cumulative effect of a continued dependence on an export sector which was vulnerable to cyclical prices and on a development strategy of import substitution became painfully clear in the latter 1970s. The managers of the state and the state-controlled industries began to turn to debt financing to keep the industries and the state solvent. Here the political class in Zambia began to be entrapped in a new dependency — this time upon the financial institutions of the West. It took half a decade, however, before the outlines of this new dependency were clearly visible.

Growing financial weakness, 1970–1980

The financial position of the Zambian government in the late 1970s stood in stark contrast to that in the 1960s. When Zambia came to independence in 1964, the new political class inherited a rather favourable financial situation. There was a relatively low external debt and good promise of foreign exchange to pay off any and all debts and to keep the national balance of payments in surplus.[26] In 1971–72 temporarily depressed prices for copper meant less foreign exchange for the country. The gap between revenues and expenditures in international accounting was filled by 'running down reserves'. Consequently, these reserves were not available to pay off new debts accrued by the state in the later 1970s. Little new foreign direct investment came into the country, and despite the first nationalisation (1969) the economy was being drained of income. The foreign minority partners were averaging from K11 million to K13 million per year for their service fees.[27] After 1975 this outflow was staunched when the mines became 'self-managed'. Yet, in order to purchase that self-management privilege, the Zambian government had paid $226.3 million to the minority partners. This cash was raised by the government's borrowing $150 million on the Eurodollar market, which at that time carried an interest rate of around 13 per cent. The difference between the loans and the re-nationalisation costs was bridged by the government officials and banks using the remaining national reserves, temporarily fattened by income from the 1973–74 mini-boom in copper.

No matter how attractive such debts may be at the time of borrowing, they still have to be repaid with interest and on someone else's schedule. If the copper market had remained 'firm', there would have been far less problem in repaying these debts. As has been made clear above, however, this did not happen. These economic difficulties beginning in 1975 were exacerbated by geopolitical events which put heavy pressures upon the Zambian political economy and upon the political class.

Continued attacks on the Benguela railway insured that it remained closed. Strife over Namibia and Angola meant that portions of Western Zambia were often vulnerable to attack and even occupations by South African troops. The war in and around Rhodesia (now Zimbabwe) disrupted rail and road routes as well as dislocated some vital trade links, for South Africa was still a major supplier of goods to the Zambian economy. Since most South African goods travelled to Zambia via Rhodesia, this put the Smith regime astraddle Zambia's primary trade routes. Even after independence for Mozambique in 1975, which lessened the strain along Zambia's eastern border, the problems were not over. The decision of the FRELIMO government in Mozambique to shut down the railway from the Rhodesian border to Beira in 1976 affected Zambia as well, effectively squeezing yet another vital transport link. The transportation bottleneck became so severe that, at times when the price of copper went through a cyclical upturn and there was plenty of copper available in Zambia's stockpiles, the mine managers still could not guarantee that the copper would make it to its Western European and Asian markets. NCCM and RCM lost these potential sales at a time when they needed the cash flow.

For a measurement of the disastrous financial effects upon Zambia of the combination of a transport squeeze and low prices for copper, one can look at revenues from the mineral sector to the state. From 1969 to 1974, the combined incomes from the mining sector contributed 32—48 per cent to the GDP and were responsible for over 90 per cent of the total foreign exchange earnings of the economy. Between 1975 and 1979, however, mineral taxes, income taxes on the companies, and dividends to the state were either non-existent or miniscule. In 1977 and 1978, the contribution of the copper industry to the GDP dropped to 11 per cent.

As the costs of producing Zambian minerals continued to rise, their attractiveness to consumers declined, despite devaluations of the Kwacha in 1976 and again in 1978. When the additional 'costs of sales' (insurance, freight, sales commissions, etc.) were added to the production costs, the Zambian mines found themselves producing and selling copper near the break-even point and sometimes even at a loss. By the end of the decade (1979) Zambia was listed as a high-cost ⹁ producer of copper. The pressure to export did not abate, however, because the companies needed the revenues and the state needed the foreign exchange generated by the sales of minerals abroad. A final blow to the financial solvency of the state came when overall production on the mines began to decline. Instead of producing 900,000 tonnes per year, in the late 1970s, the mines produced barely 700,000 tonnes of copper for export.

In reaction to the economic dislocations, the government announced a set of austerity budgets, cutting back deeply in such programmes as food subsidies and putting tight controls over import licences. How the domestic economic disarray affected the global economic reputation of Zambia is discernible in the polite words of the 1977 Special Parliamentary Select Committee Report:

> Your Committee further noted that in addition to the price of copper the rapid deterioration in the balance of payments in recent years has been due to the increase in the import cost (like oil and machinery), inflation, increased external debt obligations, increased net transfers of income (from K33.4 million in 1970 to K86.0 million in 1976) and to increased cost of invisible services (transport, freight, insurance and travel) from K75.7 million in 1967 to K155.0 million in 1976. As a result *since 1975 the country has not always been able to meet its short-term external obligations promptly.*[28]

In other words, Zambia was coming close to defaulting on its loan payments abroad.

Equally important was who this Select Committee represented. It was composed of new entrepreneurs who had come into parliament in the 1973 elections plus a few technocrats. They made a series of recommendations of actions to alleviate some of the most severe of the economic and political aspects of the crisis. Some of their suggestions, such as the rationalisation of purchasing policies of the mines, were enacted. There was also some decrease in the rate of growth of governmental expenditures to compensate for the fall in minerals revenue. According to the Bank of Zambia, however, the increase in total expenditure which had taken place year after year had led to a persistence of overall deficits in the government budget. Without the additional revenues from mineral sales to offset the expenditures, government officials turned to deficit financing and to the multilateral lending and aid institutions of the market economies of the West. In particular, I refer to the private commercial banks, the IMF and the IBRD.

Hence, the political class which, before the mid-1970s, had not had extensive dealings with these foreign financial centres, now had to assemble a set of policies to cope with its new situation as representing a large-scale debtor nation.

The international debt position of Zambia

Before 1975, Zambia had not resorted to the multilateral funding institutions extensively; in all the years but one between 1970—79 the economy had a positive balance of trade with the rest of the world. Under the careful eye of civil servants and technocrats, the state maintained sizeable foreign and domestic reserves. Traditionally, export credits and guarantees to the mines, some private commercial loans and an occasional bilateral loan, as well as the banks' own internal reserves had proven sufficient to serve the country's needs.

After 1975 those foreign and domestic safety nets had weakened and torn. The balance of payments slipped into a chronic deficit with invisibles taking up more and more of a role in the movement of the accounts from surplus to deficit. From 1973 to 1979 the balance of payments was only in surplus twice and the overall payments arrears were sizeable. In good years (such as 1979) these payments arrears were almost paid off, but the overall external debt of the state continued to rise. Facing a likelihood of frequent and possibly steep balance of payments deficits, officials of the Bank of Zambia and the Ministry of Finance negotiated a compensatory financial facility with the IMF in 1976. Such a facility did not oblige the Zambians to draw on it. Rather, these funds were available and earmarked to offset the balance of payments deficits and payments arrears to foreign debtors. The IMF extended this facility with the proviso that Zambia devalue the Kwacha, reduce domestic spending, and invoke a series of 'money-saving' policies.

Whether these actions were taken because of the pressures from the IMF or the conservative fiscal and monetary policies of technocrats and civil servants is unclear. Despite such actions, the economy continued to stumble and the debt increased as did debt servicing ($150 million in 1976; $173 million in 1977).[29] Given the scale of the Zambian mining industry and the GDP, a debt of this size is not particularly large or onerous. With a deep recession in the copper market, however, and with the GDP beginning to decline (down 3 per cent in 1977 according to one source),[30] the foreign exchange receipts to the state continued to decline and the ability of the Zambian government to repay the debts became more uncertain. Debt servicing began to consume growing percentages of the export income of the state (18 per cent in 1977), thus taking it away from such areas as capital expenditures.

In March 1978 Zambia returned to the IMF for another tranche. This time, it received a promise of SDR $390 million. In return, Zambian officials promised to devalue the Kwacha again (10 per cent); reduce the money supply (8.07 per cent); and cut back even further on government spending. Yet the total debt continued to climb; debt services reached $190 million in 1978. In June of 1978 the Zambians also turned to the sister agency of the IMF, the IBRD (World Bank). A consulting group meeting was held in Paris in 1978 under the auspices of the World Bank to discuss balance of payments and development loans. According to rather vague reports, these talks were quite successful. But the scale of the debt was large and the needs of the Zambians for more capital was pressing. In December of 1978 the Zambian government negotiated another Eurodollar loan, this time for $57 million. Such loans were difficult to obtain on good terms.

The growing indebtedness of the state is mirrored in the mineral industry. As an indicator of financial stress, the Zambian government became a major lender to its own state-owned industries, NCCM and RCM. By March of 1978 RCM and NCCM owed the Bank of Zambia over $200 million.[31] Later, the state indirectly lent money to the mines in a complex trade of debt for equity. Despite loans from the government, the long period of low copper and cobalt prices and low profits for the companies, meant that earnings were too small to finance the companies from within.

One tactic to lessen the financial pressures on the companies was to try to reduce costs. To lessen the mines' expenses and to plan for more efficient capital outlays, the management of NCCM and RCM invoked a series of cost-cutting policies and merged various operations of the mines. As part of the $400 million stand-by loan to Zambia in 1978, the IMF had requested that the mining companies restrict their borrowing to rather strict limits and try to cut costs. While the IMF cannot force such restrictions, since ultimately the state is the authority over the mines, it does appear that pressures were brought to make the mines cease their foreign borrowing and to take some deep cuts in operating and technical areas. Most deeply affected were the capital expenditure programmes of the mines, which will be discussed later. More visible was the announced move to merge the two companies, NCCM and RCM in 1981 to create a new company, the Zambian Consolidated Copper Mines Ltd (ZCCM).[33] In the short run, some money was saved. But the financial squeeze affected Zambia's foreign policy.

Changes in Zambian foreign policy

While engaging in financial negotiations on the global level, government officials would also have to ask a series of difficult questions about the efficacy and pragmatism of Zambia's regional foreign policies. The economic and social crises in the post-1973 era lent credence to the claims of the technocrats and entrepreneurial factions that Zambia's foreign policy had to reflect the exigencies of the moment, rather than ideological support for the liberation struggles in Southern Africa *if and when* the two were in conflict. The political leadership should then reassess its options. The parameters of what was possible and desirable for the Zambian political economy became clearer.

On the basis of pure economic self-interest, the Zambian political class would have to minimise the costs to the state from all foreign policy activities, regional and global. Some costs were fixed and difficult to reduce, such as increases in military expenditures. Others were more subject to minimising. A settlement of the Zimbabwean war, for example, would lessen the costs to the Zambian state for support of the liberation groups as well as permit Zambian businesses to resort to the cheapest and closest source of supplies — South Africa and Rhodesia in particular — for their manufacturing industry, mines and consumers. Entrepreneurs were forceful on this point as their own enterprises were being strangled by lack of supplies and constricted markets. Problems of transport also would have to be settled and the most reliable route was through Rhodesia. But that border had been sealed to traffic between Zambia and Rhodesia since 1973. Any reopening of that border would have to be invoked under the threat of physical assault across the bridges from the Rhodesian side and would face opposition from the national politician faction. So this option was bound up with some resolution to the war and a constitutional regime coming to power in Rhodesia.

On the global level, technocrats and entrepreneurs in the Zambian government and the parastatals as well as private business railed against inefficiencies in production in the country. Direct foreign investment should be encouraged. Foreign policy began to include guidelines for extended negotiations with external financial institutions, an area previously conducted by the Bank and by the private mining companies. Members of the technocrats and entrepreneurs became the chief spokesmen for these strategies despite their unpopularity with the national politicians and some civil servants. Although President Kaunda soundly denounced several of these proposals — for example, the reopening of the border to Rhodesia — over time, many of these pragmatic ideas became policy though rarely were they acknowledged as changes.

Some new policies were hardly new at all. Détente with South Africa, for instance, was a perennial in Zambian politics since independence. The economic crisis which began to build after 1975, however, when combined with upheavals in the region and actual fighting within or along Zambia's borders, meant a growing insistence by some of the political class on these policies. A temporary problem was that these proposals often conflicted with prior rhetoric or even current policy. As signatory of the OAU Declaration on Southern Africa in 1975, Zambia was committed to bringing about majority rule in Zimbabwe. Would some sort of joint government between the African and European politicians fit such a goal? As a Front Line State, Zambia's diplomats and politicians were active participants in an apparently never-ending round of public and private negotiations trying to resolve the Rhodesian war. Economic pressure upon the Smith government via the railway seemed to be one of the few tools that the government had to use. Yet in October of 1978, well before a final settlement and the bringing to independence of the Mugabe government, Zambia announced a partial reopening of the border with Rhodesia to permit some vitally needed goods to be conducted. Despite denunciations of South Africa's behaviour over Soweto and even some claims of South African-sponsored sabotage within Zambia, imports from South Africa grew markedly after the reopening of the border.

Under strong encouragement from the IMF and other external lenders, Zambian technocrats and civil servants were developing a set of policies to create a more attractive investment climate in Zambia for foreign capital; build a larger and more productive agricultural sector on commerical rather than peasant farmer or cooperative lines; expand the manufacturing sector; and resuscitate the mines. The linchpin of these policies appeared to be opening the economy further to foreign capital. This, in turn, required some adjustment of the prior rhetoric of economic nationalism that had been contained in the Mulungushi reforms, as part of the platform of the national politicians. As late as 1975 such economic nationalism set the tone for Zambian policy towards foreign investors despite some countervailing legislation. A review by the Ministry of Development Planning, while acknowledging the 'situation', still called for 'tight foreign exchange measures to plug loopholes in the outflow of foreign exchange'.[34] Such measures are not looked upon favourably by foreign investors who certainly want to be able to repatriate a high percentage of the profits they make overseas. To rely on international aid or grants to help supply capital to the Zambian economy was unrealistic given the worldwide decline in the percentages of this aid from most of the advanced industrial states, the traditional sources of such capital.

But a turnaround in this policy was underway. Back in 1977, the Select Committee suggested politely that the

> policy of the Party and Government regarding investment in the economy has in the past been misunderstood. As a result an impression has been created both in Zambia and abroad that the country does not welcome private investment. It was the view of your Committee that this impression has badly affected the economy especially in recent years. Potential investors have been hesitant in spite of the great opportunities available in Zambia. Steps taken recently (1977) however, and in particular, steps taken by the enactment of the Industrial Development Act should improve the investment climate.[35]

These steps included lessening income taxes, customs and excise taxes and a loosening of prior foreign exchange controls. The Emergency Development Plan (invoked in 1977) specifically was designed to 'attract foreign investment and boost development activity based on local materials while stimulating a heavy export of our products especially from the land'.[36] A new policy towards commerical agriculture was also announced. Such policies to rebuild and to energise the manufacturing and agricultural sectors required extensive negotiation and promotion on a global level. Although no heavy influx of capital has been apparent so far, these new policies were very much in line with the suggestions of the IMF and commercial lenders.

Regional foreign economic policies vitally affected the economy in the late 1970s, and they were most subject to various political and ideological pressures. Along with the unreliable nature of the price for copper, the mines were being slowly choked by inadequate imports and shortages of skills. The opening of the border in 1978 helped loosen the import/export bottleneck. Now the question seemed to be to locate cheaper and more reliable sources of supply. The independence of Zimbabwe under an African nationalist government in 1980 opened a safety valve for the Zambian economy. In April of 1980 a Southern African Economic Summit was held in Lusaka. Zambian businessmen and parastatal managers were encouraged to avoid the more expensive United States and European markets and to turn to the least expensive sources of supply, i.e. Zimbabwe and indirectly South Africa. Although this has not been a smooth and uninterrupted pattern (particularly with reference to new trading links with South Africa), this decision should help reduce the costs to Zambian citizens and businesses of consumer and capital goods. And the long supply lines will be greatly fore-shortened. In a parallel set of policies, NCCM and RCM now rely on the South African port of East London to export some of their copper. Despite the diminution of many of these severe economic constraints, the Zambian economy continues to have balance of payments troubles and to be short of investment capital. Costs of government continue to escalate; shortfalls in revenues mean larger and larger budget gaps to be bridged. The gap has been lessened somewhat by the new tax laws which levied a higher personal tax on individuals and on companies. But mostly, the gap has been bridged by domestic borrowing and foreign financing.

Before 1978 the mines borrowed independently of the government from various sources, but in particular from private international banks. But the scale of capital now needed tested the familiar sources, and they turned to the government. Zambia, in 1980, appealed to the multi-lateral lending institutions of the West, specifically the IMF. This time Zambia obtained a massive loan of almost $1 billion (SDRs), $800 million of which was rumoured to go immediately to foreign creditors. Although the exact terms of this IMF facility were not available at the time of writing, IMF policies usually carry profound implications for the recipient state when it begins to borrow this heavily from the IMF. Deepening reliance on such international public finances traditionally carries a set of consequences briefly reviewed below.

First, there are the immediate economic effects. Although the IMF loans to offset the balance of payments deficits are extended to needy countries on generous terms (relative to private financing), these loans do carry some interest and usually must be repaid in a relatively short period. After a country returns to the IMF for a second tranche, the IMF gains a certain leverage to make strong policy recommendations to the recipient nation's planners and civil servants. Such IMF advice can be as mild as some suggestions on how to save money. Or it can be as extreme as the placement of IMF economists and bankers in control over the central bank of the host state as in Zaire. To avoid such humiliation, most states (after the second tranche, in particular) create domestic and foreign policies which have a complementarity with the IMF's known standards. Whether this 'policing of oneself' is easier on the IMF or more acceptable to the recipient state is highly debatable. These policies, I suggest, fit comfortably with the wider economic policies evolved by the Zambian political class. The goal for all is the economic recovery of the Zambian economy within the Western capitalist market for commodities and thus is heavily reliant on the health of the mines. Unfortunately, the long period of cutbacks and serious production problems has left a legacy for the mining industry which may prove difficult to overcome.

Conclusions

The political class in Zambia had managed to wrest some control over its own mineral sector from foreign capital. Independence for Zimbabwe has greatly relieved the momentary pressures upon the Zambian regime of both an economic and military character. SADCC may yet prove a very important organisation in Zambia's possible regional integration with independent states in the region in lieu of South Africa or Western countries which have their own agendas for Southern Africa. The inherited exclusive dependence that newly independent Zambia had had on the metropole, and the white-ruled regimes of the South is over. But Zambia's position remains vulnerable and the first 20 years of foreign policy have not produced greater mobility or autonomy for the political economy. Rather, Zambia seems more intensively integrated into the Western capitalist system.

The exclusive dependence of the early days has been transformed by the political class into a wider dependence on the oligopoly of copper companies, the multilateral lending institutions, and the big commercial banks. Thus a powerful set of foreign and domestic actors has expanded its power to influence the making of Zambian internal and external policies. The apparent control over the means of production, epitomised in the second nationalisation of the copper mines in 1973, did not translate to control over the means of generating and accumulating capital given the deep reliance on the needs of the Western markets, controlled by international resource companies. The earlier industrial and manpower dependencies of the Zambian raw materials-based economy is now augmented by financial reliance on public and private lending organisations linked into the capitalist system with the banks.

The freedom for any state to make foreign policy is constrained by the realities of the economic needs and vulnerability of the society.

Different factions within the Zambian political class continue to be torn by different interests, alliances and policies. Without the immediacy of the Rhodesian crisis to unify it and to bring it behind the ruling party, even less coherence and congruence appears likely for Zambian foreign policy in the future. The likelihood of a political class of this nature being able to create an autonomous and independent foreign policy is slim. The deep features of production dependency and the political class's urge to push the regime in whatever direction will permit its survival and perhaps even insure some profits will be the motivating forces in foreign policy decisions. This tendency is likely to create great strains in the region as the Zambian regime draws closer to more conservative allies and away from some of the more radical experiments of other Front Line States.

Notes

1   The setting for early Zambian foreign policy is well described in Douglas G. Anglin and Timothy M. Shaw, *Zambia's Foreign Policy: studies in diplomacy and dependence* (Boulder: Westview, 1979). Another source is Jan Pettman, *Zambia: security and conflict* (Devizes: Davison, 1974).
2   See Richard Hall, *The High Price of Principles: Kaunda and the White south* (London: Hodder and Stoughton, 1969).
3   The troubled relations between the various Zimbabwe liberation groups and Zambia is documented in David Martin and Phyllis Johnson, *The Struggle for Zimbabwe* (London: Faber and Faber, 1981). For another view of Zambia's role, see 'Zambia and Southern African Liberation Movements, 1964–1974', in Anglin and Shaw, *Zambia's Foreign Policy* (note 1), pp. 169–233.
4   Richard Sklar, 'The Nature of Class Domination in Africa', *Journal of Modern African Studies*, vol. 17, no. 4, December 1979, p. 550.
5   Arthur Hazlewood, 'The Economics of Federation and Dissolution in Central Africa', in his collection on *African Integration and Disintegration* (London: Oxford University Press, 1967), pp. 185–250.
6   See Richard Sklar, 'Zambia's Response to the Rhodesian Unilateral Declaration of Independence' in William Tordoff (ed.), *Politics in Zambia* (Berkeley: University of California Press, 1974), pp. 320–363.
7   This argument is presented in greater detail in Marcia M. Burdette, 'The Dynamics of Nationalisation Between Multinational Companies and Peripheral States: negotiations between AMAZ, Inc., the Anglo American Corporation of South Africa, Ltd., and the

Government of the Republic of Zambia' (unpublished Ph.D. dissertation, Columbia University, 1979).

8 Similar usage of the terms is found in Michaela von Freyhold, 'The Post-Colonial State and Its Tanzanian Version', *Review of African Political Economy*, no. 8, January—April 1977, pp. 75—89; and is applied to the European context in Nicos Poulantzas, *Classes in Contemporary Capitalism* (London: New Left Books, 1975).

9 Interviews with officials in and advisers to Zambia who were engaged in discussions and negotiations over the copper nationalisations.

10 Marcia M. Burdette, 'The Political Class in Zambia: technocrats versus nationalists', *African Studies Association*, Los Angeles, November 1979.

11 Colin Legum, *Southern Africa: the secret diplomacy of detente* (New York: Africana, 1975).

12 Vernon Mwaanga, 'Zambia's Policy Toward Southern Africa', in Christian Potholm and Richard Dale (eds), *Southern Africa in Perspective: essays in regional politics* (New York: Free Press, 1972), pp. 234—241.

13 The best work done to date on this indigenous bourgeoisie (or fraction thereof) is Carolyn Baylies, 'The State and Class Formation in Zambia', (unpublished Ph.D. dissertation, Department of Sociology, University of Wisconsin, 1978); and Morris Szeftel, 'Political Conflict, Spoils, and Class Formation in Zambia', (unpublished Ph.D. dissertation, Department of Politics, University of Manchester, 1978).

14 A general description of this group can be found in D.L. Dresang, *The Zambian Civil Service: entrepreneurialism and development administration* (Nairobi: East African Publishing House, 1975).

15 Interviews with various Zambian officials and advisers. Also see Anthony Martin, *Minding Their Own Business: Zambia's struggle against Western control* (Harmondsworth: Penguin, 1975).

16 General policies, goals and ideology are summarised in three speeches by His Excellency, Dr Kenneth D. Kaunda, *Zambia: towards economic independence,* April 1968 (Mulungushi I); *Towards Complete Independence*, August 1969 (Matero); and *Take Up the Challenge*, November 1970 (Lusaka) (Mulungushi II).

17 For references to this policy, see Mark Bostock and Charles Harvey (eds), *Economic Independence and Zambian Copper: a case study of foreign investment* (New York: Praeger, 1972).

18 *Manifesto on Southern Africa* (Lusaka: Government Printer, April 1969).

19 Sklar, 'Zambia's Response to the Rhodesian Unilateral Declaration

of Independence' (note 6).
20 A persistent proponent of this view, other than Zambian officials themselves, has been Douglas Anglin, former Vice-Chancellor of the University of Zambia; see Anglin and Shaw, *Zambia's Foreign Policy* (note 1) for his argument and data.
21 *Ibid.*
22 Chapter 7 in *ibid.* and Legum, *Southern Africa* (note 11).
23 Chapter 8 of Anglin and Shaw, *Zambia's Foreign Policy* (note 1). A journalistic and personal account of Zambia's support for FNLA and UNITA is included in John Stockwell, *In Search of Enemies: a CIA story* (New York: Norton, 1978).
24 Sam C. Nolutshungu, *South Africa in Africa: a study of ideology and foreign policy* (Manchester: Manchester University Press, 1975), and Legum, *Southern Africa* (note 11).
25 Ronald T. Libby and Michael E. Woakes, 'Nationalisation and the Displacement of Development Policy in Zambia', *African Studies Review*, vol. 23, no. 1, April 1980, pp. 33–50.
26 Ralph M. Jeker, 'Assessment of the Risks of Borrowing From a Developing Country's Point of View: Zambia', *Aussenwirtschaft*, vol. 33, nos 1–2, 1978, pp. 109–127.
27 Burdette, 'The Dynamics of Nationalisation between Multinational Companies and Peripheral States' (note 7).
28 Republic of Zambia, National Assembly, *Report of the Special Parliamentary Select Committee Appointed on Friday, 14th October 1977* (Lusaka: Government Printer, n.d.), p. 4, emphasis added. For more on this Committee see Tony Southall, 'Zambia: Class formation and government policy in the 1970s', *Journal of Southern African Studies*, vol. 7, no. 1, October 1980, pp. 91–108.
29 Jeker, 'Assessment of the Risks of Borrowing from a Developing Country's Point of View' (note 26), p. 116.
30 These calculations were made by Chislelembwe Ng'andwe 'Inflation in Zambia, 1964–80', Humanities and Social Sciences Staff Seminar, June 1981, University of Zambia.
31 *The Economist*, September 1978, p. 99.
32 Interviews with mining personnel, summer 1981, Lusaka and Copperbelt.
33 *New Africa*, no. 119, July 1981, p. 140.
34 Republic of Zambia, Ministry of Development and Planning, *Annual Review: Performance of the Zambian Economy 1975* (Lusaka, December 1975), p. 1.
35 *Report of the Special Parliamentary Select Committee*, p. 5.
36 *Ibid.*, p. 22.

13 Zimbabwe

Ken Good

The location of the independent state of Zimbabwe is of considerable strategic importance. It lies immediately above the Limpopo and below the Zambezi and, as the penultimate African settler colony to be freed, its position is simultaneously vulnerable and exemplary, a Front Line State (FLS) in every sense of the word. It is threatened by the might and intransigence of South Africa, while its own power is significantly in advance of its African neighbours: Botswana, Zambia, and Mozambique (see Chapters 2 and 12). And it is a focus for the attention of the unliberated peoples of South Africa itself. Zimbabwe's foreign policy is largely a function of the national political economy and external interaction.

Political economy as the basis of foreign policy

The specificity of Zimbabwe lies mainly in the economic sphere. At independence in April 1980 it acquired a relatively advanced, diversified, integrated, and dynamic capitalist economy. The settler economy had well-developed manufacturing and commercial agricultural sectors, the latter having both a strong export capacity and a near

348

self-sufficiency in domestic food production. It also had a rather broad-based mining sector, a comprehensive monetary system, and good infrastructure. Manufacturing was the leading sector and contributed 25 per cent to gross domestic product; per capita industrial output was in advance of all other African countries except South Africa and another former settler colony, Algeria. Gross domestic product in 1980 was an estimated US \$4.8 billion. The developed and interlinked nature of the economy was such that it possessed, for example, a large iron and steel industry based upon domestic raw materials which, in turn, supplied a large mechanical engineering industry well integrated with other domestic industrial sectors. And agriculture in Zimbabwe produced about 40 per cent of the materials used in the country's manufacturing industry.[1]

Such unusually advanced capitalist development had had a price, mainly in the subordination and exploitation of African pre-capitalist agriculture. Capitalist development in Zimbabwe was built upon the artificial creation by the settler colonial state of two distinct land-use patterns and associated cheap labour supply systems.[2] The achievements of white commercial agriculture were manifest. Between 1944 and 1976 the number of white farmers in the country had doubled (from 3,640 to 6,680), the area under crop had gone up by a larger amount (from 0.54m acres to 1.42m acres), and gross output had increased by a factor of 20 (from \$16.2m in 1944 to \$362m in 1975). Whereas in 1905 white farmers had produced only 10 per cent of marketed crops, in 1975 they were responsible for 92 per cent of a greatly increased output.[3] Near independence the number of white farmers had fallen to about 5,500, but they still produced about 80 per cent of the country's food on some 36 per cent of the land (14.5m hectares), and they earned for Zimbabwe some 68 per cent of its foreign exchange.[4]

The decline of African agriculture was also clear, and was causally related to the expansion of the capitalist system. The African peasantry was relentlessly deprived over the colonial decades of the best land in the country and was pushed into increasingly crowded, infertile, and ill-served Tribal Trust Lands (TTL). In the 1970s there were perhaps some 675,000 cultivators in the TTL, 'at least two and a half times as many as the *highest* minimum recommended number'.[5] The enforced decline of the peasantry originated near the turn of the century, but as late as 1955 African peasants had sold 30 per cent of their agricultural output. Yet they were further squeezed out of the market and by 1970 they could sell only 19 per cent of output.[6] The situation in the African purchase areas, where land was individually owned or leased and where a middle and rich peasantry could more easily rise, was slightly better. These areas covered 3.7 per cent of the total land area (3.6m acres), contained in the 1970s approximately 1 per cent of all African cultivators, and produced 2.3 per cent of total agricultural output. There were 8,102 occupied purchase area farms in 1977 and more than 440 were vacant; but these cultivators could market 66 per cent of their total production.[7] The exploitation of rural wage labour was as manifest and as important as the decline of the mass of the peasantry. Real wages in agriculture stagnated between 1893 and 1948 and in 1974 they were at the same level as they were in 1948. Moreover, wages as a percentage of gross agricultural profit fell from 12.6 per cent in 1965 to 7.6 per cent in 1974. The supply of cheap labour to commercial agriculture was a continuing factor in the success of the latter.[8]

Land was the main link between the pre-colonial, settler colonial, and independent socio-economic systems, and is indeed 'the central social and economic issue' of Zimbabwe as of Rhodesia.[9] Its use and misuse were at the heart of the inherited systems of wage labour, of food, and of commodity export production, and its output helped to fuel manufacturing industry which supplied agriculture in turn. Rural wealth was deeply intertwined with rural poverty and both were interlinked with industrial productivity. Capitalism in the country offered powerful supports and significant constraints to the independent government, as to its predecessors.

Such an economy and society operated hardly at all in terms of unfettered market forces, and the existence of a large, active, and interventionist settler state was another notable inheritance of independent Zimbabwe. State intervention into the economy was comparable with South Africa and Australia rather than with the typical administrative colony like Tanzania or Mozambique. Direct state involvement and initiative was responsible for the establishment and operation of industries and infrastructural services – iron and steel, cotton spinning, railways, airline, power generation and supply, radio and television, abattoirs and cold storage, the Sabi-Limpopo Authority, and a range of agricultural purchasing and marketing authorities, among others. Current and capital expenditures by central and local governments (but not including the spending of parastatals) represented between 27 and 32 per cent of gross domestic product between 1967 and 1975, and rose to 38.5 per cent in 1977. When such expenditure was combined with certain fiscal and other measures after the settler Unilateral Declaration of Independence (UDI) in 1965, it provided government with 'dominating control over most aspects of the economy'.[10]

State control was asserted over the economy even where – as was commonly the case – ownership either by the state or by private settler interests was not involved; ownership of capital was roughly one-third settler and two-thirds foreign. An early act of the Smith government after 1965 was legislation giving control over firms and subsidiaries to ensure that their actions were 'in Rhodesia's interests'.[11] This was used, notes David Wield, to ensure that companies continued to pay workers made redundant, thereby pressuring them to diversify and redeploy resources quickly in response to 'international sanctions'. Companies moved with state encouragement into the production of a great range of goods no longer imported. State bodies helped to channel foreign investment and reinvestment funds into industry, and government controls on direct expatriation of profits and on indirect profit export through so-called transfer pricing further reinforced domestic investment.[12]

The weight of the settler state was further indicated by the fact that some one-third of the adult white population was employed in the public service near the end of the settler period. The Lancaster House constitutional agreements provided for the maintenance of the state apparatus and the continuance of the administrative standards and career prospects within it. It committed the independent government to the payment of white civil service pensions and to the making of appointments through the Public Service Commission, with separate commissions for the judiciary, military, and police. The existing public debt became a liability of the independent state and constitutional amendment procedures were rigid. There was also the large Rhodesian military machine and quasi-military police service. This had been under direct settler control since the 1920s, and it remained intact and undefeated, although it had been deprived of effective control in the countryside and had become reliant upon obsolete equipment. The Rhodesian military and police were the effective administrative power in 1980. Overall, it was clearly a state apparatus which was capable of dominating a moderate, detached nationalist elite. But it could also provide a radical and determined leadership, one that was integrated with the mass of rural and urban African society, with significant controls over the economy.

The country's external environment at the end of the 1970s was one of acute economic and military dependence upon South Africa. The earlier support which Rhodesia had enjoyed — particularly in the Security Council of the United Nations from the British metropole and less directly from the United States — had declined under the impact of the intensification of guerrilla war. As the struggle intensified, the United States and Britain along with South Africa swung towards opposition to a rigid and intransigent Rhodesian colonialism, as indicated by the direct and dramatic entry of Secretary of State Kissinger into African affairs in 1976. Ian Smith accepted the principle of majority rule under pressure from Prime Minister Vorster and Secretary Kissinger, with the former himself influenced by rising

African anger inside South Africa. Under pressure from its own settler constituency, South Africa continued to supply a range of vital supports to Rhodesia — markets and investment funds, outlets to the sea following the closure of the Mozambique border in 1976, military equipment and personnel, financial underpinning for the counter-insurgency effort — but the dumping of settler government was but a matter of timing and technique.

In moving against the Smith government, it is interesting to note what its erstwhile allies supported. Kissinger was apparently determined to prevent what he saw as the likely 'radicalisation' of the liberation war in Rhodesia, and he recorded his views in July 1979. His strategy was: 'to co-opt the programme of moderate evolutionary reform, that is to say majority rule, and minority rights. At the same time we sought to create a kind of firebreak between those whose radicalism was ideological and those whose radicalism was geared to specific issues. We could meet the demands for majority rule; we never thought we could co-opt the ideological radicals; our goal was to isolate them'.[13]

The liberation movement was, of course, the other key element in the Zimbabwean conjuncture of 1980. Historically, this was a divided, factionalist, petty-bourgeois, and constitutional—nationalist movement. The leadership competed in terms of personal careerism and for regional—tribal supports. The various elements within it — largely but not entirely embraced by the two rival groupings from the early 1960s, ZAPU and ZANU, which were drawn loosely together as the Patriotic Front for the Geneva Conference in 1976 — moved reluctantly and hesitantly to the encouragement of armed struggle within the country in the early 1970s.[14] After 1972 the movement became a rural and peasant-based struggle, with the peasantry and the rural areas bearing the brunt of the war. Some 20,000 people were killed, well over a million were forced from their homes, and village economies were gravely disrupted. This experience sharply distinguished Zimbabwe from the pattern of constitutional decolonisation of the usual African administrative colony; but it was not so harsh a war as that waged against Algerian settler colonialism in the previous decade during which about one million Algerians died.

Despite the sacrifices of the Zimbabwean peasantry, no significant new organisations developed out of the liberation struggle through which the mass of the people — workers in the settler-controlled towns as well as rural people — might control their leaders. Perhaps two new political forms did emerge: the *pungwes*, or night-time meetings, and the *mujibas* and *chimbwidos*, the young men and women who acted as the eyes and ears of the guerrillas. But these organs served chiefly to weld together village people and guerrilla cadres; and the cadres themselves, experienced though they might be, influenced the leadership only with difficulty. The leadership was dispersed through Lusaka, Maputo, Dar es Salaam, and Rhodesian prisons, and the politicians of ZAPU and ZANU eventually succeeded in maintaining their ascendancy over the command structures of their respective military movements, ZIPRA and ZANLA, though not without some difficulty at times.[15] The latter was the larger and by far the more active of the two military formations, but it was ill-disciplined, ill-equipped and ideologically incoherent.[16] The international linkages which ZANU had established over the years were partly responsible for this. ZANU had turned to a range of countries — China, some European communist states (but not the Soviet Union), North Korea, Algeria, and other liberation organisations such as the PLO — for assistance, and the training and ideology of the ZANLA cadres reflected these differences.

Regional linkages played an important role in the ceasefire and transition to independence. Zambia and Mozambique had lost heavily through the war and, despite the differing alignment of Zambia with ZAPU and Mozambique with ZANU, both stood to gain from a Rhodesian settlement. The actual transition was effected via party electoral activity, relegating the guerrilla forces to inactivity and strengthening the position of petty-bourgeois elements — teachers, businessmen, and small officials — within the existing and re-surfacing party organisations. ZAPU ran as the Patriotic Front led as before by Joshua Nkomo, and ZANU, as ZANU(PF), under Robert Mugabe. Their respective electoral programmes did not differ markedly and each stressed regionalism and tribalism in rallying voters' support. It was redolent of a return to the politics of loyalty rather than of participation, of party competition and dominance, and of control by the educated petty bourgeoisie.[17]

The transition from settler colonialism to social democracy

Free enterprise, investment and aid

The landslide electoral victory of ZANU(PF) under Robert Mugabe in April 1980 came as a surprise to Britain, the United States, and South Africa. The Pretoria government had financially supported Bishop Muzorewa's campaign; the interim British administration under Lord Soames had at one stage contemplated the appointment of a coalition of minority African parties and Smith's Rhodesia Front; and preparations for a coup attempt had also been made within the Rhodesian military. However, Mugabe is said to have met South African political and military representatives and Rhodesian security and military men in Maputo on day two of the election and to have provided certain assurances.[18] Mugabe said later that 'socialism must be the byword' of the new government; but he also said, early in April, that he did not envisage an overnight transformation of the capitalist system.[19] Later that month the Prime Minister stated: 'There must be changes and we will take bold steps, but nothing unconstitutional'.[20]

In approaching key areas of the economy, bold steps have not been taken. Mugabe said in May 1980 that, while foreign investment was welcome in Zimbabwe, the majority shareholding must remain inside the country and profits must be reinvested. Yet it was 'not the Government's intention to legislate against repatriation of profits but rather to invite investors to join in the spirit of our Zimbabweanisation programme'. Support for the pillars of the capitalist system was stated on 1 September 1980, when the Prime Minister said that 'private initiative and private enterprise have an assured and significant role to play in the economy of the country'.[21]

While the 1980 budget was referred to as a 'people's budget', appropriate to the government's philosophy of 'mild and pragmatic' socialism, in the words of Finance Minister, Enos Nkala, and a very large boost in spending on education and health — roughly a trebling of funds — was then announced,[22] support for the capitalist structures has remained. Mugabe told a meeting of German businessmen in Bonn in May 1982 that the Zimbabwean constitution protected foreign investment and forbade expropriation without compensation, and that there was an important role for foreign capital in the country. In Paris shortly afterwards he said that he welcomed foreign private investment.[23]

Much that has occurred has been consistent with these words. *Moto*'s economic correspondent referred to a government three-year national development plan — then expected in July 1982 — which called, he said, for 38 per cent of a total of $4,600 m in investment funds to come from outside Zimbabwe, much of it from private sector sources. The economic policy paper of February 1981 — *Growth With Equity* — had already indicated official desires in the field of private investment. It particularly welcomed foreign investment in certain areas:

1 new enterprises requiring specific technology which would make an additional contribution to the economy and train Zimbabweans;
2 new enterprises in rural areas;
3 new enterprises on a joint venture basis;
4 existing enterprises where an injection of additional foreign capital or technology would mean an increase in productivity and an improvement in the end-product (but the absolute amount of existing domestic participation should not be diluted as a general rule, nor should an existing domestic control level of

equity holding be allowed to pass to foreign investers),

5 undertakings promoting the more intense use of local raw materials and processed inputs;

6 areas promoting labour-intensive technology and appropriate technology; and

7 activities in which generation of exports in a reasonable time was possible.

The document noted that investment in rural areas as an 'absolute priority'. *Moto* said that the private sector had initially seemed well pleased with this outline, but calls had subsequently been made for a more precise statement of government policy.[24]

This much delayed statement on foreign investment was referred to as finalised, but still unpublished, by the Minister for Trade and Commerce, Richard Hove, in September 1982. He described the code not so much as a system of control, but as being designed to facilitate the entry of foreign capital; and he declared that he was 'confident that it will do much to encourage foreign investment in Zimbabwe'.[25] Shortly after a partnership deal with the United States food-processing company, H.J. Heinz, was agreed to — a proposal first publicly announced in April — in which the multinational would take 51 per cent and the Zimbabwe government 49 per cent of the shares in the hitherto locally controlled Olivine Industries. Heinz planned to invest US $20m in the country — the largest single private investment since independence — and to use its Zimbabwean base to expand into growing markets in the region and elsewhere. Heinz's chief executive, Tony O'Reilly, said in a statement: 'We're acquiring a superbly-run company in an essential food business and we're assured of good dealings politically with the Government'.[26] The new government had accepted foreign majority ownership of an efficient company.

The Mugabe government had earlier decided upon a programme of reconstruction of the war-ravaged rural economy, and had accorded this policy a much higher priority than any possible structural adaption of the established and complex Zimbabwean capitalist system. Reconstruction required large investment funds, but the exigencies of Zimbabwe's international situation were not entirely favourable. ZANU's bad relations with the Soviet Union were not improved in the immediate post-independence period, and the communist states were generally seen within the Mugabe government as inadequate sources of hard foreign currency funds. Nor were the leading capitalist states as ready to help the Mugabe government after 1980 as they had seemed ready to assist a Muzorewa regime in the less certain times of a few years earlier.

Great disappointment was reported to exist within the new

Zimbabwe government in mid-1980 over the Western world's tardy reaction to their post-independence programme; aid offers from the United States in particular were regarded as derisory.[27] When opening the 'Zimcord' conference on reconstruction and development in March 1981, the Prime Minister noted:

> Whilst some may now perhaps find it inconvenient to be reminded of the aid promises that were presented to us as essential components of the Anglo-American constitutional settlement proposals of 1976 and 1977 respectively, we merely note that our immediate post-war requirements were then estimated at around US $1.5 billion. That was four or five years ago.

He said that present estimates of the costs of reconstruction were of the order of $1.23 billion Zimbabwean dollars. He stressed the saliency of land resettlement within this programme:

> The land is available, but. . .my Government lacks the requisite financial resources either for its purchase as stipulated under the Lancaster House Agreement, or for its development. If we must honour the Agreement — and we have all along indicated our willingness to do so — and if the international community, including Britain in particular, desires us to honour the Agreement — and we think that is the case — then we simply have to have the resources to enable us to discharge our obligations while doing full justice to our people. This is. . .a matter of paramount importance. . .[28]

In January 1981 United States aid stood at about US $50m. At this time the Finance Minister, Enos Nkala, was reported as saying that Zimbabwe was 'at war with Britain over aid'.[29] But the additional aid that Britain offered at Zimcord was only £25m for a grand total of £143m promised from 1980 to 1983.[30] At the end of the year the British government published its view that the Zimbabwe Development Fund had lapsed with the collapse of the Anglo-American settlement proposals in 1977, so Britain would not give more aid for land resettlement in Zimbabwe.[31]

In its 1981 budget the government announced sales-tax increases affecting almost all goods in the shops and, at the same time, increased spending mainly on social services: education would receive 14.4 per cent of total spending and health 5.4 per cent (with 13.9 for defence). The sum of US $28m was set aside for the state to buy up shares in private companies, and the government planned to spend a quarter of that to purchase some 43 per cent of Caps Holdings, the country's biggest pharmaceutical manufacturer. A controlling stake in Zimbank, the second largest banking group in Zimbabwe had already been acquired, and the establishment of a metals marketing agency was expected. The government also planned to phase out food subsidies, which were taking 8 per cent of the new budget.[32] Economic growth over this period was a partial reflection of the sobriety of government policy: GNP rose 11.75 per cent in 1980 and 7.5 per cent in 1981, a notable improvement on the last years of the liberation war, 1975–1979. But in 1981 Zimbabwe experienced a trade deficit of $68.4m, the first since 1968.[33]

Agriculture

The programme of national reconciliation which the Prime Minister was quick to announce after his election was directed not least at the white farming community. On 20 May 1980 Mugabe told a meeting of 300 white farmers that they had a guaranteed future, that the government would crack down on the reported pillaging of crops and on cattle thefts, and that full and fair compensation would be paid for any land acquired for resettlement. He repeated his call for white farmers to stay at another meeting a month later.[34] At this time, however, some three million people were believed to be facing starvation as a result of the war in the countryside, and a very large number required resettlement. It was soon apparent that what the government conceived to be its initial socialist thrust, as Mugabe himself put it, would be made in the important areas of land resettlement and peasant agriculture.[35]

Vincent Tickner had said in 1979 that the Patriotic Front appeared then 'weakly prepared for dealing with the food supply sector'.[36] The Mugabe government's approach has certainly recognised the complexities of the problem and has shown both caution and determination. The complexities of the inherited agricultural system have been referred to above, and the task which the government set for itself over a three-year period was the purchase of 60 per cent of white-owned commercial farmland on which to settle about 162,000 peasant families (or, at six persons to a family, approximately one million individuals).

With occasional lapses, it was repeatedly stressed that land purchases would be on the basis of willing-seller, willing-buyer, and that only unused and under-utilised land would be considered; land purchases on a strictly commercial basis with full compensation was, of course, the position to which the government was committed under the Lancaster House constitution. Mugabe appeared to renege on this, however, when speaking in the important farming area of Mt Darwin – scene of intense guerrilla activity in the 1970s – in November 1980. He reportedly said that white farmers would be asked to surrender some of their arable land to the government for resettlement, and they would have to look to the British government for compensation 'because we have no money to pay them and do not feel inclined to pay for land plundered from the indigenous people by the colonialists'.[37] Officials quickly explained that the speech was 'intended to apply only to unused land'; but Mugabe said much the same thing a year later. Then he told a cheering crowd at Sanyati in Mashonaland West that the government would not hesitate to expropriate land if Britain did not provide sufficient money: 'the government cannot let you pay for land which is rightfully yours'.[38] The basis for these remarks was that the government did not see the continued ownership of some 14.5m hectares by about 5,000 white farmers as either desirable or politically tenable, as the Minister of Lands, Moven Mahachi, indicated in mid-1982.[39]

The government's approach to the whole question of land was in fact a dual one: both redistribution and food production. The emphasis on production meant that land for resettlement was not intended to be given to already employed persons or those with an existing source of income,[40] and it was aimed at increasing output. Dr Sekeramayi, then Minister of Lands, said at Zimcord that redistribution was 'not merely to give land to the landless masses, but to create an agricultural community on land which will no longer be just subsistence, but commercial orientation. There is need to produce for their needs and the needs of the non-agricultural sectors of the population'.[41] Land was intended, as Mahachi said, for the farmer determined to make use of it.[42] Some reconciliation of the rather differing aims of equity and productivity, and of the contending interests of the landless African and the efficient white commercial farmer, was theoretically possible. What was wanted of white landowners, it was officially said in 1981, was that they gave government the first option on land they wished to sell.[43] And on the willing seller basis it actually had 'more land on offer than funds available [for purchase]'; as of July 1982, only 1.35m hectares had been acquired by the government.[44]

But it was doubtful if real harmony existed between the goals of land redistribution and agricultural productivity. The landless peasantry was not simply waiting patiently for the government to acquire necessary funds but was moving on to available land as squatters. 'Thousands' were said to have taken this action and in Manicaland alone in mid-1982, 'over 75,000 people had moved without permission on to commercial and state land'. Without either supervision or worthwhile resources, they then 'applied the degraded farming methods of the over-crowded TTLs, felling whole tree plantations, growing crops on river banks, ploughing vertically instead of across hillsides, grazing cattle indiscriminately, and promoting erosion and impoverishment of the soil'.[45] Squatting involved the despoilation of arable land, sometimes of existing efficient farms. It could cause a drop in the production of food, which in fact occurred in 1981 and 1982, though not entirely or even partially due to a regression in farming methods. Milk, cooking oil, and bread have been in short supply, brought on by serious falls in the production of all three basic items, the effects of drought, low producer prices (where producer prices have been high, such as with cotton, maize, and sorghum, production has also been good), and increased popular demands stimulated by higher minimum wages.[46] In October 1982 the government raised the price of bread, cooking oil, and margarine by about 12 per cent, and forecast a similar increase for maize meal, the country's staple food. Food subsidies had placed an economic strain upon the government, it was officially said, and higher prices would 'make more essential commodities available on the shelves' to 'most workers who were now getting higher wages and could afford to pay [the] full cost of food'.[47]

The criticality of agriculture in Zimbabwe has not declined in the post-independence period. The dangers inherent in a situation where land redistribution was only limited and where food production had already fallen were fairly obvious. President Banana warned in September 1982 of the relation between food supplies and the stability of a country. He noted that Zimbabwe, because of its unusually developed agricultural economy and its existing capacity as a granary state, had been given special responsibilities in food production within the regional grouping — SADCC — which had got to be met. He stressed the need for 'every person using the soil' to do so 'rationally and efficiently', and for the encouragement of 'intensive agricultural production along scientific lines'.[48] An even more critical analysis was made by the Minister for Home Affairs, Dr Herbert Ushewokunze, when addressing the annual congress of the Zimbabwe National Farmers' Union. Security was a grave problem facing most farmers, and the government would provide training in police methods to people's defence groups. But farmers had to be guaranteed a continuous supply of labour at a price they could afford. And the minister also criticised 'telephone farmers', like civil servants, businessmen and even ministers whom, he said, indulge in land speculation and conduct their farming over the phone.[49] Hope appeared to have been placed upon efficiency and rationality within the peasantry generally, and in the exploitation of wage labour by commercially orientated, fairly large-scale growers.

An agricultural system like that in Zimbabwe was not to be changed quickly. It involved the articulation of pre-capitalist and capitalist modes of production, each displaying quite different levels of efficiency — with the former in fact in subordination to the latter — and with only a small minority of owners and producers but a vast majority of consumers concerned with the operation of the capitalist mode. The system was in existence for no less than 100 years (if one excludes the long history of pre-capitalist agriculture), and state aid and investment supported its development. The characteristic cautiousness of the Mugabe government was appropriate to the adaptation of such complexities. The government's initial socialist thrust was well directed into agriculture; it was broad in scope, but limited in the extent of resettlement achieved after two years. But for the transformation of the poor peasantry to go steadily ahead, production of food in particular had to be maintained. The frustration of the landless and the shortages of food called for quick solutions.

The state: civil and military bureaucracy

'No unconstitutional acts' has here been the byword. White civil servants were given assurances about their jobs and asked not to leave soon after the government took office. This conciliatory attitude was to some extent forced upon the government by the weight of the white presence in the bureaucracy. The highest post held by an African just after independence was only senior administrative officer, and even many of the junior posts, as was typical in Rhodesia, were held by white wives or pensioners; even when black rule was obvious, the Public Service Commission failed to embark on an effective Africanisation programme.[50] Whites were brought into the ministry, including a member of the Rhodesian Front and a leading representative of white commercial farming interests who was made Minister of Agriculture. In September 1980 the Prime Minister praised his white ministers for the 'wonderful contribution' they were making.[51] Even by 1982, the Africanisation of the top of the bureaucracy had advanced only partially. The number of black Permanent Secretaries was then thought by Mugabe to be 'slightly more than that of the whites', and he was pleased that the government had 'managed to ameliorate the problems'.[52] It may be noted that one thing Zimbabwe did not lack was a large pool of black university graduates, many in possession of post-graduate degrees.

The 'bold steps' which Mugabe had planned to take towards the inherited state appear to have been realised largely in terms of additions to the system: the creation of a Ministry of Lands, Resettlement and Rural Development in addition to the existing Ministry of Agriculture, for example. Parastatals have also been established which promised greater control over the economy; a new Minerals Marketing Agency was set up in 1982 to take over the selling of the country's minerals, with leading white capitalist interests well represented on its board. The Mugabe government had within two weeks of taking office ruled out the possibility of the nationalisation of minerals production, emphasising instead simply the need to train Zimbabwean management and technical personnel quickly.[53]

A result has been of course the sheer increase of bureaucracy; but the scope for patronage has been enlarged as well. The Mugabe government contains approximately 32 ministers and 25 deputy ministers, chosen from a lower house of 100 and an upper chamber of 40. It is also increasing the number of senior bureaucratic positions. The government has, moreover, chosen to maintain the generous wage-scale system in operation before. Permanent heads in the public service enjoy a salary of approximately $27,000 per annum (in 1982 some US $36,000); wages for domestic and farm workers – by far the largest category in the country – are only some $600 a year. Significant perks are also available. A government housing loan of approximately $70,000 is available to senior bureaucrats and ministers. Therefore splendid houses in the former exclusively white suburbs of Harare are easily obtainable, and the new petty bourgeoisie which now controls the state experiences a way of life quite unlike that of the mass of the population. Housing for most urban blacks is still rudimentary shelter on the periphery of the towns.[54]

Mugabe has made plain his preference for a one-party system in Zimbabwe. But he has repeatedly ruled out the possibility of introducing the system before the 1985 elections and has spoken of prior consultation with the people perhaps through a referendum. ZANU(PF) was, however, characterised by a lack of effective and coherent organisation in 1980,[55] and no significant improvements have been made since then. A party congress is overdue, but the Prime Minister is sanguine about the situation. Mugabe said that 'at the moment the exercise is really to reorganise the party'. He believed that new structures must be established in all provinces before a congress could occur: 'One wonders whether 1983 will be the year of the first congress after the war, or perhaps 1984'.[56] If it was held in 1984 it would be but one year before scheduled national elections, and ZANU has a record of internal divisiveness and conflict when congresses and elections are at hand. The future of ZANU as a vehicle for effective participatory politics is problematic at best.

Greatest change has occurred within the military forces. Certain of the most repressive and notorious Rhodesian units, such as the Selous Scouts and Greys, were quickly disbanded or disbanded themselves with the decampment of their personnel, presumably to similar employment in South Africa. Reorganisation has focused on the bulk of Rhodesian forces, ZANLA, and ZIPRA, and has aimed at the integration of these disparate groups, chiefly with the aid of British instructors and advisors. Orthodox colonial units were to be integrated with two distinct guerrilla armies, with hostilities between them having ceased but a few months before. By July 1980 it was reported that of a total of 3,500 regular white officers and non-commissioned officers in the Rhodesian forces at the ceasefire, only 1,900 remained; and at this time Lieut.-General Peter Walls, commander of the nominally combined forces, resigned. One combined unit of former ZIPRA and ZANLA guerrillas had then been formed, another was undergoing training, and it was planned to produce further integrated battalions every fortnight until all 35,000 guerrillas in assembly-points had been absorbed into the Zimbabwean army or had been demobilised.

Tensions already existed within the joint high command comprising the white commanders of the former Rhodesian army and air force, and the ZIPRA and ZANLA commanders.[57] It was expected in August that the overall Zimbabwean army would be large — some 45,000 to 50,000 men — and that it might be divided into regular, full-time fighting units, and those engaged in rural reconstruction and development. An accelerated integration programme was, however, announced next January, designed to create a force comprising 33,000 former guerrillas and three battalions of the Rhodesian military by August 1981.[58]

The demobilisation of the guerrillas emerged as one of the greatest problems facing the government in Mugabe's assessment. The goals of earlier programmes have not been met. At the end of 1981, Zimbabwe had an army of 65,000 men, costing about 20 per cent of the national budget to support. It was intended to persuade 20,000 ex-guerrillas to leave the army and return to civilian life through extremely attractive financial inducements (they would receive their regular army pay of some £75 and an additional £50 a month for two years after they left).[59] The Prime Minister has aimed at a high degree of demobilisation: 'the psychological disaffiliation of every cadre who was affiliated to any political party or leadership'.[60] But the promised demobilisation pay has not always been met, and the result has been the exclusion from the new social order of many of those who fought to free Zimbabwe. 'People treat us as if we're sick and need a doctor,' one former guerrilla was reported as saying, and another explained: 'It pains us to see our schoolmates who remained behind to finish their education. They now have good jobs, big houses and cars, while we have nothing. Everywhere we go to apply for a job we are reminded that we don't have the necessary qualifications'. Many of these young people, it was said, expressed discontent and bitterness.[61]

The reorganisation of the military has been carried out chiefly by the British military advisory and training team. It has composed some 130 personnel most of the time, but had declined to about 80 towards the end of 1982. Its cost was £3m annually in 1980 and £4.3m more recently, and it was the largest British military aid programme in Africa.[62] Mugabe was 'delighted that we have had the assistance of Britain: British instructors, who stood neutral in relation to any of the three forces'. Britain was equally willing to maintain the group.[63] A

362

North Korean military advisory group arrived in August 1981, with the particular task of training the fifth army brigade of some 5,000 men based near the Mozambique border. The North Korean team totalled about 100 and equipment worth some £12m was also supplied.[64]

The reorganisation of the military has, however, been far from perfect. Some 2,500 former guerrillas — approximately 2,000 ex-ZIPRA and 500 ex-ZANLA — were said to have deserted from the national army in 1982.[65] Former ZIPRA commanders were taken into detention, and various insurrectionary actions occurred, including an attack on Mugabe's house in Harare, abduction of foreign tourists, and the burning of tractors. So-called 'dissident' action was estimated to have resulted in the deaths of more than 50 people by October 1982. The government then claimed to have captured 425 dissidents in South-western Zimbabwe, indicating the significant scale of the problem.[66] But serious sabotage attacks on military bases have also occurred, carried out very probably by former Rhodesian military personnel subsequently in the employ of the South African military;[67] and in the case of the sabotage at the Gweru air force base, possibly by former Rhodesian elements within the national air force.

The government's existing problems of landlessness and agricultural production were greatly compounded. The frustrations of the poor peasantry could be combined with the disillusionment of the ex-guerrillas; and the latter were capable of offering a focus for the dissatisfactions of the former. The earlier peace and stability which the Mugabe government had done much to provide for the country had been lost. And the national character of the government was undermined by the high incidence of dissident activity and government counter-action within Matabeland. The government could not safely rely on its reorganised military force to meet the security problems in their immediate, short-term sense. It was caught in a scissors situation by the security problem as it was with agriculture. A reduction in the size of the military was desirable on financial grounds, but it threatened to increase the problems of security.

Foreign relations

Much of what has happened in the broad area of foreign affairs since April 1980 was summed up by the then Deputy Minister of Foreign Affairs, Simbarashe Mumbengegwi, in October 1981: 'We are trying to catch-up with 90 years of not having a Ministry of Foreign Affairs. What we only had [sic] was a Ministry of South African Affairs'.[68] By the second anniversary of independence in 1982, 19 foreign missions had been established; and 50 states and six international organisations had established diplomatic relations with Zimbabwe.[69] The general principle influencing the establishment of these relations was the well-known one of non-alignment. Zimbabwe, said the Minister of Foreign Affairs Dr Witness Mangwende, would 'not automatically take sides on the critical issues of world politics — and the country's position would be dictated by its own national interests first and foremost'. The latter had, however, a particularly important role to play. Mangwende believed that it was also an accepted fact that, 'while nations [we] re free to choose their friends, they cannot, however, choose their neighbours'. Economic dependence often imposed constraints on the extent to which an underdeveloped country could genuinely pursue a policy of non-alignment 'without compromising some ꭓf its most cherished ideals'.[70]

Zimbabwe has not escaped from the inherited, systemic, and geographical situation of heavy South African influence in its internal and external affairs. In 1982 South Africa remained the country's number one trading partner, with Britain, the United States, and West Germany each of much lesser importance. Within the exigencies of this situation, the Mugabe government has endeavoured to maintain a principled policy. Mugabe ruled out Zimbabwe's participation 'at this juncture' in any sanctions against South Africa, but he added that his country would 'not stand in the way of the international community' if it imposed sanctions.[71] Zimbabwe would give military, political, and moral support for SWAPO fighting for independence in Namibia, but would not provide it with bases, said the Prime Minister. Nor would the government 'create conditions in this country which can be used by any organisation for carrying out military attacks against. . . South Africa'.[72] Mugabe more recently denied that contradictions existed in Zimbabwe's position of both calling for sanctions against South Africa and continuing trade with that country itself. For certain African countries to participate in such sanctions, he said, provision would first have to be made to alleviate the hardship that would inevitably be faced by them. Zimbabwe's relations with South Africa were 'only of an economic nature and other governmental relations would never occur, whether of a political or informal nature'.[73]

South Africa's reaction to this reasoned and moderate position has been described as one of alternatively squeezing and helping Zimbabwe; efforts at economic and military destabilisation fairly steadily pursued combined with the occasional grant of assitance. In quick succession through 1981, Pretoria

1 withdrew 25 locomotives and 150 mechanics on loan to Zimbabwe, gravely jeopardising the export of the country's tobacco and maize over war-damaged infrastructure;

364

2   slowed down the turnround times of Zimbabwean rail traffic through South Africa;

3   began to repatriate some 20,000 black Zimbabweans working in South Africa;

4   struck at Zimbabwe's tourist trade by introducing visa requirements that had to be reciprocated; and

5   gave notice of intention to terminate the existing preferential trade agreement between them.

The ending of this trade agreement would have involved the loss to Zimbabwe of £34m a year in foreign exchange.

Pretoria belatedly announced its willingness to renegotiate an extension of the trade agreement for an indefinite term. But it intensified its 'railway war' on Zimbabwe through sabotage attacks on the country's only alternative routes to the sea through Beira and Maputo – not necessarily by direct South African military assault, but through the Mozambique Resistance Movement (MRM) with which Pretoria is closely associated. The reopening of the oil pipeline from Beira to Mtare, in August 1981, promised to cut Zimbabwe's oil dependence on South Africa, but it was sabotaged in October and did not resume pumping until late-1982. Shortages of essential fuels combined with the other railway problems meant that at one stage Zimbabwe was losing £4m a week in export earnings.[74] In August 1982 the government appealed to South Africa to stop its campaign of destabilising neighbouring countries. Mugabe said: 'We have not sponsored subversive activities against South Africa, none whatsoever'; and he added: 'We hope that the posture we have shown will be reciprocated'.[75] But Zimbabwe has not been pressured as Pretoria would seem to have intended, into closer relations with South Africa, nor coerced by the display of South African power into a compromised position in regional affairs. Its position is much the same in regard to SWAPO and the African National Congress, and it has not adopted the accommodationist tactics of Zambia (see previous chapter).

Mozambique is next in importance to Zimbabwe in regional affairs. This is based largely on the earlier links between ZANU and FRELIMO, and on the shared interest in the routes to the sea at Beira and Maputo, in harbour facilities, and in the oil pipeline. Relations with Zambia are of a different order. The development of Rhodesian capitalism was partly based upon the underdevelopment of Zambia and the latter's near total reliance on a mono-commodity export economy, intended to serve as a market for the manufactured products and verdant agriculture of its stronger Southern neighbour. Further, the Mugabe government has not had any notable reason to admire President Kenneth Kaunda given the Zambian leader's relations with Ian Smith and with

Prime Ministers Vorster and Botha, and his actions against those elements within Zimbabwean nationalism with which Mugabe had been closely associated.

In its relations with the communist states, those with China and North Korea are especially prominent, while in Europe continuing links exist with Romania. All three had given important assistance to ZANU during the liberation war. Romania provided substantial quantities of arms and trained some 2,000 people; Mugabe said, in November 1981, that 'if it were not for that assistance we would still be languishing under the colonial yoke'.[76] China pledged aid to Zimbabwe worth US $30m in May 1981, and the greater part of North Korea's post-independence assistance has been noted: military aid. The Soviet Union, however, is in a category of its own. Zimbabwe says it is friends with both China and the Soviet Union and non-aligned in their disputes. But Mugabe referred as recently as September 1981 to the fact that the Soviet Union 'assisted ZAPU exclusively' in the 1970s. The Russian ambassador to Zimbabwe said, however, in November of the same year, that bilateral relations had 'now settled down', and the Soviet Union was 'beginning to do [its] best to take part in the development of this country'. Zimbabwean students have been accepted at Soviet colleges, and a senior Soviet official said, in August 1982, that his country was 'determined to develop relations with Zimbabwe in every area'.[77]

No communist state has the importance to the established Zimbabwean economy that South Africa and the major capitalist states enjoy; nor are they seen by the Mugabe government as possessing the same capacity for providing economic assistance as the latter group. Britain was the second largest supplier of Zimbabwe's imports (10 per cent) and the United States was third (7.3 per cent) in 1981, while the United States held the same position as an export market for Zimbabwe (7.9 per cent) and Britain held only fourth place (6.9 per cent). Britain is Zimbabwe's major source of foreign aid but, as has been noted already, it is not seen to give enough by the Mugabe government either in relation to promised grants under the earlier proposed Anglo-American Zimbabwe Development Fund, or to the restrictive terms of the Lancaster House constitutional agreement. Aid from the United States is seen as derisory.

The Mugabe government works within the country's established linkages with the capitalist world. It wants large foreign private investment funds to support the country's advanced economy. But it has tried to establish a relatively independent position in its relations with the communist states and with the Third World; military assistance from North Korea is a counter-weight to a heavy reliance upon Britain; and Zimbabwe recognises and supports the Polisario Front and has no relations with Israel. It is a foreign policy that is as reasoned and as cautious as domestic policy. But South Africa and the major capitalist powers had neither expected nor obviously welcomed the electoral victory of the Mugabe government; the end of settler intransigence and majority rule under the compliant leadership of such as Muzorewa was the desired outcome. Zimbabwe has faced continuous harassment from South Africa, and its policies have not received the economic returns from the West which the Mugabe government optimistically expected.

Social welfare and the decline of political participation

Big advances have been made in health and education in Zimbabwe. Both have been made available in more appropriate forms to an increasing proportion of the population. On the one hand, minimum wages for most workers have been raised by considerable amounts. The wages of agricultural and domestic workers were increased by 66 per cent from $30 to $50 a month, and for industrial and commercial workers by 23.5 per cent from $85 to $105 a month, in January 1982. These increases were in line with proposals made by the Riddell Commission on incomes, prices, and conditions of service. But, as Mugabe acknowledged, these new wage figures did not take workers up to the estimated urban poverty datum line for a family of six on $128 a month.[78]

On the other hand, the government has, however, taken a hard line towards organised action for improved pay and conditions by workers. The strikes by nurses and teachers in October 1981 were met by a refusal to concede on the part of the government. Strikes by railway-men in January 1982 met even more uncompromising action: workers were arrested and fined through the use of the emergency regulations of the settler regime. While most urban workers were finding increased minimum wages eaten up by rising inflation, some groups were faced by particular hardship. When 150 drivers, conductors, and mechanics at a bus company in Harare went on strike in August 1982, it was revealed that most had not been paid for 15 weeks, and one mechanic said that he had 'had no rise since joining this company 16 years ago'.[79] Relations between the government and the trade union leadership do not appear to be good, Mugabe complaining that 'the trade union move-ment leadership is not sufficiently enlightened on the policies we wish to pursue [to develop the worker]'.[80]

Discontent appears to exist among workers in the towns of Zimbabwe and at a deeper level in the countryside. Popular partici-pation in the liberation movement was terminated largely with the ceasefire agreement. ZANU has not offered a replacement for this nor, on its record, could it reasonably be expected to do so. Urban and rural people do not stand in an organised relationship with the Mugabe government, as the latter faces serious internal economic and political problems affecting the very framework of Zimbabwe. These are combined with the destabilisation tactics of South Africa and the relative disinterest of Britain and the United States. The Mugabe government is, therefore, in a precarious position, and so too are its policies of moderation, rationality, and multi-racialism. However, there has been no descent into the obscurantism of 'African socialism.' or 'humanism', and distribution with productivity has been stressed. Neighbours like Tanzania and Zambia experience an unending agony of underdevelopment and enjoy a shared poverty at best. The material achievements and legacy of Rhodesian settler colonialism are notable; and it is the social democratisation of these which the Mugabe government is attempting.

Notes

1 David Wield, 'Manufacturing Industry', and Colin Stoneman, 'Agriculture', in Colin Stoneman (ed.), *Zimbabwe's Inheritance* (London: Macmillan, 1981), pp. 151–152, and 136 respectively. Dollars are Zimbabwean unless otherwise noted.
2 Roger Riddell, *The Land Problem in Rhodesia*, (Gwelo: Mambo Press, 1978), p. 2.
3 *Ibid.*, p. 13.
4 *Moto*, July 1982, p. 5.
5 Riddell, *The Land Problem in Rhodesia* (note 2), p. 10. His emphasis.
6 Vincent Tickner, *The Food Problem* (Gwelo: Mambo Press, 1979), p. 21.
7 Riddell, *The Land Problem in Rhodesia* (note 2) pp. 3 and 52–53.
8 *Ibid.*, p. 13.
9 *Ibid.*, Preface.
10 Colin Stoneman and Rob Davies, 'The Economy: an overview', in Stoneman (ed.), *Zimbabwe's Inheritance* (note 1), pp. 112–113.
11 Quoted in David Wield, 'Manufacturing Industry', in Stoneman (ed.), *Zimbabwe's Inheritance* (*ibid.*), p. 155.
12 *Ibid.*, pp. 154–157.
13 Quoted in David Martin and Phyllis Johnson, *The Struggle for Zimbabwe* (Harare: Zimbabwe Publishing House, 1981), pp. 235–236.
14 Two subjective but detailed accounts of Zimbabwean nationalism are *ibid.* and Masipula Sithole, *Struggles Within the Struggle* (Salisbury: Rujeko Publishers, n.d.). There is also the informative

and compelling work by Maurice Nyagumbo, *With The People* (Salisbury: Graham Publishing, 1980).

15 The frequent divisions within and between ZANU and ZANLA are referred to in Martin and Johnson, *The Struggle for Zimbabwe* (note 13), and in Sithole, *Struggles Within the Struggle* (note 14). The ultimate dominance of the 'old guard' in ZANU is considered in T.O. Ranger, 'The Changing of the Old Guard: Robert Mugabe and the revival of ZANU', *Journal of Southern African Studies*, vol. 7, no. 1, 1980.

16 Palley says that ZANLA 'operate[d] through separate commanders who behave[d] more like medieval barons than officers in an integrated army. After the ceasefire and even after the elections ZANLA soldiers were engaged in pillaging the countryside and in brigandage'. Claire Palley, 'What Future For Zimbabwe?', *Political Quarterly*, vol. 51, no. 3, 1980.

17 Lionel Cliffe, 'Zimbabwe's Political Inheritance', in Stoneman (ed.), *Zimbabwe's Inheritance* (note 1), pp. 32–33, and, with Joshua Mpofu and Barry Munslow, 'Nationalist Politics in Zimbabwe: the 1980 elections and beyond', *Review of African Political Economy*, no. 18, May–August 1980, pp. 44–67.

18 Palley, 'What future for Zimbabwe?' (note 16), p. 287. She gives no details of the meeting and no sources for the statement.

19 *Ibid.*, p. 291.

20 (London) *Times*, 29 April 1980.

21 *Times*, 8 May and 2 September 1980.

22 *Times*, 25 July 1980.

23 (Harare) *Herald*, 26 May and 3 June 1982.

24 *Moto*, June 1982, p. 37; and *Growth With Equity* (Harare: Government of the Republic of Zimbabwe, February 1981), pp. 15–17.

25 *Herald*, 24 September 1982.

26 (Singapore) *Straits Times*, 9 April 1982; *Moto*, August 1982; and *Times of Zambia*, 13 October 1982.

27 *Times*, 23 May 1980.

28 *Zimcord: Report on Conference Proceedings* (Salisbury: Government Printer, 1981), pp. 30–32.

29 *Times*, 28 and 31 January 1981.

30 Noted in a speech by Lord Soames which concluded: 'We see this . . .as a demonstration of our attachment to Zimbabwe and of our profound interest in its future', *Zimcord*, pp. 64–65.

31 *Times*, 2 December 1981.

32 *Times*, 30 and 31 July 1981; and *The Economist*, 8 August 1981, p. 64.

33 *Economist*, 1 May 1982, p. 67; and *Herald*, 23 September 1982.

34   *Times*, 21 April and 20 May 1980.
35   *Times*, 26 May and 10 September 1980.
36   Tickner, *The Food Problem* (note 6), p. 58.
37   *Times*, 3 November 1980.
38   *Times*, 4 November 1980 and 6 November 1981.
39   *Moto*, July 1982, pp. 5—6. The Ministry's full title is Lands, Resettlement and Rural Development.
40   Statement by Mahachi, *Herald*, 2 September 1982.
41   *Zimcord*, p. 124. Sekeramayi referred to three models for 'resettling developing farmers': 'Intensive village settlements with individual arable allocations and communal grazing areas; intensive settlement with communal living and co-operative farming; intensive settlement combined with a centralised estate farm.'
42   *Herald*, 2 September 1982.
43   Statement by Sekeremayi, *Times*, 1 September 1981.
44   *Herald*, 23 September 1982.
45   *Moto*, July 1982, pp. 6—7.
46   *Times*, 14 October 1981; *Moto*, August 1982, p. 17; and *Herald*, 23 September 1982.
47   *Zambia Daily Mail*, 8 October 1982, and *Times of Zambia*, 9 October 1982.
48   *Herald*, 29 September 1982.
49   *Herald*, 24 September 1982.
50   *Times*, 4 June and 5 July 1980. Not all was sweetness and light; e.g., the then Minister of Manpower Planning and Development, Edgar Tekere, accused senior (white) civil servants in mid-1980 of 'sabotage' over failure to circulate certain questionnaires seeking information about civil servants' qualifications. *Times*, 4 June 1980.
51   *Times*, 10 September 1980.
52   From an interview with Mugabe, *Moto*, August 1980, p. 7.
53   *Moto*, August 1982, p. 39; Statement by the Minister of Mines, Maurice Nyamgumbo, *Times*, 30 April 1980.
54   See, e.g., D.H. Patel and R.J. Adams, *Chirambahuyo: a case study in low-income housing* (Gwelo: Mambo Press, 1981).
55   Palley, 'What future for Zimbabwe?' (note 16), p. 292.
56   *Moto*, August 1982, p. 9.
57   *Times*, 18 July 1980.
58   *Times*, 1 August 1980 and 30 January 1981.
59   *Times*, 28 November 1981.
60   *Moto*, August 1982, p. 5—6.
61   'Comrades Return to a Cold Front', by a special correspondent, *Moto*, June 1982, p. 16.
62   *Times*, 6 June 1980; *Herald*, 28 September 1982.

63   *Moto*, August 1982, p. 5; *Herald*, 28 September 1982.
64   *Times*, 8 August and 30 October 1981.
65   *Africa Now*, June 1982, pp. 31–34 and 40–43.
66   *Zambia Daily Mail*, 5 October 1982.
67   Soldiers of the former Rhodesian army in the South African military revealed in September that they had 'regularly been used on raids into neighbouring African states' including Zimbabwe: 'We know the ropes. We operate in Zimbabwe because we obviously know the country well. We also go into Mozambique. . .', the South African paper, the *Sunday Mail*, reported (*Zambia Daily Mail*, 7 September 1982).
68   *Herald*, 16 October 1981.
69   The 19 were: Algeria, Belgium, Britain, Canada, China, Ethiopia, France, Japan, Mozambique, Nigeria, Romania, Senegal, Sweden, Tanzania, United Nations Organisation, United States, West Germany, Yugoslavia, Zambia (*Herald*, 18 April 1982).
70   *Herald*, 4 November 1981.
71   *Herald*, 20 March 1981.
72   (Harare) *Sunday Mail*, 7 June 1981; and *Herald*, 9 June 1981.
73   *Herald*, 31 May 1982.
74   *The Economist*, 16 January 1982, p. 53.
75   *Herald*, 19 August 1982.
76   *Herald*, 17 November 1981.
77   *Herald*, 7 November 1981 and 13 August 1982.
78   *Times*, 5 December 1981.
79   *Herald*, 28 August 1982.
80   *Moto*, August 1982, p. 8.

Conclusion: The future of a political economy of African foreign policy

Timothy M. Shaw

As it enters its third decade of independence, Africa faces a troubled future. Its troubles are directly related to the growing pains associated with attempts to establish polities, economies, and societies under a second and third generation of leadership. . . The third decade is a time for diplomacy, with all the art and skill that the calling can carry.

I. William Zartman[1]

The triangular alliance among feudalism, the domestic bourgeoisie, and the foreign imperialist bourgeoisie is to be understood in its dialectical unity. There are areas where their class interests converge, and also areas where they clash.

Ranjit Sau[2]

The introduction to this collection was concerned with the past (deficiencies) and present (opportunities) of foreign policy behaviours and studies in Africa, while outlining a possible new path for progressive analysis. The conclusion seems to be an appropriate place to go beyond contemporary caution and to speculate somewhat on future trends in both statesmanship and scholarship. For the second 20 years of 'independence' on the continent, to the year 2000, are likely to be even more troubled than the first two decades.[3]

This projection of increasing and intensifying difficulties is, alas, likely to come true whether one's mode of analysis is radical or not: interstate conflicts and intrastate contradictions are widely expected to multiply given Africa's inauspicious inheritance and current conjuncture. This concluding chapter overviews some of these potential problems and suggests possible remedies based on insights derived from the sort of critical scholarship presented in this collection.

Into the second 20 years: maturation and marginalisation

At the continental level, the past two decades, particularly the most recent one, have been characterised by two dominant trends, aside from the intra-African divergencies which will be discussed in the next section: the somewhat contradictory tendencies towards *maturation* on the one hand and *marginalisation* on the other. The progress towards maturation has taken place primarily in the area of process, or politics, whereas the decline into marginalisation has occurred especially in the area of production, or economics. These two phenomena are interrelated although the former is essentially an internal process whereas the latter is an external effect: maturation has produced a less abrasive and more mellow reaction to marginalisation.

The maturation apparent in African foreign policy is in part a function of time — African states may still be small and weak but they are no longer 'new' — and in part a function of learning — African statesmen now have 20 years of post-independence diplomatic experience behind them. The idealistic and aggressive stances of the early 1960s have yielded to more pragmatic and reasoned positions. And the apparently relentless process of marginalisation has almost led to a sense of resignation rather than expectation. To be sure, African diplomats individually and collectively continue to blame and berate the world, especially its Western parts, for both imperialistic and disinterested policies yet nowadays they rarely threaten economic sanctions or diplomatic breaks. Typically, President Shehu Shagari defended his own foreign policy for Nigeria (see Chapter 8) on grounds of 'studied restraint' rather than a 'primitive military retaliatory raid' in response to real regional threats:

I think that our reaction to these events should. . .be judged against the background of the principles of our foreign policy. . . [which] has been meticulously geared towards promoting good neighbourliness and a healthy respect for the principle of non-interference in the mutual affairs of others. . . I am also conscious that Nigeria, like most other regional powers, must learn to contend with problems associated with leadership and the attendant responsibility. This is the classic constraint which Nigeria will increasingly be called upon to live with.[4]

The other dominant trend — that towards marginalisation — is less important to the Nigerian case than to almost all other African states. For the majority, however, the world system is much less promising than 20 or even 10 years ago. Despite discussions and resolutions about the Third UN Development Decade the unavoidable reality of the continent is decline rather than development. Just as relatively optimistic assumptions held at independence about prospects for growth have been discarded, to be replaced by widespread notions of dependence, so commonplace notions of neo-colonial linkages should now be superseded by an appreciation of isolation.

Indeed, Africa may have chosen 'self-reliance', the motif of the OAU's *Lagos Plan of Action,*[5] by default. Its growing marginalisation — it is no longer exploited as its products and markets are, by and large, insignificant — has led to resignation as well as to maturation. Only a few African states and statesmen are relevant to world politics and economics. The African caucus may still exhibit a residual cohesion but its salience is minimal. African political economies may have lost their innocence and newness; yet on the whole, they are weaker and poorer than ever. Only a few matter to the global power and growth calculus of the 1980s: a competitive and protectionist world.[6]

Towards divergence: new hierarchies and coalitions

Given the prevalent and seemingly irreversible trend towards global and continental — let alone regional and national — inequalities, two types of state actor would seem to have become more important and influential than others because of two sets of salient criteria. First, the pregnant division of African states into a majority at the periphery and a minority at the semi-periphery. And second, the emergent distinction between those at the centre of intra-African coalitions and those who follow rather than lead. Both of these sets of distinguished states — the semi-periphery and the coalition centres — have realised the status of *primus inter pares* because of position in the world system rather than impressive leadership or compelling ideology.[7] And because their eminence is structural rather than individual it is likely to last longer than previous forms of hierarchy on the continent.

The new division of Africa into periphery and semi-periphery is more fundamental, then, than previous distinctions between, say, multi- and one-party states or between civilian and military regimes. As Henry Bienen recognises, for instance, 'although military factors are increasingly important in Africa':

> . . .looking at substantive foreign policy outcomes, we do not find that African military regimes align themselves in clear-cut ways in either inter-African affairs or global politics. Such regimes do not seem to have a bias for particular foreign policy stances.[8]

Moreover, in recognising the increasing distinction between more radical and conservative political economies we need to go beyond superficial ideological distinctions. But the chic critique of Michael Radu is hardly reflective of this new reality:

> Ideological considerations, as a result of their domestic power structure, are now dominating the foreign policy of a number of African states . . . the myth of an innocent Africa, preoccupied only with economic development, should finally be discarded.[9]

Likewise his cute characterisation of their alignment is beside the point: their (international) diplomacy is less crucial than their (developmental) strategy: 'The foreign policies of the African Marxist regimes. . .are increasingly inconsistent with their proclaimed allegiance to non-alignment'.[10] Moreover, they lack both the coherence, consistency and impact that Radu alleges:

> Internal militarisation, the increasing level of cooperation among African revolutionary regimes and between them and the communist states, and the presence of foreign military and security personnel on their territory are all factors of regional and continental instability.[11]

Rather, relating the two sets of criteria of distinctions indicated above, the fundamental basis of alternative coalitions in African international affairs today is position in the world system — i.e., periphery or semi-periphery — from which other features follow, such as national strategy — i.e., self-reliance or further incorporation — and national ideology — i.e., state socialism or state capitalism, respectively. And coalitions based on such sub-structural position, which tend obviously to correlate quite highly with super-structural features such as type of regime or ideology, are unlikely to change as quickly as coalitions tended to do in the 1960s because they now reflect continuing rather than transitory interests.

However, the leadership of such coalitions may be somewhat more fluid, the reflection of individual or institutional qualities rather than just political economy. So the major national or personal actor in the conservative coalition can shift from Leopold Senghor to Shehu Shagari while the mantle of the radical coalition can be passed from Kwame Nkrumah to Julius Nyerere. Such transitions can occur also at the regional as well as the continental level, with Zimbabwe succeeding Zambia or Tanzania as the heart of the Front Line States and the Ivory Coast challenging Senegal for leadership of Africa's francophones.

While neither type of distinction — semi-periphery and coalition centre — is liable to precipitous change both can still evolve over time in response to evolutions in either or both global and national political economies. First, the centrepiece of any state at the semi-periphery is the 'triple alliance' among national, state and multinational capital with particular emphasis on the 'national' component of the bourgeoisie.[12] If this balance changes then the place of the national political economy in the world system may shift. And second, the crucial feature of any country aspiring to be a coalition centre is its leadership's connections with African and extra-African countries. If such distinctive 'comprador' elements are squeezed out by either national or external fractions then the state's intermediary position and role may be jeopardised. In any event, the metamorphosis in mode of analysis is much less transitory: if political economy helps to explain the present better than alternative approaches it surely will do so in the future as well.

The future and foreign policy studies

The type of future projected through a political economy form of analysis — marginalisation rather than maturation and divergency rather than unity — may be contrasted with the limited insights derived from more traditional projections. Whilst it is clear that inter-state conflict will continue, we clearly need to go beyond orthodox notions to identify intra-state and transnational forms of struggle, by contrast to Raymond Copson's recent formulation:

> . . .it is clear that armed international violence is possible, primarily at four major flashpoints: the regions bordering South Africa and Namibia; the Horn of Africa; Libya's borders and the borders of the Libyan sphere of influence, now extending into Chad; and Morocco's borders, including the borders of Morocco's sphere of influence in the former Spanish Sahara.[13]

Conflict in Africa is likely to be increasingly 'unconventional' in the sense that it may not be among orthodox military formations; rather it is likely to consist of debates and activities from nuclear to guerrilla strategies including class struggles.[14] In the mid-term future, conflict will arise from 'internal' tensions (including their transnational

376

connections) and 'spill-over' into a variety of 'international' forms: border conflicts, regional alignments, and broad intercontinental coalitions involving extra- as well as intra-African actors. The character of foreign policy as well as of conflict will change as modes of relation and analysis evolve.

In particular, when viewed from a more radical perspective, foreign policy will come to reflect and advance the distinct class or fractional interests of African states always rationalised and legitimised, of course, by reference to 'national interest' or 'pan-African solidarity'. In any event, despite the particularistic imperatives of foreign relations for social formations under pressure, it is easier than ever to reject the simplistic and paternalistic assertions of Africanists such as J.F. Maitland-Jones who were still arguing less than a decade ago that 'the essential ingredient of a coherent foreign policy (in Africa), that is continuity of aim, circumstance and the means for carrying it out, are in all cases (except that of South Africa), almost totally lacking'.[15]

There are, of course, limits to the relative power of African states and to the relative influence of African statesmen. But the basis of these limits is structure rather than personality: Africa's place in the international division of labour rather than incompetent and unintelligent leadership. A few states — the semi-periphery — may have enhanced capabilities and a few statesmen may have superior skills but overall Africa's place in the world system remains marginal.[16] Notwithstanding growing sophistication, African diplomacy will remain forever uninfluential if the continent fails to resolve its crisis and achieve enhanced growth, and thus visibility, through self-reliance, collective and national.

However, even if the existential future for the African continent appears at present to be less than bright, the analytic future may be considerably improved as African studies comes to reconsider its assumptions and expectations. Situating foreign policy within the context of national and international divisions of labour represents a considerable advance over the simplistic and uncritical forms of diplomatic history and ideological investigation characteristic of the 1960s. Such a relatively radical endeavour also means going beyond orthodox assumptions about the undifferentiated nature of African political economics and to identify salient class and interstate struggles. Despite Maitland-Jones' assertions, African leaders have not always been domineering, eclectic or transitory; rather they increasingly reflect continuing and rooted fractional concerns: 'The conduct of foreign affairs (in Africa), like that of much of the rest of government, is too frequently the province of one man, the head of state, whose preoccupations amid the urgencies of one- party, one-person rule must accordingly be many and fleeting'.[17]

However, we should be careful not to go too far in the other direction of seeing leaders as both diverse and predictable given their distinctive class and country positions. To be sure these will continue to diverge — the semi-periphery will grow away from the periphery at an exponential rate — yet pan-African pressures to conform will not disappear entirely: collective as well as individual as well as common class interests will restrain excessive divergencies. In short, foreign policy in the future, as in the past — even if we failed as scholars at the time to recognise it as such — will reflect the rise and fall of particular interests and issues internally and externally, along with transitory coalitions and contradictions. But these dialectical relationships cannot really be understood without situating them within the context of more continuous, structural features of political economy, both global and peripheral.[18]

The particular outcome of substructural economic change on superstructural political life can never be plotted with great confidence. However, to ignore the former by concentrating only on the latter is to prejudice chances of reliable explanation and extrapolation. Situating foreign policy within the *problematique* of international and national divisions of labour is difficult; but the advantages, even imperatives, of doing so are now clear and compelling. So we can conclude this collection positively in regard to the continent's analytic future even if projections about Africa's existential future remain considerably more problematic.

Notes

1   I. William Zartman, 'Issues of African diplomacy in the 1980s', *Orbis*, vol. 25, no. 4, Winter 1982, p. 1025.
2   Ranjit Sau, *Unequal Exchange, Imperialism and Underdevelopment: an essay on the political economy of world capitalism* (Calcutta: OUP, 1978), p. 141.
3   For an overview of these two decades see Timothy M. Shaw (ed.), *Alternative Futures for Africa* (Boulder: Westview, 1982), *passim*.
4   President Alhaji Shehu Shagari, 'Annual foreign policy address', *Nigerian Forum*, vol. 1, no. 6, August 1981, p. 204.
5   See OAU, *Lagos Plan of Action for the Economic Development of Africa, 1980–2000* (Geneva: International Institute for Labour Studies, 1981).
6   See Timothy M. Shaw, 'Which way Africa? ECA and IBRD responses to the continental crisis' (Uppsala: Scandinavian Institute of African Studies, 1982).
7   Cf. Timothy M. Shaw and Naomi Chazan, 'Limits of Leadership:

Africa in contemporary world politics', *International Journal*, vol. 37, no. 4, Autumn 1982, pp. 543–554.

8   Henry Bienen, 'Military rule and military order in Africa', *Orbis*, vol. 25, no. 4, Winter 1982, p. 965.

9   Michael Radu, 'Ideology, parties and foreign policy is sub-Saharan Africa', in *ibid.*, p. 992.

10 *Ibid.*, p. 990.

11 *Ibid.* Cf. Timothy M. Shaw, 'The political economy of African international relations', *Issue*, vol. 5, no. 4, Winter 1975, pp. 29–38 and 'Class, Country and Corporation: Africa in the capitalist world system' in Donald I. Ray *et al.* (eds), *Into the 80s: proceedings of the 11th annual conference of the Canadian Association of African Studies, Volume 2* (Vancouver: Tantalus, 1981), pp. 19–37.

12 See Peter Evans, *Dependent Development: the alliance of multinational, state and local capital in Brazil* (Princeton: Princeton University Press, 1979), *passim*, especially pp. 299–313.

13 Raymond W. Copson, 'African Flashpoints: prospects for armed international conflict', *Orbis*, vol. 25, no. 4, Winter 1982, p. 904.

14 See Timothy M. Shaw, 'Unconventional Conflicts in Africa: nuclear, class and guerrilla struggles, past, present and prospective', *Jerusalem Journal of International Relations* (forthcoming).

15 J.F. Maitland-Jones, *Politics in Africa: the former British territories* (New York: Norton, 1973), p. 191.

16 See Shaw and Chazan, 'Limits of leadership' (note 7).

17 Maitland-Jones, *Politics in Africa*, (note 15), p. 191.

18 For one attempt to do this see the analytic essay in Timothy M. Shaw, *Africa's International Affairs: an analysis and bibliography* (Halifax: Centre for Foreign Policy Studies, 1983), pp. 1–43.

Bibliography on African Foreign Policy

Note: For a more comprehensive bibliography on African international relations and foreign policy see Timothy M. Shaw *Africa's International Affairs: an analysis and bibliography* (Halifax: Centre for Foreign Policy Studies, 1983), pp. 45–102.

Overviews

Akindele, Rafiu A. 'Reflections on the preoccupation and conduct of African diplomacy', *Journal of Modern African Studies* 14(4), December 1976, pp. 557–576.

Akpan, Moses E. *African Goals and Diplomatic Strategies in the United Nations* (North Quincey, Mass.: Christopher, 1966).

Aluko, Olajide 'The determinants of the foreign policies of African States', in his collection on *The Foreign Policies of African States* (London: Hodder & Stoughton, 1977), pp. 1–23.

'African responses to external intervention in Africa since Angola', *African Affairs* 80(319), April 1981, pp. 158–179.

Bienen, Henry 'African militaries as foreign policy actors', *International Security* 5(2), Fall 1980, pp. 168–186.

Boutros-Ghali, Boutros 'The foreign policy of Egypt in the post-Sadat era' *Foreign Affairs* 60(4), Spring 1982, pp. 769–788.

Clapham, Christopher 'Sub-Saharan Africa', in his collection of *Foreign Policy Making in Developing States: a comparative approach* (Farnborough: Saxon House, 1977), pp. 75–109.

Daddieh, Cyril Kofie and Timothy M. Shaw 'The political economy of decision-making in African foreign policy: the cases of recognition of Biafra and the MPLA' *International Political Science Review* 5(1), January 1984.

Dei-Anang, Michael 'Foreign policy of the independent African states', in Christopher Fyfe (ed.) *African Studies since 1945: a tribute to Basil Davidson* (New York: Africana, 1976), pp. 66–76.

DeLancey, Mark W. 'Current studies in African international relations', *Africana Journal* 7(3), 1976, pp. 194–239.

African International Relations: an annotated bibliography (Boulder: Westview, 1981).

'The study of African international relations', in his collection on *Aspects of International Relations in Africa* (Bloomington: Indiana University, 1979), pp. 1–38.

Dessouki, Ali E. Hillal 'Domestic variables in inter-state conflict: a case study of the Sahara' *Armed Forces and Society* 7(3), Spring 1981, pp. 409–422.

and Bahgat Korany *Foreign Policies of Arab States* (Boulder: Westview, 1983).

Dolan, Michael B., *et al.* 'Foreign Policies of African states in asymmetrical dyads', *International Studies Quarterly* 24(3), September 1980, pp. 415–449.

Gaudier, Maryse *Africa 2000: an analytical bibliography on African proposals for the 21st century* (Geneva: International Institute for Labour Studies, for OAU, 1982).

Gitelson, Susan A. 'Why do small states break diplomatic relations with outside powers: lessons from the African experience', *International Studies Quarterly* 18(4), December 1974, pp. 451–484.

Johns, David H. 'The normalisation of intra-African diplomatic activity', *Journal of Modern African Studies* 10(4), December 1972, pp. 597–610.

'Diplomatic activity, power and integration in Africa', in Patrick J. McGowan (ed.) *Sage International Yearbook of Foreign Policy Studies, 3* (Beverly Hills: Sage, 1976), pp. 85–105.

'Diplomatic exchange and interstate inequality in Africa: an empirical analysis', in Timothy M. Shaw and Kenneth A. Heard (eds), *Politics of Africa* (London: Longman, 1979), pp. 269–284.

Khapoya, Vincent B. 'Determinants of African support for African liberation movements: a comparative analysis', *Journal of African Studies* 3(4), Winter 1976/7, pp. 469–489.

Kirk-Greene, Anthony H.M. 'Diplomacy and diplomats: the formation of foreign service cadres in Black Africa', in Kenneth Ingham (ed.) *Foreign Relations of African States* (London: Butterworths, 1974), pp. 279–319.

Korany, Bahgat 'The take-off of Third World studies? The case of foreign policy' *World Politics* 35(3), April 1983, pp. 465–487.

Mayall, James 'Black-white relations in the context of African foreign policy', in Peter Jones (ed.) *International Yearbook of Foreign Policy Analysis, Volume 1* (London: Croom Helm, 1975), pp. 181–205.

'Foreign policy in Africa: a changing diplomatic landscape', in Peter Jones (ed.) *International Yearbook of Foreign Policy Analysis, Volume 2*, pp. 188–208.

Mazrui, Ali A. 'Nationalists and statesmen: from Nkrumah and de Gaulle to Nyerere and Kissinger' *Journal of African Studies* 6(4), Winter 1979/80, pp. 199–205.

McGowan, Patrick J. and Klaus P. Gottwald 'Small state foreign policies: a comparative study of participation, conflict and political and economic dependence in Black Africa', *International Studies Quarterly* 19(4), December 1975, pp. 469–500.

and Thomas H. Johnson 'The AFRICA project and the comparative study of African foreign policy', in Mark W. DeLancey (ed.) *Aspects of International Relations in Africa* (Bloomington: Indiana University African Studies Programme, 1979), pp. 190–241.

Mugomba, Agrippah T. *The Foreign Policy of Despair: Africa and the sale of arms to South Africa* (Nairobi: EAPH, 1977).

Nweke, G. Aforka *Harmonisation of African Foreign Policies, 1955–75: the political economy of African diplomacy* (Boston: African Studies Center, Boston University, 1980. African Research Series Number 14).

Ogunbadejo, Oye 'Conservatism and radicalism in inter-African relations: the case of Nigeria and Tanzania' *Jerusalem Journal of International Relations* 4(1), 1979, pp. 23–33.

'Non-alignment in Africa's international relations: the case of Angola' *Jerusalem Journal of International Relations* 5(2), 1981, pp. 16–45.

Ottaway, David and Marina *Afrocommunism* (New York: Africana, 1981).

Radu, Michael 'Ideology, parties and foreign policy in sub-Saharan Africa' *Orbis* 25(4), Winter 1982, pp. 967–992.

Shaw, Timothy M. 'Review article. Foreign policy, political economy and the future: reflections on Africa in the world system'. *African Affairs* 79(315), April 1980, pp. 260–268.

(ed.) *Alternative Futures for Africa* (Boulder: Westview, 1982).

and Naomi Chazan 'Limits of leadership: Africa in contemporary world politics', *International Journal* 37(4), Autumn 1982, pp. 543–554.

Stremlau, John J. 'The foreign policies of developing countries in the

1980s', *Journal of International Affairs* 34(1), Spring/Summer 1980, pp. 161–178.

Vengroff, Richard 'Instability and foreign policy behaviour: Black Africa in the UN', *American Journal of Political Science* 20(3), August 1976, pp. 425–438.

'Domestic instability and foreign conflict behaviour in Africa' *African Studies Review* 23(3), December 1980, pp. 101–114.

Zartman, I. William *International Relations in the New Africa* (New York: Praeger, 1966).

'Decision-making among African governments in inter-African Affairs', *Journal of Development Studies* 2(2), January 1966, pp. 98–119.

'Issues of African diplomacy in the 1980s' *Orbis* 25(4), Winter 1982, pp. 1025–1043.

West Africa

Addo, M. *Ghana's Foreign Policy in Retrospect* (Accra: Waterville Publishing House, 1967).

Akindele, Rafiu A. 'Review article: on the operational linkage of external and internal dimensions of Balewa's foreign policy', *Odu* 12, July 1975, pp. 110–122.

Akinyemi, A. Bolaji *Foreign Policy and Federalism: the Nigerian experience* (Ibadan: Ibadan University Press, 1974).

'Mohammed/Obasanjo foreign policy', in Oyeleye Oyediran (eds), *Nigerian Government and Politics under Military Rule, 1966–1979* (London: Macmillan, 1979), pp. 150–168.

(ed.) *Nigeria and the World: readings in Nigerian foreign policy* (Ibadan: OUP for NIIA, 1978).

and Margaret Vogt 'Nigeria and Southern Africa: the policy options', in Douglas G. Anglin, Timothy M. Shaw and Carl G. Widstrand (eds), *Conflict and Change in Southern Africa* (Washington: University Press of America, 1978), pp. 151–168.

Aluko, Olajide 'Israel and Nigeria: continuity and change in their relationship', *African Review* 4(1), 1974, pp. 43–59.

Ghana and Nigeria 1957–70: a study of inter-African discord (London: Rex Collings, 1976).

'Ghana's foreign policy' and 'Nigerian foreign policy' in his collection on *The Foreign Policies of African States*, pp. 72–97 and 163–195.

'Oil at concessionary prices for Africa: a case study in Nigerian decision-making', *African Affairs* 75(301), October 1976, pp. 425–443.

'After Nkrumah: continuity and change in Ghana's foreign policy', *Issue* 5(1), Spring 1975, pp. 55–62.

'Nigeria and the superpowers', *Millenium* 5(2), August 1976, pp. 127–141.

'Nigeria and Britains since Gowon', *African Affairs* 76(304), July 1977, pp. 303–320.

'Nigeria, the United States and Southern Africa', *African Affairs* 78(301), January, 1979, pp. 91–102.

'Necessity and freedom in Nigerian foreign policy', *Nigerian Journal of International Studies* 4(1 & 2), January and June 1980, pp. 1–15.

Essays in Nigerian Foreign Policy (London: Goerge Allen & Irwin, 1981).

Aluko, Olajide 'Nigeria and Southern Africa' in Gwendolen M. Carter and Patrick O'Meara (eds), *International Politics in Southern Africa*, pp. 128–147.

Amin, Samir *Neocolonialism in West Africa* (Harmondsworth: Penguin, 1973).

Ade, Bassey Eyo 'The presence of France in West-Central Africa as a fundamental problem to Nigeria' *Millenium* 12(2), Summer 1983, pp. 110–126.

Carlsson, Jerker *The Limits to Structural Change: a comparative study of foreign direct investment in Liberia and Ghana, 1950–1971* (Uppsala: Scandinavian Institute of African Studies, 1981).

Dei-Anang, Michael *The Administration of Ghana's foreign relations, 1957–1965: a personal memoir* (London: Institute of Commonwealth Studies, 1975. Commonwealth Papers No. 17).

Delorme, Nicole 'The foreign policy of the Ivory Coast', in Olajide Aluko (ed.) *The Foreign Policies of African States*, pp. 118–135.

Dudley, Billy *An Introduction to Nigerian Government and Politics* (London: Macmillan, 1982) pp. 274–306.

Fasehun, Orobola 'Nigeria and the Ethiopia-Somalia conflict: a case study of continuity in Nigerian foreign policy', *Afrika Spectrum* 17(2), 1982, pp. 183–193.

Gambari, Ibrahim 'Nigeria and the world: a growing internal stability, wealth and external influence', *Journal of International Affairs* 29(2), Fall 1975, pp. 155–169.

Party Politics and Foreign Policy: Nigeria under the First Republic (Zaria: ABU Press, 1980).

Henderson, Robert D'A. 'Nigeria: future nuclear power?' *Orbis* 25(2), Summer 1981, pp. 409–423.

Herskovits, Jean 'Nigeria: Africa's new power', *Foreign Affairs* 52(2), January 1975, pp. 314–333.

'Dateline Nigeria: a black power', *Foreign Policy* 29, Winter 1977–78, pp. 167–188.

Idang, Gordon J. *Nigeria: international politics and foreign policy, 1960–1966* (Ibadan: Ibadan University Press, 1973).

Ihonvbere, Julius O. 'Resource availability and foreign policy change: the impact of oil on Nigerian foreign policy since independence', *Afrika Spectrum* 17(2), pp. 163–181.

Kofele-Kale, Ndiva 'Cameroon and its foreign relations', *African Affairs* 80(119), April 1981, pp. 197–217.

Legum, Colin 'International involvement in Nigeria, 1966–70' in Y.A. Tandon and D. Chandarana (eds), *Horizons of African Diplomacy* (Nairobi: EALB, 1974), pp. 45–85.

Libby, Ronald T. 'External co-operation of a less developed country's policy-making: the case of Ghana, 1969–1972', *World Politics* 29(1), October 1976, pp. 67–89.

Mayall, James 'Oil and Nigerian foreign policy', *African Affairs* 75(300), July 1976, pp. 317–330.

Ofoegbu, Mazi R. 'Nigeria and its neighbours', *Odu* 12, July 1975, pp. 3–24.

Ogunbadego, Oye 'Nigeria and the great powers: the impact of the civil war on Nigerian foreign relations', *African Affairs* 75(298), January 1976, pp. 14–32.

'Nigeria's foreign policy under military rule 1966–1979', *International Journal* 35(4), Autumn 1980, pp. 748–765.

Ogwu, U. Joy 'Nigeria and Brazil: a model for the emerging South-South relations?' in Jerker Carlsson (ed.) *South-South Relations in a Changing World Order* (Uppsala: Scandinavian Institute of African Studies, 1982) pp. 102–127.

Ojo, Olatunde J.B. 'Nigerian-Soviet relations: retrospect and prospect', *African Studies Review* 19(3), December 1976, pp. 43–63.

'Ideology and pragmatism: the Soviet role in Nigeria, 1960–1977', *Orbis* 21(4), Winter 1978, pp. 803–830.

'Nigeria and the formation of ECOWAS'. *International Organisation* 34(4), Autumn 1980, pp. 571–604.

Ostheimer, John M. and Gary J. Buckley 'Nigeria' in Edward A. Kolodziej and Robert E. Harkavy (eds), *Security Policies of Developing Countries* (Lexington: Lexington, 1982), pp. 285–303.

Philips, Claude S. *The Development of Nigerian Foreign Policy* (Evanston: Northwestern University Press, 1964).

Polhemus, J.H. 'Nigeria and Southern Africa: interest, policy and means', *Canadian Journal of African Studies* 11(1), 1977, pp. 43–66.

Sesay, Amadu 'Sierra Leone's foreign policy since independence', *Africana Research Bulletin* 9(3), 1979, pp. 3–43 and 11(1–2), 1981, pp. 3–49.

Shaw, Timothy M. 'Nigeria's political economy: constitutions, capitalism and contradictions', *ODI Review* 2, 1980, pp. 76–85.

'A problematic power: the debate about Nigerian foreign policy in the 1980s', *Millenium: Journal of International Studies* 12(2), Summer 1983, pp. 127–148.

'Nigeria in the international system', in I. William Zartman (ed.) *The Political Economy of Nigeria* (New York: Praeger, 1983), pp. 207–236.

and Orobola Fasehun 'Nigeria in the world system: alternative approaches, explanations and projections', *Journal of Modern African Studies* 18(4), December 1980, pp. 551–573.

and Olajide Aluko (eds.) *Nigerian Foreign Policy: alternative perceptions and projections* (London: Macmillan, 1983).

Skurnik, Walter A.E. *The Foreign Policy of Senegal* (Evanston: Northwestern University Press, 1972).

Sotumbi, A.O. *Nigeria's Recognition of the MPLA Government of Angola: a case study in decision-making and implementation* (Lagos: NIIA, 1981. Monograph Series, Number 9).

Stremlau, John *International Politics of the Nigerian Civil War* (Princeton: Princeton University Press, 1977).

'The fundamentals of Nigerian foreign policy', *Issue* 11(1 and 2), Spring and Summer 1981, pp. 46–50.

Turner, Terisa 'Nigeria: imperialism, oil technology and the comprador state', in Petter Nore and Terisa Turner (eds.) *Oil and Class Struggle* (London: Zed, 1980), pp. 199–223.

White, P.V. 'Nigerian politics: class alliances and foreign alignment', in Ukandi G. Damachi and Hans Pieter Seibel (eds.) *Social Change and Economic Development in Nigeria* (New York: Praeger, 1973).

East Africa

Biersteker, Thomas J. 'Self-reliance in theory and practice in Tanzanian trade relations', *International Organization* 34(2), Spring 1980, pp. 229–264.

Clark, W. Edmund *Socialist Development and Public Investment in Tanzania, 1964–73* (Toronto: University of Toronto Press, 1978).

Cliffe, Lionel 'Underdevelopment or socialism? A comparative analysis of Kenya and Tanzania', in Richard Harris (ed.) *The Political Economy of Africa* (Cambridge: Schenkman, 1975), pp. 137–185.

Fransman, Martin (ed.) *Industry and Accumulation in Africa* (London: Heinemann, 1982), pp. 60–231.

Gitelson, Susan A. *Multilateral Aid for National Development and Self-Reliance: a case study of the UNDP in Uganda and Tanzania* (Nairobi: East African Literature Bureau, 1975).

'Major shifts in recent Ugandan foreign policy', *African Affairs* 76(304), July 1977, pp. 359—380.

'Policy options for small states: Kenya and Tanzania reconsidered', *Studies in Comparative International Development* 12(2), Summer 1977, pp. 29—57.

Godfrey, Martin and Steven Langdon 'Partners in underdevelopment — the transnationalisation thesis in a Kenyan context', *Journal of Commonwealth and Comparative Politics* 14(1), March 1976, pp. 42—63.

Gordenker, Leon *International Aid and National Decisons: development programmes in Malawi, Tanzania and Zambia* (Princeton: Princeton University Press, 1976).

Gupta, Vijay 'Ugandan foreign policy dimensions: enmity to friendship', *Foreign Affairs Reports* 31(1), January 1982.

Hatch, John *Two African Statesmen: Kaunda of Zambia and Nyerere of Tanzania* (London: Secker & Warburg, 1976).

Holtham, Gerald and Arthur Hazlewood *Aid and Inequality in Kenya* (New York: Holmes and Meier, 1976).

Hoskyns, Catherine 'Africa's foreign relations: the case of Tanzania', *International Affairs* 44(3), July 1968, pp. 446—462.

Ismael, Tariq Y. 'The Sudan's foreign policy today', *International Journal* 25(3), Summer 1970, pp. 565—575.

Johns, David 'The foreign policy of Tanzania', in Olajide Oluko (ed.) *The Foreign Policies of African States*, pp. 196—219.

Kaplinsky, Raphael (ed.) *Readings on the Multinational Corporation in Kenya* (Nairobi: OUP, 1978).

Karioki, J.N. 'Tanzania and the resurrection of Pan-Africanism', *Review of Black Political Economy* 4(4), Summer 1974, pp. 1—26.

Langdon, Steven *Multinational Corporations in the Political Economy of Kenya* (London: Macmillan, 1980).

Leys, Colin *Underdevelopment in Kenya: the political economy of neo-colonialism* (London: Heinemann, 1975).

Makinda, Samuel M. 'From quiet diplomacy to Cold War politics: Kenya's foreign policy', *Third World Quarterly* 5(2), April 1983, pp. 300—319.

Mathews, K.S. and S.S. Mushi (eds.) *Foreign Policy of Tanzania: a reader* (Dar es Salaam: Tanzania Publishing House, 1982).

Mayall, James 'The Malawi-Tanzania boundary dispute', *Journal of Modern African Studies* 11(4), December 1973, pp. 611—628.

McMaster, Carolyn *Malawi: foreign policy and development* (London: Friedmann, 1974).

Mushi, S.S. 'Tanzania foreign relations and the policies of non-alignment, socialism and self-reliance' *Taamuli* 9, December 1979, pp. 4—40.

Niblock, Timothy 'Tanzanian foreign policy: an analysis', *African Review* 1(2), September 1971, pp. 91–101.

Nnoli, Okwudiba 'Autonomy in Tanzanian foreign policy', *Africa Quarterly* 17(1), 1977, pp. 5–36.
Self-reliance and Foreign Policy in Tanzania: the dynamics of the diplomacy of a new state, 1961–1971 (New York: NOK, 1978).

Okumu, John J. 'Some thoughts on Kenya's foreign policy', *African Review* 3(2), June 1973, pp. 263–290; revised version in Olajide Aluko (ed.) *The Foreign Policies of African States*, pp. 136–162.
'Foreign relations: dilemmas of independence and development' in Joel D. Barkan and John J. Okumu (eds.) *Politics and Public Policy in Kenya and Tanzania* (New York: Praeger, 1979) pp. 239–266.

Pratt, Cranford 'Foreign policy issues and the emergence of socialism in Tanzania, 1961–1968', *International Journal* 30(3), Summer 1975, pp. 445–470.
The Critical Phase in Tanzania, 1945–1968: Nyerere and the emergence of a socialist strategy (Cambridge: Cambridge University Press, 1976).

Sathyamurthy, T.V. 'Tanzania's non-aligned role in international relations', *India Quarterly* 37(1), January–March 1981, pp. 1–23.
'Tanzania's role in international relations and non-alignment: an interpretive essay', *Geneve-Afrique* 19(2), 1981, pp. 73–101.

Seaton, E.E. and S.T. Maliti *Tanzania Treaty Practice* (Nairobi: OUP, 1973).

Shamuyarira, Nathan 'Tanzania', in Douglas G. Anglin, Timothy M. Shaw and Carl G. Widstrand (eds.) *Conflict and Change in Southern Africa*, pp. 15–32.

Sharkansky, Ira and Denis L. Dresang 'International assistance: its variety, coordination and impact among public corporations in Kenya and the East African Community', *International Organisation* 28(2), Spring 1974, pp. 153–178.

Shaw, Timothy M. and Ibrahim S.R. Msabaha 'From dependency to diversification: Tanzania '1967–1977', in Kal Holsti (ed.) *Why Nations Realign: foreign policy restructuring in the post-war world* (London: George Allen & Unwin, 1982) pp. 47–72.
'Tanzania and the New International Economic Order' in K. Matthews and S.S. Mushi (eds.) *Foreign Policy of Tanzania, 1961–1981: a reader*, pp. 67–79.

Shivji, Issa 'Capitalism unlimited: public corporations in partnership with multinational corporations', *African Review* 3(3), 1973, pp. 359–381.

Stevens, Richard 'The 1972 Addis Ababa Agreement and the Sudan's Afro-Arab policy', *Journal of Modern African Studies* 14(2), June 1976, pp. 247–274.

Swainson, Nicola 'The rise of a national bourgeoisie in Kenya', and Steven Langdon 'The state and capitalism in Kenya', *Review of African Political Economy* 8, January–April 1977, pp. 39–55 and 90–98.

Tandon, Yash 'An analysis of the foreign policy of African states: a case study of Uganda', in Kenneth Ingham (ed.) *Foreign Relations of African States*, pp. 191–209.

Wai, Dunstan M. 'The Sudan: domestic politics and foreign relations under Nimeiry', *African Affairs* 78(312), July 1979, pp. 297–317.

Yu, George T. *China's African Policy: a study of Tanzania* (New York: Praeger, 1975).

Southern Africa

Anglin, Douglas G. 'Zambia and Southern Africa "detente",' *International Journal* 30(3), Summer 1975, pp. 471–503.
'Zambian versus Malawian approaches to political change in Southern Africa', in David S. Chanaiwa (ed.) *Profiles of Self-determination: African responses to European colonialism in Southern Africa, 1652-present* (Northridge: California State University Foundation, 1976).
'Zambian crisis behaviour', *International Studies Quarterly* 24(4), December 1980, pp. 581–616.
and Timothy M. Shaw *Zambia's Foreign Policy: studies in diplomacy and dependence* (Boulder: Westview, 1979).

Azevedo, M.J. 'Zambia, Zaire and the Angolan crisis reconsidered: from Alvor to Shaba', *Journal of Southern African Affairs* 2(3), July 1977, pp. 275–293.

Barber, James *South Africa's Foreign Policy, 1945–1970* (London: OUP, 1973).

Baynham, S.J. 'International politics and the Angolan civil war', *The Army Quarterly and Defence Journal* 107(1), January 1977, pp. 25–32.

Bender, Gerald, J. 'Angola, the Cubans and American anxieties', *Foreign Policy*, 31, Summer 1978, pp. 3–30.

Bone, Marion 'The foreign policy of Zambia', in Ronald P. Barston (ed.) *The Other Powers: studies in the foreign policies of small states* (London: George Allen & Unwin, 1973) pp. 121–153.

Carter, Gwendolen M. and Patrick O'Meara (eds.) *Southern Africa: the continuing crisis* (Bloomington: Indiana University Press, 1982. Second Edition).

Dale, Richard 'President Sir Seretse Khama, Botswana's foreign policy and the Southern African subordinate state system', *Plural Societies* Spring 1976, pp. 69–87.

'The challenges and constraints of white power for a small African state: Botswana and its neighbours', *Africa Today* 25(3), July–September 1978, pp. 7–23.

Davidson, Basil, Joe Slovo, Anthony R. Wilkinson *Southern Africa: the new politics of revolution* (Harmondsworth: Pelican, 1976).

DeLancey, Mark W. 'The international relations of Southern Africa: a review of recent studies', *Geneve-Afrique* 15(2), 1976, pp. 82–135.

Fodor, Erika 'Sub-imperialist tendencies in the international system: the case of the Republic of South Africa', *Development and Peace* 3(1), Spring 1982, pp. 233–247.

Grundy, Kenneth W. 'Intermediary power and global dependency: the case of South Africa' *International Studies Quarterly* 20(4), December 1976, pp. 553–580.

'Black soldiers in a white military: political change in South Africa,' *Journal of Strategic Studies* 4(3), September 1981, pp. 296–305.

Hallett, Robin 'The South African intervention in Angola, 1975–76', *African Affairs* 77(308), July 1978, pp. 347–386.

Henderson, Robert D'A. 'Relations of neighbourliness – Malawi and Portugal, 1964–1974', *Journal of Modern African Studies* 15(3), 1977, pp. 425–455.

'Principles and practices in Mozambique's foreign policy', *World Today* 34(7), July 1978, pp. 276–286.

Hill, Christopher R. 'The Botswana-Zambia boundary question. A note of warning', *Round Table* 252, October 1973, pp. 535–541.

Hirschmann, David 'Changes in Lesotho's policy towards South Africa'. *African Affairs* 78(311), April 1979, pp. 177–196.

Hodges, Geoffrey 'Zambia: opening the gates and tightening the belts', and Tony Southall, 'Zambia: class formation and detente – a comment'. *Review of African Political Economy* 12, May–August 1976, pp. 87–98 and 114–119.

Jones, David *Aid and Development in Southern Africa* (New York: Holmes and Meier, 1978).

Kamana, Dustan 'Zambia' in Douglas G. Anglin, Timothy M. Shaw and Carl G. Widstrand (eds), *Conflict and Change in Southern Africa* pp. 33–68.

Legum, Colin and Tony Hughes *After Angola: the war over Southern Africa* (New York: Africana, 1976).

Makgetla, Neva Seidman 'Finance and development: the case of Botswana', *Journal of Modern African Studies* 20(11), March 1982, pp. 69–86.

Marcum, John 'The anguish of Angola', *Issue* 5(4), Winter 1975, pp. 3–11.

'Lessons of Angola', *Foreign Affairs* 54(3), April 1976, pp. 407–425.

The Angola Revolution: Volume II: exile politics and guerrilla warfare, 1962—1976 (Cambridge: MIT Press, 1978).

Markakis, John and Robert L. Curry 'The global economy's impact on recent budgetary politics in Zambia', *Journal of African Studies* 3(4), Winter 1976—77, pp. 403—427.

Martin, Anthony *Minding Their Own Business: Zambia's struggle against Western control* (Harmondsworth: Penguin, 1975).

Martin, David and Phyllis Johnson *The Struggle for Zimbabwe* (Harare: Zimbabwe Publishing House, 1981).

Mbeki, Moeletsi 'Southern Africa's strategies of disengagement from South Africa' and Centre for African Studies, Eduardo Mondlane University, Maputo 'The constellation of Southern African states: a new strategic offensive by South Africa', *Review of African Political Economy* 18, May—August 1980, pp. 93—98 and 102—105.

Minter, William *Imperial Network and External Dependence: the case of Angola* (Beverly Hills: Sage, 1972).

Portuguese Africa and the West (Harmonsworth, Penguin, 1972).

'Major themes in Mozambique foreign relations, 1975—1977', *Issue* 8(1), Spring 1978, pp. 43—49.

Mittleman, James H. *Underdevelopment and the Transition to Socialism: Mozambique and Tanzania* (New York: Academic, 1981).

Mtshali, Benedict V. 'The Zambian foreign service, 1964—1972', *African Review* 5(3), 1975, pp. 313—316.

Morton, K. *Aid and Dependence: British aid to Malawi* (London: Croom Helm with ODI, 1975).

Nolutshungu, Sam *South Africa in Africa: a study in ideology and foreign policy* (New York: Africana, 1975) especially pp. 191—258.

Nyathi, V.M. 'South African imperialism in Southern Africa', *African Review* 5(4), 1975, pp. 451—472.

Ogunbadejo, Oye 'Angola: ideology and pragmatism in foreign policy', *International Affairs* 57(2), Spring 1981, pp. 254—269.

Pettman, Jan *Zambia: security and conflict* (London: Friedmann, 1974).

Scheidman, W. 'FRELIMO's foreign policy and the process of liberation', *Africa Today* 25(1), January—March 1978, pp. 57—67.

Seidman, Ann and Neva Seidman Makgetla *Outposts of Monopoly Capitalism: Southern Africa in the changing world economy* (Westport: Lawrence Hill, 1980).

Seiler, John 'South African perspectives and responses to external pressures', *Journal of Modern African Studies* 13(3), September 1975, pp. 447—468.

Shaw, Timothy M. *Dependence and Underdevelopment: the development and foreign policies of Zambia* (Athens: Ohio University Papers in African Studies Number 28, 1976).

'Zambia: dependence and underdevelopment', *Canadian Journal of African Studies* 10(1), 1976, pp. 3–22.

'Zambia's foreign policy', in Olajide Aluko (ed.) *The Foreign Policies of African States*, pp. 220–234.

'Kenya and South Africa: 'sub-imperialist' states', *Orbis* 21(2), Summer 1977, pp. 357–394.

'Dilemmas of dependence and (under)development: conflicts and choices in Zambia's present and prospective foreign policy', *Africa Today* 26(4), Fourth Quarter 1979, pp. 43–65.

and Agrippah T. Mugomba 'The political economy of regional detente: Zambia and Southern Africa', *Journal of African Studies* 4(4), Winter 1977–78, pp. 392–413.

and Lee Dowdy 'South Africa' in Edward A. Kolodziej and Robert Harkavy (eds.) *Security Policies of Developing Countries* pp. 305–327.

Sklar, Richard L. *Corporate Power in an African State: the political impact of multinational mining companies in Zambia* (Berkeley: University of California Press, 1975).

Spence, J.E. *Repuhlic under Pressure: a study of South African foreign policy* (London: OUP, 1965).

'South African foreign policy: changing perspectives', *World Today* 34(11), November 1978, pp. 417–425.

'South Africa: the nuclear option', *African Affairs* 30(321), October 1981, pp. 441–452.

Strack, Harry R. *Sanctions: the case of Rhodesia* (Syracuse: Syracuse University Press, 1977).

Index

OAU 16, 27, 31, 34, 41, 51, 52,
70, 98, 102, 104, 124, 158,
198, 202, 235-258, 272-274,
278, 341, 374, see also FLS,
ECA
OCAM 138-139, 168-173
Oil 36-37, 53, 203, 209, 245,
264, 300, and Angola 36-37,
53

Pan-Africanism 99, 101, 104,
197-198, 278, 377-378, see
also OAU
Parastatals 174-180, 224, 231,
290-294, 329, see also
Indigenisation, State
capitalism
Political economy 3, 4, 8-10,
11-12, 147, 165-167, 183,
192, 378, see also Marxism,
Radical
Portugal 25, 35-36, 47, 226,
238-239, 241-242, 246, 326,
see also Angola, Mozambique

Radical 17, 375-377, see also
Marxism, Political economy
Rhodesia see Zimbabwe
Rawlings, Jerry 106-111, see
also Ghana, Nkrumah
Roberto, Holden 45, see also
Angola

SADCC 60, 71-74, 257-259,
344, 359, see also FLS,
Southern Africa
Sahel 173, 180
Savimbi, Jonas 53-54, see also
UNITA
Self-reliance 264, 266, 271-272,
275, 278, see also
Indigenisation
Semi-industrialising 14, see also
NICs

Semi-periphery 193, see also
Sub-imperialism
Senegal 5-6, 139, see also
ECOWAS, OCAM
Shaba 46, 229, 294-295, 304,
305-306, 311, see also Zaire
Skurnik, W. A. 5-6
Socialism 55, 146-149, 266,
277-278, 333, 368, see also
Self-reliance
Somalia 13, 85, 91, 154-155,
156, 157
South Africa 14, 29, 64-75,
101, 124, 125, 135, 136-137,
147, 153, 158, 221-259, 272,
285, 319, 321, 323, 325-332,
336, 340-344, 348, 353, 361,
364-368, 378; and Angola 25-
55; and Botswana 61-75; outward policy 232-239; detente
239-251, 259; destabilisation
246-257; see also Sub-
imperialism, Southern Africa
South African Customs Union
64-72, 235, see also SADCC,
South Africa
Southern Africa 41, 69, 71-74,
136-137, 233, 247, 251-259,
327, 340-344; destabilisation
251-257; see also FLS,
SADCC, South Africa
Soviet Union 29-43, 48-55, 84-
92, 124, 133, 136, 149, 156,
158, 245, 275-276, 301, 353,
355, 366; and Angola 29-43;
and Neto 35-52
State capitalism 13, 139, 222-
232, 350; see also
Indigenisation, Parastatals
Sub-imperialism 147, 229-239;
see also NICs, semi-periphery
Substructure 4, 7, 165, 375
Sudan 80, 81, 82, 91
Superstructure 4, 7